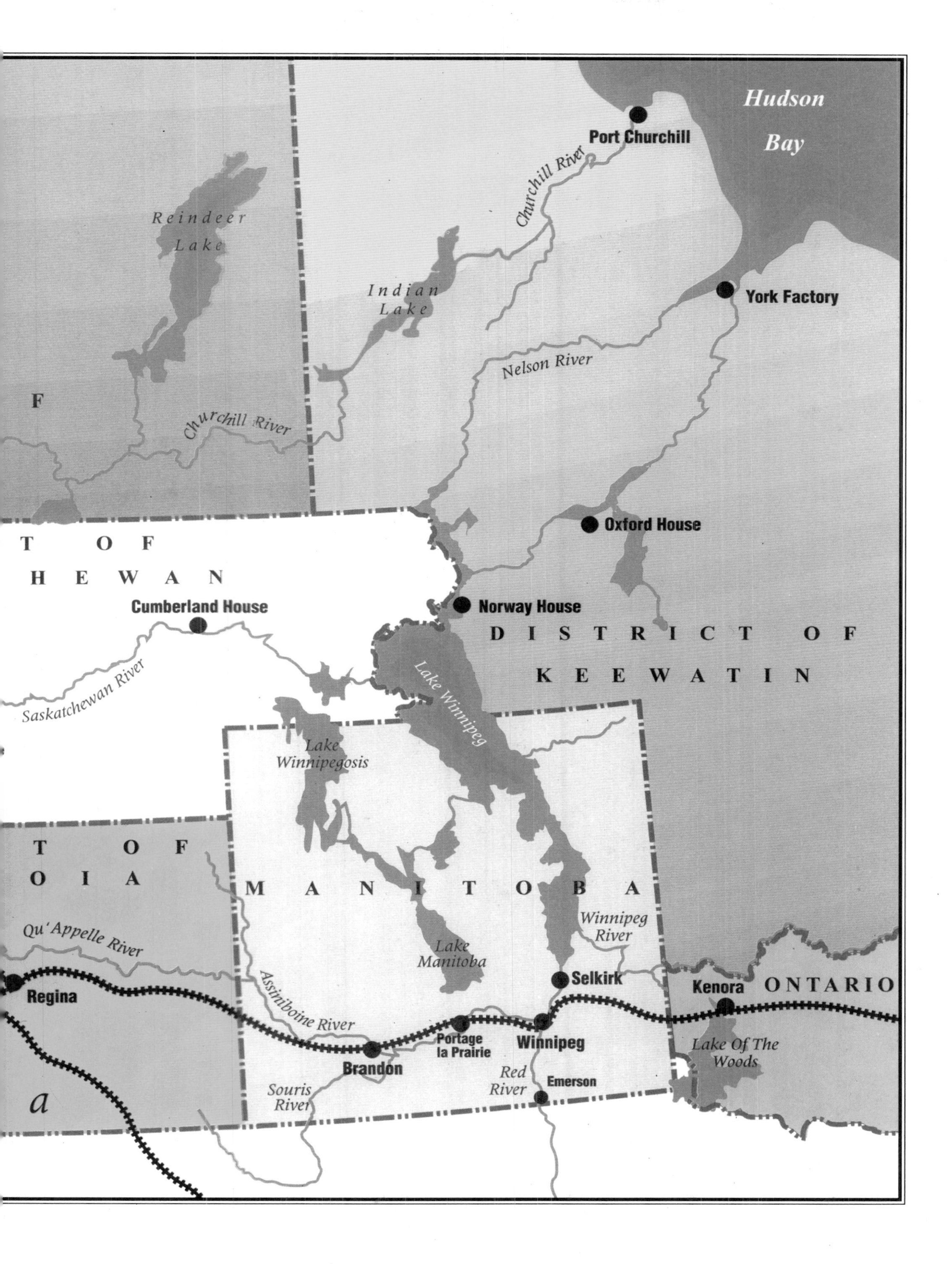
Hudson
Bay
Port Churchill
Churchill River
Reindeer
Lake
Indian
Lake
York Factory
Nelson River
F
Churchill River
Oxford House
T O F
H E W A N
Cumberland House
Norway House
DISTRICT OF
KEEWATIN
Saskatchewan River
Lake Winnipeg
Lake
Winnipegosis
T O F
O I A
MANITOBA
Winnipeg
River
Qu'Appelle River
Lake
Manitoba
Selkirk
Kenora
ONTARIO
Regina
Assiniboine River
Portage
la Prairie
Winnipeg
Lake Of The
Woods
Brandon
Red
River
Emerson
Souris
River
a

ALBERTA
IN THE 20TH CENTURY

A JOURNALISTIC HISTORY OF THE PROVINCE IN 12 VOLUMES

Volume 1

THE GREAT WEST BEFORE 1900

United Western Communications Ltd.
Edmonton
1991

The Great West Before 1900

ISBN 0-9695718-0-1
Printed in Canada
Bound in the U.S.A.

Canadian Cataloguing in Publication Data

Main entry under title:
The Great West Before 1900
(Alberta in the 20th century; no. 1)
Includes bibliographical references and index.
1. Alberta, District of (Alta.) — History.
2. Canada, Western — History. I. Series.

FC3217.G74 1991 971.23'02 C91-091827-9 F1060.9.G74 1991

Third Printing

The staff
of *Alberta Report* Newsmagazine
gratefully dedicate this history
of our province
to John A. Scrymgeour,
an Albertan,
without whose help and direction
neither this history
nor *Alberta Report*
would be.

The Great West Before 1900

Consultative Committee: Donald M. Graves, a Calgary businessman; Hugh A. Dempsey, curator emeritus of the Glenbow-Alberta Institute in Calgary; Martin A. Lynch of Kaslo, B.C., former Chief of the Copy Desk of the Globe and Mail; Richard D. McCallum, president of Quality Color Press Inc. of Edmonton.

Editor Ted Byfield
Production editors Virginia Byfield, Paul Bunner, Link Byfield
Designer and photo editor Craig Wiwad

Writers
Virginia Byfield
Brian Hutchinson
Brad Clark
Gregg Shilliday
Link Byfield
Rick Bell
Terry Johnson
Ted Byfield
George Koch
Mike Byfield
Mark Stevenson
Celeste McGovern
Greg Heaton

Researchers
Kathleen Wall
Chris Jukes

Art assistant Barbara Olmstead
Proofreader Carolyn King

Lithographer Guideline Graphics Inc., Edmonton

Printer Quality Color Press Inc., Edmonton

The publisher gratefully acknowledges the generous assistance of the Glenbow-Alberta Institute in Calgary and the Provincial Archives of Alberta in Edmonton.

Table of Contents

Section One NEW YEAR'S EVE, DECEMBER 31, 1899

Section Two THE INDIANS

Section Three THE FUR TRADERS

Section Four THE RAILWAYMEN

Section Five The Ranchers

Section Six The Sodbusters

Section Seven Drillers and Diggers

Section Eight The Politicians

List of Maps

Alberta in the 20th Century

VOLUME I	THE GREAT WEST BEFORE 1900
VOLUME II (1900 - 1910)	THE BIRTH OF THE PROVINCE
VOLUME III (1910 - 1914)	THE BOOM AND THE BUST
VOLUME IV (1914 - 1920)	THE GREAT WAR AND ITS CONSEQUENCES
VOLUME V (1920 - 1930)	BROWNLEE AND THE TRIUMPH OF POPULISM
VOLUME VI (1930 - 1939)	
VOLUME VII (1939 - 1945)	
VOLUME VIII (1945 - 1960)	
VOLUME IX (1960 - 1970)	
VOLUME X (1970 - 1980)	
VOLUME XI (1980 - 1990)	
VOLUME XII (1990 - 2000)	

Foreword

It's true, I think, that the way we use pronouns often reveals our inner loyalties. Inside an office, for instance, the employees will usually speak of the company as "they." You'll hear people say, "They're giving us a holiday next week," or "They'll never be able keep the schedule they've set." But outside the office, the same people might do one of two things. Referring to the company, they might continue to say, "They're doing this," or "They're doing that." Or they might say, "We're doing this," or "We're doing that." The former group plainly do not entirely identify themselves with the company, the latter plainly do. Whether we say "they" or "we," in other words, often discloses where our heart really lies.

The same holds true of our other allegiances. When we at *Alberta Report* were preparing to work on this history project, a young Texan happened to be visiting us. I asked him why Texas was called "the Lone Star State." His reply went something like: "Oh you see, back in the 1830s and '40s, we were a republic for about 10 years. That's when we had the war with Mexico, the Alamo and all that. After that we entered the union." Utterly unconscious of what he was doing, this young man identified himself with events that occurred nearly a century and a half before he was born. It wasn't what "they" did, it was what "we" did. Whatever happened to Texas then, he was somehow involved in it. He was part of Texas and Texas was part of him.

Now you don't often hear Albertans, or any Canadians, talk this way. I don't hear Calgarians say something like, "Well, back in the Riel Rebellion, we actually raised two cavalry units here." Or Edmontonians observe: "We really got going when we ran a portage over to Athabasca Landing, what we used to call Fort Assiniboine." Or Medicine Hatters mention, "We used to be part of Saskatchewan, you know, until we joined Alberta in 1905." Some people talk like this, I know, but most do not. We do not identify with our own past. Insofar as we mention it at all, it's nearly always as "they."

Some would argue that this is a good thing. They would say we are "preserving our objectivity," or "demonstrating our resistance to flag-waving propaganda," or "holding ourselves dispassionately above the past, rather than becoming beholden to it." This, anyway, must have been the aim in educating our people away from the kind of commitment which the young Texan was educated towards.

Unfortunately, however, what so often has resulted is not the cool, dispassionate objectivity to prior events which the educators sought, but almost total indifference to and ignorance of them. Rather than being able to see several views of the farm revolt on the Prairies, for instance, their students scarcely know there ever was such a thing, and they could hardly see its connection with anything that might be going on now. The man who fought in a war might not be able to see many aspects of it as accurately as the man who later studies the war. Both, however, are preferable to the man who doesn't know there ever *was* a war. And the latter, it appears, is what our efforts at objectivity have all too often achieved.

Our society was very aware of the disadvantages of "commitment" to the past. We could see the dangers of jingoism and blind tribal loyalty only too clearly. What we did not see was the danger on the other extreme, that rootlessness could be every bit as destructive as partisanship, and that the man who "belonged" too fiercely to one society only, was perhaps not as dangerous as the man who belonged to no society at all.

We at *Alberta Report* are publishing these histories to help correct that error. Candidly, we want the Albertans who read them to come away from them saying "we" not "they." This does not mean approving of everything that "we" did, any more than recalling the events of our own lives necessarily means approving of everything we did in them. There are things I am glad I did, and things I am ashamed of having done, but there is no question I did them. The same is true when we look back on the deeds of our own society, and our own province. Some of the things described in these books were simply awful. They ought not to have happened, but they did, and "we" did them. Other things described were intelligent, visionary and courageous, and of those, by the same rule, we have every right to be proud.

More than ever, we think this identification with the past is now urgently needed. As this is written, in 1991, the future of the whole country is triply endangered. One province has declared itself so fundamentally different from the other nine that it can only remain in Confederation if certain conditions are met which the others believe unacceptable. While this receives the most attention, it is probably the least of our three problems. Of even graver import is the fact we have so burdened ourselves with debt that we cannot effectively compete with other countries around the world. Worst of all, our education system is in chaos, our schools hurled one way then another as successions of "new" teaching technologies are applied, and all the while the skills we impart to the next generation slip farther and farther behind those achieved by school systems elsewhere.

We face, in other words, a challenge every bit as formidable as that which confronted our forebears, whether white or red, on these Prairies a century or more ago. Their challenge was one of survival. At first they didn't know it, but they very soon did. So is ours one of survival. We may not know it, but economic reality will force us to know it very soon. Of that we may be certain.

Of one other reality we may be equally certain. Government — our old crutch and supposed helper, upon which we have placed so much confidence and learned so habitually to lean — cannot solve this problem. What is required is not a change in our government but a change in *us*. We have to become what we once were; we have to regain what we once had. We have to recover the same toughness, resilience, imagination and resolve that "we" once possessed. These virtues can only arise, of course, out of necessity. But that necessity seems now at hand.

To meet this need, first and foremost we must know who "we" are, how we got here, what we believe, what values we hold in common, what are our strengths, and where we are prone to err. All this our history can show us. And when it does, we may find we come away with a certain assurance, a strange sense of common purpose, a feeling of continuity with our past. No longer are we homeless. We know now where we live. We belong.

That the first volume of a history of Alberta in the 20th century should deal only with the 19th and earlier, and cover material widely beyond the boundaries of the province requires some explanation.

When the curtain goes up with the creation of the province in 1905, the stage is already crowded. Countless stories are already unfolding, and many of the leading characters have already established their roles. To make sense, therefore, of what was going on in 1905, you have to go back beyond this, indeed back to the first written records left by people who lived in or visited the lands that would one day constitute the province.

If it is impossible to make sense of an Alberta that begins abruptly in 1905, it would be even more difficult to explain Alberta in isolation from other parts of western Canada, or Canada, or North America as a whole. In the late 19th century, the area embraced by the present province was part of the North West Territories, its affairs wholly entwined with what is now Saskatchewan and related as well to the provinces of Manitoba and British Columbia. As a result the history of Alberta in fact involves the history of a whole lot else.

Hence, the history of Alberta is the history of the Plains Indians, of the Hudson's Bay Company and the fur trade, of the American Civil War, of Canadian Confederation, of the building of the Canadian Pacific, of the Riel Rebellion, and of the long struggle of the North West Territories to achieve provincehood. And that is how we have told it.

The reader will notice another, more immediately visible unorthodoxy. These volumes look more like magazines than history books. The use of hundreds of pictures and "sidebar" stories is akin to journalism, not history. We can hardly deny this; we are journalists, not historians. We are therefore describing the series as "a journalistic history," meaning a newsmagazine about events that occurred many years ago.

But our hope is that the reader will go from this popularized version to the real thing, to the real historians, of which Alberta has many fine ones, and to the primary sources. At best, we aim to tantalize, to whet the palate. The real banquet of the past will be found elsewhere. This is merely an appetizer.❦

Ted Byfield

Calgary policemen and townfolk gather with Police Chief Tom English (at centre, wearing medal) in 1900
Glenbow Archives, NA-1075-26

Section One
New Year's Eve, 1899

Chapters by Virginia Byfield
Sidebars by Brian Hutchinson, Brad Clark and Gregg Shilliday

Calgary Herald Collection, Glenbow Archives, NA-2864-13233

Calgary's Stephen Avenue in 1889, looking east from Scarth, or 1st Street S.W. A city noted for sandstone elegance and wandering cattle.

So much, in just 25 years, what could stop Calgary now?

FIRST THE MOUNTIES, THEN THE RANCHERS, THEN THE CPR ❦ CALGARY'S 4,000 CITIZENS FIGURED THEY HAD IT MADE AND THE STAMPEDE GROUNDS WERE WORTH EVERY CENT OF THAT $235

The sun broke through clouds that Sunday morning to shine briefly over the several hundred frame homes that lined the mud streets of the Canadian Pacific Railway divisional point called Calgary. Wood and coal fires in iron stoves were laying their haze of smoke over the town. Cows in backyard sheds mooed to be milked. Soon the bells of all eight churches would be ringing out across the Bow River valley. But this was no ordinary Sunday. It was December 31, 1899. In a few hours Calgary and the world would be entering the 20th century.[1]

A visitor to the place could not help but be impressed by its cocksure confidence in the coming era. True, it was a typical frontier establishment, founded only 25 years earlier as a North-West Mounted Police fort. But it had been bolstered by ranchers for whom it was a kind of headquarters, and by the CPR which made it the maintenance depot for the mountain region. Now, with a popu-

[1] At the time, as a matter of fact, there was a good deal of debate on this point. Did the 20th century begin on January 1, 1900, or on January 1, 1901? The argument was that if the 1st century started with 'year one' and ended with 'year 100,' then the 19th century must have started in 1801 and would close at the end of 1900. Historian Hugh Dempsey, former director of Calgary's Glenbow Institute, says that to his knowledge the matter was never resolved.

lation of 4,000 and by far the biggest prairie centre west of Winnipeg, how could it help but boom?

Coming into town from, say, Fort Macleod, the visitor would first encounter the home grounds of the Calgary Cricket Club: Victoria Park,[2] a fenced-off, 94-acre tract honouring the great Queen who had given her name to the era and who would die within 13 months. For many Calgarians, however, the park was chiefly distinguished as the site of the Agricultural Society's annual exhibition, which drew competing crop and livestock exhibits from all over the North West Territories. There they would marvel at sideshows featuring bearded ladies and Siamese twins, at palm readers and at hawkers of miracle cures for backaches and baldness, along with dazzling displays of the latest agricultural technology by the Massey Manufacturing Company of Toronto.

People still told how Major James Walker, a former North-West Mounted Police officer, got the grounds for the exhibition back in '84 with the help of a horse that threw its rider. The unfortunate victim, who broke his collar bone, was A.M. Burgess, deputy minister of the Department of the Interior at Ottawa. Walker took the badly shaken deputy to his home on the Bow, then used the opportunity to impress upon him Calgary's need for an agricultural fair, and how ideally the federally owned Victoria property would suit it. Burgess persuaded his political masters in the Tory government of John A. Macdonald to sell it to the society for $235. So the horse became a hero and the *Calgary Herald* nominated it for a seat in the territorial legislature.

Glenbow Archives NA-4778-1

Major James Walker, Mountie, ranch manager, businessman and mayor. He did the negotiations, but a horse got half the credit.

The real hero, if there was one, had to be the tireless town promoter Walker. A graduate of the Royal Military College at Kingston, Ontario, he served seven years with the NWMP, ending as superintendent. He then became the first manager of the Cochrane Ranche, and through Bow River Mills supplied much of the lumber for the new city's wooden buildings and sidewalks. Walker "quickly became the best-known figure in and about early Calgary," says Grant MacEwan in *Calgary Cavalcade*. Besides the Agricultural Society, he helped organize the school district, and formed and commanded the unit that protected the city when insurrection was feared in 1885.

Calgary had another lumber mill on the Bow River, operated by Peter Prince, just upstream from what came to be called Prince's Island. In its early history lay a major tragedy. Men from Prince's Eau Claire Lumber Company floated pine and spruce down the Bow from the forests to the west, a business fraught with danger. In July 1888, six of them drowned when their boat shot over a six-foot waterfall near Morley. Three had wives and children in Calgary; the others were transient Scandinavian workers. Prince's men removed a logjam where the men were believed to be trapped but the bodies were never found.

Calgary pedestrians appreciated their wooden sidewalks. Even in December there could be mud, although on the last Sunday of 1899 the temperature was 15 below zero Fahrenheit. Nothing like the terrible winter of 1886-87, however. People still shuddered over it as "the one without the chinooks," when it was already 40 below in November. By January fuel was so low Central School on Northcote Avenue[3] was shut down, and feed so short horses were too weak to haul wood from beyond the city limits.

Most Calgarians worked for the CPR and lived in frame homes, some one storey high and some two. Although these were modest enough, the residents at least had a water supply. It was hauled in by Tom Brennan who filled his horse-drawn tank each day from a well in front of City Hall. The affluent had their own wells. The decidedly unaffluent who inhabited clusters of shacks along the city's outskirts drew water from the Elbow, a tricky chore in winter.

Calgary did, however, have a waterworks of sorts. In 1889, after two years of haggling, the town signed a $75,000 contract with British capitalist George Alexander to steam-drive water through a four-inch main a mile and a half from a headworks on the Bow, supplying four fire hydrants, two drinking fountains and several troughs. It was a disappointment from the start. The pump kept failing and the firemen complained of inadequate pressure. The system, wrote city commissioner A.G. Graves in 1899, was "in a demoralized condition."[4] The next year the disgusted city took it over, replacing it in 1907 for $340,000 with a gravity line from up the Elbow.

Water inadequacies notwithstanding, Calgary's better-off citizenry could boast telephones and

[2] Over the next century, Victoria Park would become a dilapidated neighbourhood in the shadow of downtown Calgary, and the site of a large sandstone school built in 1918. In 1923, the Calgary Exhibition and Stampede was moved from Victoria Park to a new location a few blocks to the south-east. By the 1990s, however, the Stampede Board was seeking to expand its grounds and reoccupy Victoria Park.

[3] Central School was located on what later became James Short Park. The building was demolished in 1938 and replaced with a larger school, named after one of Calgary's first principals, James Short.

[4] The old waterworks' small sandstone pump house had a future none would have predicted, however. It survived as a theatre, known as "The Pumphouse," and became a National Historic Site.

electric lights. The Calgary Electric and Calgary Water Power companies had been selling power since 1890. But the price confined the service to the well-to-do. At 40 cents to a half-dollar a month for a single 16-candlepower lamp, it was far beyond the means of, say, a police constable who made $30 monthly. So most homes were lit by kerosene lamps.

Some 200 yards north of the CPR tracks stood the NWMP barracks. In 1882 prosaic frame buildings had replaced the spruce and pine fort that once provided security and lodging for up to 15 officers, 73 constables and 58 horses. (In the next century the tract would become a city-owned historic park.) F-Troop had come to the confluence of the Bow and the Elbow in 1875, under the command of Inspector E.A. Brisebois. This was the land of the Blackfoot who had been decimated by alcohol provided by roving fur traders from United States territory. F-Troop's job was to get rid of the whisky traders and keep peace with the Blackfoot.

I.G. Baker and Company of St. Louis supplied materials and built the fort in a matter of weeks, then opened a drygoods store.[5] A year later, Brisebois' commanding officer, Colonel A.G. Irvine, gave the outpost the name Fort Calgary, which may derive from the Gaelic for "bay farm." Inspector Brisebois had already taken to calling it Fort Brisebois, but as Tom Ward recounts in *Cowtown: An Album of Early Calgary*, he was sternly ordered to desist. Fort Macleod had been

[5] Expert at setting up frontier posts, the American firm was already well established on the Canadian side of the border by 1875.

This buckskin-clad father of 14 was the first Calgarian

Sam Livingston was on hand to greet the Mounties

Calgary's first settler was there waiting, so to speak, when the North-West Mounted Police rode in and decided to build their fort in 1874. On hand to greet them was a wild-looking man, dressed in buckskin and living in a cabin with his wife and a cluster of children.

An Irishman, Sam Livingston by name, he was as untamed as the land on which he lived. According to the Catholic missionary Father Albert Lacombe, he was "brimful of Celtic fire, with grizzled hair worn long, down to his shoulders. Leather trousers and red shirt, and a gay handkerchief knotted about his throat with another on his sombrero, completed a striking picture of a frontiersman."

Livingston's story typified the West of those times. Born in 1831, he left Ireland for America at 17, searched for gold, hunted buffalo and avoided hostile Indians for 20 years. The mid-1860s found him trading buffalo hides in the North Saskatchewan River country, and in 1865 he married Jane Howse, a granddaughter of Joseph Howse, the first Hudson's Bay man to cross the Rockies.

The couple settled at Victoria Mission, on the North Saskatchewan northeast of Edmonton, where the Hudson's Bay Company had recently established an outpost. Livingston became a freighter, carrying supplies between Edmonton, Winnipeg and Fort Benton in Montana. But he was enchanted by the rolling foothills of the south and in 1873 moved his family to a location on the Elbow River upstream from its confluence with the Bow.

Alex Ross, photographer, Glenbow Archives, NA-94-1

Livingston in 1890.

"Those aren't Indians," Livingston is supposed to have said to his wife when he spotted F-Troop riding towards them. "They're sitting different in their saddles." After the Mounties chose their site, Livingston moved downstream, establishing a grain and livestock farm that many years later would be submerged under the Glenmore Dam Reservoir.

Sam Livingston became a regular sight in Calgary, visiting the I.G. Baker store and the Windsor Hotel on Atlantic Avenue (later 9th Avenue) and chatting with the citizenry. He also contributed to the city's early population growth: he fathered 14 children, the last one born in 1896 when Livingston was 65.

The following year, making one of his usual stops at the Windsor, he suddenly complained of chest pains. A doctor was summoned and found Livingston, no churchgoer, kneeling over a mattress. "On your knees at last, Sam?" quipped the doctor. "Yes," came the reply, "and only just in time." Therewith the first Calgarian fell forward, dead. *B.H.*❦

C.I. Soule, photographer, Glenbow Archives, NA-1075-26

Calgary's first CPR station.

named for NWMP Colonel James F. Macleod, it was true, and Fort Walsh in the Cypress Hills for Superintendent James Morrow Walsh. The big difference was that Brisebois had been discredited for his lack of control of his men.

In the next eight years most of F-Troop was reassigned to forts Macleod and Walsh, where the whisky traders were more concentrated, and Fort Calgary much diminished. But the coming of the big ranches in '81 and the CPR in '83 changed the picture again. With the railway, an immediate tent town sprang into existence, providing under canvas both housing and, for a time, offices for a newspaper and a dentist. The hordes of workmen required a certain amount of policing, as did ranch hands.

Now, 17 years later, housing had undeniably improved. The firs and poplars lining the residential streets to the west of the fort had grown considerably since their planting a few years ago. Homes were still adorned with Christmas wreaths. Many were resplendent with colourful ribbons and Union Jacks for New Year's. Calgary, like most of western Canada, felt itself "British."

City Hall stood on the corner of Drinkwater[6] and McIntyre. In 1894, a mere decade after its incorporation as a town, Calgary became the first city in the territories, a distinction ill-represented by this long, low building. Adjoining it on the north was the two-storey city police station with its modest bell-tower. Even in winter, Thomas English, chief since 1890, could usually be found reclining in the rocking chair on its porch, a cigar stuck firmly in the corner of his mouth below his bushy moustache. Its four jail cells were customarily full after Saturday night's festivities, since it fell to the 12-man city force, mostly ex-Mounties, to collect the drunks and rowdies.

[6] Drinkwater Street was to become the Macleod Trail, and the future Calgary City Hall and municipal building would occupy the same site.

They also had to deal with the cattle problem. Many householders kept at least one cow to assure fresh milk. The animals habitually broke free and roamed at will through the dirt streets, the constables in determined pursuit. It did little for the dignity of the uniform. The NWMP continued to handle serious crime.

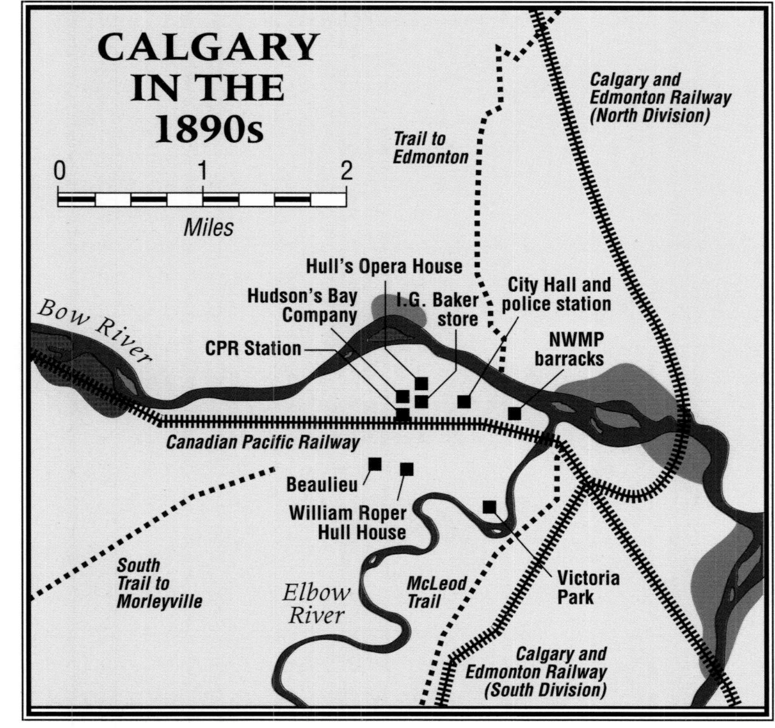

Such as murder. On February 8, 1884, for instance, James Adams, a young clerk, was found lying in his blood on the floor of McKelvie's store, steam rising into the chilly air from the gashes in his throat, a bloodied axe nearby. Alarmed Calgarians gathered in Clark and Beaudoin's music hall, at the back of the Exchange Saloon on Stephen Avenue. "A determined look marked every countenance," noted the *Calgary Herald.* "Lynching the culprit was spoken of."

But the NWMP were in charge and the investigation took them to a tepee west of town, the abode of Jess Williams, a Texas Negro recently arrived who had earlier been seen eyeing the store's open till. He was, said the *Herald*, "a short, thick man" whose "little twitch in the left eye" gave him "a diabolical appearance." Williams feigned innocence, then confessed to killing Adams and stealing around $50. A jury found him guilty and he was condemned to death.

For its fascinated readers, the *Herald* recounted his end in every grisly detail — how he spent two months at the NWMP barracks tied to a ball and chain, how Father Claude adminis-

A carpenter's son with a law degree founds a dynasty

JAMES LOUGHEED MADE GOOD FRIENDS IN THE CPR, AND FOUND A GOOD WIFE IN THE FAMED MIXED-BLOOD HARDISTYS

The 19th century was a time when men of humble origin could rise to great heights. Opportunities were everywhere, not least on Canada's western frontier, for those who knew how to seize them. James Alexander Lougheed, son of a Brampton, Ontario carpenter, knew how. When he journeyed west in 1883 at 29 he had practised law for five years in Toronto. His Calgary career would help mould the city of Calgary and the province of Alberta. It would also make James Lougheed a wealthy man and a knight of the realm.

One story would have it that the young lawyer finished his journey to Calgary on foot, a few months before the tracks got there.* In any event, he had made a valuable connection on his journey from Toronto. Meeting William Van Horne along the way, he had convinced the CPR general manager that he was the man to handle the railway's Calgary legal business.

His talent as a lawyer was matched by his talent for land speculation. In the 1880s, says Marian McKenna in *Citymakers: Calgarians after the Frontier*, "a man could prosper merely by dabbling in real estate. Lougheed did more than that; he was enough of a gambler and speculator to garner dazzling rewards from high-risk venture."

He was also well-informed. The neighbours may have been puzzled, for example, when he bought 35 lots west of the original townsite. Illumination came when his client, the CPR, announced plans to build a new station just one block from the young lawyer's property. Eventually the entire town would form around the station.

Lougheed the deal-maker did not lack for Alberta connections beyond Calgary either. Fiery Frank Oliver, a man of very different political style, had been a schoolmate of his back in Brampton. Far more important, though, was his marriage in 1884 to Belle, a member of the prominent mixed-blood Hardisty family. Her father, William L. Hardisty, was chief factor for the Hudson's Bay Company's Mackenzie district. Her uncle, Richard Hardisty, chief factor at Edmonton and inspector for the entire northern district, was appointed first senator from Alberta in 1888.

What's more, an aunt of Belle's, Isabella Sophia Hardisty, was married to Donald A. Smith, which made him a Lougheed in-law. Smith, later Lord Strathcona, was the prime mover and shaker behind the CPR, the HBC's biggest shareholder, and a major shareholder in the Bank of Montreal. The HBC subsequently became a Lougheed client, and so did the bank.

W. E. Wing, photographer, Glenbow Archives, NA-3232-7

Sir James Lougheed, speculator and senator.

After overseeing the construction of several important office buildings in his chosen city, Lougheed turned his attention to politics. At first he limited himself to lobbying for provincial status for Alberta, but when Richard Hardisty died in 1889 James Lougheed was appointed to succeed him as senator. He was 35, one of the younger senators. He would later become Conservative leader in the Senate and hold cabinet portfolios from 1911 to 1921.

Despite his frequent absences in Ottawa, the Calgary law practice continued to flourish, thanks in part after 1897 to a junior partner named Richard Bedford Bennett, another eastern fortune-seeker. (A New Brunswicker, R.B. Bennett was to become Canada's 11th prime minister.) When the senator was at home, he and Belle, besides producing six children, functioned as social arbiters at their Calgary mansion. An invitation to Beaulieu was a coveted honour.

Powerful connections notwithstanding, the James Lougheed success story was rooted in his ability to spot an unexploited opportunity. Almost a century later, grandson Edgar Peter Lougheed would notably apply the same talent in the electoral field, to steer the province through 14 tumultuous years of another boom. *B.H.*❦

* Only the barest facts of Senator Lougheed's life have ever been published. Apparently none of his personal papers have been preserved, a circumstance that has thwarted would-be biographers.

tered the last rites, how the condemned man consumed a final breakfast of beefsteak, toast and coffee, how the 16-foot scaffold cast a shadow on the fort as he was led out, how he mounted it, how the noose was placed around his neck, how the executioner with black hood covering his face swung an axe at the bolt holding the rope in place, how Williams' body plunged seven feet before the slack ran out and shook convulsively for a full seven minutes before he finally strangled to death.

For most Calgarians much of the time life held no such riveting excitement, however. Rather, there were rituals — like the open-air market[7] every Friday, 10:00 to 6:00, across McIntyre Avenue from the police station. Fresh meat, fresh fish and vegetables in season. In winter, coal and hay hawkers took it over. Or after church on Sunday there was the trooping of young people to barn-like Claxton's Rink, sometimes called the Star,[8] one block north up Drinkwater and a block west on Angus Avenue for ice-skating in winter, roller-skating in summer, to the music of the NWMP band.

Claxton's also featured the highly popular foot races, some of them 16-hour ordeals run four hours at a time over four days. It was there in 1886 that NWMP Constable James Green was pitted against two Blackfoot Indians, Little Plume and the famous Deerfoot. (His actual name is said to have been Scabby Dried Meat, but his white promoters thought "Deerfoot" would inspire more confidence and less nausea among bettors.)

W.H. Boorne, photographer, Glenbow Archives, NA-250-3

'Deerfoot' the famous Blackfoot runner, in 1887. A warrior with Sun Dance scars on his chest, his end was tragic, but his memorial magnificent.

Tall and well-muscled, Deerfoot could run for hours without tiring, and in the first two days both he and Little Plume easily outdistanced Constable Green. But wily gamblers had devised a scheme to scratch Deerfoot from the race. They got him roaring drunk, and sure enough, the third day he lagged badly. No matter, he said, on the fourth he'd win. And so he did, while the whole town roared in appreciation.

Deerfoot went on to win more big races against white opponents. But in 1887 he stole two wool blankets from a settler, then outran the Mounties for two years before finally giving himself up. While he was serving 45 days' hard labour, his spirit seemed to break. He never raced again and spent the rest of his life in and out of jail, never suspecting, of course, that one day a great Calgary freeway would honour his memory.

Farther along Angus Avenue, where it crossed McTavish Street, the 1899 visitor would come to Hull's Opera House.[9] Only three evenings ago, the imposing brick structure was the scene of Calgary's 10th Annual Firemen's Ball, one of the year's most important social events. Beneath yards of bright "Victoria Regina" bunting, a huge portrait of the Queen and the firemen's emblazoned motto, "Duty, Vigilance, Humanity, and Promptitude," the 300 guests danced to the music of Mr. Augade's orchestra. Completing the scene, noted the *Herald*, were the ladies in their ball gowns of

[7] The open-air market occupied the future 7th Avenue site of the public library.

[8] The Star, built in 1885, stood next to the site where the Calgary Police Service building would be located a century later.

[9] Built in 1893 and demolished in 1906, it was situated on what would become the corner of 6th Avenue and Centre Street.

How Joe Butlin's discovery made a new Calgary

After the Great Fire of '86 his strange porous rock led to the 'sandstone city'

In 1880 NWMP officer Joe Butlin left the force to take up ranching on a spread two and a half miles south of the little settlement at Calgary, on the banks of the Elbow River. It wasn't long before Butlin realized his ranch was sitting on an extensive seam of yellowish, slightly porous rock. He had discovered the material that by the century's end would cause admirers to dub Calgary "the sandstone city."

Timber, readily available and easy to use, had naturally been the first choice for Calgary building material. The timber fort was still the only substantial structure in the place in 1880. Around it huddled (in addition to tents and tepees) a collection of wooden cabins. Watchmaker George E. Jacques and his wife were quite typically accommodated in 1881. Their first home, 12 feet by 16 feet, had a dirt floor, a mud roof and a single, small window. They slept on straw and cooked over an open fire.

Two years later the railroad boom brought more substantial housing, along with a few three- and four-storey commercial buildings. Some homes even boasted paint or simple lattice work on windows and doors. A quite decent three-room frame house could be built for $400. Shops, though they often featured false fronts, might have large display windows. But Calgary's building style was still entirely frame and very much "frontier."

Unfortunately the wooden town was also extremely vulnerable to fire. After the "Great Fire of 1886" blazed for 24 hours, consuming much of the business district, Joe Butlin's sandstone discovery began to attract attention. Besides Butlin, men like Thomas Edworthy, John McCallum and Colonel W.B. Barwis established sandstone quarries. Several small stone structures were built in 1886, the first stone church (Knox Presbyterian) a year later.

Provincial Archives of Alberta, E. Brown Collection, B-3139

What better way to enhance a dusty prairie town than build with stone? In the 1890s, it was used extensively downtown, as in the new Hudson's Bay store (right), and in the wealthy neighbourhood to the southwest; (upper far right) the Lougheed mansion 'Beaulieu,' and (lower far right) a more modest bungalow.

Glenbow Archives, NA-4441-2

The new sandstone courthouse was completed in 1888 at a cost of $40,000. The renowned Alberta Hotel was opened at the corner of Stephen Avenue and Scarth Street (later 1st Street West), where it stood through the 20th century as well. In the 1890s the architecture became more ornate. Turrets, fancy stonework and large bay windows appeared. Perhaps the most elaborate building was the Alexander Corner (1891) erected on the site later occupied by the Hudson's Bay Company.

By the time Calgary achieved city status in 1894, main thoroughfare Stephen Avenue was becoming a sandstone strip. Construction permits totalled $300,000 annually, and almost 50% of construction workers were involved in stone masonry. Prominent citizens like William Roper Hull, Peter Prince, James Lougheed and William Pearce were using their influence and their money to reshape the urban landscape, and the urban lifestyle too.

Glenbow Foundation Library, Glenbow Archives, NA-1586-4

As Paul Voisey notes in his essay "Entrepreneurs in Early Calgary" (in *Frontier Calgary*), the city's social and business leaders tried hard to "ape the behaviour of the Eastern elite." Among other things, this involved garden parties, British-style private schools for their children and, of course, suitable housing. "Sandstone," author Voisey writes, "gave Calgary the appearance of solid respectability that was lacking in most western cities. It became a prestigious symbol for the very rich."

Brick was also admissible, it is true. British-born rancher, meat packer and land speculator Hull built a sumptuous brick mansion, Longmore, a block west of the later site of the Colonel Belcher Hospital. Hull is said to have spent $3,000 decorating its interior, including installation of a third-floor billiard room, and to have customarily worn a red velvet smoking jacket to receive guests.

But stone was considered especially appropriate. Sandstone mansions began appearing on the city's southwest fringe, about half a mile from the bald hill later known as Mount Royal. The three-storey James Lougheed home, Beaulieu, which still survives, stood on what would become 13th Avenue, amidst lawns, terraces and fountains. The interior featured marble imported from Italy, mahogany from Spain and furniture from England.

Federal government official William Pearce built his huge sandstone home on the east side of the Elbow. Ironically named Bow Bend Shack, it was heated by steam and lit by gas. The gas lighting extended to the ample grounds, where Pearce carried out some of the district's earliest horticultural experiments.

The homes of the affluent may have incited envy among less fortunate citizens. But the mansions and the warm, golden, sandstone glow of downtown Calgary were nevertheless a source of reassuring civic satisfaction for all. *B.H.*❦

Glenbow Archives, M-2271

The Officers and Members
of the Calgary Fire Department request the
pleasure of the company of
Mr. W. Smith & Ladies
at their Tenth Annual Complimentary Ball
to be given in the Opera House, on
Thursday, Dec. 28th, 1899,
at 21 o'clock.

T. Tarrant, Chairman of Committee.
Geo. Mitchell, Secretary.

R.S.V.P.
Please present this card at the door

The Firemen's Ball was a social highlight of the 1899 season.

satin and lace.

Balls were a regular feature, usually with music supplied by the NWMP band or several other local groups. The Calgary Dramatic and Musical Club performed regularly, as did the Calgary Amateur Orchestral Society. Some imported entertainment had become available too, like an 1886 performance by an Italian string band and an 1892 discussion of *Ben Hur*, complete with "stereopticon" illustrations. The Literary and Debating Society was established in 1884. By 1892 the Young Men's Christian Association reading room offered 18 different newspapers. Ladies interested in reading joined the Calgary Institute for $1 per annum.

A marked shortage of single women somewhat inhibited Calgary's social and intellectual life, however, and matrimonial prospects were poor for single men. A certain Mrs. Fitzgibbon of Ontario, the *Herald* had reported the previous summer, was trying to bring women from England to the territories to match them with bachelors. Nothing had been heard of the scheme since. So Calgary remained a decidedly male city. There were prostitutes, of course, who appeared in court from time to time. Only last March, in fact, a notorious rascal of a woman had turned up with two young Ukrainian girls, with the intent of selling them to a Chinese brothel. Her scheme was discovered and thwarted by the police.

Moving south down McTavish Street to McIntyre Avenue, the visitor might spot Cappy Smart and his family — wife Agnes, son Bud and daughter Minnie — heading home from church that Sunday morning. Smart, the fire chief, lived right next door to the large fire hall on McIntyre, whose 50-foot tower dominated the city skyline and reminded Calgarians that help was there if it was needed.

Glenbow Archives, NA-4942-4

Thomas and Fanny Bryant with their children, outside their typical home on 5th Street West in 1898.

There had been no tower and not much help a decade and a half earlier, when J.L. Bowen's house caught fire on a cold January day and a hastily recruited bucket brigade proved incapable of doing anything about it. Neighbours even tried to save the house by heaving snowballs into the blaze. The brigade was better organized but still woefully underequipped in the fall of 1886 when the "Great Fire" struck Calgary.

At two o'clock in the morning of October 15, Parrish's flour and feed store, across from the CPR station on Atlantic Avenue,[10] caught fire, no one was ever sure how. A strong wind spread the blaze to other buildings, including the Union Hotel. Soon the flames had moved a block east and a block north, towards Stephen Avenue. Fire volunteers, rushing to the scene, found that their new "chemical engine" and hose-reel had been locked in a nearby building by customs officers because city council could not pay the duty on it. The desperate firefighters broke into the building, grabbed the engine and used it to douse the fire, which by then had consumed 16 buildings. The city fathers, upon this painful lesson, built their well-equipped fire hall the next year.

A block north of the tracks, McIntyre led to Stephen Avenue, named for George Stephen, president of the CPR. This was probably Calgary's busiest intersection. Here the Hudson's Bay Company had erected a magnificent stone building, two storeys high. The HBC had gone all out that Christmas. The

[10] At Centre Street and 9th Avenue, site of the future Skyline Hotel.

A.J. Ross, photographer, Glenbow Archives, NA-298-3

Atlantic Avenue (now 9th, between Centre Street and 1st Street S.E.) after the Great Fire of 1886; first one block went up, then another. The fact the customs officers had locked up the fire engine didn't help.

grocery window featured an old-fashioned log cabin with Santa Claus preparing to hop down the chimney. The drygoods window sported a large Christmas tree, and another displayed bottles of whisky and sherry.

The prestigious law offices of James Lougheed and R.B. Bennett were located not far from here, as were the *Calgary Herald* office and the Bank of Montreal. A little to the west was the 11-year-old Alberta Hotel, located on the corner of Stephen and Scarth.[11]

Chinatown began not far to the east,[12] a motley assortment of shacks that housed some 50 of those few Chinese workers who had migrated east of the mountains, rather than west or south, when the CPR was completed. Most of them now worked in laundries and restaurants. In 1892 Chinatown occasioned an incident that stands as a blemish on Calgary's history.

Almost exclusively male, its inhabitants reputedly spent what little leisure they had quietly playing mahjong or smoking opium. But then a laundryman on Stephen Avenue was discovered to have smallpox. He was immediately quarantined on the edge of town, but the case caused panic and some sought to rid Calgary of all Chinese.

"The local feeling against the race is strong," reported the *Herald*, "and it is well for the authorities to recognize the fact." It published a letter, headed "The Chinamen Must Go," which declared them "undesirable in any white community." Several weeks later, a mob of 300 drunken whites attacked Chinatown and tried to burn it down. The NWMP rescued the inhabitants.

The "Smallpox Riot" was not a proud moment in Calgary's history and was categorically denounced elsewhere in Canada. The *Manitoba Free Press* called the mob a "cowardly pack." Calgarians remained unrepentant, however. Six hundred of them jammed Hull's Opera House to hear one Locksley Lucas deliver a vehement rebuke against the Chinese. After the lecture they formed an Anti-Chinese League.

South of Chinatown, beyond further rows of undistinguished frame dwellings, lay the homes of the gentry, the sandstone mansions of people like Patrick Burns, the millionaire cattleman and meat packer, and Senator James Lougheed. These were elegant estates with extensive lawns, servants' quarters, steam heating and indoor plumbing.

But at the heart of the city was the Canadian Pacific station, nerve centre of the railway that had given Calgary such promise. Here trains ran east, west and south. They also ran north, to another prairie centre where a very different kind of city was emerging.❦

[11] At 8th Avenue and 1st Street West, it was to survive as an office building throughout the 20th century.

[12] Chinatown began here in the early 1890s, was relocated across the railway tracks in 1900, and moved later to its more permanent location on Centre Street and 3rd and 4th Avenues.

CHAPTER TWO

In 'Old Edmonton' the new century brings a ray of hope at last

ITS BOOM WENT BUST WHEN THE CPR BYPASSED IT, THEN THE GOLD RUSH FIZZLED ❦ BUT NOW THERE WAS TALK OF NOT ONE BUT TWO RAILWAYS HEADING STRAIGHT FOR IT

Eleven hours north of Calgary by jolting and lurching train, on the far bank of the North Saskatchewan River, brooded a community of less than 2,000 souls known unpropitiously at the century's end as "Old Edmonton." It was a city of resentments. For years, at least until very recently, it had resented Ottawa. Even more than Ottawa it resented Calgary. Even more than Calgary it resented the latest of its grievances, often referred to

Provincial Archives of Alberta, E. Brown Collection, B-5542

Jasper Avenue in 1890. Because the Hudson's Bay Company had not subdivided its reserve west of 101st Street until 1880, early development spread eastward.

as "New Edmonton," the annoying little upstart community that was springing blithely into life on the south bank of the unbridged river.

Only 20 years earlier the fur station of Fort Edmonton seemed to have an assured future as first city in the District of Alberta. The great Pacific railway had been surveyed to run that way. This coincided with a Winnipeg-based real estate speculation boom involving various western towns, of which isolated Edmonton was the most bizarre.

Edmonton as a hot real estate prospect became even more bizarre after 1881, however, when the CPR suddenly opted for a southern route through an inconsiderable place variously known as "Bow Fort," or "Elbow," or "Fort Calgary." By 1899 Calgary boasted a population of 4,000, while Old Edmonton stagnated and seethed, one river valley beyond the end of the 191-mile spur known as the Calgary and Edmonton Railway. The uncertainty of C&E service was rivalled only by the uncertainty of its ever bridging the river.

Yet even in Old Edmonton there were now good grounds for optimism. For one thing, despite setbacks, it had been growing at a fairly steady pace: from an estimated 350 residents in 1887 to about 1,800 by 1899. Moreover, there was extravagant talk of not one railway through Edmonton to the Pacific, but two: not only the hare-brained dream of those two wild contractors, Mackenzie and Mann, but the far more substantial vision of the new Liberal government of Wilfrid Laurier, for whom the northern Prairies were a centre of interest and a source of votes. Build either one of 'em, said the optimists, and Edmonton would grow tenfold.

In the meantime, however, it was New Edmonton, just incorporated as the Town of Strathcona[1], that was proclaiming itself "the Railway Centre of the North." In a mere five years its population had more than doubled, from 505 to 1,156. And was the C&E likely to cross the river, gloated gleeful New Edmonton boosters, while its directors were busily speculating in Strathcona real estate? Only by three river ferries was Old Edmonton tenuously linked to the C&E terminus and to the world.

Old Edmonton was living in the past, its rivals yawned. The Hudson's Bay Company fort still dominated its sparse skyline, perched atop the riverbank on what would one day be the meticulously groomed grounds of the Legislature. The fur trade, upon which its economy had been founded, was rapidly declining in significance, though merchants on both sides of the river still prospered by supplying provisions to trappers working in the Peace, Athabasca and Mackenzie regions, and furs taken in those areas were all sold, bought and shipped through the HBC in Edmonton.

There had also been the wild, if brief, extravaganza of the Klondike rush in '97 and '98. And with rainfall higher and soil richer than that of the southern Prairies, both grain production and mixed farming were off to a promising start. Coal was abundant and being mined; over 100 years later, the riverbank coal seams would still be visible from the downtown valley trails. It sold then for $1.50 a ton, $2.50 delivered, for household use and to fuel many of the steam-powered riverboats that carried freight on the North Saskatchewan.[2] Finally, timber was being boomed down-river to Edmonton sawmills.

The net result of all this was published in the *Edmonton Bulletin* as the city's "exports" for the month of October 1899, expressed in numbers of railcars: five of coal, seven of cattle, 20 of oats, two of potatoes, two of hogs and seven of "mixed grain and mill stuffs." Among the "small lots" shipped out were 370 pounds of eggs, 2,200 pounds of beer and 1,710 pounds of wool. The foodstuffs in particular were bound for the interior of British Columbia, while the other goods were destined for markets across the country.

[1] The name Strathcona honours Donald A. Smith, Lord Strathcona, one of the founders of the CPR. By plebiscite in 1898 residents chose the name "Minto" after Canada's governor-general, the 4th Earl of Minto. The territorial government substituted Strathcona, ostensibly because Minto had already been used. Only the unincorporated community of Minto, New Brunswick, was later listed with that name, however, and not until 1904.

[2] The most famous steamer, a sternwheeler called the *Northwest*, had served the area well, bringing goods upriver from Fort Carlton. During the Riel Rebellion in 1885 it was fitted with guns and carried troops. But the C&E rendered it obsolete, and it was beached on the south side of the river on Walter's Flats. Heavy rain in the summer of '99, carried it downstream and smashed it on the centre pier of the unfinished Low Level Bridge.

Provincial Archives of Alberta, E. Brown Collection, B-5631

The sternwheeler Northwest. *After an illustrious career, she came to a sad end.*

Strathcona's local newspaper, the weekly *Alberta Plaindealer,* was disposed to the same boosterism, typical of all western publications, bragging extensively of Strathcona's various commercial assets. Not only was there the boundless promise of the railway terminal—mentioned four times in a single editorial, doubtless for the benefit of the embittered people across the river—but there were also John Walter's sawmill, and sleigh and wagon shop. The enterprising Walter toiled just east of what would become the site of the High Level Bridge, where he also operated the area's longest serving rope ferry. His partner in the mill, ironically, was Old Edmonton entrepreneur William Humberstone. About 200 men were employed in their mill, where a sign warned: "No Swearing" and "Only Irishmen need apply." Walter also built river dredgers, the editorial pointed out, for the modest gold sluicing industry on the river, and ran several coal mines along the river bank.

Another unparalleled asset, said the *Plaindealer,* was Robert Ritchie's flour mill, the first in Alberta to be equipped with steel rollers, which made possible the milling of the hard Red Fife wheat. As well, Strathcona boasted a creamery, a brewery, the territory's first iron foundry and four "first-class hotels." The Pollard brothers ran a brickyard west of John Walter's mill, right next to the tannery of Firmin Bedard.

But Old Edmonton, despite its disappointments, was still substantially ahead of its rival on the south bank. Humberstone had established a brickyard there almost 20 years earlier. On the flats later known as Riverdale, James Little operated another one; as J.B. Little & Sons it would continue production until 1956. D.R. Fraser and Richard Hardisty had flour and sawmills. Tom Cairns ran a brewery on the Ross Flats, just east of Donald Ross' Edmonton Hotel. Another brewery, owned by James Gibson, occupied the site of the future Royal Glenora Club.

Most of the banking and finance in the area was handled by the Edmonton branch of the Imperial Bank, opened in 1891 and managed for 45 years by G.R.F. Kirkpatrick. A board of trade, established in 1889 by Matt McCauley,[3] John A. McDougall and Frank Oliver, the irascible editor of the *Bulletin,* aggressively protected, promoted and protested the interests of local commerce.

By the end of 1899 both towns had most of the social institutions and major utilities expected

[3] McCauley, Edmonton's first mayor and a man of boundless energy, was to represent the constituency of Victoria, immediately northeast of Old Edmonton, in the first provincial legislature, before becoming warden of the new dominion penitentiary. In 1911 he moved to Penticton and became a highly successful apple grower. Still restless at 75, he returned to Alberta as a homesteader near Sexsmith, 12 miles north of Grande Prairie, clearing and breaking a new farm. He died there in 1930 at age 80.

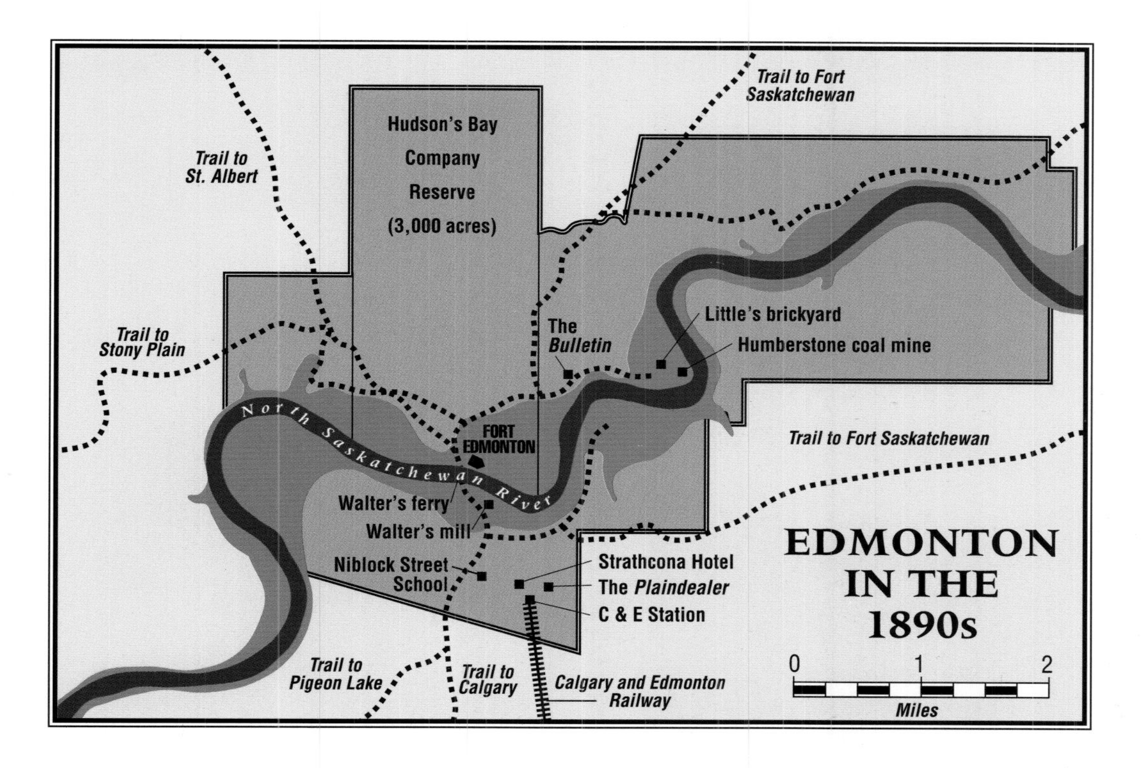

of any growing North American community. Edmonton set up its public school system in 1884, hiring Richard Secord to teach in the two-room school for a salary of $800 a year. (Dick Secord did much better than that later on, when he became a partner of trader John A. McDougall.) Southside children had to cross on Walter's ferry to attend school, season permitting, until 1891, when a log cabin schoolhouse was built next to the C&E hotel. A frame building finished in 1892 was replaced by the brick Niblock Street School on the northwest corner of Whyte Avenue[4] and 105th Street in 1894, the same year that farmer and community leader Laurent Garneau founded a Catholic school division.

Edmonton's hospital, built and run by the Grey Nuns, served the district's medical needs from 1896. Alex Taylor, who had brought the telegraph to Edmonton in 1879, had also introduced a telephone system (1886) and an electric power plant (1891) that served both communities. Sewage systems would not become a municipal priority until early in the coming century; for the time being, backyard plumbing prevailed.

Though the economy of both Edmontons was essentially the same, the two nevertheless differed in character. Old Edmonton, as the site of the fort, was nearly a century older and its French-Canadian element made it seem more cosmopolitan. The fevered enthusiasms of the *Plaindealer* notwithstanding, it was also more commercial. Old Edmonton produced people whom its boosters would call "resolute" and "tenacious," men like Frank Oliver, Donald Ross, Alex Taylor, Matt McCauley and John A. McDougall. Strathconans, of course, saw these same qualities rather differently, as "pig-headed" and "stubborn."

So, to put it mildly, did William Pearce, the Dominion Lands Board inspector who was assigned by Ottawa to

Provincial Archives of Alberta, E. Brown Collection

Matt McCauley. A tenacious Edmontonian (some would say pig-headed).

[4] Strathcona's Whyte Avenue is named for Sir William Whyte, general superintendent of the CPR's western division (1886) and the company's second vice-president (1904).

Provincial Archives of Alberta, E. Brown Collection, B-5184

Edmonton's zany Klondike caper

MERCHANDIZING 'THE BACK DOOR ROUTE' GAVE THE CITY A SHORT-LIVED BOOM BUT 70 PEOPLE DIED TRYING TO USE IT

There is a tide in the affairs of men which taken at the flood leads on to fortune: Omitted, all the voyage of their life is bound in shallows and miseries.

With this goading challenge, borrowed from Shakespeare's *Julius Caesar*, Edmonton merchants John A. McDougall and Richard Secord urged prospectors in 1897 to take the "Great Back Door Route" to the boundless wealth of the Yukon gold fields. Their enthusiastic advertisements described the Edmonton-Yukon journey as "the Shortest, Cheapest and Best." It was not, and hundreds suffered terribly or perished finding out. But it produced a riotous two years that the future Alberta capital would long remember and would one day commemorate with an annual "Klondike Days" festival.

A McDougall & Secord leaflet outlined for the bold and daring the various trails and waterways of the Edmonton route, with the distances from one point to the next. Equally important, it listed the requisite provisions — which McDougall & Secord were naturally prepared to supply. Distributed across North America, the leaflet brought thousands of gold-hungry prospectors to town.

Over the next two years this advertising campaign, allied with the promotional zeal of *Bulletin* publisher Frank Oliver and the Edmonton Board of Trade, brought to town an extraordinary conglomeration of people, who were largely accommodated in a tent city on the flats of the North Saskatchewan, along with their dog teams and packhorses. They included a rich assortment of oddballs, some of whom brought with them or manufactured such strange transportation contrivances as to tax local credulity.

The idea was to reach the Klondike as quickly and painlessly as possible, of course, so amphibious craft were particularly popular. One ark-like device was equipped with a keel for river travel and runners for snow. A similar "boat-sled" had a wheel that doubled as a rudder. A chap known

Provincial Archives of Alberta, E. Brown Collection, B-5265

Klondikers on Jasper Avenue in 1898 (opposite page). It was 'incomprehensible' that sane men should try this, said Sam Steele. (Left) a Klondike-bound contraption. Everything collapsed, first the machines, then the whole venture.

as Texas Smith had a horse-drawn, all-terrain vehicle he called "the Duck." Topped with a sleeping platform, it used wooden barrels as wheels. When Smith rumbled off to find his fortune, the hoops were jolted off the barrels and the Duck collapsed.

George Glover of Chicago brought a steam sleigh, a locomotive of the snows christened the "I Will," intended to tow cars of supplies to the north. A spike-studded, 400-pound steel drum drove the sleigh. When Glover fired up the machine to begin his journey the heavy drivewheel spun furiously, hurling snow and dirt at the nervous crowd of onlookers. But the mighty I Will would not. It succeeded only in digging an impressive hole in the frozen ground.

Irish peer Viscount Avonmore (known unkindly to the locals as "Lord Have One More") was no less dauntless. He came to Edmonton with a party of former British Army colleagues, servants, 10,000 pounds of supplies and (according to legend) a hundredweight of toilet tissue and 75 cases of vintage champagne. But the Avonmore party, like its expensive bubbly, couldn't handle the rigours of the winter; it broke up shortly after departure. The champagne also froze, it was said, and was sold on the streets for 25 cents a bottle.

While the gold rush brought cash and merriment to the town, it had a very different outcome for the prospectors. Two routes to the Klondike from Edmonton had been worked out, both extremely arduous. The "water" route followed the Athabasca River to Great Slave Lake, then the Mackenzie River, and went west over mountains from the Mackenzie's delta — almost 5,000 miles in all. The "overland" route, the short one, took Klondikers to either Fort St. John or Fort Nelson in British Columbia, then on to the gold fields via the Pelly and Yukon rivers, about 1,500 miles but hard foot-slogging through tough terrain.

Superintendent Sam Steele of the NWMP once said it was "incomprehensible that sane men" would take the Edmonton route to the Klondike. Trails were almost nonexistent. The forests were thick with fallen timber that ripped the shins of horses. Feed for pack animals was hard to come by. And most of the hopefuls who tried the trip were anything but seasoned woodsmen.

One historian counted 766 men, nine women and 4,000 horses who set out by the overland route: only 160 men made it, and not a single woman or horse. The water route had a better success rate. Some 565 souls reached the Yukon that way, out of an estimated 885. Historian James G. MacGregor estimates that the two routes took 35 lives apiece. Two starved, four froze, six died in accidents, 20 drowned, 32 fell victim to scurvy and six people died after reaching Dawson or other Yukon points. He concludes that only 725 men got to the Klondike from Edmonton, and only 20 of those came back with anything more than their lives.

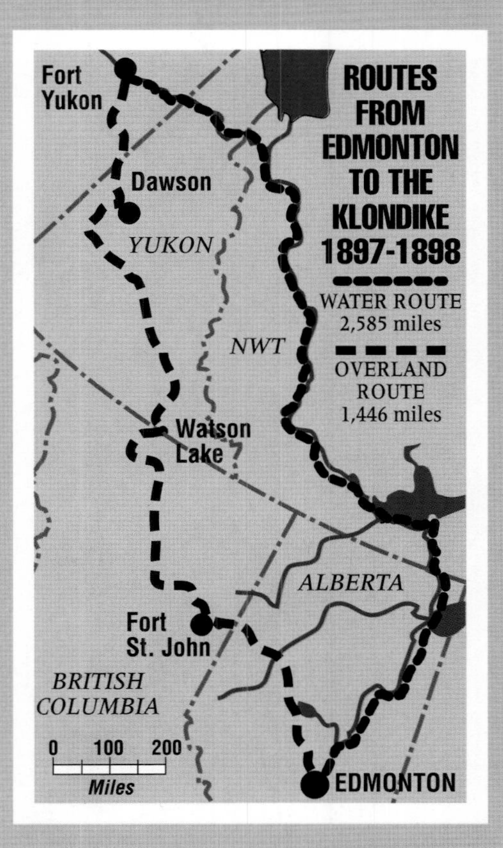

The vast majority of gold seekers, not deceived by Edmonton blandishments, took a train to Vancouver or Seattle, boarded a boat to Alaska, and then crossed the Chilkoot Pass (also admittedly very difficult). On the map the Edmonton route looked much shorter — but the prospectors weren't travelling on a map. *B.C.*

settle some 30 disputed property claims around Edmonton in 1884. The dominion government had finally got around to surveying the area, but some land had been occupied for generations although no one could prove either ownership or the precise location of property lines. Disputes were heated and not all Pearce's decisions were universally accepted. McDougall for one objected, taking his case to court where it remained in dispute well into the next century, with all the claimants still uncertain as to who owned what.

Nor was McDougall the only Edmontonian Pearce tangled with. Oliver, who quarrelled with virtually everyone associated with the dominion Tory government, was another. So was Laurent Garneau. (Garneau was also arrested in 1885 on suspicion of spying for rebel Louis Riel but was not prosecuted.) Father Hippolyte Leduc of the Catholic Mission, discerning an anti-French bias in his decisions, called Pearce a racist.

Pearce responded in like terms. "As to the people in the vicinity of Edmonton, that is the white population, they are about the worst class one can meet with on Canadian soil," he wrote. "I presume there is more whiskey drank per head than any place...There are private stills at work and I must confess I can see no way to stop the traffic. These people, many of them, put in a bare existence, their chief occupation seems to be anything to create a row between the difficult elements of the community, or as against the government. Even the clergy do not keep themselves from that style of thing as they should. I can see that the community generally is a tough one."

Pearce, who settled in Calgary after his Edmonton experience, there to pursue a long and honourable career, would not have lacked for other evidence of northern obstreperousness. He could well have drawn his impressions from some of the provocative personal ads appearing in the *Bulletin* at about that time. These have no real parallel in modern journalism. People simply bought space in the newspapers to vent their ill-feelings.

Typical was one run by J.R. Matheson, local merchant and settler: "J.R. Matheson is at home now. Can be found at any time at his place on the Sturgeon River. Bark now, ye sneaking curs who have so much to say behind his back. Or shut your mouths before he has to shut them for you."

The J.B. Little & Sons brickyard on the Riverdale flats. Despite Strathcona's railway, Old Edmonton kept ahead of its upstart rival.

Provincial Archives of Alberta, E. Brown Collection, B-1343

[5] The *Plaindealer* was edited by R.P. Pettipiece between 1894 and 1896 and J. Hamilton MacDonald from then until it folded in 1912. "Parm" Pettipiece went on to the mining boom town of Ferguson, British Columbia, in 1901, where as editor of the *Ferguson Eagle* he jousted with J.L. Langstaff of the *Trout Lake Topic.*

[6] Jasper Avenue gets its name from Jasper Hawes, an independent trapper with an Indian wife who joined the Hudson's Bay Company at Brûlé Lake in the Rockies in 1813, a post soon identified on HBC maps as Jasper House. Speculation that he was the fair-haired man for whom the Yellowhead Pass was named is likely not warranted, although he and his family are said to have drowned while rafting down the raging Fraser, whose headwater valley provides the Yellowhead's western exit. But David Smyth, in "Tête Jaune" (*Alberta History*, Winter 1984), conclusively demonstrated that "Yellowhead" was an Iroquois Indian.

The *Bulletin* carried a reply several issues later: "I wish to inform Mr. Matheson that I think if there is a sneaking cur in the country, he is one. Signed, George Gagnon."

Vitriol was in good supply among the editors themselves. They could seldom resist the opportunity to taunt their competitors, and did not shrink from allusions to the physical. On Oliver's pipsqueak physique, the *Plaindealer*[5] said, "He is the smallest editor of the smallest newspaper" in the territories. On his eyesight: "The *Bulletin* man has so long been staring with jealous eyes from Edmonton, upon the railway, the mills...and other modern improvements of the rising star of the Saskatchewan that his organs of vision refuse to do their duty in a straightforward manner." Oliver, for his part, dismissed the voices from across the river as the yapping of mongrels. "The business of the country was practically done at Edmonton," he observed, "the only and original Edmonton, spelled with a large capital 'E,' and don't forget it."

Hockey afforded even greater vent for inter-city rivalry. The clubs of New and Old Edmonton customarily met on Christmas Day at Strathcona's Shamrock rink and on New Year's at the Thistle rink in Edmonton. The Thistles, as Edmonton historian Tony Cashman recounts in *More Edmonton Stories*, were notorious for high sticking. But player violence hardly equalled that of the fans, among whom fights were frequent. Puck-sized lumps of coal would cascade onto the ice when a forward for the visiting club worked his way into scoring position. Then too, there were the women who, though it might be 30 below at rinkside, frequently showed up with summer parasols, used for tripping opposing players as they skated by.

In other words, the sports passion that would become endemic to the whole province was already in evidence. Curling was a popular pastime, often played on a cleared section of the frozen river with kettles full of sand for the stones. Both communities also went in for cricket, soccer and baseball. Old Edmonton had a bowling alley, and a five-hole golf course behind the fort.

Nor was all culture physical. Old Edmontonians attended dramas and recitals, mostly produced locally but occasionally provided by a touring company, at Robertson Hall on Jasper Avenue.[6] Strathconans patronized amateur theatrical productions at their five local churches and concerts by the town's brass band. They seem to have credited themselves with possession of a deeper appreciation than their neighbours to the north for the finer things in life, and they may have been right.

At any rate, Strathcona in 1899 was undoubtedly more reserved and more "British." Its population included a higher proportion of Ontarians, well-heeled and educated, who came out to make

One of three ferries that plied the North Saskatchewan before the first bridge.

Provincial Archives of Alberta, A-1420

How Edmonton met Ottawa's challenge and lost anyway

The town finally got a bridge but learned a new government doesn't mean a new attitude

On February 4, 1897, it looked as though long-suffering Old Edmonton had finally won a victory. Twice in 16 years it had suffered major reversals. First, in 1881, the Canadian Pacific announced its main line would not pass through Edmonton, but 200 miles to the south. Ten years later, the connecting spur from Calgary stopped short of crossing the North Saskatchewan River. Edmonton had lobbied the CPR and the dominion government ever since for help in building a bridge, with no apparent effect.

But in early 1897 it began to look as though the Liberals might have been sincere in promising that they would do things differently. In the crucial 1896 election they had finally replaced the old Tory regime in Ottawa. Now came a telegram from the new minister of Public Works to the Edmonton town council: If the town would contribute $25,000 towards the $65,000 bridge, the new "West-conscious" regime in Ottawa would put up the other $40,000.

There were sceptics, of course, one of whom was the newly elected mayor, John A. McDougall. Ottawa knew full well, he observed, that a town with less than 2,000 people could not likely raise $25,000. At least two private ventures had failed in attempts to bridge the river and pay for it by toll. Thus the federal acceptance might in fact conceal a federal refusal.

"But we called their bluff by clubbing together and raising the amount on a joint note through the Imperial Bank," Mayor McDougall wrote in his memoirs, "and we wired the money the same day the wire was received by us." The money was put up by a handful of local businessmen, including the mayor, through a company called the Edmonton and District Railway Co. that they had incorporated the previous year to further a number of railroad enterprises.

At its next meeting town council voted to have the ratepayers assume the liability. The following week the Liberal *Bulletin* confidently reported that "the long-felt want of a combined railway and traffic bridge, and extension of the railway system across the North Saskatchewan at Edmonton, is in a fair way of being attended to in the present season."

Another five years would pass before enough dominion money actually came through to finish the job, however. Construction of the Low Level Bridge, as it was later to be known, began in 1897 all right but proceeded slowly. By the summer of 1899 the centre pier was in. But the delays gave Edmontonians time to learn two crucial lessons. Lesson One came that August, when heavy rain caused the river to exceed previous flood levels. The engineers watched in chagrin as their pier disappeared under water, and then added another eight feet to their design.

Even so, the Low Level was not to be completed until 1902, and that was the second lesson. A change of government at Ottawa did not necessarily precipitate a whole-hearted change of attitude. *G.S.*❦

Provincial Archives of Alberta, E. Brown Collection, B-3273

The 'Low Level,' under construction for five years, looking north. On the horizon is the College Avenue school, soon abandoned because its foundations sank into coal mine shafts.

Glenbow Archives, NA-614-28

A Strathcona public school in 1898. After 1891, children no longer commuted by rope ferry to Old Edmonton.

their mark after the rails arrived. Gracious social functions at the home of lawyer A.C. Rutherford (later to become first premier of the province of Alberta) were typical of the high-society lifestyle. So was tennis, on three courts on an empty lot owned by the C&E Land Company south of Saskatchewan Drive on 103rd Street. The women played in long white dresses, the men in white flannels, and tea was served on Saturdays.

Not five blocks away from all this elegance, however, was the immigration shed, the shelter built next to the station in all major rail towns to provide, at government expense, communal accommodation and kitchen facilities for newcomers while they arranged to register for a homestead. When New Edmonton's first sheds were constructed in 1892, most immigrants came from the United States. By the turn of the century American settlers had been replaced by Ukrainians (then customarily referred to as Galicians) who were scorned for their unusual costumes and "unknown tongue."

Galician encounters with intolerant thugs were not uncommon and never pleasant. One night in 1899, for example, an armed band of "drunken toughs" tried to smash their way into the sheds, the *Plaindealer* reported, pounding on doors and breaking windows. When a few town residents answered the cries of the "the government's guests," the hoodlums disappeared into the night. That same year a Galician settler's wedding was disrupted by local youths singing bawdy and insulting songs. One of the songsters was knocked senseless by a "foreigner" brandishing a heavy ink bottle. The Galician was charged with assault but received only a nominal fine from a sympathetic magistrate.

Strathcona had its own Orange Hall, testament to its Anglo character, and members would march each July 12 to celebrate William III's triumph over the Catholic Irish. The largely Protestant British and the Catholic French still regarded each other with considerable suspicion and apprehension, despite the fact that some of the more prominent families of both towns were Metis and Catholic. Religion tended to reinforce ethnicity, and vice versa.

Since religion was a matter of belief rather than sentiment, these differences were taken very seriously. Sometimes they led to grievous personal tragedy, as they did for Lottie Brunette, 21, a Catholic from St. Albert, and her Protestant beau, W.P. "Peck" Rowland, 22, of the well-known Edmonton family whose name was perpetuated by the city's Rowland Road. They wished to be married. Both families objected; so did their friends. "They resolved," reported the *Bulletin*, "that if they were not allowed to live together they would die together."

Accordingly, they strolled into a field northeast of town, spread out a canvas sheet and blanket by a thicket, and drank from a bottle of strychnine. The young woman died almost immediately. Young Rowland required a second dose, and before he died he staggered to a nearby home and confessed to the suicide pact. Apparently he feared the bodies might not be found.

But love in the Edmontons didn't always end tragically. In the summer of 1897 passers-by were at first amused and then touched by the unusual proceedings outside a home on Jasper Avenue and 96th Street. A husband and wife, determined to separate, had arrived on the scene almost simultaneously with drays, to divide the household possessions. Agreeing to a 50-50 split, they stormed out of the house in turn with various belongings. The last item was a huge feather mattress, which they carried out together.

When they both tried to put the feather tick on their respective wagons, however, they became embroiled in a spirited tug-of-war, a crowd gathering to watch. The mattress suddenly ripped apart, sending feathers everywhere. The combatants stared, as though some realization had begun to dawn upon them. The crowd became hushed. She smiled; he smiled. She laughed; he laughed; the crowd laughed. The couple embraced and eventually moved their belongings back in together for good.

A not dissimilar process would one day resolve the fractious relationship between the two rival towns, and see Edmonton and Strathcona also "move in together for good." That process would be as simple, and as complex, as the building of a bridge. Even now the first bridge, to be known as the "Low Level," was partly built, although construction was stalled for the time being. But the long struggle against Strathcona had, some said, whipped Edmonton into fighting trim to take on its far more formidable competitor to the south, the centre that was now zooming ahead of it: Calgary.

This was a rivalry destined to continue for the next century. Meanwhile, south and east of the future capital, other hopeful settlements were ambitiously struggling towards municipal status. That their aspirations were overshadowed by the Edmonton-Calgary contest was a situation which would also endure.❦

Provincial Archives of Alberta, E. Brown Collection, B-6824

John A. McDougall (left), Edmonton mayor and a tireless promoter of the old city. (Below) the upstart, upscale railway city of Strathcona, looking northwest past the Strathcona Hotel on Whyte Avenue, still standing a century later. Old Edmonton resented Strathcona even more than it resented Calgary.

City of Edmonton Archives, EA-10-1291

CHAPTER THREE

A trek around a future province where a cow got into a drugstore

IN SPORTS-CRAZED MEDICINE HAT, FIVE LACROSSE PLAYERS WERE KNOCKED OUT COLD IN A SINGLE SCRIMMAGE ❦ IN LETHBRIDGE THE MOUNTIES DEFENDED THE 'SOILED DOVES'

Notwithstanding the colourful tale that Medicine Hat was so named by the Indians on account of a Blackfoot medicine man's lost *saamis* (or holy head-dress), some unromantic sceptics insist that the locale was not especially notable in native lore and was not even on a major Indian trail.[1] It was definitely on the chosen trail of the Canadian Pacific Railway, however, whose surveyors and engineers judged it the best crossing of the South Saskatchewan River. The result, as they built their wooden trestle bridge in 1883, was the first town spawned by the CPR in what would become Alberta, a tent-and-boxcar affair that sprouted almost overnight.

By the century's end 16 years later, only a few other Alberta settlements (Fort Macleod and Lethbridge in the south, St. Albert and Strathcona farther north) could even dream of challenging the pre-eminence of Calgary or Edmonton. Medicine Hat's 1,500 citizens, however, were convinced they were leading the field. They regarded their metropolis as definitely destined for future greatness: a mecca that would, among other things, become the major railway centre between Winnipeg and the Pacific. Calgary, its rival 186 miles up the line, regarded such pretensions as absurd.

Strictly speaking, Medicine Hat was not actually in Alberta at the turn of the century. The eastern boundary of the territorial district called Alberta lay 80 miles west of the 110th meridian, which would become the future provincial boundary. Until then, Medicine Hat was in the neighbouring district of Assiniboia. Provincehood, however, was not uppermost in the minds of Medicine Hatters

Probably the first picture of Medicine Hat, looking north in 1883 across the tent city to the north side of the South Saskatchewan River valley.

Glenbow Archives, NA-2622-8

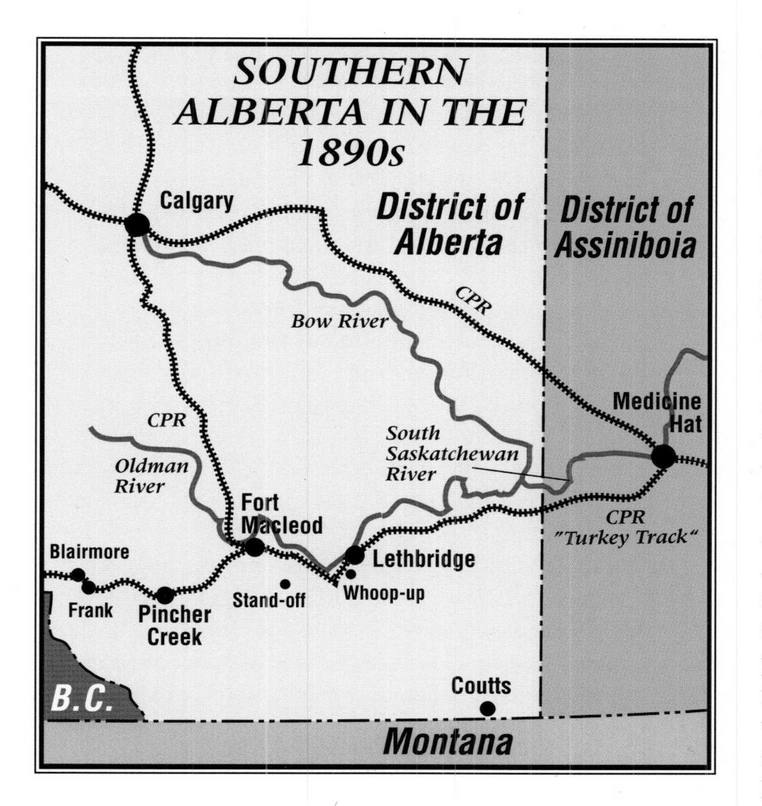

on New Year's Eve 1899.

What mattered far more were sports. The town's cricket and hockey teams had been territorial champions in 1896, the cricketers deliciously trouncing Calgary in the finals. A golf course had just been completed in 1899. There were baseball, football, turf (horse racing), gun, bicycle and curling clubs. There was a lacrosse club (so rough, writes David C. Jones in his *The Weather Factory: A Pictorial History of Medicine Hat,* that five members were once knocked out in a single scrimmage). Foot races were popular too, with heavy betting. Long-skirted young women in neat tuques and sweaters played in their own hockey matches, which men were barred from watching. (One newspaperman did watch, though, producing a predictably patronizing account.)

Thus the town's program for New Year's Day 1900 was typical. It had rained on Christmas and was expected to continue mild. Slated New Year's sports festivities included a hockey game (male variety), a football game played in shirtsleeves, and golf. Socially it had been a quiet holiday season, the *Medicine Hat News* noted. The Masonic Lodge had held an "At Home" for 50 couples. Societies like the Masons, the Orange Order and the Oddfellows Lodge were important in the town's social life. There was also the Opera House, located above A.C. Hawthorne's Clothing and Furniture store. It featured such extravaganzas as "The Regular Down South Darky Cake Walk," performed by the Georgia Minstrels, a troupe of local residents in blackface.

The other major preoccupation of Medicine Hat's citizenry, circa 1899, seems to have been "progress." Visitors, true enough, might miss the metropolitan aspects of the town. They might not

[1] In his history of Medicine Hat, *All Hell for a Basement*, author Ed Gould quotes pioneer William Henry McKay as insisting that it was William Van Horne of the CPR who actually named the place Medicine Hat. According to McKay the Indians called it Ka-As-It-Ah-Ta-Wah-Tik, "where it runs against" (i.e., where the river runs against the Cypress Hills). But at the McKay home in 1883, he said, a Cree called Thunder Bear told Van Horne of a personal experience he had while camped there. He had eloped with the youngest wife of a chief at the Red Deer Forks, and she dreamed that if they presented her erstwhile husband with a head-dress made from the feathers of seven eagles, he would accept the situation peaceably. Thunder Bear did so, and they were forgiven. The story caught Van Horne's fancy. That was "good medicine," said he. "I will call this place Medicine Hat."

get past the superficial shortcomings of its business district. South Railway, Main and Toronto Streets (the last two later renamed Second and Third) were dusty or muddy according to season and often notable, the *News* complained bitterly, for "loathsome, foul-smelling accumulations of filth." Every spring, the paper said, the place looked like "a Hottentot kraal."

There were untoward incidents, too, like the episode of the cow that wandered into the storeroom of Dr. J.G. Calder's drug store, ending up in the basement when the floor collapsed. There was also the water supply, delivered by wagon at 25 cents a barrel and sometimes, according to one finicky customer, "with appalling bits of debris therein."

Nevertheless, Medicine Hatters would counter, what other town in the West — or anywhere else for that matter — had street lamps fuelled by reserves of natural gas so vast they burned night and day, because it was cheaper than hiring someone to shut them off? And what about the hotels: the Brunswick, the American, the Lansdowne and, since 1898, the imposing Assiniboia[2] (rates "$1 a day upwards") with no fewer than 63 rooms, many with the unusual luxury of their own complete bathroom? The Assiniboia, moreover, offered a bowling alley, barber shop, steam heating and (naturally) gas lighting. In its "gentlemen's sitting room," in fact, the new town council had held its first meeting.

In the Assiniboia's dining room, just before New Year's Eve 1899, a gala farewell supper was held for six men who had signed up with the new Canadian Mounted Rifles, to fight in the Boer War (1899-1902). Canada was about to send a second contingent of troops to South Africa; the call had gone out for good marksmen and horsemen between 20 and 40 years old. As one local paper editorialized, Mounties and cowboys are "the kind of material that is needed," and across southern Alberta they were hastening to enlist.[3]

The economic mood was buoyant too, as North America emerged from the depression of the mid-1890s. The CPR was advertising special $50 return fares to Ontario and Quebec. The Merchants' Bank, second biggest in the country, had opened a Medicine Hat branch. The town was well-supplied with retail shops, including Cousins Dry Goods and Furniture, established in 1883 by young William Cousins. As Ed Gould tells the story in *All Hell for a Basement*, Cousins and his partner arrived late one May evening, so broke that they flipped to see which of them would get to spend their last dollar on a meal. Cousins lost. But next morning they started selling; by 1899 Cousins, a future mayor, was a prosperous leading citizen and owner of an attractive two-storey

[2] **The Assiniboia survived until 1944 when it burned down. It had been built as the Alberta Hotel for Captain Horatio Hamilton Ross. Reputedly one of southern Alberta's notable British remittance men, he was called captain by virtue of his unsuccessful efforts to establish steamships on the South Saskatchewan.**

[3] **The first contingent, 1,000 infantrymen, sailed from Quebec on October 30, 1899. The second was to total 6,000 men, all mounted. The third, Strathcona's Horse, 500 mounted riflemen, was entirely funded by CPR financier Donald Smith and commanded by the redoubtable Sam Steele, late of the North-West Mounted Police and the Riel Rebellion. This regiment was later renamed Lord Strathcona's Horse (Royal Canadians), and one squadron of the CMR incorporated into it. Another CMR spin-off was the Alberta Mounted Rifles, which in 1931 became the South Alberta Light Horse and the Alberta Dragoons.**

Provincial Archives of Alberta, E. Brown Collection, B-6536

A Medicine Hat women's hockey team at the turn of the century. Men, of course, were barred from watching on account of their insufferably patronizing comments.

Provincial Archives of Alberta, E. Brown Collection, B-2433

Looking south down the main street of Lethbridge in 1884. The clergy should reform their own congregations if they want to rid the city of vice, said the NWMP officer.

frame house with a wide verandah.

Meanwhile ranchers had been setting up in the surrounding countryside. A sawmill and a brickyard had been established. Drillers were eagerly seeking more gas. Allied to local supplies of good clay for brick and pottery, this surely promised a bright future. The railway bridge had been replaced by a steel one in 1885. A ferry (20 cents a trip) took care of other traffic, except on Sunday, although pedestrians kept on using the railway bridge despite dire warnings that sometimes were tragically fulfilled. In June 1899, for example, the *News* reported that little Louis Bray, 6, had been killed by a train on the bridge. Not until 1907 would one be built for non-rail traffic.

Railway work accounted for many accidents, fatal and non-fatal. Gas explosions, including domestic ones, also provided patients for the 25-bed Medicine Hat General Hospital, imposingly built of stone in 1889 after four years of fund-raising by the Ladies Aid.

The gas had been discovered when a CPR crew looking for water in 1883 found methane instead. The city soon drilled municipal wells, but pressure in the first ones was too low to supply all residents. Consequently many citizens just drilled for their own domestic supply, improvising some shockingly unsafe arrangements. The fire hazard was high. But even by 1899 the only fire-fighting potential was provided by a wagon with a hose and a pump, and a volunteer fire brigade that worked on an incentive system: a dollar for the first man to reach the wagon with a horse to pull it.

After its incorporation in 1898 Medicine Hat hired a constable, to back up the efforts of the NWMP detachment that came in 1883 to keep order among railway workers and Indians. In the main the Mounties had succeeded remarkably in their task. A principal function of the town constable was to help them enforce the territorial liquor laws among the townsfolk. These had produced a war between bootleggers and teetotallers that the former had been largely winning. The whisky peddlers had quite a few supporters, the clergy of Medicine Hat's five churches conspicuously not among them.

John Niblock, CPR divisional superintendent, was not among them either. A thorough-going Methodist with autocratic tendencies, he strongly disapproved of gambling and profanity as well. CPR employees known to indulge in such vices would feel his wrath.[4] This incensed *Medicine Hat Times* editor J.D. Drinnan. Niblock should be told, he thundered, that "he does not own the bodies and souls of the free and independent citizens of Medicine Hat..." Drinnan also accused the super-

[4] To discourage blasphemy, Niblock had a poem posted in CPR cabooses: "It chills my blood to hear the blest Supreme/ Appealed to lightly on each trifling theme./ Maintain your manhood; profanity despise./ To swear is neither brave, polite, nor wise."

Recipe for a hotel: Enlarge one shack and add beds

That's what they were at first, but soon some elegance appeared along with the 'Queen of Garbage'

Pioneer Alberta was transient and transitional. At the turn of the century, most people were newcomers, many on their way to homesteads or gold-fields, or briefly in from the wilds. Hence hotels were among the first businesses, and the first social centres where men shared frontier yarns over a beer, where courts held session or town councils met, where remittance men spent their allowances. At their bars assembled the colourful, the corruptible and the conniving — including the hoteliers themselves.

The crudest shelter could be transformed into a hotel simply by adding beds. Calgary's first was just that. Called Calgary House, the bare-board, mud-caulked structure appeared a little before the CPR in 1883. "If you don't like it," was the management attitude, "try the next hotel...in Winnipeg." In 1886 Calgary's three-storey Royal vastly improved the comfort level, even if cotton sheets were all that divided male from female quarters on its top floor.

In 1899 the Royal was surpassed in turn by the Alberta Hotel, a fine sandstone structure financed by cattle interests and adopted as a watering hole both by them and the city's accumulating eccentrics. It was here, for instance, that Mother Fulham, Calgary's "Queen of Garbage,"* once wrestled with a Chinese employee she accused of stealing "her" trash behind the hotel. The filthy, feisty Irishwoman had the poor man charged with assault and the case went to trial. Contradictory evidence suggested he was actually trying to conceal a chicken he had swiped from the kitchen; ultimately all charges were dropped.

Future prime minister R.B. Bennett appreciated the Alberta's dining room, where he lunched almost daily, just off the austere lobby. Understandably he avoided the notably less respectable bar, where some carried guns, revellers on occasion brought in their horses, and the 125-foot bar was reputed the longest in western Canada. It was here that *Eye Opener* publisher Bob Edwards would some years later hold court with the renowned defence lawyer Paddy Nolan, meat magnate Pat Burns or cattle baron George Lane.

Edmonton's first notable hotel arrived with the steel in 1891, and was located therefore on the south side of the river. Owned by the CPR-operated Calgary &

Glenbow Archives, NA-654-4

Edmonton Railway, the Hotel Edmonton lay a mere hundred yards from the station. It boasted 45 rooms, a dining room and a bar, and a special display area for travelling salesmen. The building was to survive through the coming century as the Strathcona Hotel or, more familiarly, the Strath.

For its first five years Hotel Edmonton was managed by an English couple named Sharples. "Dad" Sharples, as he was called, had been fired as a CPR steward when the railway's western division superintendent, William Whyte, caught him hanging the hand-washed linen to dry on the bell-ropes of the dining cars. (At the Edmonton, of course, Sharples was still working for the CPR, and in a hotel located on an avenue named for the man who fired him.)

Ma Sharples, an accomplished pastry cook, made a capable partner. But both were known to indulge on occasion in late-night drinking binges, says Agnes Teviotdale in her biography of her pioneer father, Harry Wilson. Sometimes, she adds, that meant leaving the guests to forage in the kitchen for their own breakfasts. The Sharpleses were considered advanced because they provided Hotel Edmonton with one of the six phones in the area. But they took it out because there was almost no one the guests could telephone.

Soon there were half a dozen hotels in the two Edmontons, their horse-drawn conveyances meeting the four trains a week to vie for the business of bone-weary passengers. Sharples was always there, and Donald Ross. Ross was a good-natured Scot from the north side who in 1876 had converted the top floor of his house at the foot of McDougall Hill into a dormitory, thereby making himself a hotelier.

Ross's establishment was called the Edmonton Hotel. (If he resented the similar name of the later southside competition, there is no record of it.) The Edmonton Hotel advertised the outstanding amenity of a bath, not mentioning that only a communal roller-towel was supplied. Edmonton historian Tony Cashman recounts in *More Edmonton Stories* how a customer complained the towel was soggy. "Strange," replied Ross, "twenty men have dried their hands on that towel this morning and you're the first to complain."

Another customer, finding the Ross place full, agreed to sleep on the pool table, then balked when Ross charged him the regular 50-cent room price. "Well if you don't like that," snapped Ross, "I can charge you pool-room rates, which are 60 cents an hour." In the western hotel industry of the late 19th century, it was definitely a sellers' market. *B.C.*❦

*Mother Fulham, whose seldom-used real name was Caroline, visited the hotel regularly to collect restaurant scraps for her pigs, and also to drink. Women weren't ordinarily served at the long bar, but then, Mother Fulham was not exactly ordinary. She was usually served until her vituperative language got her thrown out.

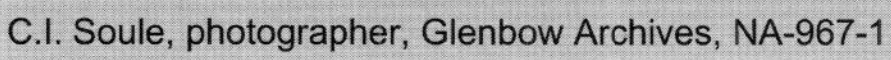
C.I. Soule, photographer, Glenbow Archives, NA-967-1

Provincial Archives of Alberta, E. Brown Collection, B-3177

The longest bar in Alberta—guns and horses discouraged (opposite page); (upper left) Calgary's first hotel in 1883; (lower left) the Halfway Hotel between Edmonton and Ft. Saskatchewan, typical of turn-of-the-century establishments.

Sir Alexander Galt Museum, P19672953001

intendent, an Orangeman, of anti-Catholicism and other transgressions. The town divided into anti- and pro-Niblock factions. The *Times* (founded in 1885) ceased publication in 1894 and was replaced by the *News*, which backed Niblock. Drinnan sparked a citizens' committee that petitioned the CPR to remove Niblock forthwith. Niblock's supporters countered with another petition calling the superintendent "our best citizen." Not until 1899 was Niblock transferred.

For all the power he may have wielded over the morals of the citizenry, Niblock does not seem to have possessed much pull with his company on behalf of the town. Medicine Hat, one CPR divisional point among many, aspired to become a veritable hub of railroading. Unaccountably in the local view, the CPR seemed to favour Calgary for this role on the main line.

McCord Museum, Notman Collection

Interior of the A. Macdonald & Co. general store in Lethbridge, 1900; Indian commissioner and town-founder Galt.

Calgarians saw the matter differently, of course. As early as 1885 the *Calgary Tribune*, under the heading "Good News for Calgary," was writing of an expected CPR decision to locate the regional headquarters and shops there. This could mean 300 to 500 permanent jobs. An 1899 *Medicine Hat News* story despondently quoted William Whyte, then manager of western lines for the CPR, as saying he did not wish to "dampen Medicine Hat's prospects," but any new shops would likely go to Calgary.

But railroad prospects were not limited to the CPR main line northwestward through Calgary, Banff and the Rogers Pass. In the past two decades rumours of six or seven possible lines had circulated round town, and one of these had actually become a reality. It led to Lethbridge, 108 miles west on the banks of the Oldman River.[5] Formerly known as Coal Banks, by 1899 Lethbridge was a town of 2,000, supplying coal for CPR locomotives.

A narrow-gauge railway, derisively dubbed the "Turkey Track" for its wobbling progress across the prairie, had run from Lethbridge to Dunmore, 7.5 miles east of Medicine Hat, since 1885. In 1890 the Turkey Track was extended from Lethbridge to Coutts, on the Montana border. Broadened to standard-gauge in the mid-1890s, it became the first leg of the CPR's southern line, westward through the Crow's Nest Pass.

Coal was not the initial attraction in the Lethbridge district, however. It was buffalo hides that brought American traders there in the 1860s, wreaking social havoc among the Bloods and Blackfoot with their staple trade item: rot-gut whisky. Fort Hamilton, better known as Fort Whoop-up and the most notorious of several dozen "whisky forts" on the southern Prairies, was located at the confluence of the Oldman and St. Mary rivers, eight miles south of the site of Lethbridge. Hides and supplies were transported by wagon on a regular route to Fort Benton, Montana, until the North-West Mounted Police clamped down on the whisky traders in 1874. Some of the traders, turning to different pursuits, became the first residents of Lethbridge.

Their new pursuits were not necessarily all that different. George Houk, for example, originally from Pennsylvania, had been at Whoop-up in the early 1870s, and became a Montana deputy sher-

[5] The Oldman was also named Arrow, Livingstone or Belly on early maps. The name Oldman may derive from the Indian designation for the place where the river leaves the mountains. They called this the "Old Man's Playing Ground," the Old Man being a supernatural entity.

Glenbow Archives, NA-3251-18

John Black, the rebel merchandiser. Black came to Fort Macleod in 1884 with I.G. Baker and Company, and worked for the HBC when it took the store over. He later turned competitor and opened his own shop, photographed here in 1898. He is shown just left of centre, holding the horse. He died in 1899 at age 43.

iff after that. He set up in Lethbridge as a wholesale merchant in liquor and fine cigars. Houk was also a great baseball enthusiast; in her *19th Century Lethbridge*, Anne Laurie Stafford Peat credits him with bringing the game to town. By 1899 his team, Houk's Savages, were famed as district champions.

Another first citizen was New York-born Nicholas Sheran, whose career is said to have included being shipwrecked in the Arctic and serving with the Union Army in the American Civil War, in Meagher's Irish Brigade. In 1874 Sheran began the first mine on the Oldman, selling the coal[6] to the NWMP at Fort Macleod and shipping some to Fort Benton. But markets were limited and transport costs high.

That situation changed in 1879 when Elliott Torrance Galt (eldest son of Sir Alexander Galt, one of the Fathers of Confederation) noted the five-foot-thick outcroppings, or coal banks, while travelling in the region as assistant Indian commissioner. Hearing of CPR plans to develop the Crow's Nest route, he lined up financing in Britain and incorporated the North Western Coal and Navigation Company.

The "navigation" element in the company's name derived from its plan to ship the coal by river to Medicine Hat. It built two steamers, the 173-foot *Baroness* and the 120-foot *Alberta*, a tug called the *Minnow* and a fleet of barges. But the low water of the Oldman and the South Saskatchewan defeated them all. The Turkey Track proved far superior.

Miners came streaming into Lethbridge, named for NWC&NC shareholder William Lethbridge, a London barrister who never did see the place. Shopkeepers and a few professional men came too. Among these was a young Ontario apothecary and amateur historian named John D. Higinbotham, who moved over from Fort Macleod. He recorded what he saw and heard, providing an admirable source for early southern Alberta history, and for years kept one of the two brass cannon from derelict Fort Whoop-up in his garden.

In 1899 Lethbridge remained a fairly rough town despite the anti-vice efforts of some of its clergy. Especially prominent in these battles was the Presbyterian minister, the Reverend Charles McKillop, a big Ontario Scot whose unfailingly formal attire did not restrain him from actually

[6] The Blackfoot knew coal could be used for fuel. They also knew its fumes could kill, say Alex Johnston and Andy den Otter in *Lethbridge, A Centennial History*, and frowned on using it, especially inside tepees. They preferred dried poplar and buffalo dung.

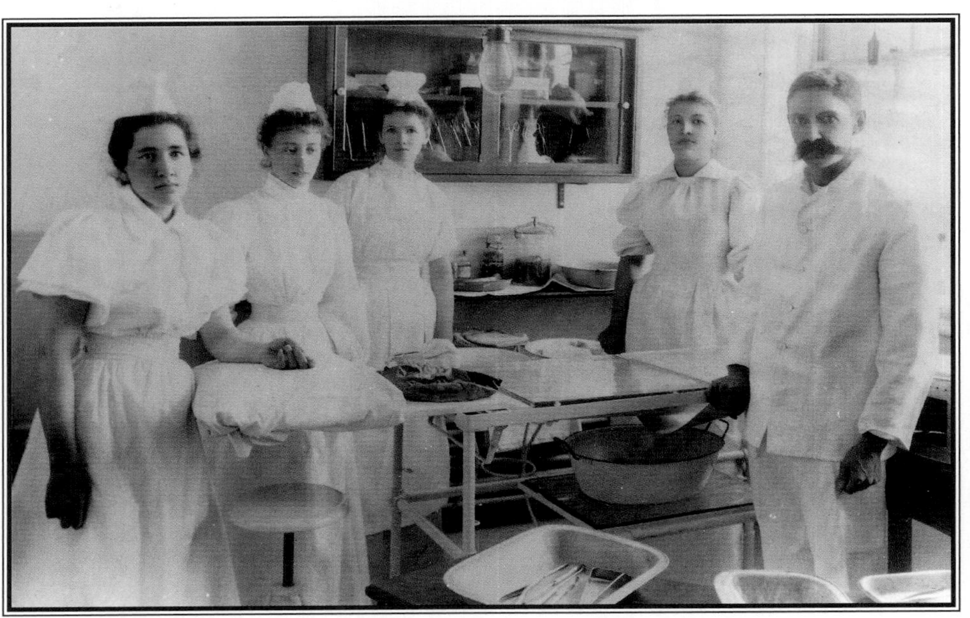

Sir Alexander Galt Museum, P19737730000

thrashing an errant citizen when he thought a thrashing was warranted. The Lethbridge NWMP, however, failed to appreciate the clerical campaigns against drinking, gambling and prostitution.

"The Presbyterian and Methodist ministers have been of late making a great deal of talk about prostitutes being allowed in town," NWMP Superintendent R. Burton Deane noted in an official report in July 1894. "If they would turn their attention to the juvenile depravity and promiscuous fornication that is going on under their own eyes and in their own congregations, they would be kept so busy they would have no time to think of the professional

The legend-shrouded frontiersman who started Waterton Park

Kootenai Brown was indeed soldier, Indian fighter and bounty hunter, but he never created scandal at court

The Indians called John George Brown "Inuspi" (Longhair), for his hairstyle; his countrymen called him "Kootenai," the old name for the lakes 50 miles southwest of Fort Macleod where he made his isolated home after 1874. No townsman, Kootenai Brown was a sometime soldier, adventurer, prospector, Indian fighter, express rider, buffalo hunter, wolfer and trader; but he spent the last 25 years of his life campaigning for a national park in the Kootenai Lakes region, by then known as Waterton.[a] Ultimately he was successful.

Legend attached itself to Kootenai like barnacles to a boat. Biographer William Rodney, in *Kootenai Brown: His Life and Times*, has dismissed some of the stories. He found no evidence that scandal forced the well-born young Irishman to flee the court of Queen Victoria, for example, or that he killed a fellow British officer in India. But Brown's subsequent career, after he resigned his commission in the Imperial Army and headed for Canada's west coast in 1863, was adventurous enough.

With four companions he trekked through the mountains into Alberta in 1865, via the pass named South Kootenay on later maps, and into Blackfoot country. They were soon set upon by a band of young warriors. Although two of the attackers were killed and the rest fled, Brown took an arrow in the back. In Manitoba in 1867 he and Edmonton trader James Gibbons barely survived an attack by two dozen angry Indian customers. When he signed on as an express rider carrying the United States mail through Montana Sioux country from Fort Stevenson to Fort Benton, that job proved equally hazardous.

Kootenai Brown. The Sioux took his clothes but left his sca

One day in 1868 a Fort Stevenson sentry saw what he thought were two naked Indians approaching the gate. As Harold Fryer tells the story in *Alberta: The Pioneer Years*, the sergeant of the guard recognized Brown and a fellow pony express rider. "What's up?" he demanded. "Nothing much," Brown replied. "The Sioux have your mail, horses and our clothes and came mighty near getting us."

The pair had been captured but not scalped, Brown used to

ladies, who at all events are orderly, clean, and on the whole not bad looking."

The two ministers had tackled the town council about these ladies, referring to them as "soiled doves," Deane continued, but had chiefly succeeded in entertaining the citizenry. "The whole town was there to see and hear. The 'doves' had a lawyer present to watch the case for them."[7]

The NWMP was doubtless preoccupied with more pressing problems that year. The coal company, stricken by the recession of the 1890s, had suddenly laid off 580 men. Fewer than 150 left town, notwithstanding the company offer of a free pass to Great Falls, Montana. The company also wanted to hire back 130 men at a 17% lower wage, but miners willing to accept were beaten up by their fellows, and the mine superintendent was threatened.

By the end of 1899, however, times were better and Lethbridge was prospering. Amenities included: a telephone line from the mine to the home of manager William Stafford; public baths heated by the boiler from the abandoned *Baroness*; a company-financed hospital; a rudimentary electric plant; and plank sidewalks in the business district. Elliott Galt had built a handsome home named Coaldale.

That year an annex was added to the Lethbridge Hotel, causing the *Lethbridge News* to proclaim it "the best hotel west of Winnipeg." Construction was booming, hampered only by a shortage of bricks. Retail holiday sales were brisk in everything from men's laced boots (90 cents, reduced from $1.50) to Christmas gift hampers of plum pudding, raisins, apples, tea and "1 Bottle of Good Rye Whisky" ($3 a hamper).

(Opposite page) the operating room of the Galt Hospital in Lethbridge. For victims of mining accidents and labour disputes, among others.

[7] This report is included in *The Prairie West to 1905*, a collection of essays and original documents edited by Lewis G. Thomas, the first chairman of the University of Alberta history department born in the province.

explain, because the other rider was part Sioux and convinced the Indians that Brown was too. Stripped and imprisoned, they managed to escape and walk back to the fort, much bitten by mosquitoes. The next year, 1869, he survived a blizzard that killed three companions. Despite all this, he carried on with the pony express for another five years, then joined the Metis in their vast buffalo hunts.

He had married a Metis, Olive Lyonais, and liked her people's way of life. He always claimed the Metis were in effect conservationists. Father Albert Lacombe, the great Oblate missionary they so respected, taught them that waste was a sin. So they made use of the entire carcass, Brown said, not just the hide like white hunters, or the hide and tongue like the Blackfoot.

But as the buffalo became scarce he had to take up the despised trade of wolfing — poisoning wolves with strychnine — to support his wife and two small daughters. It was in an argument over wolf hides in Montana, according to the stories, that he killed a trader named Louis Ell. Jailed at Fort Benton, he was tried for murder and acquitted. It was then he took his family back to live by the Kootenai Lakes he had first seen 10 years earlier.

There they stayed, and Kootenai acquired his name. He traded, hunted and fished. "Mr. Brown of Kootenai Lakes brought to town on Saturday a trout weighing 30 pounds," reported the *Fort Macleod Gazette* in 1883. He worked as guide for the railway surveyors and packed in supplies for the track crews. In 1885, during the North-West Rebellion, he joined the Rocky Mountain Rangers, whose job was to see that southern Alberta's thousands of Blackfoot, Blood, Stoney and Peigan Indians did not join forces with the Metis. Kootenai, who spoke most of their languages, served as a scout.

Meanwhile a son, Leopold, was born in the cabin by the lake and not long afterwards Olive Brown died. Canon S.H. Middleton of the Church of England, a friend of Kootenai in the scout's later years, wrote in his reminiscences that this was in 1881.[b] A few years later Fr. Lacombe married Brown to a young Cree woman, Nichemoos (also called Isabella), who was to survive him.

Brown told Canon Middleton he also got into the oil business for a while, around 1890, working with William Aldridge of Cardston to collect and sell crude at a dollar a barrel. Preservation of the Kootenai region became his major preoccupation, however. He had seen what happened to the buffalo.

Men like Pincher Creek rancher John Herron, the MP for Macleod, and William Pearce, who was then dominion superintendent of western mines, supported his efforts. In 1895 they succeeded in getting a small forest reserve set aside there. Brown was given full charge of it in 1910. He promptly demanded a typewriter, and at the age of 71 learned to use it, to handle the attendant government paperwork.

The reserve was finally enlarged to 423 square miles in 1914, as Waterton National Park. Kootenai Brown died two years later. He lies buried in his park, his grave flanked by those of his wives. ❦

[a] Lieutenant Thomas Blakiston of the Palliser expedition renamed the Kootenai Lakes region in honour of English naturalist Charles Waterton.

[b] One daughter of Olive and Kootenai Brown died in childhood. Canon Middleton says the other daughter married and was living in Quebec in the 1950s. Leopold married Justine Bellarose, had five daughters and died at Fort McMurray in 1916, a few months after his father.

HOUSE RULES

1. Guests will be provided with breakfast and dinner, but must rustle their own lunch.
2. Spiked boots and spurs must be removed at night before retiring.
3. Dogs not allowed in bunks, but may sleep underneath.
4. Towels changed weekly; insect repellent for sale at the bar.
5. Special rates to Gospel Grinders and the gambling profession.
6. The bar will be open day and night. Every known fluid, except water, for sale. No mixed drinks will be served, except in case of a death in the family. Only registered guests allowed the privileges of sleeping on the barroom floor.
7. No kicking regarding the food. Those who do not like the provender will be put out. When guests find themselves or their baggage thrown over the fence, they may consider they have received notice to leave.
8. Baths furnished free down at the river, but bathers must provide their own soap and towels.
9. Valuables will not be locked in the hotel safe, as the hotel possesses no such ornament.
10. Guests are expected to rise at 6 A.M., as the sheets are needed for tablecloths.
11. To attract the attention of waiters, shoot through the door panel. Two shots for ice water, three for a new deck of cards.

No Jawbone.

In God we trust; all others cash.

-House rules of the Macleod Hotel, operated by Harry "Kamoose" Taylor in the 1880s. As related by J.B. Higinbotham.

Thirty miles west of Lethbridge on the Crow's Nest line, the town of Macleod had been experiencing ups and downs. The CPR main line and the Calgary & Edmonton Railway killed much of its wagon-freighting business. But the NWMP post, built by Colonel James F. Macleod in 1874, was still important, and the town had become the centre for a sometimes thriving ranch economy. By 1884, says James G. MacGregor in *A History of Alberta,* Ottawa had leased 1,785,690 acres of land thereabouts to 47 ranches. And then, in 1897, came the Crow's Nest line and a brief but lively boom.

Fort Macleod had dropped the "Fort" from its name in 1891 when the town was incorporated; residents felt it might give outsiders too wild and woolly an impression. This impression, however, had undeniable reality behind it, based in part upon characters like Harry "Kamoose" Taylor, a missionary turned whisky trader and proprietor of the Macleod Hotel. The Taylor brand of humour hardly conveyed urban sophistication. Historian MacGregor quotes some of the house rules he posted. "Guests are expected to rise at 6 a.m., as the sheets are needed for tablecloths" was one of them. Another: "Towels changed weekly; insect repellent for sale at the bar."

Urbanity was not always evident either in the news purveyed by the *Fort Macleod Gazette,* founded by former Mounties C.E.D. Wood and E.T. (Si) Saunders. (Saunders moved on to Lethbridge, where he founded the *News* as well.) Something must be done to prevent stray horses and cattle from eating the town's newly planted trees and shrubs, advised the *Gazette* at one point.

Railway construction workers had proved at least as rowdy as teamsters or ranch hands. Gunshot wounds were listed (along with typhoid fever) as one of the most frequent reasons for admission to the Macleod Hospital.[8] But labourers were making $1.50 a day, and at one stage the *Gazette* claimed the town's population had grown by 4,000 in one month. It settled to something under a thousand residents by 1899.

Some rowdiness notwithstanding, they were a cheerful lot, very enthusiastic about sport: baseball, hockey and curling, and especially the British-derived football, cricket, tennis and polo. Dancing was popular (the Red River jig, reels, polkas and round dances) despite a shortage of female partners. So was singing. One group called itself the Macleod Quintette Club, though it numbered eight or nine singers. In disguise and under cover of darkness they inflicted raucous serenades upon the populace.

As the southerly railway builders forged onward in 1897, they opened another area that would ultimately produce several more towns: the Crow's Nest communities. At the turn of the century coal was also being mined in the mountains near 10th Siding, also called The Springs. 10th Siding would shortly become Blairmore and would be followed by other mining villages: Frank and Hillcrest, Lille and Bellevue.

Embryonic settlements were also strung along the main CPR line. Between the Rockies and Calgary were Banff, Canmore, Exshaw, Morley (where the Reverend George McDougall had established a mission in 1873, named for Morley Punshon, a Methodist minister who supported his work) and Cochrane. Another dozen were dotted between

Glenbow Archives, NA-354-1

Col. James Macleod.

[8] Before the Macleod Hospital was built, Dr. Richard Nevitt had a surgery in the NWMP fort. It was here that he treated Crowfoot during one of the great Blackfoot chief's illnesses. The doctor, it is recounted in *Fort Macleod: Our Colourful Past,* wore Blackfoot medicine robes while doing so, out of respect for the chief.

Provincial Archives of Alberta, E. Brown Collection, B-2626

Wetaskiwin in 1898. The tide of settlers had yet to come.

Calgary and Medicine Hat, most of them scarcely more than sidings yet.

Northward, along the C&E Railway, more settlements were beginning to grow: places like Didsbury, Innisfail (which began as Poplar Grove), Lacombe and Wetaskiwin (16th Siding). The C&E generally followed the wagon trail, so that some of the settlements pre-dated 1891. But few were more than stopping houses on the trail or a couple of homesteads, until the trains began bringing settlers in significant numbers.

Red Deer provides an example. The wagon trail forded the Red Deer River at Red Deer Crossing, where by 1882 there was a stopping house, a sawmill and a store. In 1884 a Methodist minister from London, Ontario, the Reverend Leonard Gaetz, settled with his wife and 10 children three miles down river. Gaetz, who may have been the first to describe the region's mix of prairie and woods as "the parklands," was a determined promoter. In 1890, with samples of grain from his farm, he appeared before the parliamentary Committee on Colonization and Agriculture in Ottawa, to support the Mackenzie and Mann proposal for a railway across central Alberta.

Red Deer and District Archives

Leonard Gaetz. Piety and promotion.

Gaetz was also one of the speakers at the C&E sod-turning in 1890. In return for 600 acres of land, he had persuaded that company to cross the river at his holding, and a townsite was laid out there. The "Old Crossing" settlement faded out. The new Red Deer prospered with the district. Some 700 new homesteaders had been registered in the area by 1899. The town (population about 300) had a Methodist church, a two-room brick schoolhouse, a hall, a hotel, a brickyard, an agricultural society that held a fall fair, and a 1,500-bushel grain elevator.

Older, non-railway communities around Edmonton were also growing. St. Albert, chosen by Father Albert Lacombe in 1861 as a Metis farming refuge, had more than a thousand residents. A hundred miles northeast at St. Paul des Metis, the settlement Lacombe initiated in 1896, new francophone immigrants were beginning to outnumber the Metis. Farther north still, the Athabasca and Peace River regions were still the exclusive domain of Indians, traders and missionaries. But German-speaking settlers were homesteading around Fort Saskatchewan and Stony Plain and moving into central Alberta, where Scandinavians too were establishing colonies. And Interior Minister Clifford Sifton had begun the campaign that would bring 170,000 Ukrainians to Canada by 1914.

But if the settlers could look forward with optimism to the new century, whatever their present hardships, the same was not true for the Indians of the plains. In a mere two decades of what the coming century would learn to call "unrestricted immigration," their homeland had already been transformed. In 1881 they still outnumbered the Europeans by at least eight to one. By 1899, just 18 years later, it was *they* who were outnumbered, five to one. As Howard and Tamara Palmer put it in *Peoples of Alberta*, the West had become "white man's country." Upon this the ragged and starving red man marvelled — in anguish, anger and despair.❦

A Sarcee Indian camp in the 1890s.
Provincial Archives of Alberta, E. Brown Collection, B-37

Section Two
The Indians

Chapters by Link Byfield
Sidebars by Rick Bell, Link Byfield, Brian Hutchinson

R.B. Nevitt's painting of Indian tepees. Before the horse arrived in the 1700s, tepees were small, travel laborious, and the old had to be left behind to die.

From Dog Days to Horse Days — The golden age of the Plains Indian culture

BRITISH AND FRENCH TRADE GOODS AND THE SPANISH HORSE LIBERATED NATIVE TRIBES FROM THE TOIL OF PEDESTRIAN, STONE-AGE EXISTENCE

The neat geographic pentagon we call Alberta would have seemed a meaningless and silly fiction to the prehistoric inhabitants of northwestern North America. To the great tribal alliances that whites displaced late in the 19th century, Alberta was three separate and very mystical homelands, without a straight line anywhere, without a road or a single permanent dwelling. The land was utterly wild, and its thinly scattered inhabitants crossed it as freely and fiercely as the wolf. They led a harsh life, and violent.

Provincial Archives of Alberta, E. Brown Collection, B-11

An unidentified Cree camp in the late 1880s. Hunting, moving, praying and fighting were the mainstays of plains life in the free days.

Though their supplanters in the late 19th century often thought of them simply as "Indians," they were many tribes and nations, as different from one another as the Irish from the Turks. When white settlement began there were four language groups and 10 tribes, each numbering between several hundred and several thousand, within what is now Alberta. Northern Alberta was the homeland of the Athapaskan language group — the Beaver, Slavey and Chipewyan. Theirs was the vast boreal forest of tamarack and spruce, drained by the broad, silty-grey Peace and Slave rivers as they flowed down north to the barren country of the Eaters of Raw Flesh, the Inuit.

South of the Peace and along the rolling poplar basin of the North Saskatchewan River lived the Woods Cree and the Plains Cree, whose tribal empire stretched clear to Hudson Bay. Upriver of the Cree, as far as the Rockies, lived the Assiniboine, who spoke a Sioux dialect. And in the wide ocean of buffalo grass south of the Battle River lived the fierce Blood, Peigan, Blackfoot, Gros Ventre and Sarcee tribes. Their hunting grounds ran from the eastern slopes of the shining mountains to the Dakota badlands and the valley of the Missouri.

Although Indians had lived in North America for at least 12,000 years, tribal movements for most of that period can be known only archaeologically — by burial customs, by style of spear and arrow heads, and by "medicine wheels"(prominent, unexplained hilltop piles of stones arranged in circular patterns with spokes). How the people looked and acted we have no idea.

Other than pictographs, Indians had no method of writing, so the earliest coherent glimpse we have of them consists of cursory and anecdotal passages in the journals of 17th- and 18th-century explorers like Henry Kelsey, Anthony Henday, Matthew Cocking, David Thompson and Alexander Henry. Tribal migration and culture by then were already being driven by two new factors: English and French metal from the east, in the form of trade muskets, steel knives and hatchets, and copper kettles; and the horse from the south, an inadvertent contribution of the Mexican Spaniards. By 1800, horse herds had been spreading northward from tribe to tribe for over a century.

The most aloof and ferocious of all three Alberta groupings was the Blackfoot, the only one whose eventual tribal range would happen to fall almost entirely within the province. In 1691 Hudson's Bay Company explorer Henry Kelsey, the first white to reach the lower Saskatchewan River plains, heard from his Cree and Assiniboine companions about a fearsome enemy farther west they called the "Naywattamee Poets." Kelsey himself never saw them, but they were probably the Blackfoot. It was undoubtedly traders from New France penetrating the central Saskatchewan country in the 1730s and '40s who met them first.

The earliest written account of them, however, comes from Hudson's Bay Company explorer Anthony Henday. On a marketing mission into the plains in 1754 he visited a big Blackfoot[1] camp of 322 tepees — at an average of eight per lodge, some 2,500 people — probably a short distance southeast of Red Deer. He noted with fascination that they rode horses, complete with stirrups and pad saddles stuffed with buffalo hair, and he himself experienced the thrill of a mounted buffalo hunt. It was all he could do to control his horse, he reported, while the Indians galloped with both hands free and felled buffalo with as few as two arrows.

[1] Some historians suspect that Anthony Henday's description, the first of native life in Alberta, was probably of the Gros Ventre, staunch allies of the Blackfoot until the mid-1800s. Henday referred to them simply with the Cree word for "foreigners."

Buffalo Hunt Surround, an undated lithograph by George Catlin.
A good hunter on a skilled horse could fell a three-quarter-ton bull with one or two arrows at a full gallop.

Life revolved around the thundering glory of the buffalo hunt

Slaying and butchering the huge beasts was dirty, dangerous work, but it provided almost everything the Plains Indian needed

No Plains Indian activity was more vital than hunting the prairie buffalo. For at least 10,000 years, long before the Indians' brief history as horseback hunters, the buffalo served as their "staff of life." Its bones, sinews, horns, skull, hide, mane, hair, tail, paunch, bladder and intestines furnished them with most of their food, clothing and shelter, and many of their tools and utensils.

Killing the shaggy, skittish, dangerously horned bovines was both difficult and risky, however. The Indians from all plains tribes had developed three common methods before they were blessed with the horse by the Spaniards.

The simplest and most primitive technique was stalking. Draped in buffalo skins, the hunters would move slowly toward the grazing herd from downwind, so their own scent would not alert the quarry. Once within range of bow or spear, they would rise up and attempt a fatal volley against the nearest few, aiming always for the heart cavity behind the foreleg.

A more complex method was the pound, or corral, which, when it worked at all, was more productive. Using deadfalls, brush, travois poles and any other materials at hand, the band would construct two long, parallel fences converging down a slope, with as sturdy a corral as possible at the bottom. Sometimes the builders would surround the inside perimeter of the corral with sharpened stakes, driven into the ground and pointing inward toward the centre, to keep the animals away from the fence.

While the most potent holy man in the band remained behind in his lodge and prayed that unfriendly spirits would not interfere by shifting the winds and spooking the herd, the swiftest and most skilled hunters, sometimes dressed in wolf-skins, would then approach the target herd and slowly worry it towards the fences. This touchy business could take days. Once the lead animals were moving into the funnel, the hunters would leap into view to stampede the whole herd after them and down the slope—which might be greased with freshly peeled poles or frozen buffalo dung—and into the corral. All remaining men, old and young, then shot as many of the milling animals as they could before the buffalo broke out. Afterwards, the band chief would distribute the meat proportionately to each family.

The other method of mass slaughter was similar: the buffalo jump. A herd would be craftily herded towards a cliff along a coulee or river valley. Then, with much waving of blankets and yelling by the carefully positioned band members, the animals would be driven over the edge. Other hunters waited below to finish off survivors.

There were numerous jumps on the western Canadian plains, the most famous being the Head-Smashed-In site northwest of Fort Macleod in the Porcupine Hills. The jump method sometimes produced immense waste. Lewis and Clark passed one such site on the Missouri where "the remains of a vast many mangled carcasses of Buffalo" had filled the air with a thick stench for miles around.

As the plains tribes built up their horse herds in the 1700s, they perfected the chase. Unlike the more prosaic and practical Metis, who would execute very elaborate and disciplined surrounds for maximum slaughter, Indians preferred a straight chase at full gallop. It was probably less efficient, but a lot more fun.

Upon sighting a herd, the hunters would lead their fastest and best-trained buffalo-running horses to the closest downwind point of concealment. Once mounted, they would often form into two lines, right-handed archers on the right, left-handed and spearmen on the left. Few Indians used muskets in the hunt, because they were hard to load on the run. Most preferred a short, strong bow, and could drop an animal by sinking two or three iron-tipped arrows into the heart cavity.

With a wave from the lead hunter, the Indians would break from hiding and go straight for their quarry at full gallop. The startled buffalo would immediately stampede. Cows, being fleetest, would lead the flight, and, because they were fatter and more tender, became the targets of those hunters with the best horses. Men with slower mounts would have to content themselves with the tougher, more dangerous bulls.

Boys, meanwhile, who were usually brought on hunts to tend horses and learn the trade, practised their riding and shooting skills on the calves trailing behind. The meat was tender and calfhide was valuable for babies' garments and women's clothing.

A good outcome, of course, depended upon the horse. It had to know the hunter's intent, because he was riding at full tilt with both hands busy; usually he had a long rein coiled under his belt in case he fell off. The horse had to gallop alongside within a few paces of the thundering, panic-stricken quarry, and swerve away at the twang of the bow, because the buffalo might tumble.

Or it might not tumble, and try to gore the horse. If it ran on, the hunter signalled with his knees for the horse to come alongside again. So it went. Many men were crippled or killed by falling or charging bison, or when a horse stepped into a prairiedog hole, sending itself and its rider to the ground with shattering impact.

Collection of Glenbow Museum, 75.10.24

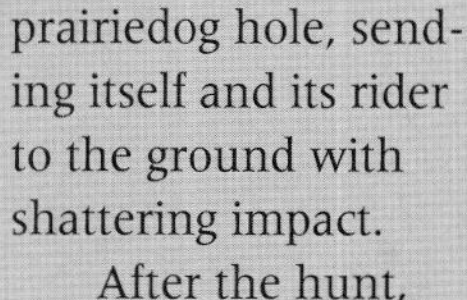

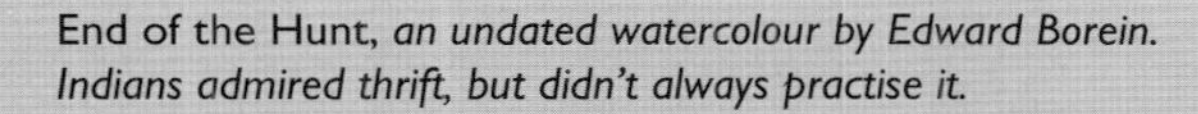

End of the Hunt, *an undated watercolour by Edward Borein. Indians admired thrift, but didn't always practise it.*

After the hunt, man and wife donned old clothing and skinned and quartered the beasts felled by that hunter's arrows. Each animal took about an hour to dress, and would typically yield 400 pounds of boned meat and useful parts — a full load for two packhorses. Depending upon the needs of the moment, utilization might be anything from very little (tongue, hump, back fat and other choice pieces) to something very close to 100%. Indians admired thrift, but didn't always practise it.

The Plains Indians were famous feasters. Mountie Sam Steele claimed to have seen men consume 20 pounds of meat each in a sitting, although such prodigious gluttony would seem physically impossible.

They also dried the meat in strips, pounded the strips to mash, mixed it with berries and rendered marrow or fat, and sewed it in a raw buffalo-hide bag (hair out) as pemmican. This was a staple for the Metis and all the prairie tribes. The constant need of the Canadian fur trade for pemmican, along with the Missouri River market for buffalo hides and robes, accounted in large part for the unsustainable level of harvest that reduced the Canadian herds to nil by 1879.

The final destruction of the American herd followed five years later. More than 150,000 skins were sold at St. Paul in 1883. The next year the figure fell to 300. A United States game inventory in 1886 showed only six animals known to be still alive. Thereafter the buffalo survived only as a protected species until buffalo-raising began appearing as a small agricultural industry in the mid-20th century. *L.B.*❦

Provincial Archives of Alberta, E. Brown Collection, B-801

A Cree warrior at the turn of the century. As the Cree pressed west and south along the North Saskatchewan, the Blackfoot drove the Shoshoni and Kutenai out of southern Alberta with single-minded ferocity.

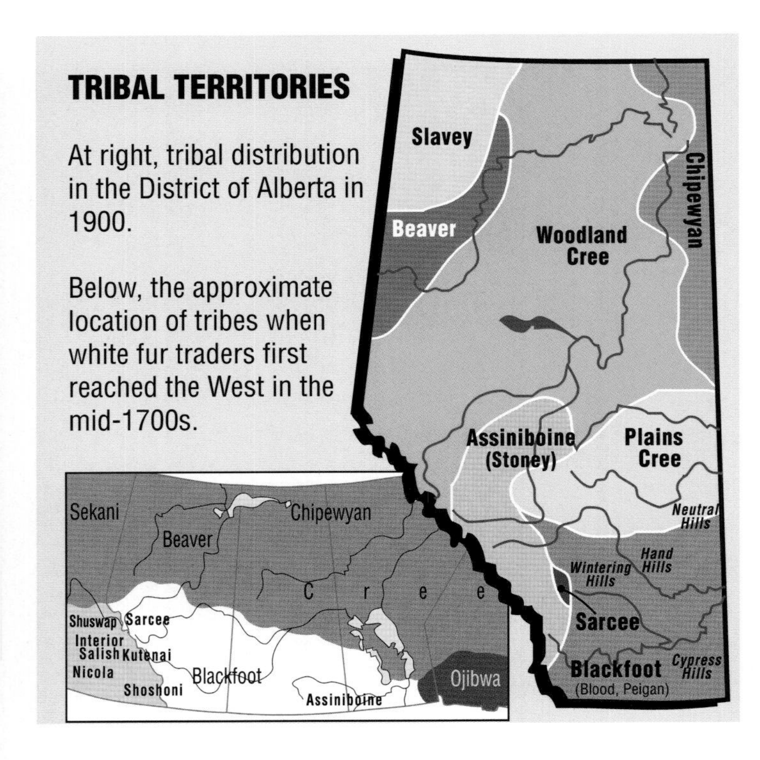

But most early observations deal with little more than the trade potential of the inland tribes, for the observers were men of action, not anthropologists. Not until explorer and cartographer David Thompson wintered with the Blackfoot in southern Alberta in 1787-88 did anyone think to write down how they came to be there, which tribes wanted to kill them, and how their society worked.

Thompson's hosts were the Peigan (pronounced pay-gahn, from the Blackfoot word Apikuni, meaning "scabby hides"[2]), one of three tribes that shared the same language. The others were (and are) the Blackfoot themselves, (a literal translation of their word Sik-sikah meaning "black foot") and the Bloods (self-described as the Kainai, meaning "many chiefs").[3] These three composed the Blackfoot Confederacy, together with a fourth, the small Sarcee tribe (calling themselves the Tso-tli-na, "earth people") who spoke a language akin to the Athapaskan tongue of the Beaver in the north, from whom they had split some time in the 1600s.

The Blackfoot language is Algonkian and springs from the same root as many others, among them Cree, Ojibwa, Gros Ventre, Arapaho and Cheyenne. It is now believed that all these westward-migrating plains tribes came earlier from the western Great Lakes country. The Blackfoot led the way into the grasslands in the north, the Sioux and Cheyenne into those in the south.

Thompson reported that the Peigans had no tribal memory of earlier migration, except that most recently they had come from the Eagle Hills (near Battleford in Saskatchewan), land that was already being occupied increasingly by the Cree. As the stocky, quiet, snub-nosed Londoner hunched that winter of 1787 by the Peigan lodge fires and chewed on buffalo meat, a few wizened oldsters recounted their parents' and grandparents' tales about an age they called "the days when we had only dogs for moving camp," or "dog days." They meant, of course, the time before the horse.

Life then had been hungry and poor, tepees small, and meat harder to get. All possessions had to be carried on the backs of women or on short A-frame "travois" poles dragged by dogs, which could haul little more than 70 pounds. This meant that a buffalo-hide tepee couldn't exceed about eight skins, making it only 10 or 12 feet in diameter, to shelter eight or more people. People too old or lame to walk had to be left behind to die alone.

A good day's march seldom exceeded six miles in dog days, making it impossible for any band to move far into the dry and windswept open plains where the biggest summer herds of buffalo grazed. And because so much time had to be spent moving camp or hunting deer, elk and moose

[2] The Blackfoot frequently use the word "scabby" much as slang English uses "lousy" to signify a poor or unsatisfactory condition.

[3] Indian legend holds that the tribes of the Blackfoot nation split into three tribes to guard their frontiers. Once when a man from the northern group visited those in the southeast he happened to cross a burned prairie, and his group were thereafter named Blackfoot. He in turn noticed how proud and independent the other tribe had become, and named them Kainai, or Many Chiefs. The whites named them Bloods, probably for the red ochre dye on their clothing. Among the Peigan, visitors found that the women were so rich in buffalo hides that they had become careless in dressing them; hence "scabby hides."

singly in the bush, the size of the Indians' summer camps on the plains was limited to perhaps 200 people at most, and winter camps in the woodlands to a few families each.

Worse still, such time-consuming hunting and moving restricted the honour men could win by raiding enemy tribes for women, holy objects and scalps. And it left less time for communing with spirits and conducting religious ceremonies. Hunting, moving, praying and fighting were the mainstays of Indian life among all tribes, at any rate for males. Of these, moving was the least interesting.

Thompson observed that Plains Indian men would sooner walk for six hours over rough ground than suffer for one hour at some camp drudgery. They worked at all only from necessity rather than choice, he said. The life and attitude of Indian women he found very different. Berries had to be picked, meat butchered, dried and pounded into the transportable form known as pemmican, roots dug, firewood broken and hauled, hides for tepees and clothing scraped, tanned and sewn. One detects the European perspective here, of course. From another perspective, men had the tasks of hunting and protecting the camp, and women did the rest. Fighting and hunting were work, and dangerous at that.[4]

Provincial Archives of Alberta, E. Brown Collection, B 1022

A Blackfoot warrior in 1881. A fierce people whose greatest virtue was not courage but generosity.

In dog days, of course, work of all kinds was accomplished with tools made either of stone, especially flint or a quartz known as chert, or bone, neither of which cuts very well. Pots were of clay and probably didn't survive many moves. Even shaping a single spoon out of buffalo horn required patient hours of boiling, cutting and grinding. In Thompson's time many such tools were still made and used, although certain stone-age skills had, for good reason, been abandoned. For three generations, items like iron arrow tips had been almost literally a dime a dozen, first through barter with friendly Assiniboine bands and after 1790 at Blackfoot forts along the North Saskatchewan. Chipping the same number of points from flint would have taken a skilful old man many weeks.

Even in dog days, however, life for the Blackfoot, Assiniboine and southern Cree centred on the buffalo. Zoologists estimate the continental herd to have numbered 50 million head or more. The lumbering, shaggy, reddish brown, three-quarter-ton ruminants ranged from northern Alberta to the Texas plains. They summered in the open prairie. In winter they retreated into the northern and western forests, and wooded prairie hill ranges and river valleys. The artist Paul Kane's description of them is memorable: "During the whole of the three days it took us to reach Edmonton House, we saw nothing else but these animals covering the plain as far as the eye could reach, and so numerous were they that at times they impeded our progress, filling the air with dust almost to suffocation."

Where moved the buffalo, there moved the pedestrian Indians, strung out in struggling columns of toiling women, larking little children and yapping dogs. Warriors, armed and painted,

[4] Despite his very different temperament, the pious, industrious Thompson admired the Peigans. "The character of all these people," he wrote, "appear[s] to be brave, steady and deliberate...almost every character in civilized society can be traced among them, from the gravity of a judge to a merry jester, and from open hearted generosity to the avaricious miser. This last character is more detested by them than by us...great attention [is paid] to those that are least fortunate in the chase, and the tent of a sick man is well supplied."

The all-encompassing spirit world of the Cree

Within the web of Indian mysticism lay a devoutness which made many ready converts to Christianity

On the broad plains, the Cree, like all prairie tribes, saw their lives intertwined with supernatural realities. Within both worlds, natural and beyond-natural, was a single, all-powerful God or Manito, along with mediating spirit powers in the natural world that assisted mankind. Manito remained aloof, but every prayer and ritual addressed to the other powers began with an invocation asking him to witness it.

Manito was not personal. He did not appear in visions and was never asked directly for his blessing because he was too awesome. The lower spirit powers were more approachable — rather like the saints in Catholic tradition. Spirits dwelled within every living thing: a horse, bear or tree. Special characters, such as Wisakichak, the trickster who had many adventures when the Earth was created, also had spirit power. So too did the "little people," who the Cree believed made flint arrowheads and lived in river banks and sand hills. Inanimate objects, stones for example, could have spirit power. Natural phenomena like thunder, wind and the sun were among the mightiest spirit powers.

Man was also part of the supernatural world. His soul entered his body at birth, lived along the nape of his neck, and left when the body died. During visions, the soul could leave the body and travel with a spirit power. After death the soul wandered about for four days, then followed the Milky Way and entered the Green Grass World where, if the person had lived worthily, his reward was a carefree afterlife. Some holy men actually visited there. Although souls might return, especially in a ceremony involving the Carried on the Back Bundle, they didn't appear in visions and could not grant any power. Sometimes souls returned to haunt certain places, making their presence known through weird noises. These were called ghosts.

The spirit powers resided in each of their kind; for example, the bear spirit lived in every bear. But the powers also lived in an ideal realm, remarkably akin to what western philosophy knows as the Platonic "forms." The Great Parent of Bear was never seen, except partly and imperfectly in the form of earthly bears.

The Plains Cree received their spirit helpers through vision quests. When a boy approached puberty, his father or grandfather would send him out to fast for several days in a secluded spot, to pray and to mortify his bodily cravings and weaknesses. One boy, for instance, was said to have looked at the sun for four days. Alone in the wild the quester might cry, but once sufficiently exhausted, thirsty and hungry he would sleep. His appointed guiding spirit would pity him (the appeal to pity was often made when calling upon the spirits) and would appear, speaking in great kindness, calling him grandchild.

The spirit would become his protector and give him power to perform certain deeds: some questers would be hunters, some leaders of ceremonies, some warriors and some, worthiest of all, healers. The guide would reveal the particular songs and "medicine tokens" through which the boy could call upon one or several spirits for future supernatural assistance. Receiving a spirit helper was a mixed blessing, for the person might displease the spirit by violating one of the ordinances or by reneging on promises made. Obligations went along with asking for a spirit helper's assistance.

Girls never deliberately sought a vision but, particularly during their first menstruation, might have one anyway. The spirit power then usually appeared as a female. Though women could acquire spirit help, they couldn't lead or vow to perform ceremonies except through their husbands. The presence of menstruating women defiled a religious ceremony of any sort. Some people never had a vision and therefore had no spirit helper, but these were still under the guardianship of Manito.

Vision recipients would make a sacred "bundle," comprised of layers of cloth or hide encasing sweetgrass, tobacco or particular charms, such as special stones, claws or bones. It was hung on a tripod at the back of the owner's tepee. Any item designated by the spirit helper as protective would be kept in the bundle. Big Bear, the great chief of the Plains Cree, had a bundle called the "Chief's Son's Hand," a tanned bear paw with claws, sewn on a piece of scarlet flannel and worn as a neckpiece. The bear spirit had told him to make the bundle.

A bundle was highly prized if it worked, and it could be purchased. Each had a song and a particular ritual which were taught to the new owner. Other types of bundles had different purposes. The Pipestem Bundle was given by Manito to the first human, Earth Man. This bundle's holder was chosen by the band for the merits of fearlessness and evenhandedness. The holder could not quarrel and could intervene in disputes. It was a three- to four-foot pipestem with no bowl, decorated with quills, beads, fur and feathers. The Carried on the Back Bundle was not granted by a spirit helper, but was passed from father to son. It contained the braids of deceased relatives and was carried on the back when the family moved.

Gaining contact with the spirit world required that one be pitied, and the normal means was self-torture and mortification, such as in the Thirst Dance — which other tribes like the Blackfoot and Sioux called the Sun Dance. Usually held in spring or early summer, it involved the worship of Manito through the Thunderbird spirit or the Sun spirit. Because it was the most difficult dance it was the most likely to get results. A central pole in a lodge was erected, with a Thunderbird nest near the top. Beside the pole on a white cloth was a buffalo skull (a sign of trust in Manito's care). There were innumerable prayers, singing, dancing by both sexes, cloth offerings and self-torture. Male dancers who had vowed to do so would be tethered to rawhide lines connecting the top of the pole to skewers pushed through the skin of the dancer's breast. The dancer fell back on the lines, trying to tear the skewers from his skin as he circled the pole.

If he failed to tear out the skewers, he could be released after one song. Alternatively, a buffalo skull might be hung from skewers set in the back. Other worshippers offered bits of cut skin or perhaps a little finger. Sexual intercourse was forbidden during a Thirst Dance, as were eating and drinking, except for raindrops. Rain was a sign of pity by the spirit power. Dances involving mutilation were banned by the 1895 Indian Act.

Cree spirituality found its inspiration in the hunting and warring life, and when these disappeared in the late 19th century, Cree religion soon changed direction. Indian belief shared some elements with Christianity, which may explain why so many Indians became converts after their old medicine was rendered powerless.

Christianity, especially Catholicism, demanded strict adherence to ritual. It believed in divine intervention in daily life. It was highly moralistic. Much scriptural material used nature for illustration and effect. And Christianity acknowledged that in identifying one's suffering with that of Christ, the sufferer gains a closer relationship to the supernatural. *R.B.*❦

A rare photographic glimpse of the Blackfoot Sun Dance in 1887. Skewered through the breast, the warriors aspired to receive pity and help from the spirit world.

Provincial Archives of Alberta, E. Brown Collection, B-990

Provincial Archives of Alberta, E. Brown Collection, B-53

A Sarcee woman, Omuxapop O-Krista, probably in the 1880s. A life of unremitting hard labour.

guarded the flanks and swift-running scouts reconnoitred ahead for signs of enemies and meat.

Inter-tribal enmity abounded. Most of the time the Blackfoot were at war to the north and east with the Cree, Ojibwa and Assiniboine[5], all of whom were following them into the plains. On the southeast they faced the populous multi-tribal confederacy of the Sioux, or Lakota, although their Gros Ventre allies in southern Saskatchewan bore the brunt of that. Likewise, the Cree, Ojibwa and Assiniboine were themselves ancient adversaries of the Sioux from Great Lakes days.[6]

On the south and west the Blackfoot fought the Crow and Flathead. But their deepest and harshest animosity they reserved for the Kutenai[7] and the Shoshoni (sometimes called the Snakes) who lived on both sides of the Rocky Mountains and foraged eastward far into the open plains. In the late 1700s, the Peigan, who were the most numerous and militant of the Blackfoot nation, faced the Kutenai and Shoshoni along the Bow River. It fell to the Blackfoot tribe to keep the Cree alliance out of the upper North Saskatchewan River country, from Fort Edmonton to the Eagle Hills. The Bloods lived south of the Blackfoot and east of the Peigan, and supported both fronts; they also frequently fought the Crow Indians to the southwest.

According to Blackfoot tradition, the metal and horse revolution came upon them suddenly one summer — probably in the 1730s. In dog days there were two types of warfare: the surprise attack on a camp, which could have fatal consequences to the surprised; and the formal battle, in which warriors lined up behind shields and shot arrows at each other until nightfall, when both sides usually went home with only minor casualties. On this occasion, a war party of Peigan encountered a contingent of the hated Shoshoni. Contrary to all custom, however, these Shoshoni did not line up. Whooping and waving their stone war clubs, they came racing across the grass astride large, magical animals, as fast as buffalo and as obedient as dogs. The Peigans broke and fled, losing several of their best men.

The Peigan were mystified by this terrifying new Shoshoni "medicine," and sought support from a few neighbouring and co-operative Cree and Assiniboine bands. These arrived with another marvel: a steel pipe that could spit a lead ball faster than the eye could follow, and so hard it could smash bones. Armed now with this stupendous high-tech weapon, warriors from the three tribes set out for revenge upon the Shoshoni. They soon encountered a larger Shoshoni force, this one on foot. Both sides lined up in the usual way, but the Peigan ranks suddenly loosed a thundering, smoky blast. Ten Shoshoni fell, and by dusk the Peigan and their allies had cut 50 Shoshoni scalps in a single day.

Not long after this battle the Blackfoot got their own first horses, whether through raiding or trading is not remembered. Their first firearms they purchased from the Assiniboine, and after 1795 from the Hudson's Bay Company fort at Edmonton. Thus armed and mounted and with a single-minded ferocity, they drove the Shoshoni and Kutenai back over the Rockies. Not until the early 1800s did the Shoshoni and Kutenai get their hands on trade flintlocks, and by then the Blackfoot had occupied all of southern Alberta and northwest Montana. But they relinquished the North Saskatchewan River country to the oncoming Cree and Assiniboine, and thereafter the dividing line between them ran roughly on a northwest-southeast line across the Neutral Hills, north of Consort, Alberta.

Now the Blackfoot tribes had a homeland they wanted to keep. They wintered in the western foothills, and in the prairie hill ranges as far east as the Bearpaws and Little Rockies in Montana, the Cypress and Great Sand Hills in Saskatchewan and the Hand Hills, Neutral Hills and Three Hills

[5] The Assiniboine were also known as the Stoney or Stony. Hence Stony Plain, Alberta. The Ojibwa, sometimes spelled Ojibway, were known to the whites by two other names. The French called them the Saulteaux. To the Americans they were the Chippewa. Both Ojibwa and Chippewa are attempts to render their Indian name in English.

[6] There was a further bitterness in the Assiniboine conflict with the Sioux. The Assiniboine were actually a Sioux-language tribe that had switched sides, probably in the 1600s.

Provincial Archives of Alberta, E. Brown Collection, B-34

Blackfoot boys with bows around 1890. Fighting and hunting were hard, dangerous tasks, learned early.

in central Alberta. Though they had plenty of beaver, valuable for trade, in their mountain streams, they were ill-disposed to the laborious winter work of trapping. Also, to many the beaver was sacred. Had not the spirit of the beaver helped their holy men "call" the buffalo to their roving hunting bands or into the wooden-fenced pounds to be slaughtered?

Besides, with horses they could usually kill a big surplus of buffalo. The dried meat they sold to the Canadian fur trade, and the hides they sold as tanned robes to trading forts built on the Missouri by the American Fur Company after 1831. Robes were too bulky to be profitably paddled eastward by traders to Montreal or Hudson Bay, but flatboats and later steamboats travelled the navigable Mississippi and Missouri.

Americans started trespassing in the tribal lands of the Blackfoot Confederacy after the Lewis and Clark expedition of 1804-06, which reached the source of the Missouri to stake out the western limit of the Louisiana Purchase. That foray was followed by an invasion of American trappers, and war quickly developed with the Peigan. Until then, the Blackfoot had seldom molested British and French traders, who provided useful goods and ventured forth from their forts only as polite guests among them. But these newly arrived mountain men, or "Big Knives," were quite something else. They behaved like marauders and poachers. Meanwhile, from the east came other unwelcome interlopers, buffalo hunters from Red River who were half Indian and half white. These too the Blackfoot considered enemies.

The half-breeds travelled in cavalcades of oxcarts in military formation, and were hard to annihilate. The Big Knives moved in ones and twos, however; they could be hunted down. And they were. The annual depredation went from 20 trappers killed in one winter after the invasion began in 1810 to 40 or 50 a year in the 1820s. There were heavy losses on the Peigan side, too, but the number isn't known. So ferocious was the Blackfoot warfare that it led the Americans to open the Oregon Trail, farther south, for westward commerce.

The North West Company trader Alexander Henry noted in 1811 that a party of Bloods had

[7] From the Kutenai come many names on Alberta's western flank: Kootenay Plain west of Rocky Mountain House, the Kootenay River in British Columbia (known when it flows south of the United States border as the Kootenai), and the two Kootenay regions of British Columbia. These are the East Kootenay immediately west of the Rockies including Fernie, Cranbrook, Kimberley, Windermere, Invermere and Golden; and the West Kootenay, which includes Creston, Nelson, Castlegar, Trail and the communities around Kootenay Lake and Slocan and Arrow lakes.

arrived at Rocky Mountain House showing off steel traps, New Jersey and Trenton bank notes and other American accoutrements. Henry suspected that they had eaten one of the slain.

In the 1830s the Americans finally saw reason and agreed to leave the hunting grounds alone if the Blackfoot would patronize their posts. For their part, the Indians were anxious for trade competition, now that the Hudson's Bay Company had absorbed the rival North West Company. The HBC traders had cut the prices they paid for fur, and increased the prices they charged for everything they sold. Besides, the Cree and Assiniboine were increasingly strong in the North Saskatchewan valley, and the Blackfoot could now go north to trade only in very large bands.

The HBC tried to establish a profitable trade fort on the Bow in 1832, but failed. The following summer, outside the Montana post of Fort McKenzie, 600 roving Cree and Assiniboine warriors struck at dawn a small Peigan camp consisting of 18 lodges. Soon some 500 Peigan tribesmen counter-attacked from a much larger camp 10 miles distant. A mounted battle ensued, with heavy slaughter on both sides. The Cree and Assiniboine fled all the way to the Bearpaw Mountains, 60 miles away.

Although whites were not usually involved in Indian warfare, at least in the Canadian territo-

The glories of the war trail

Inter-tribal killing and pillage was an ancient and honoured feature of the nomadic life

The ferocious warfare between the Blackfoot and Cree, which climaxed in the 1860s, generated countless tales of legendary heroism on both sides. Many were recorded by sympathetic whites such as James F. Sanderson, son of a Red River fur trader who moved west to run a freighting business in the 1870s. Others were retained in tribal lore and recorded much later by trustworthy writers such as Joseph Dion (*My Tribe the Crees*), Mike Mountain Horse (*My People the Bloods*), Peter Erasmus (*Buffalo Days*), David Mandelbaum (*The Plains Cree*), Hugh A. Dempsey (biographies of Big Bear, Red Crow and Crowfoot) and Edward Ahenakew (*Voices of the Plains Cree*), among many others.

One such tale concerns the two great Plains Cree chiefs at Fort Pitt, Sweetgrass and Big Bear. By the 1860s, both were old enough to prefer peace. Big Bear was in his 40s, Sweetgrass in his 50s and a recent convert to Christianity. But when peace was impossible, they were of a mind to fight, as honour and tribal tradition demanded. They were both short, muscular men, and in ready communion with the spirits who guided such raiding to a successful result.

The spirit helper of Sweetgrass (who was actually a Crow Indian, not a Cree) was the mosquito. Big Bear, who was born an Ojibwa but grew up among the allied Crees of the North Saskatchewan River, was under the pre-eminent protection of the bear spirit. He was therefore assumed to be virtually indestructible — an assumption supported by his enviable war record.

On this occasion, the two chiefs organized a raiding party of 18 young men and set out southwest on foot (as raiders seeking horses often did) for the Blackfoot country south of the Red Deer River. Within a few days they had reached enemy territory, but were forced to tarry in a creek-bottom to wait out an unseasonable snowstorm. Afterwards they sent one of their number to find and kill a buffalo for food.

The youth quickly returned and reported a lone Blackfoot on the plains above rounding up horses. The Cree rushed out to attack him, but the young Blackfoot stampeded his horses and fled into the valley of a nearby river. When the Cree followed him over the brink they were horrified to find an enormous Blackfoot camp spread out in the cottonwoods below.

While the excited Blackfoot warriors snatched their weapons and war ponies (usually tethered beside lodges) the Crees turned tail and bolted for another gully nearby, only to find that it too was thick with enemy tepees. So

Glenbow Archives, NA-1677-10

The great Cree Chief Sweetgrass in 1872. 'They fear you now.'

ries, its frequency and savagery terrified them. At the height of the northern plains buffalo trade, whites numbered no more than perhaps 200, while the Blackfoot Confederacy alone numbered almost 17,000. The scourge of smallpox, a hideous virus carried by the white newcomers, ravaged tribal populations in 1781, 1837 and 1869, wiping out entire villages in a few days. But even that did not diminish the vigour of the prairie Indians.

The explanation lay in their improved technology. Trade and horses had made the Indians more powerful, prosperous and proud than any of their dog days forebears would have imagined possible. In fact, the tools of the white man had introduced a "golden era" for the Plains Indians. Across their immense and beautiful grassland their war parties struck like lightning. Their women were rich in meat and hides and metal tools. The horses and tepees at tribal festivities in summer were so numerous as to thrill the heart. They lived on their ability to kill buffalo and kill enemies. They were rich and they were free, as the Great Spirit intended them to be.

As their unfettered happiness reached its zenith in the 1850s, however, none of them — and few of the fur traders either — could foresee the catastrophe that was about to overtake them in the next quarter-century.❦

they ran for their lives towards the only protection in sight, a tiny stand of spruce nearby on the snowy plain. As the Blackfoot came whooping up to surround them, they desperately scratched out hasty pits and flung a few dead-fallen trunks in front of them.

Apart from the chiefs, the only proven warrior among the Crees was a man named Half Sky; the other 17 were callow teenagers, whose job it now was to load the flintlocks for the warriors to shoot. And shoot they did, all that day and all the next. The Blackfoot lost many men trying to dislodge them, but succeeded only in setting fire to some logs of the barricade and shooting Half Sky in the shoulder. Big Bear being exhausted, that left only Sweetgrass still firing the second night.

At dawn of the third day a Blackfoot chief led a mass of warriors to the burned shell of the logs and fired into the Crees' pit. Sweetgrass fired a ball through the gutted log and into the Blackfoot's heart. Dismayed by such potent Cree medicine, his warriors dragged his body away and began to parley. One called: "Who are you?"

Came the defiant reply: "Cree!"

"I recognize some chiefs."

"No chiefs here," lied the Cree, chuckling, hoping the enemy would give it up.

"How many of you have been slain, O Cree?" asked the respectful Blackfoot.

"None. And you?"

"Seven great chiefs of the Blackfoot you have slain; and six Blood chiefs you have slain; and four Sarcee chiefs you have slain, and two Peigan chiefs. There are not many Peigan here, but of them you have killed many chieftains. Now they will cease. They fear you now."

Against orders, a curious Cree boy poked his head up to see the departing enemy and was immediately shot in the spine. His companions rebuked him for stupidity. The boy pleaded that they not abandon him, and as they set out for home they let him think they were merely going to find water. He would be dead within a few hours, and they could not dally. When they got home, they counted 32 bullet holes in Sweetgrass's coat and blanket, though he himself had not been scratched. Even a very lowly spirit such as the mosquito's, it was concluded, must nevertheless be very powerful.

L.B.❦

Provincial Archives of Alberta, E. Brown Collection, B-52

Armed and mounted, the Blackfoot were feared far and wide. This photograph was taken about 1904, when the hair was still long and memories of raiding for horses and scalps still fresh.

CHAPTER TWO

Starvation and defeat—the humbling of the prairie tribes

PLAINS INDIAN LIFE SUCCUMBED SUDDENLY TO DISEASE, STARVATION, DEBAUCH, A NEW RELIGION AND CATASTROPHIC INTER-TRIBAL WARFARE

As the 1860s opened, the western Canadian Prairie looked much as it had for a century. White trading establishments were small, few and distantly separated. The Hudson's Bay Company ran the posts on the North Saskatchewan, and the American competition ran others on the Missouri. All lands remained thoroughly Indian, and the only scars on the landscape were the double ruts dug by travois poles in the winding trails between springs and creeks across the dryland plains. The sun rose and the sun set, spring followed winter, and only the glories of occasional inter-tribal pillage and mayhem disturbed the certainty of a fairly secure and comfortable life.

A Sarcee encampment outside Calgary in the 1890s. From proud warrior culture to social problem in two disastrous decades.

J.A. Cockburn, photographer, Glenbow Archives, NA-395-15

Few would have believed that in the next two decades, this whole world was to collapse into squalor. Joyful, laughing children were to become gaunt, socket-eyed, skeletal spectres who died in their mothers' arms. Happy, busy, muscled women would shrink into wasted zombies, sitting, staring, starving, too weak to stand. Boasting, powerful hunters and warriors would haunt the white man's forts in rags, begging for food, or lie transfixed in an alcoholic stupor, every shred of dignity gone. The 1880s, observes popular historian Pierre Berton in *The National Dream*, marked the dawn of a new Canada: "Triumph lay just a few short years ahead." However, for the native peoples of Canada's lately acquired West, the 1880s were not a dawn. They marked the onset of a long and terrible night.

As the two disastrous decades began, the indispensable dark-humped buffalo grazed the plains and adjacent woodlands in what seemed an eternal abundance. By the late 1860s, some had noticed a decline. The herds were not quite as big this year — thousands where there used to be tens of thousands. By the mid-1870s, almost none could be found north of the Red Deer. By 1879, the buffalo was gone — it, and the meat you ate, the clothes you wore, the home in which your wives and children slept, and the hides you sold. The golden era of the Plains Indians had vanished as rapidly as it had appeared those four or five generations ago. The proud warrior of the prairies had become the new Canada's first major welfare problem, a subject for administrative study, an object of bureaucratic assistance programs. And all within 20 years.[1]

In 1860 the nomadic chiefs of the plains knew virtually nothing of the crowded, smoky cities growing up in the East that were using western buffalo hides for industrial machine belts. They knew even less of the territorial presumptions of governments in Washington and London. Nevertheless new themes and thoughts were spoken at the lodgefire councils. There were the mis-

[1] Historian George F. G. Stanley in *The Birth of Western Canada* points out that where the Indians of eastern Canada had 200 years to adjust to the changes brought by the white man, the Indians of the western plains had to make the adjustment in two decades.

Provincial Archives of Alberta, E. Brown Collection, B-8

Red Crow, head chief of the Bloods, in 1895. 'I got mad, peeled out my knife and told them I had killed three Cree in one day.'

sionaries, for instance. Whole bands of Plains Cree and Assiniboine were harkening to these strange, tough, holy men, and were abandoning the warpath to camp forever beside little log missions, to sing hymns and grow potatoes. Some were saying that all Indians would one day be farmers and Christians.

The Blackfoot tribes, for their part, had heard as much from American commissioners when a few of their headmen had signed a treaty in Montana with the United States government in a cottonwood grove at the confluence of the Judith and Missouri rivers in 1855. Other signatories were some of the more southerly "British" Cree, and the American tribes of the Gros Ventre, Flathead, Pend d'Oreille and Nez Perce.

The Americans had needed guarantees of the safety of railway surveyors for a proposed line from St. Paul to Puget Sound that would be known as the Northern Pacific. In exchange for abandoning inter-tribal war and giving up much of their territory, the Indians were to retain a large common hunting lease for 99 years and each tribe receive an annual cash payment. Money was in itself something new and mysterious. Although many signed, the treaty was ill-conceived and soon broken by both sides. For one thing, it failed to include the main Blackfoot enemy tribe in the south, the Crows. For another, the accustomed pattern of all inter-tribal pacts was that the peace chiefs would negotiate them one year, and smoke together to ratify them, and the war chiefs and young men within each tribe would break them the next.

A further problem was the idea of owning land. Indians had a very real appreciation of tribal possession, an understanding reinforced by centuries of warfare over hunting grounds. But it was unlike the whites' conception of ownership, because individual holding and a static farming economy were unknown to Plains Indian culture. The only thing the buffalo-dependent tribes had ever cultivated in the old days was a poor quality of tobacco, which the fur trader Anthony Henday had described unhappily as "dried horse dung." Except for wild onions, turnip and berries, almost every want — including trade goods among which was numbered whisky — was satisfied by the buffalo. The Blackfoot later found beef to be a coarse and sickly sweet substitute for buffalo, and salt pork they rejected as unfit for human consumption.

As the whites moved steadily west, they discovered that Indian society neither recognized nor understood the concept of binding political authority, at least as it applied to Indians. This made treaties a difficult business for both sides. An Indian either followed the decisions of his band chieftain or moved to some other band with whose chief he felt more content. Not infrequently a family switched tribes.

In addition to a civil chief, every band also had a war chief, who instantly assumed leadership when the band was attacked, and who also pressed for horse and scalp raids during times of peace, often (but not always) against the vehement resistance of the civil chief. Sometimes the fighters, typically excitable men in their teens and early twenties, broke the peace against the considered consensus of the older, more circumspect band members.

Within each tribe there were usually several acknowledged tribal chiefs with many winters of wisdom. But beyond their power of moral suasion they enjoyed even less final authority over the tribe than did the lesser chieftains over their individual bands. Even their own wives were free to divorce them, as Plains Indian women might do to any husband who beat them beyond tolerance or failed to provide.[2]

It was a fluid and chaotic system suited only to a roving way of life. Red Crow, later head chief of the Bloods, once recounted how tenuous were such inter-tribal treaties as the one signed in the Montana cottonwood grove. Shortly thereafter a Cree party raided the Bloods, stealing some horses. Red Crow led six fellow Bloods out to avenge the raid and found the culprit Cree in a camp of

[2] A woman divorced her husband simply by pitching his weapons, clothing and medicine bundle out of her tepee into public view. She would then normally return to her own family. However, unless her motives were generally known to be good, she brought shame upon her family by the act, and it might take longer for her relatives to arrange another marriage. While a Plains Indian woman might easily divorce a husband, her fidelity within marriage was strenuously enforced. If she dallied with another man, her husband was expected to cut or bite off the end of her nose, permanently and painfully disfiguring her. He was also expected to kill or drive from camp his male competitor.

Assiniboine, with whom the Bloods were tentatively at peace. As Red Crow sat with the Assiniboine chief in his lodge, a Cree entered, sat near the door and chanted that he would have revenge for a Cree slain in the horse raid. Red Crow scoffed at him that the Bloods had not asked the Cree to break the treaty and steal.

Pushing for a showdown, the Cree performed a war dance that night in their hosts' camp. They danced near the watching Bloods, pointing rifles and boasting of all the Bloods, Peigan and Blackfoot they had killed over the years. One Cree recounted in Blackfoot a particularly gratifying kill, describing it in great detail. Red Crow later recalled what came next: "I got mad at once, peeled out my knife and walked into the circle, shouting, 'You are no good! You are no good!' I then began to yell and sing and count coups at them [i.e., touch them]. I told them that I had killed three Cree in one day. It was a lie on my part, but I was an eye witness of the event that I referred to and could discuss it to their satisfaction...I told them lots of lies about the Cree I had killed, scalped and taken guns from...." He then tore down an HBC flag the Cree had mounted on a pole and seized a bow and 30 arrows lying beside it. He challenged the Cree to fight. When the latter silently declined, the Bloods haughtily left with their captured flag.

It was the misfortune of Red Crow to rise to the chieftainship of the Bloods during the two dreadful decades of their capitulation to white civilization. His was the role of leading a retreat, of deriving the best possible outcome from the worst possible circumstances, an unenviable but essential task if his people were to survive at all. Chiefs of the other tribes must do the same. This thankless challenge produced some remarkable Indian leaders whose biographies have been carefully pieced together by Hugh Dempsey of the Glenbow Museum out of contemporary documents and latter-day Indian tales and traditions.[3]

Red Crow typified them. A redoubtable and dangerous fighter in his youth, he went on 33

[3] **The Dempsey biographies are: *Crowfoot: Chief of the Blackfoot; Red Crow: Warrior Chief;* and *Big Bear: The End of Freedom.***

Glenbow Archives, NA-3970-8

A cut-nose Peigan adultress. The customary penalty was for the husband to cut or bite off the end of the nose.

Glenbow Archives, NA-4035-159

Chiefs of the Blackfoot Confederacy in 1884. (From left) Three Bulls of the Blackfoot, Sitting on Eagle Tail Feathers of the Peigan, Crowfoot of the Blackfoot and Red Crow of the Bloods.

raids, many of which he led, and killed five enemy Indians, four men and one woman. Though he never admitted it, he may have killed American whites as well. Born into a prominent Blood family in 1830, he escaped the smallpox epidemic of 1837 unscathed. He grew into a robust warrior, clever, courageous, generous, cheerful, pious, and physically ugly, something he often joked about. He had seven wives during his long life, several at a time.[4] Despite his exceptional war record, Red Crow was never wounded. He became head Blood chief in 1870, one year after the last major smallpox devastation claimed his predecessor and uncle, Seen From Afar.

Probably the best known to Albertans among those pivotal Indian figures, however, was the Blackfoot Chief Crowfoot, whose name if translated literally would be "Crow Indian's Big Foot." He was born a Blood in the Belly River country west of modern Lethbridge about 1830. His father, Packs a Knife, was killed in a raid against the Crow tribe when Crowfoot was two, and his grieving mother, Attacked Toward Home, moved back in with her father, Scabby Bull. Several years later she married a visiting Blackfoot warrior, Many Names. Soon after, the whole family moved north to live with the Biter band of the Blackfoot tribe in the Bow River valley.

Crowfoot went as a horse guard on his first raid when he was about 14, the typical age and method of warrior apprenticeship. As with other great fighters, his exploits soon became legendary. Before he was 20 he earned his adult name while besieging a Crow camp. The Crow had stolen a striped tepee from the Peigan, allies of the Blackfoot. Whoever can get in there and touch it, said the war chief, will one day be a great chief. Crowfoot darted forward. A musket ball struck him in the shoulder. He fell. Painfully, he regained his feet. To the astonishment of the Crow he kept coming, dodging like a halfback as he plunged into their camp. In a flash, he struck the tepee with his whip and was away, balls whistling past him as he fled. Afterwards, he told his admiring companions that his name was henceforth Crow Indian's Big Foot.[5]

By the time he was growing too old for war he had 19 battles to his credit, but his exploits were far from over. When he was 36, a grizzly bear attacked a party of women picking saskatoon berries

[4] Polygamy was widespread among pagan Indians. Women needed husbands for provision and protection, and a great many men died young on the war trails or in the buffalo hunt.

[5] Crowfoot's boyhood name had been Shot Close. His adoptive name was that of an earlier Blackfoot hero. The original "Crow Indian's Big Foot" was a chief who got the name while leading a raid against the Crow in the early 1800s. Prowling around an abandoned camp, the Blackfoot found a huge enemy footprint in the mud, which none but the chief could fill with his own foot. He was treacherously slain in 1828 by the Shoshoni while leading a peace delegation across the Missouri.

in a poplar bluff.[6] It badly mauled a young boy who stood with his little bow to defend the women. Crowfoot and a party of men from the All Brave Dogs society rode to the rescue. Crowfoot told the others to go to the far side of the bluff and bait the bear to come out. When they shouted that they had the grizzly's attention, Crowfoot rode calmly into the grove behind the massive beast and plunged his spear into its back. His horse shied, so he dismounted and continued stabbing the bear until it finally fell.

Unlike most Indians, Crowfoot was little interested in religion, though he did attend all tribal ceremonies and bore a personal totem, an owl's head, in a visible knot of hair upon his head until he died. He was handsome, reserved, imperious, short-tempered and prudent (but generous) with his considerable wealth of horses. He lacked the physical stamina to remain on the war trail after his teens and was an indifferent hunter. But the Biter band and many other Blackfoot knew that Crowfoot was courageous, morally just, spiritually blessed, and an effective thinker and speaker. In 1865 he became chief of a breakaway band of Biters called the Moccasin. In 1869, after the same epidemic that carried off Seen From Afar took the Biter Chief Three Suns as well, Crowfoot became one of three head chiefs of the Blackfoot tribe and was soon its most respected.

As early as 1866 clouds were beginning to form in the hitherto bright skies of the Blackfoot. They could not go south to the Missouri to trade because they had been at war there with a rush of incoming white settlers, arriving in the wake of the American Civil War. Nor could they reach Fort Edmonton; their Sarcee friends had seen an even stronger camp of Cree nearby.

The latter mattered greatly. For more than 40 years, the Cree around Fort Edmonton commanded the deep respect of the Blackfoot. In 1824 a large war party of Cree had surprised a big Blackfoot camp near the fort and, to the horror of the HBC traders, butchered more than 400 of them. Hitherto, all four Cree tribal groups, three of which were based in the near and more remote bush, had been considered by the traders as more tractable than the often hostile and headstrong Blackfoot. Now they saw that their own nearby Plains Cree were no less wild, haughty and militarily adept.

Since they could trade neither north nor south, the Blackfoot Confederacy came up with another idea. The Blood Chief Seen From Afar sent word to the traders at Fort Edmonton to bring a cart-train of goods south to the Red Deer River country. Thirty Red River carts arrived. They were accompanied, however, by 15 half-breeds — half white, that is, and half Cree. The party was led by trader John Cunningham. It came uneasily to a halt in the middle of a camp filled with several thousand Cree enemies — Sarcee, Bloods, Peigan and Blackfoot.

The Blackfoot War Chief Big Swan promptly began haranguing his men that the Cree half-breeds should be killed, and an angry confrontation developed. Seen From Afar was himself no lover of whites and half-whites, but inviting the traders had been his idea. He stepped forward in their defence. Big Swan shouted to the Blackfoot to ignore the Blood leader. The factor of Fort Edmonton would later describe what followed in a letter to a colleague in Rocky Mountain House:

"Mr. Cunningham gave it as his opinion that not one of them would have been spared. [Big Eagle] did all he could to incite the Blackfoot to kill them, Big Swan was the next worst, Three Suns did nothing, the Circees looked on and said nothing, but afterwards said the Blackfoot were Dogs. There was only one Blackfoot who spoke like a man, and if ever I see him I will give him a present — Crowfoot, a friend of yours...."

In fact, Crowfoot had stepped forward and shouted at his own tribesmen, "You people are dogs! The whites should wipe you off the face of the earth!" That encouraged the Bloods and Peigan to step en masse between the Blackfoot and their intended victims. But the only Blackfoot among their defenders was Crowfoot.

[6] Grizzly bears, which can stand seven feet tall and weigh up to 900 pounds, were spotted on the open prairie of eastern Montana by the Lewis and Clark expedition in 1805. They were driven off the Prairies by settlement and had retreated completely into the mountains by 1900. Their estimated population in Alberta in 1991 was approximately 1,000 and in British Columbia 7,000.

Crowfoot, head chief of the Blackfoot. On the war trail by 14, a seasoned warrior at 20, he carried an owl's head in a knot of hair all his life.

Glenbow Archives, NA-3700-3

Glenbow Archives, NA-235-1

Indian travois on Stephen Avenue in Calgary about 1887. Devastating warfare erupted with the Cree in the 1860s, culminating in several hundred dead on the Oldman River in 1870.

Warfare with the powerful Plains Cree, Crowfoot noted, was becoming as vicious and disastrous as it had been in the 1820s. This was not true of the more northerly Woods Cree, who also traded at Fort Edmonton. Many of these had submitted to baptism and forsworn the war path. Lapotac and Maskepetoon (Broken Arm) of the Beaver Hills Cree were Methodists, and the fierce Chief Bobtail of Buffalo Lake had become a Catholic. Farther down the North Saskatchewan, the important Chief Little Hunter and the lesser Chiefs Pakan (Nut) and Kehiwin (Eagle) were now hymn-singers. In fact, only a few of the smaller Battle River Cree bands still were of a fighting disposition. But the Plains Cree trading at Fort Pitt near the future Alberta-Saskatchewan border, and at Fort Qu'Appelle in central Saskatchewan, were still unreservedly pagan and warlike.

One notable missionary had actually visited the Blackfoot, but it had been an inauspicious occasion. In 1865 the buffalo had become strangely scarce along the Bow. Crowfoot's Moccasin tribe and Three Suns' Biters decided to risk wintering farther north in the wooded hills along the Battle River, on the very borders of Cree country. There, on December 3, they received a visit from the Catholic Oblate Father Albert Lacombe on his first mission to the Blackfoot. He was sleeping in Three Suns' camp the following night when, piercing the air amid a silent snowfall, came the blood-curdling war cry of the Plains Cree.

Shouting *"Assinow! Assinow!"* [the Cree! the Cree!], Three Suns and his startled warriors sprang from their buffalo robes to defend their unguarded camp. "In an instant," recorded the missionary, "some score of bullets came crashing through the leather lodge, and the wild war whoop of the Cree broke forth through the short and rapid detonation of many muskets...the groans of the dying, the yelling of the warriors, the harangues of the chiefs, and the noise of dogs and horses all mingled, forming a kind of hell."

The Blackfoot, outnumbered in warriors 800 to 80, repelled three assaults that night. Lacombe awed his hosts by crawling forward in his black cassock through the snow toward the Cree attackers. At mid-point he stood up, waving a white flag bearing a red cross, and implored the attackers in Cree to desist. The enemy ignored him, and a ricochet bullet struck his shoulder and grazed his forehead, knocking him senseless. Two Blackfoot rescued him. Only when day broke and the snow stopped could the fighting be heard in Crowfoot's camp nearby. He led his warriors into a fierce counter-attack, and the Cree, becoming disorganized, withdrew. The Blackfoot had suffered 12 dead, 15 wounded, two children captured and the loss of all 300 Biter horses. They would now be hard put to survive the winter. The Cree had 20 dead.

And so it went as the 1860s unfolded, raid for raid, reprisal for reprisal: battle and slaughter in the Red Ochre Hills, on the South Saskatchewan, and in the Sweetgrass Hills of Montana. In 1869 the Christian Cree Chief Maskepetoon[7] went south to sue for peace, but was slain by the Blackfoot War Chief Big Swan. Plains Cree under Piapot, Little Mountain, Little Pine and Big Bear, along with some Assiniboine, came thirsting for revenge in the fall of 1870. Just before dawn one morning they struck Red Crow's camp of Fish Eater Bloods on the Oldman River near the whisky fort Whoop-up. Notwithstanding the ravages of the '69 smallpox epidemic and the debauchery of American whisky trade, the Fish Eaters were strong enough to hold them off, losing only one man and several women. And in their haste for blood, the Cree had made a serious mistake.

At the St. Mary River, unbeknownst to the invaders and near enough to hear the gunfire, was camped the whole Peigan tribe, including the Montana-based South Peigan, who nine months earlier had been chased north after the U.S. Cavalry slaughtered 173 men, women and children in a surprise midwinter attack on their Marias River camp. They now came swarming to the aid of the Bloods, armed with new repeating rifles. Against these the outnumbered Cree and Assiniboine had only the old, slow, single-shot muzzle-loaders. The carnage carried on past the present site of Lethbridge as the Cree desperately retreated, losing between 200 and 300 men, compared to 40 dead among the Bloods and Peigan.

The fight on the Oldman was to be the last great tribal battle on Canadian soil. Indians now had a new evil with which to contend. Before the lands of the Hudson's Bay Company were sold to Canada in 1870, Americans had stayed away from the HBC's Indian country because they knew the British traders would incite the natives to chase them out. After the transfer of the land to Canada they invaded the Blackfoot territory, setting up whisky forts with apt names like Whoop-up, Stand-off and Slide-out.

Although the tribes had been accustomed for over a century to drinking stupendous quantities of Canadian trade rum and American whisky on their annual trading forays, never had they enjoyed constant access to it in the heart of their homeland. And unlike the established fur traders of old, these newcomers for the most part were dishonest, cynical and violent opportunists, impossible to admire and almost asking to be killed, which several were. However, within three years they had reduced all three Blackfoot tribes to social and economic degradation.

Life in the confederacy's camps became a hitherto unexperienced horror. The Blood Chief Red Crow, reckless when drink was available, drunkenly killed his younger brother Kit Fox. His first and favourite wife (his "sits-beside-him-woman") Water Bird was slain when another of Red Crow's brothers shot at the chief and missed. The Lone Fighter band Chief Calf Shirt was shot dead by whisky trader Joe Kipp, and the Buffalo Followers band Chief Bull Back Fat was killed while quarrelling drunkenly with a tribesman.

All morality and discipline broke down. In a single winter, according to one observer, liquor accounted for 70 dead Blood Indians. An American visitor to Whoop-up remarked approvingly in 1871: "[The whisky peddlers]...keep the Indians poor, and kill directly or indirectly more Indians...at no cost to the United States Government, than the entire regular army did in ten years!" A Catholic missionary, Fr. Constantine Scollen, deplored the unprecedented debauch: "...Hundreds of the poor Indians fell victims to the white man's craving for money, some poisoned, some frozen to death, and many shot down by American bullets." They sold their robes, their horses, their guns, their women's virtue — anything for more whisky. Inevitably, recounted the priest, "they began killing one another, so that in a short time they were divided into small parties, afraid to meet."

While the Blackfoot were coping with liquor, by the mid-1870s a catastrophe none had foreseen nor could possibly have imagined commanded Indian attention, first of the Cree and later of

[7] Maskepetoon was a lesser chief of the Cree reputed to have a violent temper; he is said to have scalped alive his own young wife. As he grew older, however, he befriended the Methodist missionaries—first Robert Rundle and later Thomas Woolsey, who taught the chief to read and baptized him in 1865. Thereafter he became a strong advocate of peace, forgave the Blackfoot who had slain his father, carried his Cree syllabic gospel with him everywhere on the plains, and often consulted it for advice. He was martyred after entering Big Swan's camp unarmed to plead for peace. He had others with him, including a son and grandson, all of whom were killed. Maskepetoon Park, a wildlife sanctuary near Red Deer, was named in his honour in 1957.

The westward trek of the North-West Mounted Police

How 300 fresh-faced Ontario greenhorns founded the finest wilderness police force in the world

On June 12, 1874, at 10:00 in the morning, a Montreal journalist named Henri Julien stepped off a train in the dusty Dakota town of Fargo and looked west. He could see nothing but flat, desolate Prairie. "Behind us lay the works of man with their noises," he wrote in his diary. "Before us stretched out the handiwork of God, with its eternal solitudes."

Julien was accompanying 16 officers and 201 fresh-faced young farm boys, blacksmiths, carpenters and office clerks from Ontario, Quebec and the Maritimes. They were on their way to Manitoba, where a further 150 men of similar background awaited them. These were to be the dominion government's North-West Mounted Police. Their mission: to march to the Rocky Mountains and establish the Queen's peace in the Dominion of Canada's turbulent new possession. Not a man among them suspected how gruelling a task they had undertaken.

British and colonial authorities had pondered putting some kind of peacekeeping force in the Hudson's Bay Company territory for 13 years, when the "great lone land" was the company's private property. The Canadian government had purchased it in 1870, and within three years much of it had succumbed to lawlessness, mostly fostered by American traders selling whisky to the southern Indian tribes. In May 1873, 20 Assiniboine Indians were massacred by a group of American wolf hunters in the Cypress Hills in an argument over some stolen horses. Calls for a police presence in the West could no longer be ignored.

The NWMP had no trouble finding applicants. "Everybody around here thinks it is a splendid thing for a young man to go into," wrote 20-year-old William Parker to his parents back in Kent, England. Parker, who had come to Canada three years

F-Troop on parade at Fort Calgary in 1876. The grasshoppers were so numerous they ate the canvas tents.

earlier and worked as a farmhand, noted that the pay would be 75 cents a day, "travelling expenses paid, a bully good horse to ride upon, and if I serve three years, I shall get a grant of a hundred and sixty acres of land." Who could resist?[a]

Quite a few could, as it turned out. As the date of departure drew near, some recruits had a change of heart. Stories of hardship on the Prairies and of murderous Sioux caused 31 men to desert the force on July 4, 1874, three days before the troops marched out of Fort Dufferin.[b] One day into the trek, five more bolted for the American border, never to be heard of again. More men would consider doing the same, but once they were on the endless ocean of waving buffalo grass, with no one around but wild Indians, none dared.

Under the stern direction of Lieutenant-Colonel George Arthur French, NWMP Commissioner, the troops in their scarlet serge tunics cut an impressive slash 2 ½ miles long across the landscape. "A" Division led the way astride dark bays, then "B" atop their browns, then "C" on bright chestnuts, and "D" astride greys, then "E" on blacks and "F" on light bays. The police were followed by a string of oxcarts and wagons, all driven by Metis, along with cattle and their calves, and sundry machinery such as cast iron hay mowers.

Glenbow Archives, NA-354-10

A surprising number of recruits had no meaningful experience of horses. One sub-constable, Joseph J. Carscadden, complained in his diary that "they content themselves with a snail's pace for they have not yet learned to ride."[c] Adding to the misery were swarms of mosquitoes, grasshoppers so thick they attacked the canvas tents to consume them, and the flat monotony of the hot, thirsty plain, relieved only by brackish springs trampled muddy by buffalo.

Henri Julien noted wearily that "the eye dwells on vacancy, tired at glancing at the blue sky above or the brown earth beneath...The silence is oppressing...It is a real desert, a land of desolation; and it will remain such until the white man settles upon it and turns the waste into a garden."

A friendly encounter with some Sioux in mid-August provided a temporary diversion, even though the civilized Julien recorded disapprovingly that the men "are dirty and ugly, low-browed, dull-eyed and brutish in appearance. The women, even the budding girls, have not a single feminine grace."[d]

The NWMP marched for six more weeks under a hot summer sun. They had been inaccurately assured that spare mounts and grain fodder would be unnecessary, and now they found grass and water were insufficient. Their fine-blooded animals were playing out. Forty of them died on the journey. By early August the men's boots had worn out and they had begun to complain of low rations.

"Had nothing to eat all day but oatmeal made into porridge," wrote Carscadden on August 5. A few weeks later the situation had become so desperate he noted that "it looks very much like starvation, so much so that we must keep moving ahead or sure death awaits us." The next day he wrote that "there is an old proverb which says that 'there is no black cloud but has a silver lining.' Well, it may be true but it seems very much like a lie just now."

But by September the men had penetrated the buffalo country, and for the remaining few weeks of the trek they hunted the awesome beast and dined on its flesh. The NWMP reached the confluence of the Bow and Oldman rivers, 45 miles west of present-day Medicine Hat, on September 11. Though they were in the heart of Crowfoot's homeland, neither the Blackfoot nor the notorious whisky traders were anywhere in sight, and the arid landscape looked "little better than a desert." Soon, however, they would find both Indians and whisky traders aplenty.

The 251 troopers and 24 officers who had completed the westward trek dispersed by division and rode off in search of suitable fort sites. Their first and most memorable journey was over, though the adventure had just begun. But the disciplines they had learned in their great trek west, and the many more they were about to acquire, would in due course earn them a reputation as the finest wilderness police force in the world. *B.H.*❦

[a] Although Parker started on the original trek west, he did not finish. Five days into the journey, he was sent back, suffering from typhoid. Another recruit who turned back with him died of it. Parker recovered and enjoyed a distinguished career in the NWMP. In 1903, he became an inspector.

[b] Fort Dufferin, on the west bank of the Red River at the United States border, opposite the settlement of Emerson, was one of the last "forts" established by the Hudson's Bay Company. It was opened in 1872, two years after the company's lands had been transferred to the Dominion of Canada.

[c] Carscadden's journal is remarkable for its sarcastic wit and unrelenting grousing about the conditions along the trail. He thought of deserting but never did. Instead, he was discharged in March 1875, after becoming "invalided." He is believed to have settled later in the Red Deer area.

[d] Such an opinion of the Sioux was far from unanimous. The NWMP's Sam Steele, for instance, described them as "handsome," mentioning in particular "the dark and piercing eyes peculiar to the Sioux."

Provincial Archives of Alberta, E. Brown Collection, B-822

Indians celebrating Queen Victoria's 1897 jubilee in downtown Edmonton. When the buffalo vanished in the 1870s, there was no alternative but to seek terms from the invader.

all the plains nations. The buffalo, the indispensable buffalo, simply disappeared.

When the end came, the vast North American herds, estimated to have once numbered 50 million head, seemed to vanish in three seasons.[8] As the herd neared extinction, the pressure on it grew worse. The natives, frantic with hunger, sought it out ever more desperately. Starvation came first to the Cree, then spread southward. Within three years the warriors of the plains descended from a life of abundance to a life of helpless want.

Famine was reported everywhere by 1878. "Poverty, want, privation and distress reigned supreme," says historian George Stanley. The great hunters of the plains were reduced to eating their horses, their dogs, even gophers and mice. They picked clean the bones of rotting animals. Indians gathered by the hundreds at Forts Carlton and Pitt to beg for flour, of which the whites had

[8] Historian George Stanley points out that the decline of the buffalo had begun before white settlement spread west of the Red River country. Reports of dwindling numbers were made to a British parliamentary committee on the HBC in 1857. Two years later Plains Indians told the Palliser expedition that the herd was going down. The Earl of Southesk in another report made in the 1850s found the Indians "almost starving" one winter in the Saskatchewan country, and an 1862 report describes the decline of fur-bearing animals around Fort Carlton. The annual "take" on the buffalo was staggering. The Metis hauled in 1,210 cartloads of hides in 1840, and thousands of carcases were left to rot on the plains.

precious little to give them. "The winter has been most trying to us," wrote the factor from Carlton. "The whole of the Indians on the five reserves have been in a state of semi-starvation, causing me great care and anxiety at times...I foresee that this is only the beginning of the end."

At St. Albert near Fort Edmonton, Father Hippolyte Leduc reported an instance of cannibalism. At Blackfoot Crossing old people and children were discovered abandoned and dying. The missionary Father Leon Doucet wrote of the Blackfoot: "What a change since last year. I could scarcely recognize in these victims of hunger, emaciated, all their flesh gone, no vigour and no voice left, the magnificent savages, the veritable Colossuses I had known before. These were not men but moving skeletons."

By the middle of the 1870s, even before the end came in 1879, it was obvious to all, even to those unwilling to face the implications of it, that the old life was no longer sustainable. Repulsive though it was, there seemed only one option: retreat to the missions and the North Saskatchewan forts, and plead with the Canadian government to negotiate some kind of deal in exchange for their land.

Not all the chiefs immediately surrendered to this disgraceful but inescapable fate. The Plains Cree, many of them now under the head chieftainship of a tough, homely, pockmarked strategist named Big Bear, would settle neither easily nor first, although other Cree bands, especially the Christian bands, did. Next came the turn of the once-proud Blackfoot Confederacy, hungry, besotted, humbled beyond recognition. The land transfers would be dignified with the designation of treaties. But they were in every sense surrenders, and nobody knew that better than the starving, ruined and bewildered chiefs who signed them each with his mark.

In 1874 Ottawa began the process of pacifying and subduing the wild west, by negotiating Treaty 4 with the eastern prairie tribes. That same year, in the autumn, the process began in the even wilder western Prairie, when a column of ill-equipped eastern Canadian horsemen in red coats wound through the plains and valleys of the Blackfoot country and built a fort on the Oldman River. The first act of the North-West Mounted Police was to shut down and arrest two men at Pine Coulee, 50 miles to the north. Both were trading in rot-gut. The others soon fled. Civil law had come to the prairie West.❦

By the turn of the century, all that remained of the vast buffalo herds were scattered bones. Sodbusters, like the unidentified pair here, gathered them in piles and sold them for fertilizer.

Provincial Archives of Alberta, E. Brown Collection

Lacombe – the 'Man of the Good Heart'

His parish covered 250,000 square miles, and he spent 50 years ministering to its turbulent inhabitants

Provincial Archives of Alberta, E. Brown Collection, B-9527

Lacombe – Ars-Okitsiparpi to the Blackfoot – in 1899.
A 'conquistador for the faith' and a tireless preacher of inter-tribal peace.

He may have been better known than anyone else in the Canadian North West, white or Metis, Blackfoot or Cree — the Oblate order's crucifix tucked into the belt of his tattered black cassock, his canoe flying a banner bearing a red cross. This was Father Albert Lacombe, who journeyed for more than 50 years in a "parish" covering 250,000 square miles. A trusted adviser, a writer of both Cree and Blackfoot texts, and a man with unflagging love for the natives, he was, as the Blackfoot called him, Ars-Okitsiparpi — The Man of the Good Heart.

Most of the Oblate priests came from France to preach in a new and strange world, but Albert Lacombe had been a Quebec farm boy thirsting for wild adventure. Born in St. Sulpice, just outside Montreal, he heard stories of his half-breed grandmother and his wandering great-uncle Joseph Lacombe who had worked for the North West Company. While studying theology in Montreal the young Albert met a missionary who told him of buffalo hunts, wars between the tribes, and the struggles of the first missions in the West.

Lacombe was ordained in 1849 and he yearned to be a missionary. He served in the Red River for two years, followed by six months in Montreal. But he wanted more. "I did not relish the life of a parish priest and I would rather return to the world if I could not be a missionary," he said. "I wanted to make all the sacrifices — or none at all." He got his wish in September 1852. He was sent to Fort Edmonton. There he gained the confidence of many of the natives because of his trace of Indian blood. A few months later he moved to nearby Lac Ste. Anne, where he ministered to Metis families and learned Cree. In the spring of 1855 the industrious Lacombe continued to expand his parish to include Lesser Slave Lake. Then, realizing his pioneering missions could be better supported with the help of others, he joined the Oblates of Mary Immaculate.

In 1861 Lacombe made the move that secured a prominent place for him in Alberta history. He selected a mission site overlooking the Sturgeon River about eight miles northwest of Edmonton. At this place, named after St. Albert, his patron saint, he established a settlement for the Metis. He directed construction of a grist mill and Alberta's first bridge, a 300-foot wooden span wide enough for an oxcart. He also helped Fr. Constantine Scollen open Alberta's first school at Fort Edmonton.

But St. Albert and Fort Edmonton soon became too quiet for Lacombe's questing temperament. Having worked in the woods, he now wanted to tackle the Prairie. Bishop and fellow Oblate Vital Grandin said of Lacombe: "Father Lacombe was a pioneer, a conquistador who prefers battle to inactivity." On New Year's Day 1865 he was given the assignment he'd always yearned for, "the mission of roaming the prairies in an attempt to evangelize among the ever-wandering Cree and Blackfeet."

His first self-assigned task was to found a colony for the Cree, St. Paul des Cris (St. Paul of the Crees) located at Brosseau, five miles north of present-day Two Hills. Then he learned Blackfoot and preached throughout central and southern Alberta. It was here that he was grazed in the forehead by a bullet and knocked unconscious during a Cree-Blackfoot battle when he tried to stop the fighting.

He witnessed many stirring conversions, none more thrilling than that of the Cree Head Chief Wikaskokiseyin (Sweetgrass). For many years the great warrior had rebuffed Lacombe's prodding. "Leave me alone!" he would say. "I will tell you if I need your white man's religion." One day, however, Sweetgrass brought in his son-in-law, who had blown off two fingers in an accidental musket discharge and had amputated the stumps with his knife; his hand was now infected with gangrene. Sweetgrass asked Lacombe to operate. The Oblate replied, "I am not a doctor, nor do I have the equipment." Sweetgrass haughtily rejoined, "If we were Christians you would do something. For us you do nothing."

Lacombe relented, made an incision, cleansed the wound and in three weeks the son-in-law recovered, much to the missionary's surprise and relief. When the Christian Indians next assembled for mass, Sweetgrass was there too. "My friends," he told them, "you know who I am. You have seen me presiding at our medicine feasts. Today in the presence of the Great Spirit, I turn away from all the beliefs of our fathers to follow those of the man of prayer. His religion is one of kindness, and I want to join. I have spoken." Sweetgrass later renounced his many battle honours as "what evil I once did."

After 15 years on the plains Lacombe was sent to Ontario as chaplain to the Canadian Pacific construction crews building the line between the Lakehead and Winnipeg. It was a task he didn't relish and it all but defeated him. Though many of the navvies were French Catholics, their drinking and brawling, their blasphemy and whoring left him pleading with God to return to his beloved Indians.

He doggedly stuck it out nonetheless, travelling the line in an open handcar despite recurrent pleurisy, celebrating mass daily, talking of God to the workmen, hearing confessions and watching the supposedly penitent go out and sin some more. His attempts to prohibit the bawdy dances staged by a madam at Rat Portage, now Kenora,[a] met only with scorn and jeers. So it went until the line was finished. Then, to his astonishment, the workmen took up a huge collection for him and sent him away with a new horse, buggy, harness, tent and camping outfit. Whether he had won their souls, he did not know. He had certainly won their affection.

Lacombe returned to establish a mission at Fort Macleod, finding that by then the Blackfoot decline had begun and the great hunter-warriors were reduced to penury, living on government handouts and dog meat. He moved quickly, starting an industrial school at Dunbow and serving as its first principal. It was here that he helped persuade Chief Crowfoot to stay out of the North West Rebellion, winning the gratitude of the CPR and a lifetime pass.[b]

By now he was 67 and his concern lay with the Metis. Their rebellion a failure, they were homeless. They were given no land reserve and were unable to even earn a living in the new white society. He secured land for an agricultural mission at St. Paul des Metis, 120 miles northeast of Edmonton, but their dislike of farming and their inexperience caused it to fail. In 1908 the area was opened for general settlement.

After founding the Midnapore Old Folks' Home in 1909, Lacombe retired at 82. He died on December 12, 1916, two months short of 90. The ancient foes, Cree and Blackfoot, shared him in death. His body is buried at St. Albert in the country of the Cree. His heart was removed and remained at Midnapore, in Blackfoot country. *R.B.*❦

Provincial Archives of Alberta, Ob-540

The Dunbow Industrial School in Calgary, founded by Lacombe and operated by the Grey Nuns, pictured here with students in 1888.

[a] The name "Kenora" is an acronym of KEewatin, NOrman and RAt Portage, respectively the territory to the north and two adjoining communities. It is not related to Canora, Saskatchewan, which is an acronym of CAnadian NOrthern RAilway.

[b] Lacombe frequently gave his railway pass to others, as he gave everything he owned to others. In CPR lore, three nuns handed a train conductor two tickets and a pass for their fare. "Which of you ladies is Father Lacombe?" inquired the grinning conductor.

Ripe for the Gospel of Methodism

For much of the 19th century the McDougall family shared the joys and hardships of the Cree and Assiniboine

Degraded and oppressed by the white man, thirsting for the fire water, full of all the uncleanness of heathenism, they are fast passing away. Nor are they ignorant of it. Many of them are now ripe for the gospel.

With that declaration, George McDougall headed west with his wife and five children in 1860 as the newly appointed superintendent of the Methodist western missions. He was 39 and had already spent 10 years among the Indians of central Ontario. Thus began the McDougall family mission to the Plains Indians, a two-generation endeavour that would anchor Methodism for many years as the dominant Protestant denomination in the future Alberta.

The McDougalls first spent two years at Norway House, on the Nelson River immediately north of Lake Winnipeg. But George wanted in particular to visit the North Saskatchewan River country where Methodism had already taken root. The Upper Canada-born Ojibwa missionary Henry Steinhauer was bringing many converts to the fold. At the same time, the Cree Chief Maskepetoon carried his syllabic gospel everywhere over the plains, and often consulted it during councils.

In 1862 McDougall travelled up the Saskatchewan River into the heart of the wild Indian territory. Accompanied by his 20-year-old son John, he visited the Methodist mission of Whitefish Lake, 90 miles northeast of Edmonton, manned by pastor Steinhauer. There he conducted a series of "camp meetings" that reveal his evangelizing style. The devout Christian Indians sat near the front, the curious pagan onlookers at the back. Steinhauer led prayers in Cree, the Christian Indians and the missionaries sang hymns. Then McDougall preached, with an interpreter's help; he was not yet fluent in Cree.

He told of the coming of Jesus, how true civilization originated with Christianity, and how missionaries came for the good of the people. He foretold the buffalo's extinction and the necessity to prepare for that day. He told of the ultimate settling of the country and assured the Indians the Queen would be fair. Finally, McDougall urged them to "have faith in the Great Spirit and in his son, Jesus." Promising that he would return to live among them, he concluded with

George McDougall shortly before his death in a blizzard in 1876. A hearty disdain for Catholicism.

"farewell all ye simple children of the plains. May the Holy Spirit accompany with converting and sanctifying power the living truths to which you have listened."

The following year McDougall kept his promise. With his family he established a mission on the North Saskatchewan, 70 miles downstream from Edmonton, and named it after the reigning queen, Victoria. (It is now Pakan, honouring a Christian Cree chief of the area.) Starting in tents and moving to a crude, one-room cabin, they cleared the land, built a school and a church, and ran a thriving Cree mission for seven years.

During that time John joined in his father's work. He reopened the Pigeon Lake Methodist outpost, 50 miles southwest of Edmonton. Then, after two years at Fort Edmonton, father and son moved south and forged a strong connection with the Assiniboine who wintered at Morley, west of the future Calgary. By now John, too, had found his way into the hearts of the Indians. One major reason was his Indian wife, Abigail, the daughter of Henry Steinhauer.

Abigail gave John added credibility, but she died of smallpox in 1871. John remarried the next year and in 1873 his new wife,

Elizabeth, arrived as the first white woman in the foothills. Throughout John's career she travelled with him by wagon, canoe and dog-sled, ultimately with six children in tow. In 1896 Elizabeth McDougall was president of the Southern Alberta Pioneer and Old Timers Association. She lived until 1941.

Though the new partnership of John and Elizabeth flourished, the father and son team came to an untimely end. In January 1876, the 55-year-old George became lost and died in a blizzard near Calgary, during a buffalo hunt. The elder McDougall, who had little theological training, wrote no books and left no printed sermons. He had emphasized a robust, living faith, tough as the plains he had come to love, and thus he died.

The Cree thought his death fitting, for they knew him as a warrior for the faith, and they told for years the story of how he took the Iron Stone. They had discovered back in the summer of 1866 that this much-venerated object, a 400-pound meteorite made almost entirely of iron so soft it could be cut with a knife, was missing from its hill on the Battle River, 100 miles south of Victoria Mission. The Indians believed the sacred stone had been placed there by the Ojibwa great spirit, Nanabozo. Not only could it protect Indians who left spirit offerings, but it grew in size as the years passed. Long ago, they said, a person could lift the stone but now it was impossible. Then the Iron Stone vanished.

Cree medicine men predicted that as a consequence the buffalo would soon disappear and a fierce war would ensue. Subsequent events, of course, proved them right. But its disappearance was no mystery to the Reverend George McDougall. Regarding the Iron Stone as a pagan idol, he had simply loaded it on a cart, hauled it to Victoria and shipped it to an Ontario Methodist college. It is now on display at the Royal Ontario Museum in Toronto.

The Catholic missionaries would not have done that, McDougall knew, but he regarded their veneration of saints symbolized in statues as close to idolatry anyway. He once admitted, "These priests are hard workers: summer and winter they follow the camps, suffering great privations." Nevertheless, "by them the sabbath is desecrated, polygamy [among Indians] tolerated, and the Bible ignored. Their churches are the toy shops where the poor heathen get their play things, such as idols, beads and charms."

John continued his father's work for a further 33 years. With his trader brother David he brought the first cattle to southern Alberta in 1873, and acted as an adviser to the Assiniboine who signed Treaty 7 in 1877. In contrast to his less lettered father, John wrote a five-volume memoir, two adventure books and several magazine articles. He also penned a Cree handbook, language lessons in Cree and English, and translated the first five books of the Bible from the Swampy Cree to Plains Cree dialect. He died in Calgary at the age of 74.

In his memoirs, John McDougall describes the wandering Indian ministry he shared with his father. "We accompanied them in sorrow and in joy, in fasting and in feasting, in peace and in war; we were in all things like them, without in any sense compromising principle or manliness. We were nomads or permanents, as our work needed. We hunted and trapped and fished, and engaged in all manner of athletics, foot races, horse races, anything for real fun and common brotherhood. Thus we found out men, and these in turn saw us and read us as a book, until they knew that on every page of our life was written friendship and the true desire to help them. More than this, they saw we believed in them, and at last they grew most heartily to believe in us." *R.B.*❦

Provincial Archives of Alberta, E. Brown Collection, B-9556

On an 1886 Ontario tour for non-combatant Indian leaders. (From left) John McDougall; Cree Chief Samson of Hobbema; Cree Chief Pakan; Rev. Robert B. Steinhauer (Henry's son); Assiniboine Chief Jonas Goodstoney.

Provincial Archives of Alberta, E. Brown Collection, B-847

Rev. John W. Tims, Anglican missionary to the Blackfoot and later, pictured here, the Sarcee. All denominations were frankly competitive.

A remarkable corps of men and women

Despite their denominational feuding, the Christian missionaries strove to help Indians adjust to the white invasion

The first missionaries into the future Alberta were Methodists and Catholics and they arrived more than 40 years ahead of the railway. Their purpose was to win the souls of Indians for the Christian faith. These evangelists, and those who followed them, approached their vocation with single-minded dedication. They had to contend with formidable obstacles: the Indians' pagan beliefs, the untamed land and (not least) each other.

Though Catholic priests travelling to Fort Vancouver stopped at Fort Edmonton in 1838, Alberta's first resident missionary was a Methodist, the Reverend Robert Rundle. He was sent west in 1840 by the Reverend James Evans, then chairman of the Methodists' western missions, who had created a syllabic Cree alphabet. Syllabics were symbols representing whole syllables, and it was said that some Indians could learn to start reading the Bible in their own language in less than a week.

Rundle was initially welcomed by the HBC authorities, but it was not long before he showed Fort Edmonton's chief factor John Rowand that the missionaries would change the way things were done. In one conflict, Rundle clashed with Rowand about how Sunday was observed at the fort. The Methodist preacher wanted prayer, not work, on the Sabbath. Rowand, a Catholic, was infuriated and for the rest of his career railed against what he saw as the meddling clergy of all denominations. Rowand's most bitter clash was with a Catholic, the famed Father Albert Lacombe, who publicly rebuked him for the pitiless manner in which he drove his men.

Rundle struggled to learn the phonetic subtleties of Cree and eventually mastered the language. He travelled widely in Cree

Glenbow Archives, NA-659-43

Methodists Robert and Mary Rundle in the 1860s. Popular with the Cree, but not the fur traders.

country, to Lesser Slave Lake Fort, Fort Assiniboine, Rocky Mountain House and Gull Lake. Rundle also made two trips to the Blackfoot, who were amazed at his presence and believed he'd stepped from a piece of paper that had fallen from the sky. After eight years in Alberta, suffering from ill health, Rundle went back to England. He never returned, but other Methodists soon followed.

One of these was an Ojibwa Indian. The Reverend Henry Bird Steinhauer (also Shahwahnegezhik or Southern Skies) arrived in Lac la Biche in 1855. Born in Upper Canada in 1818, Steinhauer was sponsored at the Methodist seminary by a Philadelphia banker named Steinhauer whose son had died. The Indian seminarian took his name. In 1858 he established the Whitefish Lake mission, about 90 miles northeast of Edmonton. In a wooded area away from Blackfoot war parties but close enough to the food of the plains, he sought to Christianize the Cree. A learned man, fluent in Greek and Latin, he was confident Christianity would make the Indians "crave and desire the blessing and comfort of civilized habits." Even more, it would redeem them from their "dark and chaotic minds." He worked at Whitefish until his death in 1884 and translated much of the Bible into Cree.

Catholics were far from idle meanwhile. The influence of Catholic missionaries in Alberta, particularly of the French Oblate order, can be seen on any road map, which reads like an honour roll of the Oblate priesthood: Lacombe, Leduc, Vegreville, Grouard, Legal. Father Jean-Baptiste Thibault arrived in Edmonton in 1842 and set up a mission at an Indian "medicine lake," christened Lac Ste. Anne in 1844. Missions soon sprang up at outposts such as Lesser Slave Lake (1845), Fort Chipewyan (1848), Lac la Biche (1853) and Dunvegan (1866).

The Lac la Biche mission was particularly important. Located along the divide of the Churchill and Athabasca river watersheds, it became the post linking the south with the missions of the Mackenzie. From this pivotal position the mission's warehouses supplied the Oblates' Arctic endeavours. Catholics also established themselves in the south, through such initiatives as Father Vital Fourmand's and Father Constantine Scollen's mission on the Elbow River near Bragg Creek, started in 1872.

Another important group of Catholic missionaries was the Montreal-based order known as the Grey Nuns. Working alongside the Oblates they staffed schools, orphanages and hospitals. The first three nuns came by Red River cart to Lac Ste. Anne in 1859, and moved to Fr. Lacombe's St. Albert mission in 1863. They were the first group of educated white women in the Alberta territory.

Other denominations came later. The Reverend William C. Bompas laboured in the Peace River area beginning in 1867 and was consecrated Anglican Bishop of Athabasca in 1874. Anglicans also evangelized the Bloods during the 1880s under the guidance of the Reverend Samuel Trivett. The Reverend Andrew Baird, a Presbyterian, reached Edmonton in 1881.

Glenbow Archives, NA-352-4

Southern Skies, an Ojibwa who took the missionary name Steinhauer. Fluent in Cree, Latin and Greek.

All these denominations were frankly competitive, each persuaded its own version of Christianity was closest to the truth. This conflict did not seem to deter the conversion of the Indians, however, who were impressed by the obvious depth of the missionaries' convictions. Therefore, when they adopted a denomination, they adopted whatever prejudices against rival denominations came with it. A Methodist Indian was just as persuaded the Catholics were wrong as a white Methodist was, and vice versa. *R.B.*❦

Chapter Three

Under Ottawa's heel—containment of the tribes and suppression of the culture

FEDERAL TREATY COMMISSIONS BOUGHT THE LAND AT THE CHEAPEST POSSIBLE PRICE, AND BUREAUCRATS SUBJECTED THE INDIANS TO ARBITRARY AND HUMILIATING DEPENDENCY ON GOVERNMENT

The last two decades of Plains Indian history in the 19th century represent a passage into dependence and subservience. Canadian textbooks tell the story positively — how the dominion government acquired the Hudson's Bay Company territory in 1870 and quickly secured a series of benevolent treaties with the western tribes to make way for the railways and agriculture. Colourful paintings depict the solemn ceremonies, the regally uniformed commissioner representing the Queen, the chiefs in full regalia, the tribesmen looking on in awestruck wonder. In these crucial agreements, it is explained, some 50,000 nomads exchanged their tribal lands for reserves where they would receive schools, seed, cattle and farm equipment. Thus, through Canadian sensitivity and foresight, the Indians of the Canadian North West were spared the gruesome warfare that engulfed their less fortunate brothers south of the border.

By the late 20th century, however, a very different interpretation of these proceedings had emerged. Historians like James R. Miller, John L. Tobias and John Leonard Taylor[1] have discovered that when Canada acquired the HBC lands, it had no coherent plan whatever for the western tribes. Thereafter treaties were signed on the basis of immediate expediencies. Negotiators took full advantage of Indian gullibility and ignorance, starvation was employed or even planned to extort compliance, talks were often held in the absence of senior chiefs, and the choicest land was deliberately withheld. Finally, when Ottawa had taken over, it attempted to implement a lately fashionable sociological theory about "yeoman agriculture" that effectively destroyed the very genuine effort some bands were making to engage in farming.

This pattern unfolded from the first treaties onward. Ottawa initiated Treaties 1, 2 and 3, covering generally the lands east of the future Manitoba-Saskatchewan border, only after the Indians there were demanding compensation for their losses, and menacing westbound settlers.

[1] **James R. Miller, professor of history at the University of Saskatchewan, is the author of *Skyscrapers Hide the Heavens* and editor of *Sweet Promises: A Reader on Indian-White Relations in Canada*. John L. Tobias is an instructor in history at Red Deer College. John Leonard Taylor wrote a doctoral thesis on the Indian treaties entitled *Approaches to Native History in Canada*.**

Glenbow Archives, NA-4035-151

Blood Indians and travois south of Ft. Macleod in the late 1890s. The Mounties brought peace, the bureaucrats brought misery.

Provincial Archives of Alberta, E. Brown Collection, B-975

Indians lined up at the whisky fort Whoop-up in 1881, after the liquor trade was shut down by the NWMP.

The first treaty on the territorial Prairies, Treaty 4 at Fort Qu'Appelle in 1874, was negotiated in the absence of the senior chief involved, Piapot of the Cree. When he returned after it had been signed without him, he angrily demanded better terms: more farm machinery, the inclusion of grain mills, blacksmith and carpentry shops, and more money. Only after he was told these changes were not being ruled out did he agree to touch the pen.[2] When they were not forthcoming, he repudiated the treaty.

Treaty 5, signed in 1875, covered northern Manitoba. It was seen as necessary to open steam navigation on Lake Winnipeg and use a tramway to bypass Grand Rapids where the Saskatchewan River enters the lake, among other things. In addition, Icelanders had already settled at Gimli on the lake's western shore.

Then in 1876 and 1877 came Treaties 6 and 7, ceding to the Canadian government the whole of Alberta and Saskatchewan south of the North Saskatchewan River. These involved the western Cree, Assiniboine and Blackfoot. In 1875 Methodist missionary George McDougall brought word to the 22 Cree and Assiniboine camps between Fort Edmonton and the forks of the Saskatchewan east of Prince Albert that Ottawa would treat with them next summer, first at Fort Carlton 50 miles upriver from Prince Albert, then at Fort Pitt near the future Alberta border. The Christian chiefs seemed pleased, but Big Bear rejected the clergyman's goodwill offerings from Ottawa with a famous rebuke: "We want none of the Queen's presents! When we set a fox trap, we scatter pieces of meat all around, but when the fox gets into the trap we knock him on the head. We want no baits! Let your chiefs come like men and talk to us."

McDougall reported that Big Bear was a troublemaker, an upstart "Soto." It was true he was a Saulteau (the French word for Ojibwa). But it was also true he then led the biggest Cree band on the plains. The determined and wizened little warrior made an unfavourable impression on many whites. One was the bluff Sam Steele of the NWMP, who early on decided that Big Bear's whole band was a "bad bunch." In fact, however, Big Bear was neither anti-white nor anti-agriculture; he

[2] The signatories' names on the Indian treaties were normally spelled out in Indian and in English translation, but the chiefs did not actually sign them. Even the "X" was written for them. All they did was literally touch the pen to signify consent. Crowfoot, for one, later stated that he had never actually touched it, to avoid what he seemed to consider spiritual vulnerability.

Provincial Archives of Alberta, E. Brown Collection, B-2426

Assiniboine Indians buying provisions from the HBC store at Pincher Creek around 1882. Signatories to Treaty 7, they stayed out of the 1885 Riel Rebellion in Saskatchewan. The Cree didn't.

was merely pro-buffalo as long as he could be, and pro-freedom.

For a century it has been disputed, legally and historically, whether the chiefs really understood what they were undertaking. Even at the time, a few whites considered it an unconscionably bad deal for the Indian. "Our laws declare him a minor," objected Dr. John Christian Schultz, then a Manitoba MP and later a senator,[3] "and yet we drive as hard a bargain with him as though he were a land-jobber..." He calculated with no great pride that the standard treaty allowance, one square mile per five Indians, worked out to a land surrender of 200 to one. This, he said, was in exchange for a $12 cash payment and $5 a year per Indian, a few farm supplies and implements that arrived either late or not at all. Moreover, policies would be established by dominion bureaucrats under orders from a capital thousands of miles away.

What historians do not dispute, however, is that the Indians preferred the Canadian approach, however frustrating, to the violence of the American one. Quite simply, they respected the new North-West Mounted Police, though the Cree were less fond of them than were the Blackfoot. Thinly dispersed from Fort Macleod to Shoal Lake in what is now western Manitoba, the 300 red-coats had sent the whisky traders packing within a few months and had established inter-tribal peace throughout the buffalo country.

Their most notable officer was Lieutenant-Colonel James Farquharson Macleod, who had brought them west and who spent his first few years gaining the trust of the Blackfoot, Bloods and Peigan. The Blackfoot tribes dubbed him Stamixotokan (Bull's Head). He had promised justice for Indian and white man alike, they said, and that was what he dealt. His men, with a few exceptions, were admired for cool-headed and even-handed resolve when staring down and arresting truculent warriors, returning stolen horses to their rightful owners, and delivering the Indians from troublesome whites — and this in a wild, lonely country in which they had recently arrived as helpless greenhorns. Without the Mounties' good record, neither the Cree nor the Blackfoot alliances would have settled as passively as they did.

Apart from the Mounties, however, the Indians found Ottawa unresponsive, ignorant, callous and brutal. Both the Cree and Blackfoot, through their missionaries and fur trade friends, had been

[3] Schultz, a physician, fur trader, publisher and politician, was a complex character. He first achieved prominence in the 1869 Red River Rebellion in Manitoba as the implacable foe of Louis Riel and ultra-Protestant leader of the "Canada First" Party. Later as an MP, however, he appears to have acquired deep sympathy for the Indians and grave doubts as to the morality of the country he had championed. Alarmed at the loss of the buffalo, he fought for and won conservation policies that came too late to stem their decline. He later became lieutenant-governor of Manitoba and died in Mexico in 1896 at the age of 56.

Provincial Archives of Alberta, A-5412

The supplanters and the supplanted. Unidentified whites and Indians at the Lethbridge Land Office in about 1885.

pressing the Macdonald government for treaties since 1871. It took Ottawa three years to send the police and two more to send the first western treaty commission.

In the meantime, white homesteads were spreading westward up the Assiniboine and Qu'Appelle valleys into Piapot's country, surveyors were running the international boundary through the Assiniboine and Blackfoot territories, and telegraph crews were stringing a line right through the heart of the western Cree lands to Hay Lakes near Edmonton, in preparation for the railway which, all the whites assured them, would soon follow. As the western tribesmen watched their bison herds dwindle and their people become hungrier, they demanded with increasing urgency that someone negotiate with them, because it was, after all, still their land.

Treaty Commissioner Alexander Morris seems to have avoided a confrontation by inviting only the more pliable chiefs to Treaty 6 negotiations at Carlton and Pitt in 1876. By the time Big Bear arrived at Fort Pitt from hunting, the bargaining (what little there was) was over. Sweetgrass and the other Cree chiefs had already signed. Big Bear angrily refused, as did Little Pine, and together with Piapot they went south to hunt around the Cypress Hills, taking with them over half the Treaty 6 Cree and many of those from Treaty 4, which had been signed two years before.

The Cypress Hills, south of the future Medicine Hat, offered three advantages. Some buffalo remained there. The Cree could dart south of the United States border, what they called the Medicine Line, and the NWMP couldn't follow them, then dart back into Canada where the U.S. Cavalry couldn't follow them. Finally, at Fort Walsh in the Cypress country, in what is now southwestern Saskatchewan, the NWMP would feed them if they were starving and pay treaty money to those that were covered. Hence Fort Walsh and the surrounding Cypress Hills became a gathering ground for thousands of recalcitrant, independent-minded Indians from both sides of the border and from all over the Canadian West.

The Blackfoot tribes, along with the Methodist Assiniboine of Morley and what little remnant smallpox had left of the Sarcee, signed Treaty 7 in September the following year. Due mainly to the stabilizing police influence of the past three years, Red Crow and Crowfoot kept control of the lesser band chieftains and war chiefs, and everyone signed. As with the Cree, however, the sentiment of the younger men was to drive the whites out, as the Sioux and Cheyenne were attempting to do to the south.

Those tribes had wiped out General "Long Hair" Custer's 7th Cavalry in southern Montana the previous summer. But the older Blackfoot knew that the Sioux victory was illusory, as did the Sioux themselves. Sitting Bull's Teton Sioux, followed by 900 lodges of Medicine Bear's Yankton Sioux, had fled to the Cypress Hills the previous winter, where they were now competing for buffalo with the Cree, under the watchful eye of the small Mountie patrol at Fort Walsh. Chief Joseph and a large band of Nez Perce fugitives from northeastern Oregon were meanwhile trying to fight their way into the same vicinity through three U.S. Cavalry columns; a few actually made it. The whole northwestern United States was in an uproar, and the Blackfoot chiefs knew which side was going to win.

The Cypress Hills Cree held out for six long years, while small white farming settlements sprang up all around the northern periphery of the buffalo country from Red Deer to Prince Albert. After

Collection of Glenbow Museum, NA-40-1

A. Bruce Stapleton's painting of the Treaty 7 negotiations of 1877. Col. James F. Macleod and Lieut.-Gov. David Laird seated; Crowfoot standing. Without Macleod, known to the Blackfoot as Stamixotokan, the confederacy probably would have refused.

Provincial Archives of Alberta, Pollard Collection, P-135

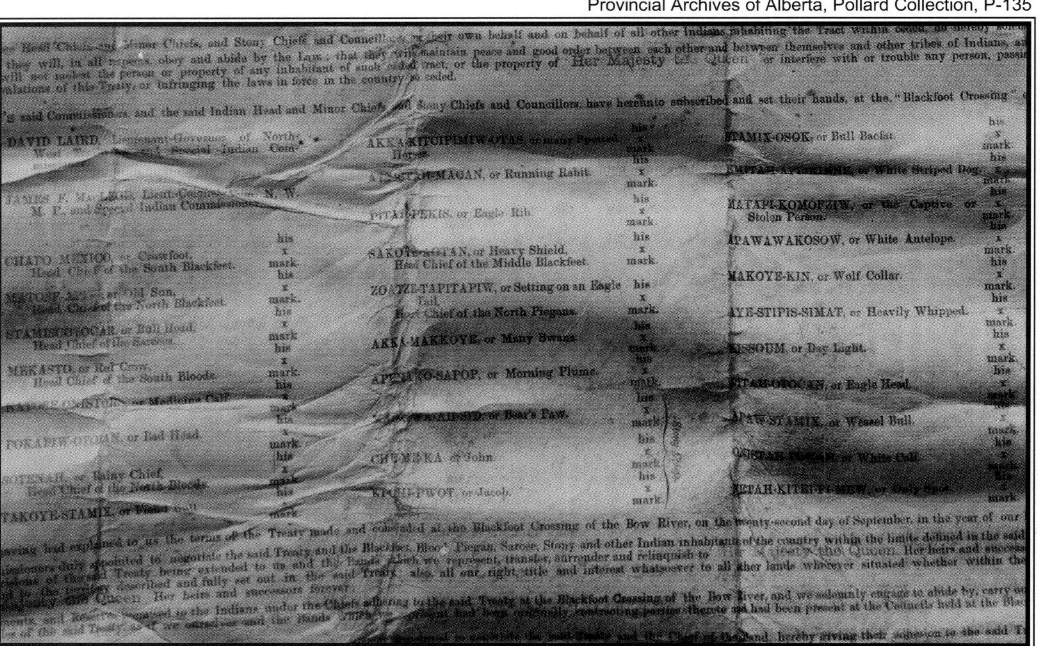

Head Chiefs and Minor Chiefs, and Stony Chiefs and Councillors, on their own behalf and on behalf of all other Indians inhabiting the Tract within ceded, do hereby ... they will, in all respects, obey and abide by the Law; that they will maintain peace and good order between each other and between themselves and other tribes of Indians, ... will not molest the person or property of any inhabitant of such ceded tract, or the property of Her Majesty the Queen or interfere with or trouble any person, passing ... stipulations of this Treaty, or infringing the laws in force in the country so ceded.

...'s said Commissioners, and the said Indian Head and Minor Chiefs and Stony Chiefs and Councillors, have hereunto subscribed and set their hands, at the "Blackfoot Crossing" ...

DAVID LAIRD, Lieutenant-Governor of North-West T... and Special Indian Commissioner.

JAMES F. MACLEOD, Lieut.-Colonel, ... N. W. M. P., and Special Indian Commissioner.

CHAPO-MEXICO, or Crowfoot, Head Chief of the South Blackfeet. his x mark.

MATOSE-APIW, or Old Sun, Head Chief of the North Blackfeet. his x mark.

STAMISCOTOCAR, or Bull Head, Head Chief of the Sarcees. his x mark.

MEKASTO, or Red Crow, Head Chief of the South Bloods. his x mark.

...-OMISTOR, or Medicine Calf. his x mark.

POKAPIW-OTOIAN, or Bad Head. his x mark.

SOTENAH, or Rainy Chief, Head Chief of the North Bloods. his x mark.

TAKOYE-STAMIX, or Fiend Bull. his x mark.

AKKA-KITCIPIMIW-OTAS, or Many Spotted Horses. his x mark.

...-MAGAN, or Running Rabit. his x mark.

PITAH-PEKIS, or Eagle Rib. his x mark.

SAKOYE-AOTAN, or Heavy Shield, Head Chief of the Middle Blackfeet. his x mark.

ZOATZE-TAPITAPIW, or Setting on an Eagle Tail, Head Chief of the North Piegans. his x mark.

AKKA-MAKKOYE, or Many Swans. his x mark.

APENAKO-SAPOP, or Morning Plume. his x mark.

...-AH-SID, or Bear's Paw. his x mark.

CHEMEKA, or John. his x mark.

KI...-PWOT, or Jacob. his x mark.

STAMIX-OSOK, or Bull Backfat. his x mark.

...-AYISKONNE, or White Striped Dog. his x mark.

MATAPI-KOMOFZIW, or the Captive or Stolen Person. his x mark.

APAWAWAKOSOW, or White Antelope. his x mark.

MAKOYE-KIN, or Wolf Collar. his x mark.

AYE-STIPIS-SIMAT, or Heavily Whipped. his x mark.

KISSOUM, or Day Light. his x mark.

PITAH-OTOCAN, or Eagle Head. his x mark.

APAW-STAMIX, or Weasel Bull. his x mark.

ONISTAH-..., or White Calf. his x mark.

PITAH-KITEPI-MEW, or Only Spot. his x mark.

... having had explained to us the terms of the Treaty made and concluded at the Blackfoot Crossing of the Bow River, on the twenty-second day of September, in the year of our ... Commissioners duly appointed to negotiate the said Treaty and the Blackfeet, Blood, Piegan, Sarcee, Stony and other Indian inhabitants of the country within the limits defined in the said ... provisions of the said Treaty being extended to us and the Bands which we represent, transfer, surrender and relinquish to Her Majesty the Queen, Her heirs and successors ... to the territory described and fully set out in the said Treaty; also, all our right, title and interest whatsoever to all other lands wheresoever situated whether within the ... Majesty the Queen, Her heirs and successors forever ... the said Treaty at the Blackfoot Crossing of the Bow River, and we solemnly engage to abide by, carry out ... ments and Reserves ... to the Indians under the Chiefs adhering to the said ... had been originally contracting parties thereto and had been present at the Councils held at the Bla... ... of the said Treaty ... and the Band hereby giving their adhesion to the said T...

Treaty 7 signatures. In reality, the Indian signatories made no mark; they merely 'touched the pen' to indicate consent.

the last few Canadian buffalo were shot off in 1879, Big Bear, Little Pine and many Cree went south into the Missouri River country to hunt the last American herds. The Montana Indian territory was a wild and violent place in the 1870s, but the Cree held their own. Big Bear kept abreast of events back home by having copies of the *Saskatchewan Herald*[4] read to him. It was being published in the new white settlement at Battleford. In this way he could see that (a) the white newcomers, unlike the missionaries, police and fur traders of old, held the Indians in the most scathing

[4] Big Bear, struggling to sustain his people in the Missouri River country and dreaded as a monster by many settlers, used his subscription to the *Saskatchewan Herald* to great effect, and once sent a letter to the editor in his own defence, saying he was still waiting to see if the government would keep its promises. He had discovered, that is, the news media, something his descendants a century later would learn to make full use of.

contempt, and (b) they were in terror of an uprising.

When the Cree returned starving and destitute to Fort Walsh in 1883, they soon had the grim consolation of knowing that their compatriots who had obediently taken to the reserves were little better off. They too were starving and were about to starve far more. This was due to the disappearance from Indian life of one species and the appearance of another. The buffalo was gone. What emerged in its place was a phenomenon with which the Indians (and whites) of the next century would become altogether familiar: the Ottawa mandarin.

The first instance of the new species was Lawrence Vankoughnet, member of a United Empire Loyalist family prominent in Tory circles. In 1878, with the return to power of the government of Sir John A. Macdonald, he was made deputy superintendent-general of Indian Affairs. By a provision of Treaty 6 the government had agreed to support the Indians in the event of "pestilence" or "famine." At first it had done so frugally, but adequately enough to keep most Indians alive. Government beef was dispatched west from St. Paul, or purchased locally from the ranchers who were now appearing near the Mountie stations of Fort Macleod and Fort Calgary. But by 1883 the Canadian economy had slackened and Macdonald called for cutbacks in all dominion departments. What, he wondered, ought to be done with the Indian support program?

Vankoughnet made a brief tour of the West and decided, against the advice of the fur traders, the NWMP and virtually every dominion Indian agent in the field, that substantial cuts in the ration could be made. "Careful consideration after personally visiting localities convinced me that there has been much needless expenditure," he wrote to Macdonald. Departmental administration must be centralized in Ottawa, he said. The discretionary powers of the local agents must be reduced. The result on the reserves and at the forts, around which the starving Indians still congregated and begged, was appalling. The new rule became: "Feed one day, starve the next."

Glenbow Archives, NA-4452-1

The Eagle, a Blackfoot headman who consented to Treaty 7. 'Our laws declare him a minor,' protested MP Schultz, 'and yet we drive as hard a bargain as though he were a land-jobber...'

From Carlton came the agent's report that the Assiniboine were now in dire danger. The agent in the Touchwood Hills to the south wrote: "I fear that many of these people will not see spring." The agent at Edmonton urged desperately that the cut not be instituted. The agent among the Blackfoot resigned. "I cannot undertake to do this work," he wrote. At Battleford, where an industrial school had been established, the ration was cut from a pound and a half of beef a day to a quarter of a pound. At Qu'Appelle, the dominion medical officer reported that the death rate, already very high, was now being "accelerated."

From their posts all over the West, NWMP officers advised against the policy. Superintendent L.N.F. Crozier wrote: "It would seem as if there was a wish to see upon how little a man can work and exist." He warned that if the option of restoring the ration was not taken, "there is only one other and that is to fight them." At Battleford, the *Saskatchewan Herald* asked the simplest of questions: "Does it not seem the most sensible to suppose that the agents who are in daily contact with the Indians should be better acquainted with their requirements?" No, in Mr. Vankoughnet's office at Ottawa, it did not seem the most sensible.

Big Bear realized all this when he returned to the Cypress Hills. He knew also that the local Indian agents feared his Cree and were determined to distribute them to as many small, scattered reserves as possible, to cut off communications between them, and to break their old tribal attitudes. Big Bear, Little Pine, Piapot and (increasingly) the young Battle River Chief Poundmaker were of an opposite determination on all points. When they failed to wrest from Ottawa a large contiguous reserve at the Cypress Hills and were deliberately starved into dispersing north and east, they tried to establish a critical mass near Fort Qu'Appelle and in the Battle River valley.

By 1882, a pitiful plight

GIVE US BACK THE LAND AND THE BUFFALO, CRIED THE DESTITUTE CHIEFS, AND WE WON'T ASK FOR FOOD

Destitution had always been a periodic hazard of Plains Indian life, but with the buffalo herds gone it became an inevitability.

In the summer of 1882, five to six years after most prairie tribes had made treaties with the Canadian government and been promised farming tools and sustenance, there were still some 2,000 free-roaming Indians, mostly Plains Cree, camped near Fort Walsh, south of modern Medicine Hat — which was to appear on the map the following year.

Some had been killing the last surviving Canadian buffalo in ones and twos east of the Cypress Hills. Others had been hunting the last big herds on the continent in Montana's Yellowstone country. This was now a chaos of whisky traders, angry ranchers, U.S. cavalrymen, half-breed hunters talking about another Canadian uprising, and enemy tribes from both sides of the border clinging to the last vestige of their ancient freedom.

In mid-October NWMP doctor Augustus Jukes conducted a medical tour of the Indians camped around Fort Walsh. "They are literally in a starving condition," he wrote, "and destitute of the commonest necessities of life. The disappearance of the buffalo has left them not only without food, but also without robes, moccasins and adequate tents or 'teppees' to shield them from the inclemency of the impending winter. Few of their lodges are of buffalo hide, the majority being of cotton only, and many of these in the most rotten and dilapidated condition...Their clothing for the most part was miserable and scanty in the extreme.

"I saw little children at this inclement season, snow having fallen, who had scarcely rags to cover them. Of food they possessed little or none; some were represented to me as absolutely starving and their appearance confirmed the report...It would indeed be difficult to exaggerate their extreme wretchedness and need, or the urgent necessity which exists from some prompt and sufficient provision being made for them by the government."

The Fort Walsh Cree knew that life on their reserves, 200 miles to the north, was little better, but had no choice except to retreat there, many of them on foot. As one Cree, Foremost Man, had put it to a *Toronto Mail* correspondent when rebellion broke loose three years later, and many Crees joined, "We are hungry. The Great Mother [Queen Victoria] does not know it. Her agents tell her we are happy, but we are not. Where are the buffalo? Where are our horses? These are gone and we must soon follow them. Your people have our lands. These prairies were ours once, and the buffalo were given us by the Great Spirit...But they are all gone.

"Look at me; look at those round me, and say we look happy. Are these blankets warm enough for the winter; are they like the buffalo robes we used to have? Let them send the buffalo back, and take their own people to the reserve where they came from. Give us the prairies again, and we won't ask for food. But it is too late. It is too late. It is too late." *L.B.* ❦

'The disappearance of the buffalo has left them without the commonest necessities – few of their lodges are of buffalo hide, only cotton, and these in the most rotten and dilapidated condition...'

Provincial Archives of Alberta, E. Brown Collection, B-772

Meanwhile the NWMP closed Fort Walsh to discourage a return to the Cypress Hills.

The Qu'Appelle-Battle River plan didn't work. By 1884 Big Bear's own band had suffered serious fragmentation and numbered only 500. At last the old man begrudgingly touched the pen. He was consigned temporarily to a small agency at Frog Lake in present-day Alberta, some 80 miles northwest of the cluster of Plains Cree reserves around Battleford. With him went the angriest of the Plains Cree warrior faction under the War Chiefs Wandering Spirit and Little Poplar, over whom Big Bear had by now lost all influence.

Glenbow Archives, NA-3205-11

Big Bear, last head chief of the free Plains Cree, photographed in prison in 1885. 'We want no baits. Let your chiefs come and talk to us like men.'

The following year, the Cree took part, ineffectually, in the North West Rebellion, whose events are detailed in another chapter. There is little evidence of Cree collusion with Riel's Metis, however, until the latter shot and killed 12 policemen and volunteers near Duck Lake in central Saskatchewan on March 22, 1885. The Cree role was limited, brief, aimless and disastrous, as the chiefs had known it would be. None knew it better than Big Bear, whose band ended up in the middle of it after Wandering Spirit's warriors streaked their faces with crimson and black, got drunk and murdered nine Frog Lake whites. When it was over three months later, Big Bear surrendered at Fort Carlton while his warriors and their families rode hell-bent for Montana. He had done all he could to prevent fighting; he knew that the consequences for his people would be harsh.

As for himself, Big Bear was tired and heartsick. Wandering Spirit, five other Cree and two Assiniboine were convicted of murder and hanged, singing their death songs at Battleford on November 27, eight months and five days after the rebellion broke out. Big Bear was found guilty by a Regina jury of treason-felony[5] and sentenced by Judge Hugh Richardson to three years in Manitoba's Stony Mountain Penitentiary, accompanied by 24 Indians and 18 half-breeds. Like most imprisoned Indians of the open plains, Big Bear, convict No. 103, soon became ill. He was released after 14 months, a broken man at 61, abandoned by his fugitive sons and reviled as a loser by whites and Indians alike. He was put on a train to Regina, and then spent a fortnight hitching a ride north on a freight wagon in the middle of winter. He died shortly afterwards, alone in a tiny cabin on the Little Pine reserve during a blinding January blizzard in 1887.

The failure of the rebellion settled the reserve question. The Indian Department redoubled its efforts to break the Indians of their old migratory and tribal attitudes and rapidly succeeded. All Indians retreated to the reserves, where a strange bureaucratic control was now settled upon them. In this, the department enjoyed the concerted support of the missionaries and, in some respects, a good many forward-looking chiefs. In the year of the rebellion, for instance, came the "pass law," requiring an Indian to receive his agent's permission in writing to travel off his reserve.

This was aimed at suppressing inter-band politicking and pan-tribal participation in prohibited religious festivals such as the Blackfoot Sun Dance and the Cree Thirst Dance. However draconian, it was not long enforced, the NWMP quietly concluding it to be unnecessary, unwise, unfair, a waste of their time, and probably unconstitutional. As for banning pagan festivities, the Blackfoot Christians were still complaining as late as 1900 that these were being celebrated as freely as ever.

[5] Although all Indian languages were capable of soaring oratory, the august terminology of British law was virtually untranslatable. The treason-felony charge against Big Bear, Poundmaker and other rebel associates was worded "to raise, make and levy insurrection...against the peace of our Lady the Queen, her Crown and dignity." This was expressed to Cree Chief One Arrow as "knocking off the Queen's bonnet and stabbing her in the behind with a sword," prompting the accused to ask the interpreter if he were drunk.

Some agents tried to enforce the anti-paganism sanction, but the Indians had half a dozen ways around it, and again the police seldom co-operated. Most seem to have agreed with Methodist missionary John McDougall: "I altogether fail to see why in these days of our much boasted religious liberty anyone should interfere with a few Indians in the exercise of their faith."

However, in one area, and an important one, the Indians discovered themselves victims of a departmental tyranny whose effect was to destroy their early, and sometimes successful, attempts to adopt the white man's way and make a living as farmers. Behind this calamity lurked yet another Ottawa mandarin. Indians across the Prairies had been making slow but discernible progress in agriculture since the '70s. Many bands, especially in what is now southern Saskatchewan, had been hampered by chronic drought in the '80s. Unlike the Qu'Appelle homesteaders, treaty Indians could not simply move on to a more promising location because the Indian Act denied them homestead rights. Nonetheless, the most innovative among them laboured on, despite the unfamiliarity of their farm instructors with prairie conditions, despite Ottawa's tendency to send them seed too late in the year for use, and despite the ungovernable bronco character of their government-supplied draft animals. Like their new white neighbours, they were learning to be wheat farmers. By 1888 several bands had co-operatively purchased modern equipment such as hay mowers and grain binders.

Hayter Reed, the new Indian commissioner, heartily approved of all this until he became enraptured by the latest sociological theory on the resettlement of primitive peoples overtaken by advanced technological societies. The best method, said the theorists, was to reinstitute "peasant agriculture." Primitives should not farm commercially. Instead they should farm the hard way, with home-made hand tools on tiny vegetable plots. Had not the whites who invented the new machinery acclimatized themselves to the self-discipline of manual toil over many centuries? Given the natural propensity of primitive peoples to take the path of least resistance, and to seek all solutions tribally rather than individually, it would be a mistake to introduce them to jointly owned labour-saving devices all at once. The proper course would be to require all prairie Indians to farm individual family plots and strive for self-sufficiency. Then when the day came, as Reed believed it must, that the Indian "is cast upon his own resources," he would have sufficient individualistic fibre to hold his own.

This was considered the acme in advanced sociological science; Reed embraced it enthusiastically. The Indian, he concluded, must abandon his newly acquired technology, and reincarnate the "yeoman farmer." Unlike Vankoughnet, Reed had actually lived in the West. A soldier and a lawyer, he had moved to the Red River after 1871, and 10 years later become Indian agent at Battleford. His zealous attention to detail, his political adroitness and his respect for authority soon won the attention of Vankoughnet, who made him assistant Indian commissioner in 1884 just in time to execute the rationing cutback. Four years later he became commissioner.

In this role, he was remarkably positioned to put these social speculations to the test. The new policy was announced in 1889. The bewildered Indians saw immediately that this was the precise reverse of what the government had been telling them all along. Agents across the West ordered all mechanical equipment out of the field, and instructed that hay and grain henceforth be cut with scythes. Sheaves were now to be bound with straw, not with purchased twine. Men would devote their idle hours to carving their own handles and pitchforks from locally cut wood, and women must weave baskets, mats and straw hats. People too old or sick to farm their own plots would have to ask their neighbours to help. Wheat acreage too large to be cut by hand must be left to rot, and henceforth root crops were to be preferred. No band could negotiate credit. No band could purchase anything jointly. Any attempt to acquire prohibited machinery would be blocked. No band would be allowed to sell farm produce off the reserve in local markets. Any instructors heard to criticize the policy would be fired. Reed himself scrutinized all departmental provisions for the reserves, to detect prohibited items.

In her book *Lost Harvests*, historian Sarah Carter weighs the documented psychological devastation this had on Reed's brown-skinned "yeomanry," as reported by the thunderstruck agents. One Indian, very old and frail, had to abandon half of his thick 15-acre wheat crop because he and his aging wife couldn't possibly harvest it all by hand. Another man, the most progressive farmer at the Moose Mountain agency, quit in disgust and announced that he would never plough another acre. He went to work for wages on a white threshing gang. Another good farmer left 15 acres standing and moved to the United States. From Edmonton came another sharp complaint, that the short prairie season left no time for taking off both wheat and hay using such backward methods. The home-made handles, forks and grain cradles broke constantly. Prairie straw was too dry and brittle to bind grain, and the straw too short to scythe without waste.

All these complaints elicited a set series of answers from Reed. Grow less wheat, more potatoes. Peasant agriculture needs only a few animals and little hay. Whites farmed with wooden forks for millennia. Credit would prove to be the ruin of western agriculture. Manual labour was in abundant supply on reserves; one binder would destroy the initiative of all those Indians who "sit by and smoke their pipes while work is being done for them with no exertion on their part." Unquestionably, said Hayter Reed, "any loss suffered in the course of enforcing the policy will prove in the long run true economy."

Sarah Carter believes Reed's real motive was far less altruistic. With the reduction of a family's required land base by three-quarters, a great many arable Indian acres would soon be deemed surplus to band requirements. In the meantime, it kept Indian competition out of the West's inadequate local markets, a source of friction in all areas lacking railway access to the East.

Two Cree bands petitioned parliament for relief in 1893 but were largely ignored. By 1896 Indians generally were refusing to farm, and agents were beginning openly to defy the policy, the lunacy of which was becoming notorious. The following year, new Liberal Minister of the Interior Clifford Sifton threw Hayter Reed himself upon his own resources by firing him, a process that took more than six months because permanent civil servants were supposed to be protected against political "interference." With his departure, the policy ended as abruptly as it had begun. But by then the Indians were sorely discouraged, and their white neighbours were technologically far ahead of them.

Far to the north in the country of the Beaver and Chipewyan Indians, meanwhile, all these tumultuous prairie events had little effect. True, they had heard of the rebellion; some had even taken part in it by robbing the local HBC store. In 1899 their chiefs touched the pen to Treaty 8. But in the main, life remained much as it had since that day, more than a hundred years before, when a white trader descended the Clearwater River and introduced the nations of the Athabasca to the fur trade. That, however, belongs to the next chapter in the history of Alberta. ❦

Two of Reed's 'peasant' Blackfoot, Frank Tried to Fly and George Left Hand, sowing by hand in the 1880s. This was the result of an anti-machinery edict from Ottawa, the lunacy of which had become notorious by 1896.

Boorne & May, photographers, Glenbow Archives, NA-127-1

Frederick Remington's speculative portrayal of the French explorers Radisson and Groseilliers, whose illegal forays beyond the Great Lakes led to the founding of the Hudson's Bay Company and European commerce in the West.
Buffalo Bill Historical Center

Section Three

The Fur Traders

Chapters by Terry Johnson

Sidebars by Terry Johnson, Ted Byfield and Rick Bell

Chapter One

The fight for fur creates the first north-south vs. east-west struggle

Skilful diplomacy sustained the West as an HBC preserve until a twice-accused murderer discovered a bonanza in fur in the North West and 'the pedlars' began a take-over

The man who descended the Clearwater River and began the first white settlement in what is now Alberta was Peter Pond, a cocky, irascible New Englander with a knack for geography, a rapacious avarice and a fierce temper. He was one of the scores of Yankees and Scots who invaded Montreal after the fall of New France in 1760 and assumed control of the old French fur trade. His key accomplishment was the discovery of a 13-mile trail in northwestern Saskatchewan, less than 10 miles from the modern Alberta border, known to the Indians and to history as Methy Portage although sometimes called by its more poetic French name, Portage La Loche.

It remained in the late 20th century much as it was in the late 18th when Pond and his men began using it: a 10-foot-wide path bordered with blueberries crossing through an aspen and spruce forest, with a little lake, about a half-mile wide, in the middle of it. The ruts still discernible in it, according to the Indians, were made by the wheels of the Red River carts that for more than 150 years regularly traversed it.

Going west, the portage begins in a swampy patch of grass at the northwest end of Lac La

Glenbow Archives, NA-789-51

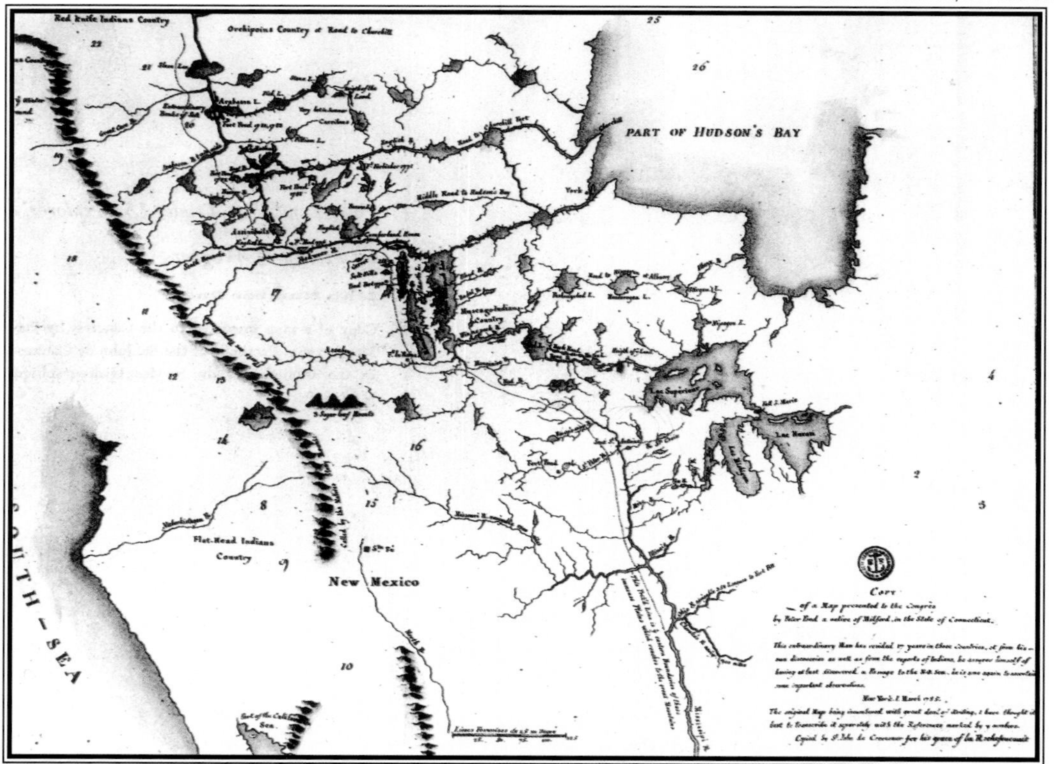

A map drawn by Peter Pond and presented to the American congress in 1785. His Methy Portage discovery near the present Alberta border ignited a four-decade war between Canadians from Montreal and the HBC.

Loche, one of the headwaters of the east-flowing Churchill River. About 11 miles into this flat, sandy trail, beyond the little lake, the traveller suddenly finds himself at the edge of a 650-foot precipice. A broad valley spreads before him to the horizon. Across the valley, a blue ribbon on a green carpet, the Clearwater River flows towards the nearby Alberta boundary. The portage trail precariously descends the escarpment to a riverside plain. A few miles downstream, the Clearwater plunges through the cauldron of Whitemud Falls, a picturesque spectacle that few Albertans have ever seen.

Pond had two interests in this river, neither of them aesthetic. For one, it flowed west — to the Pacific, he was sure. So he believed he had found the holy grail of the fur trade, the "Northwest Passage." In fact, of course, he had done no such thing. The Clearwater flows into the Athabasca whose waters go north, eventually reaching the Arctic Ocean. And second, but here he was right, he had found the source of those superb black beaver pelts that sometimes appeared on the fur markets and commanded staggering prices in London.

So Pond hastened over Methy Portage, descended the Clearwater and Athabasca, and by spring had more prime fur than he could carry out. From the local Indians he also learned how to make pemmican, the dried buffalo meat that would become the principal food of the Montreal-based traders and voyageurs. He would return each year, in 1788 building Fort Chipewyan where the Athabasca feeds the lake bearing the same name. This post, at the centre of the last untapped source of beaver east of the Rockies, was the first European settlement in what would become Alberta. The commercial rivalry that led to its establishment would ultimately pull the entire North West — and the future Alberta — into Canada.

Curiously, the region's transformation into an English-speaking society can be traced to the illegal activities of two Frenchmen a century earlier. In 1659 the *coureurs de bois* Pierre Esprit Radisson and Médard Chouart, Sieur des Groseilliers, defied the laws of New France by wintering with a party of Indians in the forests beyond Lake Superior.[1] There they discovered vast lands rich in pelts, but also that the best route to them lay not through the St. Lawrence but through Hudson Bay.

The French responded by arresting the two men for illegal trading, and by confiscating their

[1] New France, struggling hard to stimulate permanent settlement, had severely restricted travel into the Indian country that lured away its young men with promises of wealth, adventure and an unlimited supply of Indian women. The French term for the fur trade, *la traite des fourrures*, is properly translated "the fur traffic."

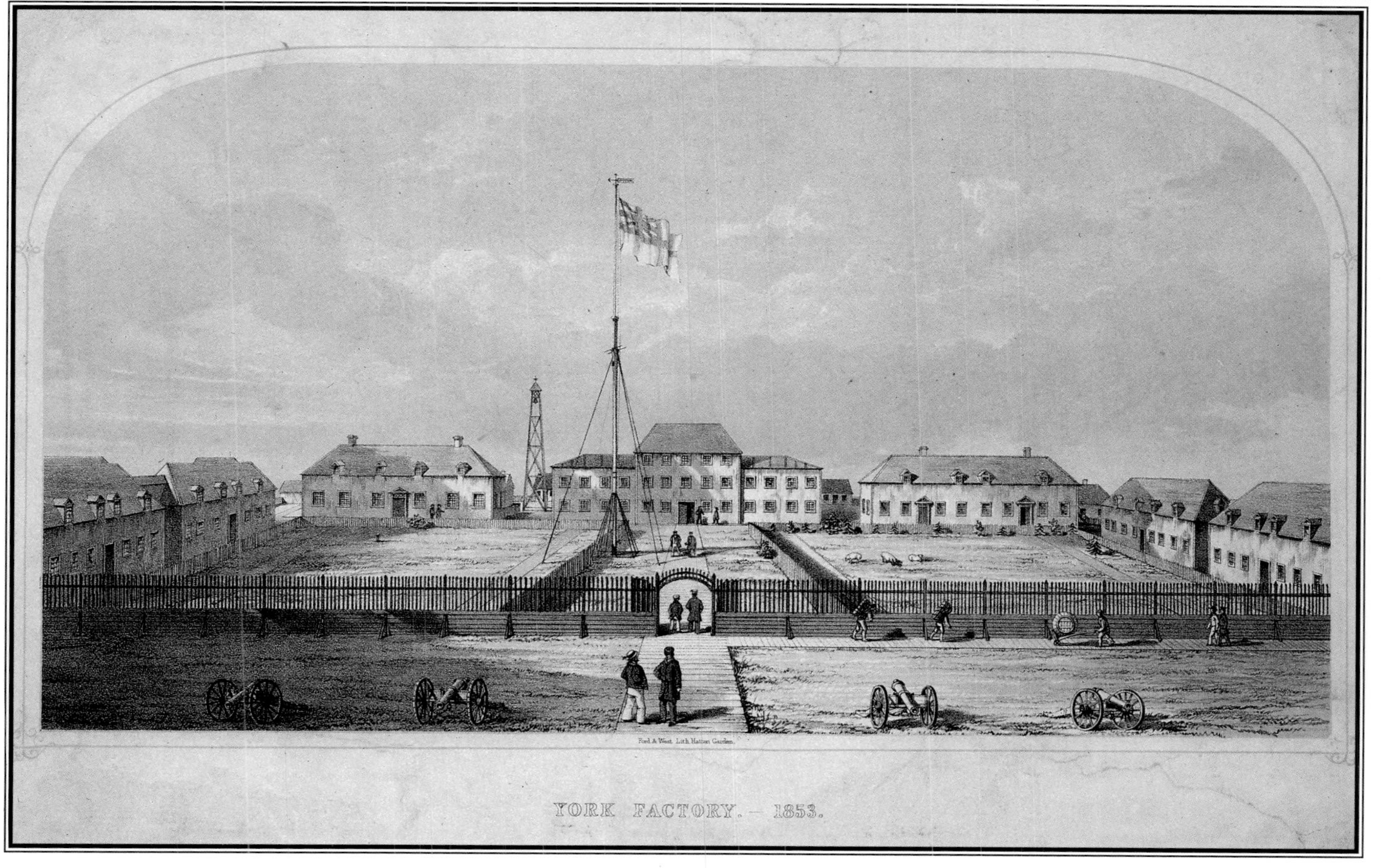

York Factory on the shore of Hudson Bay, as it appeared in 1853. It served as a saltwater gateway to the heart of the fur country, confounding the HBC's competitors from Montreal until the 1730s.

Hudson's Bay Company Archives, Provincial Archives of Manitoba

trading profits in fines and duties. So they escaped, made their way to England (where they became known by a fairly literal but unflattering translation of their names, Radishes and Gooseberries), and won the support of a loose syndicate of aristocratic investors united around Prince Rupert of the Rhine, cousin of Charles II. On May 2, 1670, the group founded the Governor and Company of Adventurers of England Trading into Hudson's Bay. For the next 300 years and more, it would be known to the world as the Hudson's Bay Company.

The HBC's royal charter made the company "true lords and proprietors" of the entire vast watershed of Hudson Bay. Named Rupert's Land, this huge, almost feudal freehold encompassed nearly 40% of modern Canada. In return, the newly formed company was required to provide two elk and two beaver to the king or his successors whenever they should enter the territory, a bizarre bounty paid only four times in the HBC's history.[2]

Within 15 years the HBC's string of posts along the shores of Hudson and James bays were doing a lucrative business, paying out dividends as high as 50% on the invested capital. The company quickly developed a corporate culture not unlike that of modern Japan. The HBC, writes Michael Bliss in *Northern Enterprise: Five Centuries of Canadian Business,* had a penchant for "stolid, unimaginative employees, the less given to drink and debauchery the better." The company recruited heavily from northern Scotland and the Orkney Islands, whose inhabitants "lived such bleak, hard lives that the numbing isolation on Hudson Bay was no special hardship." Many were apprenticed in their teens. All of them, from warehousemen to trading post factors (managers), were expected to show a lifelong loyalty to their employer. And unlike the French, whose *coureurs de bois* and missionaries lived among the Indians, the HBC forbade its employees "to convert, cohabit with or have any other intercourse with the savages."

From its posts on the Bay, the HBC tapped into an ancient Indian trading network that stretched across the continent. At its centre were the Swampy Cree who lived near the posts.

[2] This HBC ceremony last took place at Winnipeg in 1970 when Queen Elizabeth II and Prince Philip were presented with two live black beavers. Notes Peter Newman in *Company of Adventurers*: "The animals, not versed in court etiquette, released their tensions by first having a little tussle and then making love."

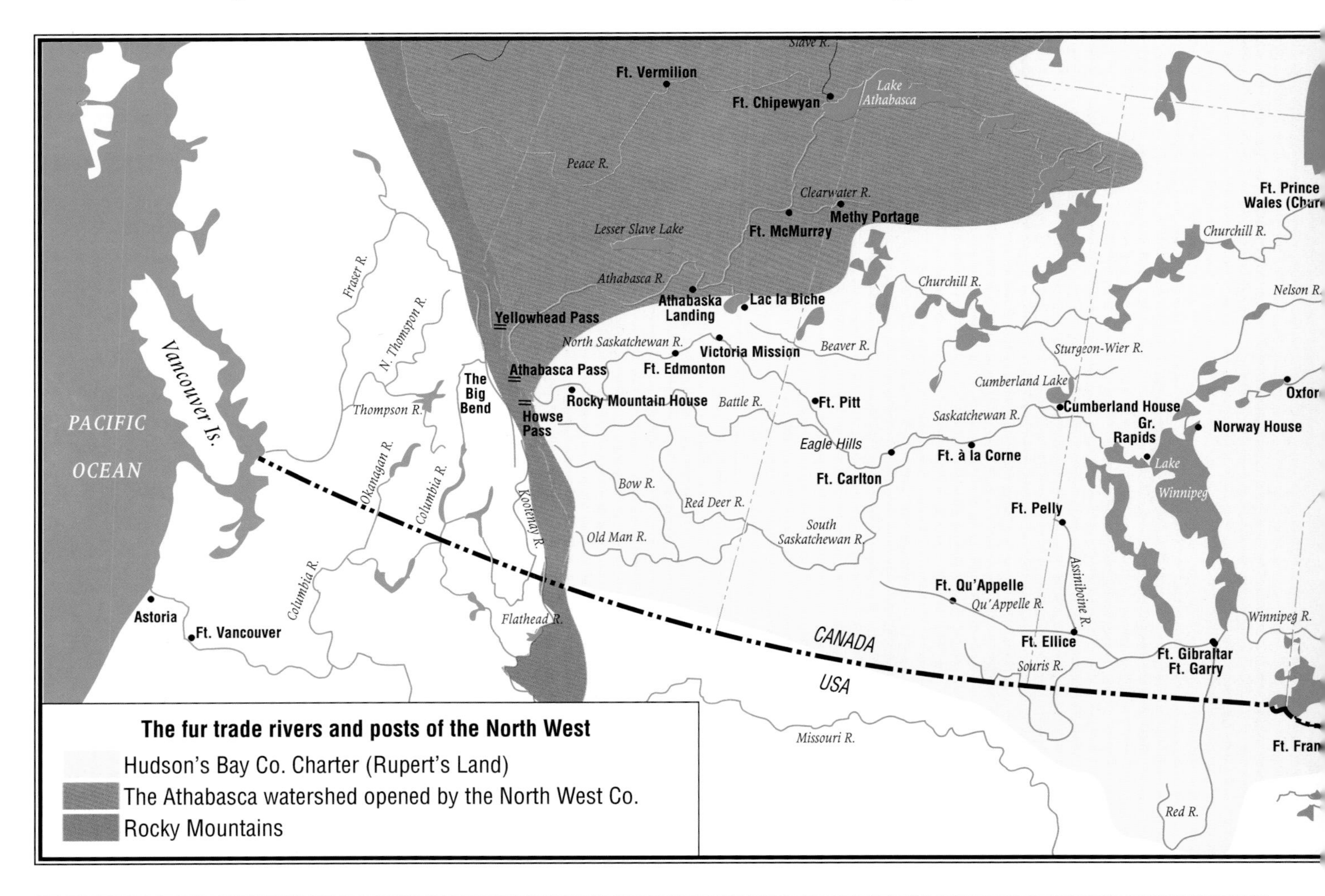

Acting as middlemen, they travelled annually to the Bay with the furs they had bartered from the Assiniboine to the south, Blackfoot to the southwest, and Beaver, Slavey and Chipewyan to the west and north. The Baymen, in turn, needed only to stock their posts with kettles, muskets, powder, knives, hatchets, blankets and tobacco, and wait for the trade to come to them.

Such conservatism so disillusioned Messrs. Radishes and Gooseberries that they returned to New France, where they promptly created a company of their own to dispute the HBC's monopoly.[3] In the intermittent, undeclared warfare that followed, a French squadron on the Bay seized every HBC fort but one. All were returned by the Treaty of Utrecht in 1713, however, and the French traders retreated to the St. Lawrence and the Great Lakes. It was the first of many victories of HBC diplomacy over frontier fact. Once again, writes Peter Newman in *Company of Adventurers*, the most readable of HBC histories, the company "reigned supreme over the territory of its choice and returned to the happy drudgery of the fur trade."[4]

For nearly a century the HBC's governing committee ignored the other requirements of the company's charter: to explore its interior holdings and search for a passage to the Pacific. The only exception was Henry Kelsey, an apprentice Bayman whose interest in Indian ways and language had at first attracted "very severe" rebuke from his superiors. Kelsey nevertheless persisted until, in 1690, he was permitted to join a party of Assiniboine trappers returning to the interior, where he was "to call, encourage and invite the remoter Indians to trade with us." He ascended the Hayes and Nelson rivers to Lake Winnipeg, and then the Saskatchewan to the open country beyond.

For two years Kelsey lived with his new companions, becoming, wrote A.S. Morton in A *History of the Canadian West*, the first example of that comparatively rare species, the "Indianized Englishman." He also became the first European to see the Prairies and meet with the Plains Indians (probably the Gros Ventres, members of the Blackfoot Confederacy), the first to witness a buffalo hunt, and the first to describe the grizzly bear. ("He is man's food and he makes food of man," Kelsey wrote in his journal.) He returned in 1692 "with a good fleet of Indians," the company noted approvingly. But otherwise the HBC paid no attention to Kelsey's travels. Some blame Kelsey himself; his journals were imprecise and written, in part, in clumsy verse:

This wood is poplo ridges
With small ponds of water,
There is beavour in abundance,
But no otter.[5]

In consequence it has proven virtually impossible to accurately retrace his steps.

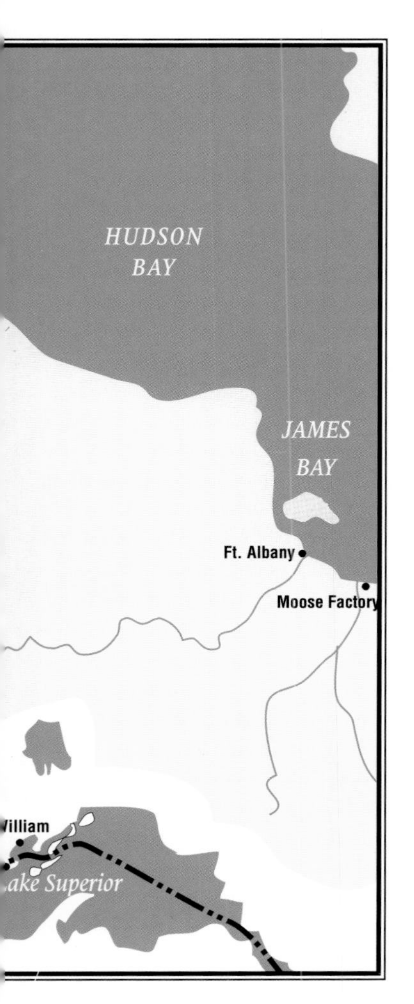

While the HBC thus sat on the Bay, the French were pushing steadily westward. In 1728 they awarded Pierre Gaultier de Varennes, Sieur de La Vérendrye, the trade monopoly over the wilderness south of Hudson Bay and beyond Lake Superior. La Vérendrye, a veteran soldier bored with running his small seigneury near Montreal, was determined to contest the HBC's control of the North West. He and his sons penetrated deep into HBC territory, beyond Lake Winnipeg to the lower Saskatchewan River, where they built a string of posts to intercept furs bound for the Bay. As a result of the new competition, pelts received at York Factory dipped by almost half, from the usual 57,000 to only 32,000 in 1732.

La Vérendrye's accomplishments were to have lasting significance. He established the first link between the West and the Great Lakes-St. Lawrence waterway, the connection that would eventually create Canada. But his basic difficulty, explained James Smith in *Wilderness of Fortune*, "was one that would always cripple and ultimately defeat every western fur trading operation based in Montreal: distance." La Vérendrye's source of money, men and materials lay 1,000 miles to the east across heavily

[3] Ultimately unappreciated by the French as well, Groseilliers retired in disgust to his seigneury at Trois Rivières after being charged a 25% duty on furs taken from the English. Radisson rejoined the HBC and fared worse. He was rewarded with a job, a silver tankard and £200 worth of HBC stock, but penurious committee men later cut his pension. Radisson was eventually reduced to begging for work as the company's London warehouseman, and died destitute in 1710.

[4] The HBC's fortified posts on the Bay would face military action only once more. In the summer of 1781, during the American Revolutionary War, a French squadron sacked Fort Churchill and burned York Factory. The ships sailed off with most of the HBC's inventory of furs and trade goods, but established no lasting presence.

[5] Henry Kelsey's journals disappeared entirely, in fact, remaining undiscovered until they turned up in a collection of private papers in Ireland in 1926.

timbered wilderness, and his men were dependent on the hunt or friendly Indians for food. The HBC enjoyed the advantage of a salt-water route to the heart of the continent, and could bring in supplies by the shipload. This was the central economic issue that would bedevil the West for centuries to come: Would the region face east-west or north-south? In the 20th century, of course, the English contestant to the north, the HBC, would be replaced by the U.S. contestant to the south.

In London, La Vérendrye's exploits and the HBC's lethargy troubled stockholder Arthur Dobbs, a wealthy Irishman with influential political connections. Dobbs "viewed the Hudson's Bay Company, like many others, as a fat, wealthy monopoly sated with profits, and sleeping in inglorious ease while the French increased their power and influence in Northern Canada," noted his biographer, Desmond Clarke. Dobbs was also convinced that the company had broken its charter by failing to look seriously for the Northwest Passage. He furiously lobbied the British parliament to rescind the HBC's trading monopoly.

Dobbs's arguments gained greater influence following the 1752 publication of *An Account of Six*

The flat-tailed engineering rat that created Canada

400 million beaver once inhabited North America, but a new European hat fashion nearly wiped them out

The 16th-century French fishermen who plied the Gulf of St. Lawrence sometimes eased their chilly trans-Atlantic trip home with the beaverskin robes they swapped for knives and hatchets with the Indians. According to explorer Jacques Cartier these deals so delighted the Micmacs that one small band danced, naked, in their canoes.[a] The fishermen soon discovered the fur was worth more in Europe than the fish. By the century's end, the fur trade was born and *Castor canadensis*, the beaver, began unrolling the map of Canada.

Some 400 million beaver then inhabited ponds and streams from the Rio Grande to the Arctic, naturalists estimate. Highly industrious, the amphibious rodents are also the only animals other than man to engineer their environment. Each family group of two 40- to 60-pound adults and their young constructs a dam to supply water for their half-submerged, multi-roomed lodge of twigs and mud with underwater entrances. In winter they eat the bark and wood of poplar, birch and willow trees, in summer the roots of aquatic plants. Their voracious appetite demands some 200 trees a year per animal.

The beaver meant more to the Indians than food and clothing. The Ojibwa believed a beaver dove into the primeval flood waters to dig up the land that became the Earth. The Algonquin thought beavers caused thunder with the slapping of their tails on the water. In a Crow legend, the beaver could speak until the Great Spirit silenced him lest he exceed man.

European furriers weren't interested in the animal's spiritual potential, however. They were preoccupied with a new fashion in hats. The unusual fibres of the beaver's undercoat are barbed, and can be matted into a lustrous, high-quality felt. "Never had the European felt-makers seen fur like this," noted Marjorie Campbell in *The North West Company*. Beaver hats soon distinguished royalty and the monied of Europe. "A fine beaver proved one's standing in the *beau monde*," said U.S. historian Walter O'Meara. "To appear without one was to be quite hopelessly out of style." In the late 17th century, a beaver hat cost four guineas, half the annual salary of a skilled tradesman.[b]

A sideline for the traders was provided by demand for castoreum, a gooey, bitter, orange-brown substance from the beaver's scent glands. First mentioned in 500 B.C. by Hippocrates as a cure for headaches and fever, it contains acetylsalicylic acid, the active ingredient in aspirin. Between 1808 and 1828 the HBC shipped 10 tons of castoreum from the Athabasca district alone.

Years' Residence in Hudson's Bay by disgruntled ex-HBC employee Joseph Robson. "The Company have for eighty years slept at the edge of a frozen sea; they have shewn no curiosity to penetrate farther themselves, and have exerted all their art and power to crush that spirit in others," he charged. Even loyal company servants complained. Wrote James Isham, factor at York: "What is the most concer'n is to see us sitt quiet and unconcern'd while the french as an old saying, not only beats the bush but runs away with the hare also." In 1752 Isham persuaded the London committee to allow him to send company servants inland to induce the Indians to trade. In 1754 Anthony Henday volunteered for the job.

Henday had joined the HBC in 1750 as a labourer and net-maker after authorities on his native Isle of Wight outlawed him for smuggling. He had no experience in inland travel or Indian diplomacy, but was aided by the Indian woman who accompanied him as guide, translator and mistress. (This liaison embarrassed Henday's superiors, who censored all references to his "bedfellow" before forwarding his journals to London.) In September 1754, three months after setting off from York

From 1853 to 1877, the HBC sold some three million beaver pelts, and only the otherwise defenceless animal's fecundity may have saved it from extinction. The creature itself became the standard of trade; everything was valued on the basis of a "made beaver" — a cured prime adult skin.

Demand began to ebb in the mid-19th century as Asian silk velour proved cheaper and more popular than beaver felt. But by then the quest for what Peter Newman would call "a glorified water rat with a flat tail," had pushed fur traders across the continent to the Pacific Ocean.

And by the late 20th century, the beaver was becoming a common nuisance. With trapping pressure eased, its dams were flooding roads and railway lines. It even learned how to live in cities. In Edmonton and Winnipeg, park maintenance staffs saw their ornamental trees routinely gnawed down. They trapped the animals and lugged them in cages to less sensitive habitats, only to see them return in greater numbers the next year. *Castor canadensis*, Canada's national symbol, was making a comeback. *T.J.*❦

[a] Any Indian band that habitually danced naked in canoes, the historian W.A. MacKay drily comments, was bound to be small.

[b] The expense indirectly inspired the Lewis Carroll character, the Mad Hatter. In the 1800s hatters made cheaper, imitation beaver felt from rabbit fur treated with a mercury compound. Many fell victim to the muscle spasms, tics, mania and "madness" of mercury poisoning.

Glenbow Archives, NA-1532-4

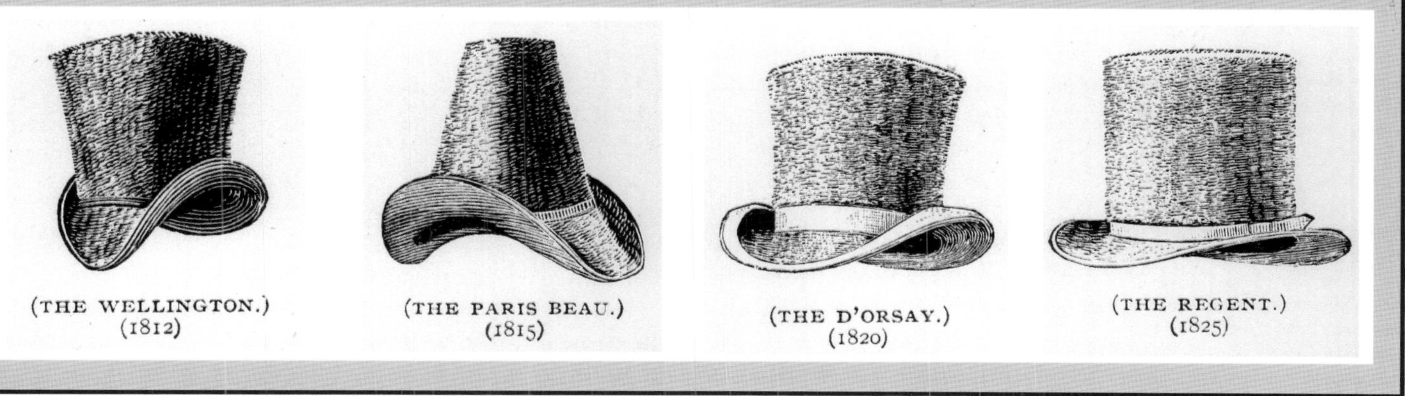

Hudson's Bay Company Archives, Provincial Archives of Manitoba

Henday Enters the Blackfoot Camp, 1754, *an HBC calendar illustration in 1951 by Franklin Arbuckle. The rumours weren't exaggerated; swaying from poles were scores of black-haired scalps.*

Factory, Henday became the first white man on record to enter what is now Alberta, canoeing up the Battle River near the future location of Wainwright. The following month, in central Alberta and almost 1,000 miles from his departure, he became the first to enter a Blackfoot camp.[6]

The encounter could have turned out badly. The Blackfoot were rumoured to be unfriendly and warlike. A French trader had written that the territory beyond Lake Winnipeg was populated by "an infinity of nations more savage than can be imagined, from whom there is everything to fear." As Henday walked down the broad avenue between the Blackfoot camp's 200 tepees, he learned the rumours weren't exaggerated: swaying from poles in front of the tents were scores of black-haired scalps. To Henday's relief, the Indians proved polite enough, although nothing he said or offered could coax them to the Bay. The HBC posts, the Blackfoot chief explained, were far off and through territory controlled by the Cree. His tribe neither owned canoes nor savoured the fish they would have to eat to survive the journey. The tobacco and other trade items Henday offered proved singularly unpersuasive.

Neither could Henday persuade his own Indian companions to hunt or trap. His mistress explained that they didn't need to harvest the pelts themselves because they could barter for more furs than they could carry, with bands too distant or otherwise unwilling to make the annual trip to the Bay. More worrisome yet was the abundant evidence Henday found that the French were successfully intercepting HBC furs in the back country. French traders, from their posts on the Saskatchewan, were plying Bay-bound Indians with brandy and coaxing them to trade away their lightest and most expensive furs. At Fort Pasquia, near the mouth of the Saskatchewan, even Henday's own Cree companions traded their best pelts for brandy. Wrote Henday: "The French talk several languages to perfection; they have the advantage of us in every shape, and if they had Brazile tobacco would entirely cut our trade off."

Henday's superiors, sceptical of his claim that the Plains Indians had horses, ignored his findings. The Seven Years' War between France and England, followed by the English victory at Quebec in 1759 that forced the closing of the French interior posts, seemed to put an end to the threat of competition for good. It proved to be only a brief respite, however. The war's end brought to Montreal a flood of Scots, English and Yankee entrepreneurs, many with experience in the fur trade to the south. They saw the removal of the French bureaucracy, with its web of feudal regulations and onerous duties, as an opportunity for the daring. The voyageurs, now idle and eager to return to their craft, were natural partners. By 1764, writes Newman in *Company of Adventurers*,

[6] Some time in November, near present-day Innisfail, Henday also became the first European to see the Rocky Mountains, but his journals are oddly silent on this. "Like other explorers of his day, Henday hoped to discover a western ocean, not a massive rock barrier," writes Newman. "Facing the immensity of the Rocky Mountains that stretched like a continent unto themselves, he may have chosen to deny their existence."

National Archives of Canada

Hudson's Bay Company, Provincial Archives of Manitoba

"the western trading routes were once again crowded with Montreal canoes." But now their managers spoke English.

Until the 1780s there were never more than a dozen or so of these new "pedlars from Canada" wintering in the North West, but for the HBC they proved much more dangerous rivals than their predecessors. "They have canoes and men at every place where Indians resort so that an Indian cannot come from any part of the country but they see of them," complained one Bayman. They were liberal with their liquor. They were flexible with their prices. And they were not "timid about knocking heads to get their way," writes Diane Francis in *Battle for the West*. At least the French had been "in a manner settled, their trade fixt, their standard moderate, and themselves under particular regulations and restrictions," grumbled the HBC master at Moose Factory.

In London HBC committee men still muttered about the danger, difficulty and cost of moving inland, but the threat was too great to ignore; in 1773 York Factory's return was only 8,000 "made beaver" (a prime beaver pelt or its equivalent in other furs), down from an average of 30,000 in the previous decade. So in June 1774, they sent a ship's mate named Samuel Hearne from York Factory with explicit instructions to establish an inland post astride the pedlars' route up the Saskatchewan.

Hearne was a natural choice for the mission. Not more than a dozen HBC servants had any experience hunting, trapping or paddling a canoe, basic requirements for a push inland. Henday had returned to England in disgust at the lack of recognition given his voyages. But Hearne was a born explorer. Six years earlier, prompted by persistent Indian tales of rich deposits of copper, he had been sent north to find the source of the ore. In three epic overland voyages ending in 1772 the young seaman followed the Coppermine River to its source and explored an area 40% the size of Europe.[7] Sent inland again, he erected Cumberland House, a low-slung log bunker with a leaky plank

Bivouac of a Canoe Party, *(above) a watercolour by Frances Anne Hopkins. For 40 years after La Vérendrye, the HBC clung to the Bay, and allowed the best fur to be diverted to Montreal by canoe.*

Samuel Hearne in 1796 (left) In 1774 he built a strategic inland post, Cumberland House, about 40 days from the Bay, compared to the five months it took to reach Montreal.

[7] In the process Hearne befriended the Indian Chief Matonabbee, the striking, six-foot-tall son of a Cree slave girl and a Chipewyan hunter. The pair met in 1770 when Hearne, lost and abandoned on the tundra by his Indian guides, seemed only a day or two away from freezing or starving to death. Matonabbee appeared out of nowhere to save him. The pair became close companions, and much of Hearne's later success can be traced to Matonabbee's help. The chief also prospered from the relationship, but his authority grew so dependent on the English presence and his friendship with Hearne, that he killed himself in despair in 1782 after a french warship captured Hearne and York Factory.

Indian women, enticing and useful, made superb wives for fur traders

GREAT FAMILIES WERE FOUNDED ON 'COUNTRY MARRIAGES'— BUT THEN CAME THE WHITE WOMEN

Collection of Glenbow Museum, ScF.6.

The Factor's Indian Wife and Child, *by Frank Schoonover in the early 1900s. Until Simpson's day, marrying a white was often a step into affluence and influence.*

Fur trader Alexander Henry the Younger vowed never to sleep with a woman out of wedlock. But in 1801, when he went to his sleeping quarters after the trading post's New Year's revels, he found there a beautiful, dark-eyed Ojibwa girl, the daughter of a chief, who refused to leave. She was "a snare laid no doubt by the Devil himself," Henry wrote in his journal. But weakened by the ever-present loneliness and isolation of a North West winter, he succumbed to one of the fur trade's basic customs: the taking of a "country wife." *

A fur trade marriage, however, was no casual liaison. These marriages *à la façon du pays* made the Canadian fur trade exceptional in its inter-racial harmony, notes Sylvia Van Kirk in *Many Tender Ties*. Elsewhere contact between European men and native women was usually illicit, an unmentionable incidental to trade or colonization. In the North West, however, "alliances with Indian women were the central social aspect of the fur traders' progress across the country."

Though the unions often lasted no longer than the husband's posting, many proved as firm and enduring as a church wedding. American-born Nor'Wester Daniel Williams Harmon, for one, retired to Vermont with his Indian wife and 14 children. The family flock eventually founded the town of Harmonsville on Lake Champlain. Other traders settled permanently in the North West with their families.

For the Europeans, the motivation to take an Indian wife was obvious. Indian women, usually married at 14 or 15, were sexually desirable. Cree girls "were very frisky when young and well shap'd, their eyes large and grey yet lively and sparkling very Bewitchen," wrote stricken Hudson's Bay Company explorer Samuel Hearne. The Ojibwa, he added, had "pretty black eyes, which they know very well how to humour in a languishing and engaging manner whenever they wish to please."

The wives also proved invaluable outside the bedroom. They were translators and guides. They provided essential labour at fur trade posts. And the marriages created "a firm friendship" with the Indians and were "a great help in engaging them to trade," noted the HBC governor of its posts on the bay, James Isham. By the mid-1700s the company, which had at first forbidden its employees on moral grounds to consort with the Indians, began to encourage the practice.

The women found benefits of their own. A woman's lot in Indian society, wrote a sympathetic Alexander Mackenzie, "was an uninterrupted succession of toil and pain." They were "subject to every kind of domestic drudgery; they dress the leather, make the clothes and shoes, weave the nets, collect the wood, erect the tents, fetch water and perform every culinary service." For Europeans, who thought of women as ill-suited for most hard physical labour, such servitude was shocking.

Marriage to a fur trader, especially one of high station, res-

roof, at a spot 60 miles west of modern-day The Pas, Manitoba. The HBC's first full-fledged inland post, it sat at a strategic point where several river routes to Lake Winnipeg converged. It was 450 miles from York Factory, about 40 days' paddling time. From the same point, the pedlars had a five-month journey to Montreal.

It came just in time. Interest in Rupert's Land rose after Captain James Cook's third and final voyage (1776-1779). This voyage, in search of the Northwest Passage, was spurred in part by Hearne's discoveries. Cook didn't find the passage, but he did discover Nootka Sound on Vancouver Island, which he took to be the estuary of a large river. It appeared to the pedlars to be a candidate for the long-sought canoe route from the North West's prime fur-bearing regions to the Pacific. Discovery of such a route would give the HBC's rivals their own, accessible salt-water outlet. And the west coast was itself rich in beaver and fur-bearing otter.

cued these women from such heavy work, and provided ready access to highly desired trade goods. It sometimes gave their children a European education and a foothold in white society. It could also occasionally give the women powerful sway over their own people.

At York Factory in the early 1700s, Thanadelthur, a forceful Chipewyan woman who had been enslaved by the Cree before coming under the protection of the post's governor, delighted in her new-found standing. Her countrymen, reluctant to trade with the English because of their close ties with the enemy Cree, succumbed to her sharp tongue. "She made them all stand in fear of her," an admiring HBC employee recounted. With "devilish spirit" she "scolded at some and pushing of others...and forced them to ye peace."

These marriages also had disadvantages for both sides, however. The woman might find herself abandoned. The children were more often rejected than accepted by white society. As for the husband, Sylvia Van Kirk writes, "In return for giving the traders sexual and domestic rights to their women, the Indians expected reciprocal privileges such as free access to the posts and provisions."

As Indian dependence on European trade goods increased, the marriage custom weakened, and prostitution and licentiousness became more common. Outbreaks of violence could often be traced to Indian anger at the theft of their women. An expedition to the Missouri plains, on the other hand, became a prized fur trade assignment; the Mandan who lived there were reputed to be especially liberal in offering their daughters to the whites, and the women's sexual prowess was a hot topic of conversation. With the establishment of the Red River colony in 1811, marrying Indian women began losing its appeal altogether. Settlement brought missionaries who preached against country marriages. It also brought white women who often disdained Indian females.

HBC Archives, Provincial Archives of Manitoba

Frances Simpson, wife of George Simpson. After her arrival in the North West, Indian wives were no longer socially acceptable.

HBC governor George Simpson, who was said to have a different girl waiting for him at every post on his annual inspection tours, snubbed the Indian wives of his subordinates as "brown jugs" or "commodities," and severed his own relationship with native wife Margaret Taylor. His 1836 marriage to his cousin Frances sent a clear signal to fur trade employees: In future, only well-bred white wives would be accepted in the upper echelons of the company.

Simpson's actions had immediate effect. "There is a strange revolution in the manners of the country," wrote James Douglas, then chief factor at Fort Vancouver, and himself the product of a liaison between a Scottish merchant in British Guiana and a Creole, in 1840. "Indian wives were at one time the vogue, the half-breed supplanted these, and now we have the lovely, tender exotic torn from its parent bed to pine and languish in the desert." A "genteel" British-born wife had become a conspicuous status symbol for an HBC officer.

But the arrival of English wives in the North West also "presaged the ultimate decline of the fur trade," Van Kirk concludes, and "symbolized the coming of a settled, agrarian order." In that world "native women would have little role to play." *T.J.*❦

* Henry seems to have succumbed not once, but twice. His will mentioned his "three reputed sons," but also referred to two daughters and a son by another woman.

For Peter Pond, Cook's discoveries were an irresistible lure. But exploiting the rich Athabasca furs he had discovered, and financing a final push to the Pacific, were undertakings well beyond his resources. Any joint undertaking by these new traders at Montreal seemed equally unlikely, however, because of the fierce rivalry they displayed for one another. In 1782, for example, Pond himself was strongly implicated in the murder of a rival trader, Jean-Etienne Waddens, who was shot while the New Englander was visiting Pond's Athabasca cabin. In 1786 another Pond rival disappeared under similarly dubious circumstances.[8] Even to the highly competitive pedlars, however, the killings demonstrated the need for greater co-operation. This led to the creation of one of the most extraordinary business enterprises in Canadian history, the North West Company. In the next 40 years the Nor'Westers would take the contest for fur over the Rockies and all the way to the Pacific in a rivalry that would very nearly destroy the HBC. The principal battleground was the land that Pond had discovered, northern Alberta.❦

[8] Pond insisted he was innocent of both murders, but the controversy, and the threat that he would be put on trial in Canada, forced him to leave the North West and retire in the United States in 1789.

Glenbow Archives, NA-1406-39

HBC and NWC Traders Competing for Fur in an Indian Camp, *an engraving by W.A. Rogers published in 1879. What began as vigorous competition ended up in bloodshed across a 4,000-mile frontier.*

The HBC defeats its rowdy rivals after competition turns into war

BUT IN A FRANTIC SEARCH FOR A CHEAPER TRANSPORTATION ROUTE THOMPSON FOUND TWO PASSES THROUGH THE ROCKIES FROM ALBERTA AND THE NOR'WESTERS MACKENZIE AND FRASER REACHED THE PACIFIC

During its 40-year history, says fur trade historian Donald Creighton in *The Commercial Empire of the St. Lawrence,* the North West Company would lay down the framework of Canada itself. "Like the makers of Confederation a century later, the company stood face to face with the problems of continental organization." Though they terrorized their rivals and bullied the Indians, it's impossible not to admire the bold vision and drive of the company's traders. "The Nor'Westers," writes Michael Bliss in *Northern Enterprise: Five*

Centuries of Canadian Business, "were among the most daring, hard-driving, ruthless and reckless businessmen in Canadian history."

The first North West Company was created in 1779 upon Pond's return from the Athabasca region of northern Alberta, but the company, never chartered or incorporated, didn't take more permanent shape until the winter of 1782-83. By 1787 it had absorbed the last of the independent Montreal-based fur trade concerns.

The contrast with the HBC could scarcely have been more startling. Where the HBC, directed from London by men who had no first-hand knowledge of the fur trade, was cautious and monolithic, the NWC — never more than a restive, loosely organized partnership of Montreal merchants and wintering traders — was flexible and aggressive. Most of its leading lights, writes Diane Francis in *Battle for the West,* had "cut their teeth on the western trade and knew every aspect of their business." This gave the company a fractious, independent spirit: "If a Hudson's Bay Company trading house typically resembled a military barracks, a Nor'Wester establishment had more in common with a rowdy tavern."

At the NWC's centre was a circle of merchants, mostly highland Scots who, after serving an apprenticeship in the "Indian country" as clerks, could graduate to a full partnership and a share in the profits. Many of these men were related to each other and to Simon McTavish, who directed the company until his death in 1804. McTavish's nephew, William McGillivray, succeeded him at the helm. Alexander Mackenzie was the cousin of fellow Nor'Wester Roderick Mackenzie, who in turn was the brother-in-law of McTavish's wife. Simon Fraser was a McTavish cousin. David Thompson, although an Englishman, was brother-in-law to a McGillivray nephew. The ties of race and family created "a degree of enthusiasm and enterprise that, for a time, completely dominated the western fur trade," Francis writes.

Collection of Glenbow Museum, 60-51-40

Simon McTavish, one of the NWC founders. Most were Scots, famous for hard travel, hard bargains and hard drinking.

In Montreal the merchant partners marketed the furs, and imported the mountain of guns, blankets, kettles and rum that fuelled the trade. French-speaking voyageurs, the workhorses of the business, paddled the canoes, hauled the supplies and built the posts. In the interior the wintering partners sought out the Indians and negotiated the prices. Each summer the two ends of the company's operations met at Grand Portage, on the northwest shore of Lake Superior, to discuss strategy for the coming season. There the fleets of heavy freight canoes from Montreal transferred their loads to the lighter "north canoes" that coursed over the height of land into the Hudson Bay watershed. (After 1801 the depot moved to Fort William, now Thunder Bay, 35 miles to the east on Superior's north shore.)

The social heart of the NWC was the Beaver Club in Montreal, open only to those who had spent a winter in the North West. There the captains of the company — many, like the McGills, the ancestors of Quebec's English-speaking elite — toasted their victories through a hectic, winter-long round of dinners, parties and liquor-flowing meetings.

The Beaver Club style unnerved George Landmann, a visitor to Montreal in the early 1800s. One night's festivities ended with the entire party whooping and dancing on the tables until all but Mackenzie and McGillivray, president and vice-president of the company, had collapsed in a drunken stupor amongst the broken plates and glasses. Wrote Landmann: "Mackenzie now proposed to drink to our memory, and then give the war-whoop over us, fallen foes and friends, all nevertheless on the floor, and in attempting to push the bottle to McGillivray, at the opposite end of the table, he slid off his chair and could not recover his seat, whilst McGillivray, in extending himself over the table in the hope of seizing the bottle which Mackenzie had attempted to push to him, also in like manner began to slide on one side and fell helpless on the floor."

The next day, no doubt, the mood would be more serious. For like La Vérendrye before them, McTavish and his partners were faced with confounding logistical difficulties. To get trading goods to such interior posts as Fort Augustus on the North Saskatchewan and Fort Dunvegan on the

The National Archives of Canada

Voyageurs' Canoe, *a watercolour by Frances Anne Hopkins. The 'north canoe' plied from Lake Superior to Great Slave Lake.*

Peace River required a vast army of voyageurs and clerks. Even in 1799 the HBC carried on their business with only 498 men posted in North America. The Nor'Westers required 1,276, with 903 of them west of Grand Portage. Thus it cost the NWC twice as much as the HBC to get out each pelt. Each push westward increased the costs, but the company could only survive by being the first to reach and exploit new, untapped sources. The Indians would be the beneficiaries (and the victims) of the NWC dilemma.

From the beginning, the fur trade had never been one-sided. Traders might try to cheat the Indians with second-rate goods, diluted liquor or arbitrarily raised prices. But the Indians proved savvy customers and expert hagglers, who would simply refuse to part with their furs if they couldn't strike a good deal. They also demanded credit, goods in the fall for pelts promised in the spring. Some also became traders themselves. Until the 1770s up to 80% of the pelts came through Indian middlemen, who procured them for as little as a tenth of the price they got from the whites.

A formal trading session began with a ritual gift-giving of tobacco, alcohol or other inducements.[1] It usually ended with the Indians' stern criticism of previous goods and a forthright demand to "give us good measure." Their opinion was taken seriously. "Never was any man so upbraided with our powder, kettles and hatchets than we have been this summer by all the natives," an HBC official at York Factory wrote to London in 1728. He implored the company to provide better-quality goods because "the natives are grown so politic in their way of trade...they are not to be dealt by as formerly." The Indians also learned very quickly how to turn white competition to their own advantage.

The Nor'Westers' go-to-the-trade policy made them a convenient and welcome alternative to the HBC for many tribes. But NWC traders, squeezed by a higher cost structure than their rivals, could prove to be unpleasant guests. They liberally doled out high-profit rum as an inducement to trade or used force to compel reluctant Indians to part with their furs.[2] It was a dangerous practice. Alexander Mackenzie described how one Indian drinking spree, at Eagle Hills on the Saskatchewan in 1780, turned violent. "One of the traders and several of the men were killed, while the rest had no other means to save themselves but by a precipitate flight, abandoning a considerable body of goods and near a half of the furs they had collected during the winter and spring."

The NWC's headlong push into the interior also upset traditional Indian alliances, sometimes

[1] From his friend Samuel Hearne the Cree Chief Matonabbee once demanded — and received — a 1,100-made-beaver inducement of 22 coats, 18 hats, 18 shirts, eight guns, 140 pounds of gunpowder, and a great quantity of hatchets, tobacco, blankets, cloth, combs and looking glasses, even before beginning to trade.

[2] By 1787, in a petition to the governor of British North America, the HBC complained that its Canadian rivals were deliberately "debauching the natives into a state of insensibility" to pilfer their goods: "It grieves us to see a Body of Indians destroyed by a set of Men merely for self interest, doing all in their power to Destroy Posterity, so we hope that your Excellency will make such regulations as will preserve Posterity and not be Destroyed by fiery double Distilled Rum from Canada." Until the 1840s, however, the moralistic HBC itself did a thriving trade in watered-down brandy.

with fatal results. In 1794 the Gros Ventre, angry that the company was supplying their neighbours with guns, destroyed a post on the North Saskatchewan, killing three men and a half-dozen women and children. "The Gros Ventres are an audacious, turbulent race and have repeatedly attempted to menace us," commented NWC trader Alexander Henry the Younger, nephew of an American-born pedlar who had joined Pond in the North West. Later the Peigan in southern Alberta would harass David Thompson as he expanded the trade over the Rockies to the Kootenays. The last thing the Peigan wanted was for their traditional enemies across the mountains to receive firearms.

Glenbow Archives NA-1733-1

Alexander Mackenzie in 1802. The first white man to reach both the Arctic and Pacific oceans overland.

Through it all, the search for a viable route to the Pacific consumed Nor'Wester energies. Pond had learned from the Indians of a great river flowing westward out of Lake Athabasca. Alexander Mackenzie, a brash NWC clerk who joined Pond in 1785, was the first to investigate this. Mackenzie had little taste for the rigours of the interior. He was so unhappy with his posting that he warned his cousin Roderick it was "the height of folly" to endure the fur trader's life, "deprived of every comfort that can render life agreeable." But he warmed to the task of discovery.

In 1789 Mackenzie descended the Slave River from Fort Chipewyan, skirted the shore of Great Slave Lake, and followed the river that bears his name from its source on Great Slave to its mouth on the Beaufort Sea. Greatly disappointed, he returned to test another Pond theory: that the source of the Peace River, which mingles with the waters of Lake Athabasca at the latter's western extremity,[3] lay near the Pacific. The source of the Peace proved to be a confusing tangle of shallow and rapid streams, one of them the Parsnip. Beyond the Parsnip, however, Mackenzie found streams flowing south and west into what is now called the Fraser. Part way down the Fraser, in today's Cariboo country, he set out westward on foot. On July 22, 1793, he reached the Pacific at the mouth of the Bella Coola River. Next day, on a rock some miles west, he recorded his triumph in vermilion paint: "Alexander Mackenzie, from Canada, by land, the twenty-second of July, one thousand seven hundred and ninety-three."[4]

The NWC next turned its attention in a more southerly direction. In 1808, after establishing a string of NWC posts along the eastern slopes of the Rockies, Simon Fraser descended his namesake river, first reached by Mackenzie 15 years earlier, to its mouth in present-day Vancouver. His journey through its canyons, with their sheer walls rising as much as 3,000 feet above the roaring rapids, was a triumph of determined endurance. To test one set of rapids, Fraser recounted in his journal, he ordered the five best men of his four canoe crews "into a canoe lightly loaded...After passing the first cascade she lost her head and was drawn into an eddy, where she was whirled about...In spite of every effort the whirlpool forced her against a low rock. Upon this the men scrambled out, saving their lives." Rescue was no easy matter either. "The situation rendered our approach perilous," Fraser wrote. "The bank was high and steep. We had to plunge our daggers into the ground to avoid sliding into the river. We cut steps, fastened a line to the front of the canoe and hauled it up...one false step might have hurled us into eternity...however, we cleared the bank before dark."

Glenbow Archives, NA-1194-8

Simon Fraser, undated. His exploration of the Fraser River proved commercially useless and almost killed him.

As his men portaged along the cliffs, carrying their 90-pound packs, loose stones and gravel would roll beneath their feet. One man lost his balance and became "so wedged amid the rocks that he could move neither forward nor backward, nor yet unload himself. I crawled...to his assistance and saved his life by cutting

[3] The Peace does not quite reach Lake Athabasca. Rather, its waters flow into the Slave River.

[4] Mackenzie returned to Montreal as a leading partner in the NWC, but quarrelled with Simon McTavish over the company's direction. Thoroughly disillusioned, he joined the upstart little XY Company in 1799. Within three years Mackenzie's prestige and aggressive management helped the new firm build a network of posts that rivalled the NWC's. But the bitter competition, driven by the personal rivalry between Mackenzie and McTavish, proved self-defeating. After McTavish died in 1804, it took only four months for the two Canadian concerns to negotiate a friendly merger.

his pack so it dropped back in the river." At times they had to climb precipices on frail ladders made of poles and withes. "We had to pass where no human being should venture," an awestruck Fraser summed up. This accomplishment proved of no commercial value either; the river was far too wild.

Finally David Thompson, the HBC man who had switched to the NWC, found the path to the Pacific. From the NWC post at Rocky Mountain House on the North Saskatchewan, he crossed Howse Pass[5] and found a major north-flowing river, which he named the Kootenae. Though he didn't know it, he had in fact found the Columbia, where it flows north before it reaches the Big Bend around the northern flank of the Selkirks and heads south towards modern Washington State and the Pacific. Rather than explore farther, Thompson concentrated on staking the NWC's claim to the region's rich furs.

Then, in 1810, his leisurely pace was disrupted. After the Lewis and Clark expedition reached

[5] The eastern approach to 5,023-foot Howse Pass is the Howse River, which flows into the North Saskatchewan immediately upstream from Saskatchewan Crossing on the Banff-Jasper Highway. The western approach is the Blueberry River, which flows into the Columbia near Donald on the Trans-Canada Highway.

The most romantic westerner the West has never known

He sang, paddled, bled and died on our rivers and trails but his language kept him from us

The cowboy emerges from the history of southern Alberta as a cultural symbol, inspiring everything from the Calgary Stampede to the Stetson hat. Northern Alberta has an equally fascinating character, though few Albertans know anything about him — partly because his language was mostly French, partly because nobody makes movies about him. He is the voyageur of the North West, workhorse of the fur trade.

His language, indeed, was not entirely French. English and a dozen Indian dialects were mixed with it. Neither did he live in Quebec. His home, insofar as he had one, was in and around the western posts of the North West Company and the Hudson's Bay Company. He was unknown on the southern prairie grasslands, where the fierce Plains Indians neither needed nor wanted his business.

The fur trade explicitly distinguished him from the men who paddled the enormous 36-foot canoes from Montreal to the ports at the head of Lake Superior. They were known as *mangeurs du lard,* pork eaters, after the dried corn and pork they lived on. To the northwest lay the domain of the *homme du nord,* the "north man," whose canoes were smaller and faster and whose life was even more arduous and dangerous.

It was he who transported fur to Lake Superior each spring and returned in the fall to a western post that might lie 2,000 miles into the interior. It was he also who carried the Nor'Westers Alexander Mackenzie, David Thompson and Simon Fraser on their amazing voyages of discovery.

He was not what we would call a big man. He was usually stocky and barrel-chested, with a short back, much better suited to carry the two 90-pound packs of fur he was required to haul over every portage going east, or the rum barrels and other goods he brought back west. His carrying device was a tumpline, a 12-foot leather thong, three inches wide in the middle and tapering to the ends. Each end was tied around the extremities of the pack, leaving a loop in the middle for his forehead.

Thus he tackled the portages with a 180-pound load. In the lands west of the Lake Superior watershed, what the trade called *le pays d'en haut,* the high country, the portages were not like modern park trails. They ran up the edges of cliffs, and forded rushing and rocky streams. They ran through waist-deep marshlands "corduroyed" with logs, which sometimes shifted and settled so that a man's leg could slip between them and be broken.

The longest trail in the trade was the 13-mile Methy in western Saskatchewan, 70 miles east of Fort McMurray. The worst was the Savanne off the Kaministikwia, northwest of Thunder Bay, where the corduroy sank year by year into the muskeg and the men cursed and groaned as they stumbled over it.

Their days began before dawn and lasted till sunset, an old fur trade rule because it was inadvisable to run past dark. But "express" canoes, those that carried company correspondence, executives and no freight, observed a very different schedule, often breaking camp at 2:00 in the morning and continuing till late at night. "Gave the men a dram and pushed on," is a familiar entry in Sir George Simpson's journals, rum being a major incentive and anodyne.

It was not the portages but the rapids that claimed most lives. By running a rapid, the voyageurs avoided the miseries of a portage, so that the inclination was to take the chance. Between the roaring and plunging waters in the middle of the river and the jagged rocks and overhanging branches along its edges, there often appeared a "water file" where the current ran free with a "V" leading into it. The steersman, *le governail,* one of the five crewmen in a north canoe, aimed the craft at the centre of the V, while the dextrous "bow man," *l'avant,* peered forward and pushed the vessel around unexpected rocks, and the three mid-men kept the craft moving to provide manoeuvrability. This way the vessel would slip down the water file and bypass the cauldron at the river's centre.

It didn't always work, as the grave markers often found below rapids evidenced. One of the worst disasters occurred on the Pacific in 1805, U.S. merchants moved to compete against the Canadians in the "new Northwest." John Jacob Astor's Pacific Fur Company launched two expeditions — one by sea, one overland — to the mouth of the Columbia. The NWC ordered Thompson to get there first. He didn't. Hostile Peigan had blocked Howse Pass. Thompson found another route over Athabasca Pass, but he did not reach the mouth of the Columbia until July 1811.[6] By then Astor's men had already built a post there, Astoria.

Then came the War of 1812, however, with Britain harassing U.S. possessions around North America. The Nor'Westers saw the war as a splendid opportunity; in the fall of 1813 the NWC sent 100 men down the Columbia to besiege Astoria. It was quite a friendly siege, as Peter Newman recounts in his second volume, *Caesars of the Wilderness.* Most of Astor's men were former Nor'Westers themselves, friends and relations of the besiegers. If one side or the other ran short of

[6] The eastern approach to 5,736-foot Athabasca Pass is on the Athabasca River, 15 miles south of Jasper, on the Banff-Jasper Highway. The western approach is the Wood River, which used to flow into the Columbia at the point the fur trade called Boat Encampment. The whole area was later flooded by B.C. Hydro's Mica Dam on the Columbia. For a map of all these passes through the Rockies, see The Railwaymen section.

Glenbow Archives, NA-1406-55

Voyageur by Frederic Remington in 1891. On the water or under a 180-pound load from dawn till dusk, there was 'no life so happy.'

the northern border of modern Alberta where the Slave River plunges over a chain of rapids near Fort Smith. According to local lore, the experienced steersman of a lead canoe offered to try the rapids first. If they were safe, he'd fire a gun to signal the less experienced steersman of a second boat to follow. Otherwise he'd walk back up the trail and have the second make the portage.

The rapid proved dangerously wild. Only with the greatest effort and luck did the first canoe survive it. Then, as he landed, a mid-man who didn't know the plan shot a deer that was drinking in the river. The steersman raced back just in time to see the second canoe start down. Ten minutes later, its whole crew, six men, were dead. They call that place "the Rapids of the Drowned."

No aptitude, however, was more important than an ability to sing. A song, the tune and words descended from medieval French culture, ended every "pipe," the short rest when the canoes came together and the men smoked. Rollicking songs eased the boredom as they paddled, rhythmic stroke upon stroke, across the West. Their songs have appeared, delicately edited, in folksong books ever since — from the swinging *En roulant, ma boule roulant* to the boisterous *Youpe! Youpe! Sur la rivière.*

Marjorie Campbell, the popular historian of the fur trade, lets a voyageur himself sum up his life in her major work, *The North West Company.* She quotes one old man's reminiscences: "I could carry, paddle, walk and sing with any man I ever saw. I have been twenty-four years a canoeman, and forty-one in service; no portage was ever too long for me. Fifty songs could I sing. I have saved the lives of ten voyageurs. Have had twelve wives and six running dogs. I spent all my money on pleasure. Were I young again, I should spend my life the same way over. There is no life so happy as a voyageur's." *T.B.*❦

Collection of Glenbow Archives 60.71.8

York Boat Running a Rapid, *an oil painting by John Innes. Like the HBC itself, the York boat was bigger and slower than its competitor, the north canoe, but proved the more durable.*

some necessity, they would help each other out in neighbourly fashion.

The Astorians began to get anxious, however, when their regular supply ship failed to appear; they thought themselves abandoned. There were also rumours that a 26-gun British sloop, the *HMS Racoon,* was on its way via Cape Horn to capture the post. On October 16 the man in charge of Astoria, whose name as it happens was Duncan McDougall, offered to sell the place to the NWC for $40,000, complete with its $100,000 inventory of beaver and otter skins. The offer was accepted, most of the Astorians readmitted as NWC partners, and the post renamed Fort George.

When the *Racoon* in fact did show up some weeks later, Captain William Black was furious at missing the chance to capture the post and seize the fur. At least there must be a ceremonial surrender, he decided, so the erstwhile defenders obligingly staged one. This was to prove a terrible blunder since Captain Black's little ceremony made the acquisition of Astoria a military capture and not a commercial transaction. Under the terms of the subsequent treaty, captured property had to be returned. The Nor'Westers had to give back Mr. Astor's fort. (The fate of the inventory was not so definite.)

For that brief interval, however, the NWC's 3,000-mile-long ribbon of rivers, portages and trading posts reached from the St. Lawrence right to the Pacific. Mackenzie was encouraged in his dream of a "vast inter-oceanic and transcontinental commerce, with trade goods from London being converted to furs in British North America and the furs shipped across the Pacific where their proceeds would buy cargoes of tea and silks from the Orient." But it was already too late for that.

For most of the second half of the 18th century the HBC had been struggling to survive. The old company had neither the men nor the expertise to match the Nor'Westers' headlong push west. HBC servants, dismissed by one NWC trader as "old women who had not courage even to defend the furs they had obtained," were terrorized by their brawling Canadian rivals. By 1800 the NWC had seized almost four-fifths of the trade. "But if the Hudson's Bay Company was at times sluggish, it was never inert," writes Diane Francis. "When it embarked in new directions, the company moved forward relentlessly, and all its advantages of organization and experience made it a formidable competitor." As the 19th century began, the HBC was ready to go on the offensive, and the man who would lead it was put into his position by the Nor'Westers themselves.

In 1806 the NWC's Mackenzie had begun surreptitiously buying HBC stock, in a bid to win a controlling voice in the rival company and transit rights to the Bay. The boardroom manoeuvre might well have worked — HBC meetings were poorly attended and proxies rarely used — but the Nor'Westers allied with the wrong man. Thomas Douglas, Earl of Selkirk, who acted for the Canadians, had a secret scheme of his own in mind. In 1810, with stock he too had surreptitiously acquired, he persuaded the HBC to award him an extensive stretch of land along the Red River valley south of Lake Winnipeg. There, in Assiniboia, the philanthropic Scottish nobleman planned an agricultural colony for those of his countrymen who had been evicted from land their families had occupied for centuries, when it was taken over for sheep farming. The first hundred settlers got there in 1811 and reinforcements followed.

Glenbow Archives, NA-2247-1

Thomas Douglas, Earl of Selkirk, about 1800. A philanthropist, he took control of the HBC and tried to wrest the West away from the fur traders in favour of settlement. The cost in lives was high.

Under Selkirk's influence, the HBC had also begun to revitalize its fur trading operations. The company had no experience with canoes, nor men who could manage them. It therefore designed a shallow-draft boat with a flat bottom — the York boat — that could carry a three-ton load (twice the capacity of a north canoe) and could be hauled over portages on log rollers. To find its way around its vast holdings, it brought in surveyor Philip Turnor to map the interior. Slowly it assembled its own network of trading posts. The Red River settlement, Selkirk reasoned, could supply these posts with food. More importantly, it would sit at the heart of Assiniboia, the vital region that provisioned the NWC's traders and voyageurs with pemmican, and through which its canoes passed on their way to and from Fort William.

With the appointment of hot-blooded Miles Macdonell as the colony's first governor, tensions rose. In 1814 Macdonell rashly forbade the export of any food, including pemmican, from the colony. Neither the enraged Nor'Westers nor their Metis allies — who considered Assiniboia their own — could let the order stand. When the NWC's canoes pushed into the region that summer, the armed Nor'Westers scattered the settlers, captured Macdonell, and went back to trading furs.

An uneasy peace stood until 1816 when Macdonell's equally impulsive successor, Robert Semple, captured Fort Gibraltar, the NWC stronghold at the future Winnipeg, and ordered it burned to the ground. "The sight of the great fort in flames was too much for the Metis," writes Marjorie Wilkins Campbell in *The North West Company.* "Soon the fire that had been smouldering in every one of them also burst into flame. To each, the destruction of Fort Gibraltar was a warning of what might happen to his own small home." Led by Cuthbert Grant, the Metis confronted Semple at Seven Oaks. In the shootout that followed, Semple and 20 HBC men were killed.

The entire North West burst into open warfare. Selkirk, with an army of 100 Swiss and German mercenaries, seized the NWC headquarters at Fort William, capturing McGillivray and 15 other senior Nor'Westers. He found evidence the Canadians had encouraged the Metis action, and he sent the NWC partners back to Montreal under armed guard, to stand trial for conspiracy to commit murder. Nothing came of the court action.

"Those fifteen minutes at Seven Oaks changed everything," writes Newman in *Caesars of the Wilderness.* "No longer a commercial contest with the occasional skirmish and post-burning, the struggle between the Nor'Westers and Baymen had turned into a guerrilla war fought along a 4,000-mile front. For the first time in the long rivalry between the two companies, the fur trade itself had become subordinate to their struggle for supremacy."

No man was more determined to win it than a red-haired Scot named Colin Robertson. An NWC clerk who had switched to the HBC, he was described by HBC governor George Simpson a

A mother and father and 13 kids gave us the map of the Wes

David Thompson's astounding work was history's biggest family project, but he died poor and in obscurity

In the 1880s Joseph Tyrrell of the Geological Survey of Canada[a] noted that virtually all the maps of the Canadian West were based on the work of a single and then-unknown cartographer called David Thompson. Marvelling at their accuracy, the young Tyrrell searched out Thompson's work in the archives. He discovered an astonishing story. In the course of 28 years this man, his wife and their brood of children (ultimately 13 of them) had traversed by canoe and dog-sled about an eighth of the North American continent and mapped it with unfailing accuracy.

In 1916 Tyrrell published Thompson's narrative of his western journeys, rescuing one of the world's greatest mapmakers from obscurity and disclosing the story of what was doubtless the biggest "family project" in Canadian history.

Thompson was a Londoner, attended the Grey Coat School for poor children and in 1784 at 14 took up service with the Hudson's Bay Company as an apprentice clerk. The account of Captain Cook's third voyage had just been published and featured "a great map of the world." It showed most of northwest North America as a yawning blank. Thompson, yearned to fill it in.

The company sent him inland as a fur trader, and from HBC surveyor Philip Turnor he learned the skills of a mapmaker. Thompson resolved to plot a better HBC route from Hudson Bay to the recently discovered bonanza beaver country around Lake Athabasca, but the HBC wasn't interested. Thompson, angry and resolute, walked the 75 miles from his post on Reindeer Lake and offered his services to the rival North West Company. They wanted maps; in 1797, he became a Nor'Wester.

With boundless energy, and at four times his HBC salary, Thompson spent seven years surveying the NWC's vast territory east of the Rockies. By now he had met Charlotte Small, mixed-blood daughter of Nor'Wester Patrick Small, and made her his wife. Though company registers usually

The Picture Gallery of Canadian History, Volume 2

C.W. Jeffreys' illustration of David Thompson taking an observation

National Archives of Canada, C-8984

Colin Robertson

decade later as "a compound of folly and extravagance," a "frothy trifling conceited man" who was "full of silly boasting." But the swaggering Robertson excelled in the struggle against his old employers, acting out again and again his cherished motto: "When you are among wolves, howl." His grand scheme was to lead the HBC into the Athabasca.

For almost 20 years the Nor'Westers had tormented, threatened and driven off every HBC attempt to exploit the rich area Pond had discovered. "Good God!" exclaimed Robertson in a forceful and persuasive presentation to the HBC's London committee. "See the Canadians come thousands of miles beyond us to monopolize the most valuable part of your territories!" Under his prodding, the company began planning an expedition to contest the NWC's control of the region.

The first attempt ended in disaster. Macdonell's capture in 1815 forced Robertson to stay in Red River and re-establish the faltering settlement. The expeditionary brigade of 100 armed men he had assembled in Montreal was placed under the command of headstrong Montrealer John Clarke instead. Clarke built Fort Wedderburn across from the NWC's main post at Fort Chipewyan, and a string of smaller trading houses, but had reached the Athabasca short on food with winter approaching. The well-stocked Nor'Westers drove away the game and forbade the Indians to trade identified a trader's wife only as "a woman of the country," Thompson insisted Charlotte be named. Their children, who began to appear annually, accompanied them nearly everywhere they went.

Gradually, point by point, Thompson pinned down the longitude and latitude of all the key posts, river junctions and other vital locations of the North Saskatchewan, Churchill, Athabasca, Slave and upper Mackenzie rivers, mapping them as he went. As the Pacific became vital to NWC plans, he crossed the mountains from his post at what is now Rocky Mountain House, Alberta, through Howse and Athabasca passes, developing the latter as a highway to the Columbia River. In 1811 he made an epic journey down the Columbia to the Pacific. By then he had traversed 50,000 miles by canoe, horseback, sled and on foot, over much of it aided by Charlotte and the children.

Among the brawling, hard-drinking Nor'Westers, Thompson was an oddity. Pious and sober, he forswore tobacco, alcohol and foul language, and regularly upbraided his peers for their dissolute and spendthrift ways. When they required him to trade rum with the natives beyond the Rockies, he strapped the kegs to the pack mules which would, he knew, cause them to be smashed against the rock faces in the passes.

"His idea of relaxing after a strenuous paddle was to gather his voyageurs around him and read aloud in French from the New or Old Testament," writes Peter C. Newman in *Caesars of the Wilderness.* He also had a deep mystical streak. He claimed to have once beaten the Devil in a game of cards, and he revered the beaver as supernatural.

Because of Thompson's regular recourse to telescope and astrolabe in his work, the Indians called him Koo-Koo-Sint, the man who looks at stars. Although he respected the Indians, devoting considerable space in his journals to a careful description of their way of life, his one failure of nerve stemmed from his fear of the Peigan. In 1810, dreading a possible clash with a Peigan war party that was jealously guarding the Rockies from intruders, Thompson took to the woods. He was found by his exasperated companions three weeks later. Too terror-stricken to hunt for game, he had nearly starved to death.

His greatest moment no doubt occurred at Fort William, now Thunder Bay. With his Pacific work complete, he proudly appeared before the NWC's hard-living Montreal bosses and wintering partners (whom he clearly respected) to present them with the greatest tool the fur traders could possess — a 10-foot-long "Map of the Northwest Territory" that plotted almost two million square miles of rivers, lakes, portages, mountains and passes between Hudson Bay and the Pacific Ocean, as far south as the Great Lakes and the Columbia River and as far north as Lake Athabasca. Today it is in the Ontario Archives.

Following his retirement from the NWC in 1812, Thompson settled in Quebec with his wife and children. He tried to continue his western mapmaking work, but he suffered near blindness. He closed his career making surveys of the streets and sewers of Montreal, and finally was forced to sell his precious surveying tools for food. In 1857 one of North America's greatest explorers died in poverty and obscurity.

Some 30 years later Tyrrell discovered him through his 39 journal manuscripts and 11 books of field notes, astronomical observations and mathematical calculations. Tyrrell found, too, Thompson's most monumental accomplishment, the map that formed the basis of most atlases of the West until well into the 20th century.[b] *R.B.*❦

[a] Geologist Joseph Burr Tyrrell (1858-1957) himself filled in a few blanks on the map during his 17 years of work for the Geological Survey of Canada. In particular he explored the Dubawnt and Thelon rivers to Chesterfield Inlet. He also discovered the dinosaur beds around Drumheller, where the Royal Tyrrell Museum of Palaeontology is named for him.

[b] There are many good books on David Thompson, including: *David Thompson's Narrative of His Explorations in Western America 1784-1812* by J.B. Tyrrell (1916); *David Thompson's Journals Relating to Montana and Adjacent Regions 1808-1812* by Catherine M. White (1950); *David Thompson's Narrative 1784-1812* by Richard Glover (1962); *David Thompson: Fur Trader, Explorer, Geographer* by James K. Smith (1971); as well as a fine children's book by Kerry Wood in the Great Stories of Canada series, *The Map Maker.*

with him. By spring 20 of Clarke's men had starved to death, and Clarke himself was on his way back to Montreal in NWC custody.

Robertson returned in 1818 with nearly 200 men, to greater success. "[Samuel] Black the Nor'Wester is now in his glory leading his bullies," he wrote. "Every evening they come over to our fort in a body, calling on our men to come out and fight pitched battles." But the Baymen won more than their share of the set-tos that followed and gained the confidence of the Indians. Not even Robertson's capture by Black that fall could break the HBC presence. Said Robertson to the Indians at the time: "That fellow was not brave enough to seize me; he stole me and would rob you of your hunt if it were not for the young men I have left in my fort. We will be revenged for this but not like wolves prowling in the bushes. We will capture them as we captured them at Fort William, with the sun shining on our faces."

From his cell at Fort Chipewyan, where he was kept for almost a year, Robertson continued to direct the war against the Nor'Westers. He even devised a secret code based on quotations from Shakespeare, and smuggled out messages in empty rum barrels to the HBC at Cumberland House. One of his dispatches noted that the NWC partners, with a season's worth of Athabasca pelts, were

National Archives of Canada, C-624

Robert Semple

C.W. Jeffreys' depiction of the fight at Seven Oaks. When Red River's Governor Semple burned Fort Gibraltar, the fire smouldering in Metis hearts burst into flame.

returning to Montreal and could be ambushed at Grand Rapids, near the entry of the Saskatchewan River to Lake Winnipeg. The successful ambush demoralized the Montrealers. "Our opponents have lowered their tone," Robertson wrote. "They talk now of conducting their business on amicable principles."

The struggle had proved too much for the Canadians. The Red River settlement formed a stranglehold over their lines of supply. The HBC's penetration of the Athabasca bit into their increasingly meagre returns. They did not have sufficient capital to develop their Pacific trade, sustain the conflict with the Bay and cover their trading losses. What ultimately decided the outcome, however, was that the staid Baymen proved they could also be as dashing, and as ruthless, as their rivals. "The moribund feudalism of the HBC took on the rampaging capitalism of the Nor'Westers and, in the process of winning, transformed itself into the mirror image of the enterprise it was trying to defeat," Newman writes. And the Nor'Westers, for all their bluster, lacked the HBC's great strengths: its access to the sea and its ties to the Bank of England.

The death of two old rivals, Selkirk and Mackenzie, 27 days apart in 1820, settled the matter. On March 26, 1821, the NWC's exhausted partners agreed to amalgamation. Later that year the British parliament granted the new Hudson's Bay Company a trading monopoly over the entirety of British North America west of the Ontario border. Mackenzie's dream of a transcontinental enterprise had come true, but the North West Company had not survived to see it, and the enterprise would run through Hudson Bay, not through Fort William, the Great Lakes and Montreal. Elegized Washington Irving in his account, *Astoria*: "The feudal state of Fort William is at an end; its council chamber is silent and desolate; its banquet hall no longer echoes to the auld-world ditty; the lords of the lakes and forests are all passed away."❦

CHAPTER THREE

Americans and the Metis destroy George Simpson's feudal empire

THIS BIRCHBARK NAPOLEON RAN THE WHOLE WEST WITH AN IRON FIST UNTIL THE METIS TOOK OVER RED RIVER AND THE MAN HE OSTRACIZED FOR DALLYING WITH HIS WIFE BECAME THE HARBINGER OF A NEW ERA

For George Simpson, the passing of the North West Company could not have come at a more opportune time. The illegitimate son of a Calvinist minister, he had so impressed the HBC's governing committee that it posted him straight from London to the Athabasca in 1820 as the company's acting governor of Rupert's Land, a seeming lamb among wolves. But George Simpson was no lamb.

The Nor'Westers scoffed at the short, humourless "gentleman from London" who appeared at Fort Wedderburn, opposite their Fort Chipewyan post, as successor to the fiery Robertson. Simpson wasted no time, however, in besting what he himself described as the "band of unprincipled, lawless marauders" he was up against. With boyish enthusiasm he captured Simon McGillivray, son of the NWC's chief executive officer; he stared down the bully Samuel Black; and he stole away most of the Athabasca trade from his veteran rivals. When word came from London that the two companies had agreed to merge, Simpson complained that the Nor'Westers could have been beaten in the field.

Still, as heir to the two companies' combined operations, he knew it would take diplomacy, not truculence, to mesh together men driven apart by a decade of open warfare. In the summer of 1821 he gathered the triumphant traders of the Hudson's Bay Company and the vanquished wintering partners of the now-defunct NWC in an edgy meeting at York Factory. "The two groups eyed each other with deep suspicion, the gaunt cast of their weather-ravaged faces and their self-conscious gestures reflecting the tensions of

Glenbow Archives, NA-841-164

The HBC's 'little emperor,' George Simpson. An iron-willed capitalist in an age of iron-willed capitalism, he closed forts, slashed wages, decimated the workforce and cut the exchange rate for Indian fur. Profits soared.

Hudson's Bay Company Archives, Provincial Archives of Manitoba

HBC York Boats at Norway House, *an HBC 1930 calendar illustration by Walter J. Phillips. The savvy diplomat Simpson summoned the defeated NWC partners to meet the victors at York Factory. The result was garrulous mutual admiration.*

the occasion," writes Peter Newman in *Empire of the Bay*. But Simpson's carefully choreographed feast developed into a "garrulous mutual admiration society." By dawn "both groups were swearing allegiance to one another — and to Simpson, their newly acknowledged leader."[1]

The 1820s found the HBC at the pinnacle of its power, and Simpson, modelling himself after Napoleon Bonaparte whose portrait adorned his offices, presided over its sprawling operations with lordly hauteur. A tireless dynamo, he engaged in furiously paced annual inspection forays that made him the master of every detail of the trade. He would push his canoe crews 16 hours a day in the hope of catching some poor factor ill-prepared for his visit. Accompanied by a bagpiper to announce his arrival at each post and bedecked in a beaver topper, he looked every inch the birchbark Napoleon. Behind the pomp, he brought a ruthless, almost inhuman devotion to his work.

The HBC's "little emperor" quickly reorganized the trade. He pruned the inherited network of 97 NWC and 76 HBC posts. He cut the company's workforce of almost 2,000 to 800, and slashed by 50% the wages of those who remained. He forbade the sale of liquor to Indians. He introduced quotas to conserve the over-trapped beaver population. Within a decade the once wild and brawling business was being run with the same cold and single-minded attention to the bottom line that had started it more than 150 years before.

Even the brigades of voyageurs and fur-laden north canoes fell to Simpson's cost-cutting. With Fort William abandoned, the entire geography of the business was re-arranged. From York Factory on Hudson Bay bulky fleets of York boats and Red River carts plied the rivers and portages. Edmonton House on the North Saskatchewan became an important regional centre. Packhorses connected the posts in what is now Alberta with those beyond the Rockies.

Such streamlining brought quick and impressive results. By the late 1820s the company was reporting annual profits of £60,000 a year on sales of £300,000, and was once again paying out 25% dividends after a century of meagre returns. But the little emperor's style could anger his peers. "The North West," lamented former NWC clerk Willard Wentzel, "is beginning to be ruled with an iron hand." Some historians still grumble about Simpson's single-minded parsimony. As Alan Cooke, former head of Montreal's Hochelaga Research Institute, says in Newman's *Caesars of the Wilderness*: "He existed only as a man of business. More than any Indian, he was a slave — a willing slave — of the exploitive machinery of 19th century mercantile capitalism. Although he achieved power, prestige and wealth, his only satisfaction came from work, and his only pleasure was in incessant, rapid travel."

For the Indians, especially those in the woodlands, where the HBC's rule was strongest, Simpson's tenure laid the roots of future dependence. Through his scornful attitude towards the Indian women he took as mistresses and the children they bore him — his "little bits of brown" — the HBC governor broke down the respected fur trade practice of taking a "country wife." In his opinion the Indians were "cunning, covetous to an extreme, false and cowardly," and had grown fat and lazy off the bounty of competition. The Chipewyan character in particular, he wrote, "is disgraceful to human nature." Simpson's solution: "However repugnant it may be to our feelings, I am convinced they must be ruled with a rod of iron to bring and keep them in a proper state of subordination, and the most certain way to effect this is by letting them feel their dependence on us."

The Indians remained indispensable partners in the fur trade, and its principal labour force. But Simpson ended the gift-giving that preceded trading, slashed credit and substituted poorer-quality

I To help ensure good relations with the Metis, Simpson even appointed old enemy Cuthbert Grant, who had led the fight at Seven Oaks, to the council that helped govern Assiniboia. The new "Warden of the Plains," wrote Simpson, was "a generous Warm-Hearted Man who would not have been guilty of the Crimes laid to his charge had he not been driven into them by designing men." But Grant's position and his £200 annual salary were "a sinecure afforded him entirely from political motives and not from any feeling of liberality or partiality," Simpson added. Grant's ensuing loyalty to the HBC, and his influence over his countrymen, would keep Metis nationalism in check for about 20 years.

Trading with the Plains Cree at Fort Pitt, 1884. The Indians (from left) are Four Sky Thunder, King Bird, Matoose (seated), Napasis and Big Bear. The trader holding a pelt is Angus McKay, flanked by Metis and white onlookers.

Glenbow Archives, NA-1323-4

Glenbow Archives, NA-1408-4

Fort Edmonton, looking west from the river flats in 1871. In the foreground, the two main vehicles of western travel: the York boat and the Red River cart.

The hard-boiled autocrat of fur trade Edmonton

His portage plan created a city but John Rowand was little loved and his death is a grisly story

Atop the North Saskatchewan River's 150-foot ramparts stood Fort Edmonton, on what would later become the lawns of the Legislature. It was a hub of activity. HBC recruits bound for beyond the mountains and veteran traders heading east on leave passed through. Boats from York Factory on Hudson Bay arrived with goods to be repacked and transported over the 80-mile portage to Fort Assiniboine on the Athabasca. It was also a food depot where buffalo meat was pounded into pemmican, where barley, oats and hundreds of bushels of potatoes were harvested and stored.

Indians came to trade, exchanging friendly gun salutes and marching in procession through the fort's wide gate to the 30- by 80-foot, three-storey "Big House" with its genuine glass windows and a gallery running the building's length. Here, in the largest building west of York Factory, they met the most notable Edmontonian of the time — chief factor John Rowand, known to the Indians as "Big Mountain."

Rowand was Canadian-born, the son of a Montreal surgeon who had emigrated from Ireland. He became an apprentice clerk with the North West Company. In 1810 he suffered a fall from a horse while hunting. When he was missed at the fort, a Metis girl went looking for him, brought him in and nursed him back to health. The accident left him permanently lame; when he used to walk around the stockade of the fort, his lame foot striking the boards earned him the derisive nickname "One-pound-one." But he married his rescuer, who became and remained the first lady of Edmonton.

Although he was not tall, Rowand was exceedingly powerful, with a rough and determined aspect that won him his Indian nickname. If a man isn't dead from an illness in three days, he used to say, then he isn't sick. He took over Fort Edmonton in 1823, and advanced the portage scheme that made it great in the fur trade and thereby positioned it to eventually become the capital of Alberta.

Eastbound trade from beyond the Rockies used Athabasca Pass, which led from the Columbia to the Athabasca River, upstream from Jasper House. It descended the relatively tranquil Athabasca to a point immediately north of Edmonton. Thereafter the Athabasca becomes a raging nightmare all the way down to Fort McMurray at the mouth of the Clearwater. By a circuitous route,[a] the traffic eventually reached Cumberland House on the lower Saskatchewan, which via Lake Winnipeg took it to Hudson Bay.

Build a fort on the Athabasca due north of Edmonton, Rowand urged HBC governor George Simpson. Then cart the goods over the 80-mile portage to Edmonton, and directly down the almost rapidless North Saskatchewan.[b] It would be cheaper and faster, and bypass the "death run" on the Athabasca.

Simpson bought the plan and Fort Assiniboine was opened on the Athabasca in 1824. The new route made Fort Edmonton the centre of the fur trade on the western Prairies. Under Rowand's iron hand its expenses fell and its profits rose. He became chief factor of the company's Saskatchewan District.

He defended his domain fiercely and cleverly. When Americans from the Missouri came north to compete for the Indian trade, Rowand dispatched men to live with the Peigan and head them off. It was no easy job. "The Peigans are the worst of all the tribes to please, expecting a great many things for nothing," Rowand wrote. "They are all chiefs who must be dressed as such, gratis of course. If not, off they go to the Americans."

Equally distasteful to Rowand were the growing numbers of missionaries. In 1843 he observ-ed: "The worst thing for the trade is these ministers and priests — the natives will never work half so well now — they like praying and singing." By mid-century, however, Rowand realized that the halcyon days of the fur trade were ending and that his life, inextricably bound to the trade, was also nearing its conclusion.

Glenbow Archives, NA-1747-1

John Rowand, Edmonton factor, in about 1847. 'Big Mountain' to the Indians, he was a hard taskmaster who detested missionaries.

That end came in the spring of 1854 at Fort Pitt, down river just inside the modern boundary of Saskatchewan, where his son, John, was factor. In a characteristic rage, Rowand was trying to break up a quarrel between two Metis boatmen when he dropped dead of a heart attack at about the age of 67. He was buried at the fort. "The old race of officers," wrote Simpson, "is extinct."

But the story doesn't end there. Rowand had asked to be buried with his kin in Montreal. At Simpson's orders, his body was disinterred, the flesh boiled off his bones (it was said that the fat was used by the Indian women at the fort to make soap), and his remains stowed in a keg, filled with rum as a preservative.

From Fort Pitt the strange cargo went by canoe to York Factory and by ship to London, where the company arranged an elaborate funeral service. Then, after being lost for a time in a Liverpool warehouse, the keg was forwarded to Montreal. On November 10, 1858, Rowand's bones were finally buried beneath a granite monument at Montreal's Mount Royal Cemetery. As for the keg, when pried open, it was discovered to be full not of rum but of water. *R.B.*❦

City of Edmonton Archives, EA-128-6

The fort's 'Big House,' also taken about 1847 by photographer Charles Horetsky. Rowand made Edmonton the capital of the North West.

[a] The rapids of the Athabasca, between the town of that name and Fort McMurray, have claimed countless lives ever since. From McMurray, the traders went upstream to Methy Portage, across to the headwaters of the Churchill and downstream to tiny Frog Portage in what would become northeast Saskatchewan. This took them across to the head of the Sturgeon-Weir, which flows south to join the Saskatchewan near Cumberland House.

[b] There were only two sets of rapids on the North Saskatchewan downstream from Fort Edmonton — the Dalles, below Prince Albert, site of an abandoned Saskatchewan power project, and the Squaw Rapids, which were flooded by a power dam. At the foot of the main Saskatchewan before it flows into Lake Winnipeg there were five, all subsequently "drowned" by the Grand Rapids Dam: the Flying Post, the Demie-charge, the Cross Lake, the Redrock and the Grand. The HBC built a horse-drawn railway around the Grand Rapids.

Collection of Glenbow Archives, 59.35.1

goods to reduce costs. The company also encouraged bands to settle in one place, preferably near a trading post, a practice hastened by the decline of game. Mobility, Simpson understood, formed the basis of independence. Even the role of the plains tribes as providers of pemmican faded in importance; the Metis of Red River, reinforced by the hundreds of fur trade employees laid off after the 1821 merger, competed for their role as company provisioners. Only the solicitude of the London committee members and of individual factors saved the tribes from the full extent of Simpson's disdain.[2] Throughout the North West the company reluctantly began to assume a paternalistic responsibility for the Indians' basic welfare.

By 1841, when Simpson embarked on a one-year, round-the-world tour (typically conducted at such a frenetic pace it was said to have inspired Jules Verne's novel *Around the World in 80 Days*), the little emperor had earned international stature. In 1838 the British government had renewed the company's monopoly for another 21 years. Simpson was knighted for his work in civilizing the frontier. The HBC, with its business secure and pocketbooks bulging, seemed ready to rule the North West in perpetuity.

Dickering with the Factor, *an oil painting by Frank Schoonover about 1912. When the HBC monopoly returned in 1821, the Indians lost.*

But a hostile world pressed relentlessly on the doors of Simpson's semi-feudal domain. "It is astonishing to see the ruined depart annually but still like the Hydra heads another succeeds," wrote one HBC officer of the competitors who steadily pushed past the borders of Rupert's Land. And the second half of Simpson's reign would be consumed in the ultimately futile task of holding back history; the industrial revolution and the rise of representative government were making the fur trade empire an indefensible anachronism.

Simpson's ruthlessness and his knack for diplomacy — and the HBC's pull with the British government — bested the first brute challenges to HBC rule. In the Oregon territory his scorched earth policy of trapping out the forests had delayed the advance of American competitors. But the United States, gripped with expansionist fever, coveted the HBC's Oregon and Pacific coast possessions.

The election of James K. Polk as president in 1844 brought matters to a head. Polk, who had won with his populist "54-40 or Fight" platform,[3] wanted the entire Pacific coast north of the Columbia to Alaska, and threatened war to get it. Only the solid HBC presence west of the Rockies allowed Britain to settle on the 49th parallel as the compromise boundary. A similar conflict with Russian fur traders, pushing south from Alaska, was also resolved just short of war.

The most difficult test, however, came in Red River. The settlement had grown from a population of 300 in 1818 to almost 5,000 by 1840. Alongside the buffalo hunt, agriculture had become a mainstay of its economy. But as the Nor'Westers had realized, the fur trade and agriculture were fundamentally incompatible activities. Both the Metis and white settlers chafed under the company's autocratic rule. They had no shortage of grievances. The struggling settlement had to buy almost all its provisions from the company, which inflated prices to guarantee itself a steady 50% profit. The company was the sole buyer of its furs and agricultural produce. Simpson's contempt for the place made things worse. The settlers, he grumbled, "are a distinct sort of beings, somewhere between the half-Indians and overgrown children. At times they need caressing and not infrequently the discipline of the birch."

Glenbow Archives, NA-1847-5

York boat under sail on the Hayes River in the 1880s.

For a time Simpson's assiduous policy of buying the loyalties of independent Metis traders, and threatening those who refused to play along, kept fur smuggling in check. But in 1843, when Canadian-born trader Norman Kittson established his American Fur Company post at Pembina, on the U.S. side of the border just 70 miles from Red River, the policy unravelled. Supplied from St. Paul on the Mississippi, the Americans offered better goods, higher prices for fur and whisky in abundance. Soon regular trains of squeaking Red River carts, carrying everything from American-made tea kettles to binder twine, were trekking north into Rupert's Land.

Since 1670 the HBC had relied on cheap transportation through Hudson Bay to subdue its Canadian competitors. Now the economic underpinning of its business was being undermined. The new American network of steam-powered riverboats and railway locomotives could move freight in and out of Red River far cheaper than could the HBC's lumbering brigades of York boats.

Furthermore, the U.S. railways were bringing in a flood of settlers to American territory. By 1858 the new state of Minnesota, south of Selkirk's old land grant, had a population of 150,000. The boisterous, entrepreneurial spirit that fuelled American expansion found a receptive audience at Red River, too, where the independent-minded Metis began to challenge the HBC's bureaucratic shackles. "The illicit traders," writes Michael Bliss in *Northern Enterprise*, "openly called for an end to the Company's privileges, labelling it a greedy, oppressive despotism."

In 1846 Simpson moved a battalion of British soldiers into Fort Garry to cow the smugglers, but that only further tarnished the company's image and increased Kittson's business. (The soldiers developed a taste for U.S. whisky and were sent home the following year.) In 1849, with "Kittson fever" raging unchecked, the company put three Metis smugglers on trial for illegal trading. That, too, backfired disastrously. Some 300 Metis buffalo hunters turned out for a boisterous protest at St. Boniface Cathedral, the most militant of them vowing to shoot the judge in his pew. Shooting proved unnecessary when a sympathetic jury found the three men guilty but recommended there be no penalty. The mob of armed Metis stormed joyfully from the courtroom.

The crowd on that occasion was assembled by the fiercely nationalist Committee of the New Nation and led by a prominent Metis miller whose efforts to establish a wool company had been frustrated by the HBC. The experience left a deep impression on his young son, a seminary student in Quebec. The father's name was Jean-Louis Riel. His son was named Louis. "*Vive la liberté!*" they shouted. "*Le commerce est libre!*" No doubt remembering his boyhood ties to the Nor'Westers, Kittson delighted in the humbling of his HBC rivals. "I shall spare no trouble in giving them the Devil," he declared.

[2] During the smallpox epidemic of 1837, for example, the Woods Cree were largely spared when William Todd, the HBC factor at Fort Pelly, distributed smallpox vaccine sent from London, and personally encouraged other factors to vaccinate the Indians near their posts. Elsewhere in the HBC's empire, and in the United States, the disease raged unchecked.

[3] Britain and the United States had long disputed the ownership of what was called the Oregon Country — in effect, the northwest quarter of the continent. The Treaty of Joint Occupation (1818) provided access by fur traders of both nations. By 1840, however, the issue had become the fur trade (largely the HBC, which was bigger and richer than its U.S. rivals) versus settlers (American). Very vocal U.S. patriots argued, moreover, that the Oregon was (or should be) all American right up to latitude 54° 40', the southern extremity of the Russian-American Company's lands near the bottom of the present Alaska panhandle.

Glenbow Archives, NA-1269-2

Upper Fort Garry in 1869, now the site of Winnipeg. By the time Riel led his Manitoba rebellion, the fur trade had passed its zenith, and the eastern prairie was drawing settlers.

The success of the free-trade movement had far-reaching implications for the HBC. The fur trade was already in steady decline, a victim of changing fashion in Europe. The ideas of the free traders were radiating outward from Red River to the most isolated Rupert's Land posts. At a mission station 200 miles from Norway House, wrote the embittered Simpson, the Indians "are receiving an education which, without improving their moral condition or rectifying the more vicious traits of the savage character, has enlightened them rapidly on the subject of free trade." Now even the company's charter was "virtually nullified," he lamented, "set at nought by the Americans and their half-breed allies." Any further attempt to enforce it, Simpson understood, would have provoked open rebellion. With its chartered rights effectively lost, the HBC was left dependent on competence alone.

The embattled Baymen, despite their singular knowledge of the North West, their pool of skilled servants, and their access to large amounts of capital, proved unequal to the task. Attempts to diversify into mining, agriculture and transportation failed, largely because of the company's deep antipathy to settlement. Simpson, health waning and spirit dimmed by the death of his wife, deferred to the inevitable. In 1858 the HBC began to ship goods for the fur trade through New York, Chicago and St. Paul to Fort Garry, abandoning Hudson Bay for all but the supply of the isolated posts there. Then, with Kittson as a partner, the company introduced the first steamship service between Fort Garry and St. Paul. Simpson retired in 1859 and died in Montreal the following year.

The turn of events delighted Alexander Kennedy Isbister. Born at Cumberland House in Saskatchewan to an HBC clerk and a Cree mother, Isbister moved to England at 21 after the company's aversion to Metis employees thwarted his ambitions. He campaigned for self-government at Red River through an organization called the Aborigines Protection Society, inflaming British opinion against the HBC's treatment of the Indians and Metis. His criticism of the company's failure to promote settlement, and to adequately defend itself against American encroachment on its territories, renewed interest not just in England but in the increasingly independent British North American colony that appeared on the map as "Canada."

With Confederation looming, Isbister-inspired newspaper editors in Ontario began to promote the North West as a fertile frontier ripe for development and to eulogize the days when the Nor'Westers carried the region's riches east. Industrialists hatched plans to save the struggling Grand Trunk Railway by extending it across the top of North America to the Pacific. The greater threat of U.S. annexation of Rupert's Land acutely worried the politicians. All that was left for Simpson's successors was to negotiate a price. On November 19, 1869, an agreement was reached with the Canadian government. In return for extinguishing its monopoly rights, the HBC was given £300,000, continued possession of its 120 posts, and an outright grant of 5% of its old empire, some seven million acres in all.

Neither the Indians nor the Metis of Rupert's Land were so much as notified of the agreement. This disdain for the opinion of the governed bewildered Cree Indian Chief Sweetgrass, who delivered a document voicing his disapproval to the HBC factor at Fort Edmonton. "We heard our lands were sold, and we did not like it," went his angry proclamation. "We do not want to sell our lands;

it is our property and no one has a right to sell them."

At Red River the reaction was far more drastic. Led by Quebec-educated Louis Riel, whose arguments for self-government echoed throughout the region, the Metis seized Fort Garry and proclaimed a provisional government. His armed followers turned back at the U.S. border the would-be Canadian governor William McDougall, as he arrived to take over the colony. The alarmed government of newly confederated Canada sent out proposals to resolve the rebellion. While these were being considered, however, Riel ordered the execution of the headstrong Ontarian Thomas Scott, who had challenged the legitimacy of Riel's government by defying it. (Riel himself would ultimately suffer the same fate, but only after leading another and much more violent rebellion farther west 16 years later.) Canada sent troops to take over the colony, the Metis fled, and in 1870 Manitoba became a province, albeit on a distinctly unequal basis.

Provincial Archives of Alberta, E. Brown Collection, B-2862

Traders from Edmonton make a deal for northern Alberta furs, at about the turn of the century.

Meanwhile, far from Red River in distant Labrador, a story had unfolded that would play a key role in the next chapter of the West's history. After his marriage to his youthful cousin, Frances, Simpson had taken her on a regal tour of the HBC's empire in the West.[4] Then he left her very much to her own devices at Montreal as he pursued his relentless annual journeys across the continent.

Here Frances, 20 years her husband's junior, became captivated with a young Scottish clerk at the HBC's Montreal office. How far this relationship went is entirely speculative. There were evenings together and walks along the shores of Lake St. Louis, however, enough to cause an apoplectic Simpson, when he returned unexpectedly and discovered it, to dispatch the young man to the Tadoussac and later the Labrador department. It was effectively a sentence to Siberia.

But the young man had great talent. He converted both departments into high profit centres, met and married the mixed-blood daughter of an HBC trader,[5] and worked out an ingenious investment scheme for his fellow factors. They habitually saved about £750 a year and invested it at a 2% return. He could get them 3%, he said. Then, working with his cousin, who was in the textile business at Montreal, he invested it at rates up to 16%, giving his colleagues their three and keeping the rest.

Thus, after 28 years, with his old nemesis Simpson now dead, he returned to Montreal in 1869 a rich man. He worked with his cousin to take over and revive an ailing bank, and bought so deeply into the HBC that he became in effect its chief officer in Canada. In this role the government of John A. Macdonald sent him west to resolve the Riel insurrection.

In February 1870, having done so, he was dog-sledding south through a blizzard, making his way to St. Paul and the railhead en route back to Ottawa. Through the sweeping snow, he saw another lone team coming north, the driver plainly having lost his way. The two men met, camped together and established a friendship that would last for the rest of their lives. Furthermore, during that long evening over a sheltered campfire, the blizzard howling around them, they developed a scheme that would eventually change, more even than the HBC had, the course of the West's history.

The young man who had once dallied with Frances Simpson was Donald Alexander Smith, later Lord Strathcona. His cousin was the Montreal financier George Stephen. The faltering bank they took over was the Bank of Montreal. The other dog-sledder was the great American railway builder James Jerome Hill, and the business enterprise they conceived over that campfire would soon become known to the world as the Canadian Pacific Railway.❦

[4] In 1830, as the governor's canoes finished traversing the length of Rainy Lake where it pours into the Rainy River, Mrs. Simpson became enchanted by the delightful setting of the HBC fort there. The chief factor renamed it for her, obviously to please Simpson. Thus Fort Frances, Ontario.

[5] Donald Smith's marriage, like so much else he did, had storybook qualities. At Tadoussac he fell deeply in love with Isabella Sophia Hardisty, a member of the mixed-blood family that played a large part in the HBC's affairs in Canada. She was already married and had been deserted when he met her. Smith was captivated by her for his whole life. She died at age 89 in Montreal, November 13, 1913. He, apparently in good health up to then, followed her two months later, on January 21, 1914, at 93. Her niece, Belle Hardisty, married the lawyer James Lougheed at Calgary.

A CPR 4-4-0 steam locomotive, number 54, in Medicine Hat in 1896.
Glenbow Archives, NA-9679-14

Section Four
The Railwaymen

Chapters by Ted Byfield
Sidebars by Brad Clark, Gregg Shilliday, Ted Byfield and George Koch

Glenbow Archives, AN-61-32-44

Weary Passengers Settling in for the Night, *artist unknown. After 1885, the West was suddenly safe and accessible. The luxury fare from Toronto to Vancouver was $18.50; the day-coach price was less.*

Vision, greed, sweat, tears and gut build the Canadian Pacific

It chose and named our towns and peopled our Prairies; but at the 'Big Hill' and at countless other horrors, builders and railroaders would pay with their lives

Donald A. Smith was one of the key transitional figures in western Canadian history, bridging two eras. He was the last great fur trader of the Hudson's Bay Company and one of the first giants of the railway era. He is the white-bearded figure in the famous photograph, driving the last spike of the Canadian Pacific main line. But the other dog-sledder Smith chanced to meet by the Red River in the blizzard that February day in 1870 (an encounter described in the last chapter) is largely unknown to Canadians, although he was born one.

James Jerome Hill, the son of Scottish immigrants, grew up near Guelph, Ontario, and moved as a young man to St. Paul, Minnesota. At 31, when he met Smith in the blizzard, he had already made a modest fortune in grocery wholesaling and general warehousing, and was heading north to investigate the feasibility of ferrying freight into the Red River colony. Minnesota had become the 32nd state in the union 12 years earlier, and its newly constructed railway connections to Chicago would easily enable it to replace frigid, inaccessible Hudson Bay as the quickest, cheapest route into the Canadian West.

Hill was a slight, wiry, one-eyed man (he had lost an eye in childhood) who possessed remarkable foresight and extraordinary energy. He was long on determination and short on patience. He needed no more than one trip to Winnipeg to persuade him that great profit would accrue from a steamboat service down the Red River from Fargo into Canada. To that end he immediately set about financing and building the sternwheeler *Selkirk* and plunged into a pricing war with Smith's HBC riverboat, the *International*. He even bribed a U.S. customs officer at one stage to block the HBC vessel at the border because it wasn't American. (Neither at this point was Hill, of course.)

This warfare ended abruptly, however, when Hill and a Minnesota associate, a fellow Canadian expatriate named Norman Kittson, formed the Red River Transportation Company with Smith as a silent partner. By ruthless price-slashing they drove all competitors off the river, then raised freight rates so astronomically that they made $75,000 in a single month, and Winnipeggers howled in protest. It was a protest that would be heard loud and often throughout the West in the decades to come, when Smith, Hill and Smith's Montreal cousin, George Stephen, would expand these riverboat beginnings into the railway that opened western Canada.[1]

Glenbow Archives, NA-1375-3

Sir Donald A. Smith, Lord Strathcona, in 1894. Always the silent partner, because the prime minister detested him, he was a key transitional figure between the old fur trade and the new era of rail.

Ironically, the syndicate that was to create the Canadian Pacific began with an American railroad enterprise. Hill, Kittson, Smith and Stephen recognized in the tottering St. Paul & Pacific the chance to produce bonanza profits that would dwarf anything earned by the Red River Transportation Company. The SP&P was intended to connect St. Paul to Emerson at the Canadian border. Manitoba's rich black soil held the promise of world-class wheat production and therefore of immense freight traffic. Furthermore, the SP&P would qualify for massive land grants promised by Minnesota if it was soon finished. But it had gone broke, and stopped abruptly in mid-prairie.

How the quartet hoodwinked the SP&P's Dutch investors into parting with their bonds at virtually give-away prices (the bonds mortgaged the company's then worthless common stock) is amusingly told by Vancouver's David Cruise and Alison Griffiths in their history of the CPR, *Lords of the Line*. At one point the crafty Stephen crossed the Atlantic ostensibly to find British financing for the take-over. He reported failure, thus persuading the bondholders their investment was valueless, although actually the British banks were prepared to take on the deal. Stephen and Smith quietly financed the SP&P acquisition through their Bank of Montreal instead. Then they completed the line to the border where it could connect with the Pembina Branch, an Ottawa-financed track down from Winnipeg. The exorbitant freight rates they charged over the ensuing decade earned them great profits and great animosity in Manitoba.

This financial success nevertheless made them prime contenders to build the Canadian railway to the Pacific. Ottawa's promise to construct it within 10 years had lured British Columbia into the Canadian Confederation in 1871, yet by 1878 the project was barely started and going nowhere. To the Macdonald government the SP&P group seemed the best bet to take it over, but there was a problem: Donald A. Smith, whom Prime Minister Macdonald had come to cordially loathe.

Macdonald had good reason. After he ushered British Columbia into Confederation back in 1871, the "Pacific Railway" was his government's most urgent priority. The great surveyor and engineer Sandford Fleming had already plotted the Yellowhead Pass route through Edmonton, and a hypothetical rail line lay across the map of the West. The contract to build it had been awarded to the Montreal shipping magnate Hugh Allan. In 1872 the Macdonald Tory government was returned, and Allan was ready to begin work. Then suddenly disaster struck.

The Liberals, by bribing one of Allan's secretaries, secured irrefutable evidence that Allan gained the Pacific Railway contract by paying large sums to Macdonald to finance the Tory campaign of '72. Fury swept the country over the "Pacific Scandal." The Commons erupted in turmoil;

[1] Norman Kittson (1814-1885) played a crucial role in helping to convince George Stephen that transforming the St. Paul & Pacific Railway into the St. Paul, Minneapolis & Manitoba was a sound idea. The Kittsons were a Lower Canada family; Norman's older half-brother William had worked for the North West Company in the Columbia district and had also been head of Kootenae House near Invermere.

a crucial confidence vote was called. Macdonald had every hope of surviving the vote so long as he could hold his Tory caucus together. Donald Smith was then MP for Selkirk in Manitoba and, although an independent, a hitherto unfailing supporter of the government. But without warning he rose in the House and loosed an onslaught upon the administration for corrupting the politics of Canada. This was enough to swing the vote and defeat the government — and also to cast Smith in the role of traitor. It wasn't the "purity of politics" that concerned him, the furious Tories charged; he wanted the Pacific contract for himself.

But Smith, characteristically, said nothing more. He endured the Tory wrath, joined the Liberal benches, then watched and waited as the Grits, under the bumbling leadership of Prime Minister Alexander Mackenzie (no relation to the fur trader) made depressingly fitful progress on the Pacific Railway. Convinced Canada was reneging on the promise, British Columbia threatened secession. With the defeat of the Mackenzie government in 1878, however, Macdonald returned triumphantly with three years left to build the line. But would his resentment of Smith prevent the SP&P group from getting the job?

Stephen, the syndicate's central financier, had been reluctant at first even to consider the project. By 1878 he was 49, very wealthy and preparing to retire to Britain. But the challenge fascinated him. In the end he out-negotiated three other contenders, and on October 21, 1880, signed the contract on behalf of four principals in his syndicate.[2] To make the syndicate palatable to the Tory government (and to Manitoba) the name Donald A. Smith was notably missing, although he was certainly a dominant fifth partner. Stephen had not informed his cousin of the deliberate omission of his name from the public document, and Smith, a man with an eye to history, was devastated. But again he said nothing, and the Canadian Pacific Railway Company was incorporated next day.

By now the central issue was not the undeclared participation of Donald A. Smith but the terms of the contract itself. The government had agreed to reward the company with $25 million

[2] The four named principals of the CPR syndicate were George Stephen, J.J. Hill, John S. Kennedy and Richard Bathgate Angus. Kennedy had supposedly been acting for the SP&P's unfortunate Dutch bondholders, whose interests Stephen had bribed him into betraying in the syndicate's acquisition of the line. Angus was general manager of the Bank of Montreal who, as an aspiring young B of M employee, had helped Smith and Stephen get control of the bank.

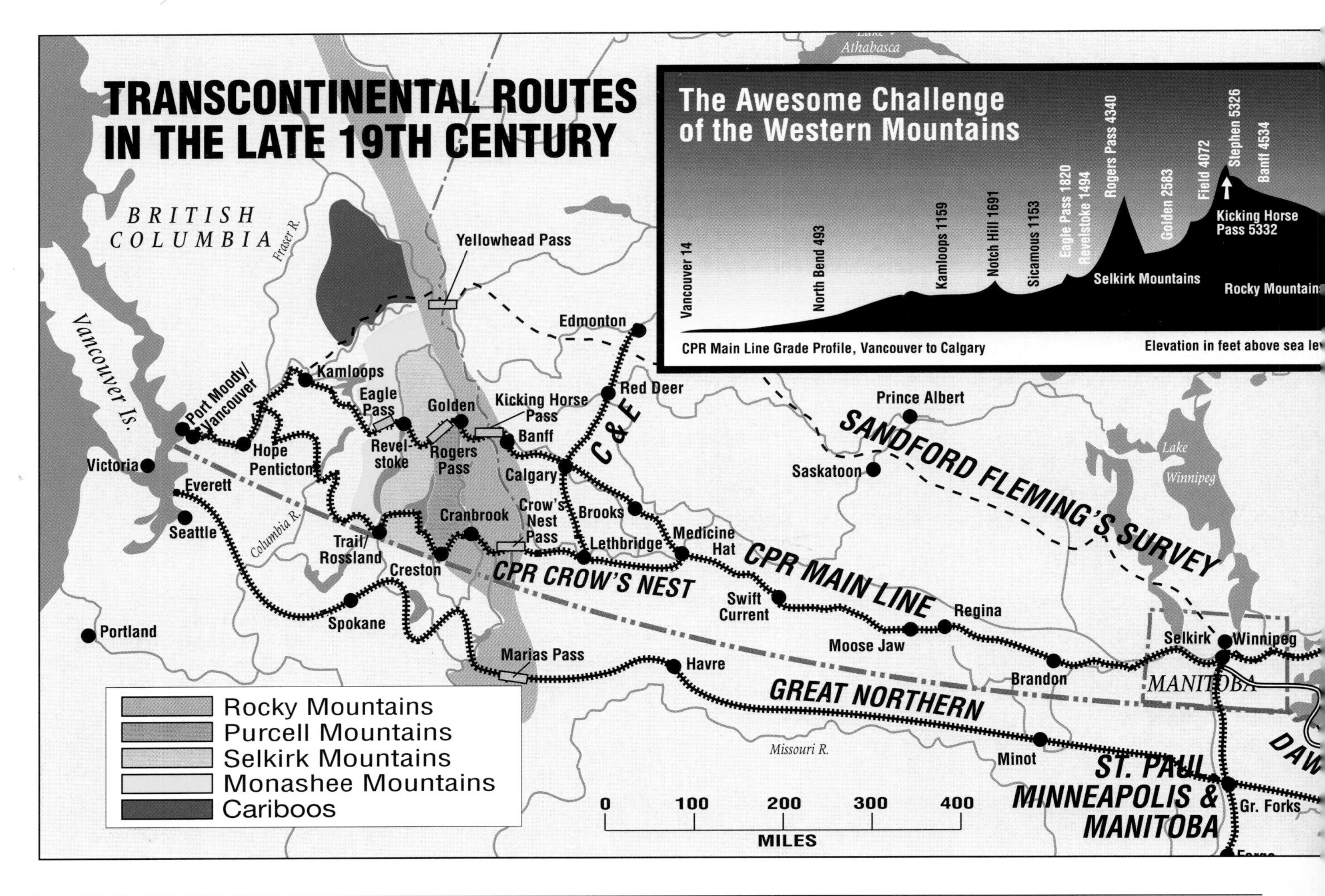

and 25 million acres of prairie land. This was considered over-generous, but bearable. Not bearable was a clause Stephen had bludgeoned the government into accepting: that no railway could operate in western Canada within 15 miles of the American border except the CPR. Western Tory members vehemently protested. The "monopoly clause," they argued, would assure exorbitant freight rates by preventing American roads from competing for Canadian traffic. In the end, however, the western Tories were whipped into line and voted for the contract. They were too few in number to resist the overwhelming caucus majority from Ontario and Quebec. Their capitulation was to have countless sequels in both parties during the years ahead.

Glenbow Archives, NA-1375-4

Financial mastermind Sir George Stephen in 1890. He was knighted in 1886 and raised to the British peerage as 1st Baron Mount Stephen in 1891. Colleague Donald Smith became 1st Baron Strathcona and Mount Royal in 1897.

Frank Oliver's *Edmonton Bulletin* foresaw grave consequences. "Unfair to the settlers in every point though the contract is," the newspaper declared, "all the power of a wealthy company, and all the strength of a political party, and all the self-interest of their myriads of hirelings will be united in its support. But every settler in the North West is, and every man who comes into the territory to make his living by his own endeavour will become the natural enemy of each and every one who is connected with it; and the time will come when not all the wealth, nor all the influence, nor all the meanness that these three powers can bring to bear will keep this bargain — procured by corruption and founded on injustice — by fair means or foul, by ballot or bullet."

The CPR in its formative years proved to be no gold mine for the syndicate, however, and taxed all the genius of George Stephen to keep it alive. Stephen had estimated the cost of building the line at $45 million. Hill, whose experience of railroad construction far exceeded Stephen's, warned repeatedly that the estimate was absurdly low. Engineer Fleming, who had far more experience than either of them, set the price at a staggering $100 million. Fleming was to prove bang-on.

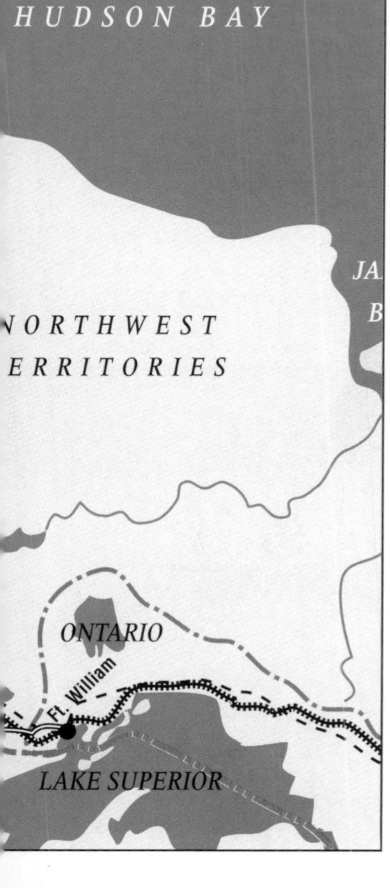

He alone fully appreciated the daunting construction challenges posed by the project. It must pick its way through the dense forest and Precambrian granite of northern Ontario, skirting the bleak, precipitous shore of Lake Superior. It must then cross the 1,000-mile expanse of trackless prairie. Finally it must find its way through the western mountains to the Fraser River and follow that cavernous cataract to Port Moody, on Burrard Inlet near Vancouver.

Making things much worse for Stephen, an influential London magazine, *Truth*, scuttled his initial attempt to raise capital in London in 1881 with a much-reprinted article depicting life on the Canadian Prairies: "The people who have gone there cannot stand the coldness of the winters. Men and cattle are frozen to death in numbers that would rather startle the intending settler if he knew, and those who are not killed outright are often maimed for life by frostbites. Its street nuisances kill people with malaria, or drive them mad with plagues of insects, and to keep themselves alive during the long winter they have to imitate the habits of the Esquimaux...The Canadian Pacific Railway has yet five and twenty million acres to sell, and it is through a death dealing region of this kind that the new railway is to run."[3]

In addition, Stephen's countering endeavours to get "positive" coverage of the CPR in the British press were driven out of the papers by a concurrent fanatic interest in the allegedly dying elephant Jumbo, then touring North America with the Barnum circus. (As it happened, Jumbo did not die just then, and did not die naturally either. He was accidentally killed — by a Grand Trunk locomotive at St. Thomas, Ontario, in 1885.)

Back in Canada, meanwhile, the railroad planners had

[3] Authors Cruise and Griffiths in *Lords of the Line* explain that the anti-CPR article was probably planted by agents of the British-owned Grand Trunk Railway, the main Quebec-Montreal-Toronto-Sarnia rail artery, which had never declared a dividend and which helped sour interest in Canadian land investment for years to come. The GTR, correctly fearing competition in its own area, bitterly opposed the CPR until the GTR was absorbed into the Canadian National nearly 40 years later.

Glenbow Archives, NA-531-5

Building an embankment cribbing below the roadbed in Kicking Horse Pass in 1885. The main problem was the near-cliff down which the river plunged.

divided the project into four sections. One had been partly completed under the old Allan contract. The American railway contractor Andrew Onderdonk had built the line from Yale to Kamloops, hewing it out of the often vertical rock that contained the Fraser and Thompson rivers. The CPR took this over, upgraded it for an estimated $5 million, then haggled for years with the government for compensation. Another section, the difficult route through northern Ontario, was postponed until 1883. The third leg was to complete the run through the mountains. The fourth, the first to get under way, was the transit of the Prairies. A contract was let to the American firm of Langdon & Shepard with orders to rush the line west from Winnipeg.

Rush was the operative word for the entire project. The CPR's contract gave it another 10 full years (implicitly adding seven to the old 10-year commitment made to British Columbia.) But for a number of reasons haste was important. For one, British Columbia had agreed to the extension but was still restive. For another, the sooner the track was laid the sooner it would make money. Finally, Ottawa feared the intrusion of American railways — and with them Americans — northward into western Canada.

But haste (and American intrusion) argued for a shorter southern route across the Prairies. This, as the CPR instantly saw, would mean abandoning Fleming's Yellowhead route in favour of some pass through the Rockies farther south, whatever the consequences for the land speculators who were already buying up lots in Edmonton. But where? Never mind where, the management decided. Just start building due west from Winnipeg, and somebody would find a way.

The "somebody" turned out to be a crony of Hill's, Albert Bowman Rogers, who had won the rank of major as an Indian fighter, and had surveyed the route of the Chicago, Milwaukee & St. Paul across the American Prairies. He spoke like a frontier rube, swore magnificently, spat with great accuracy and chewed tobacco which he carried in the rear pocket of the overalls he constantly wore back to front. All this, as Hill well knew, disguised the fact that Rogers was a Yale University-trained engineer and a surveyor of extraordinary ability.

Driving his men with a zeal some attributed to innate sadism, Rogers surveyed a route from the upper regions of the east-flowing Bow west of Banff to the head of the west-flowing Kicking Horse, which in turn dropped into the Columbia at the mid-point of its long run north to the Big Bend. This transited the Rockies. Yet there were two huge problems. First, immediately below the point where the line would reach the Kicking Horse, that river plunged down what was very nearly a cliff. How were the trains to get down and up such a hill? Second, after the Kicking Horse reached the Columbia, two other imposing mountain ranges, the Selkirks and beyond them the Monashees, must be crossed to reach the line Onderdonk had built as far as Kamloops. The Yellowhead route avoided both these ranges because it lay to the north of them. Rogers knew the more distant Monashees could be easily overcome because Eagle Pass, known since 1865, provided a relatively gentle route through them. But the Selkirks were a very different matter.

Glenbow Archives, NA-1949-1

(Right) the legendary A.B. Rogers. He was not best known for elegance. On the job, his style ran more to tobacco-chewing and startling invective, and he got the job done.

Glenbow Archives, NA-1459-55

The 'dynamo run by dynamite,' William Cornelius Van Horne (standing fourth from left in the foreground behind the tie), pictured here with CPR dignitaries and guests in Rogers Pass, 1894. He burst upon the foundering project in Winnipeg in 1882, and drove it towards completion as mercilessly as he drove himself.

The surveyor Walter Moberly, who spent years examining the Selkirks, thought them impassable for a railway. What would Rogers do about the Selkirks?[4] His answer carried his name into Canadian history and geography. He ascended the Beaver River, which comes into the Columbia from the southwest, 28 miles north of the point where the Kicking Horse joins it from the east. He found a connection, Rogers Pass, between the Beaver and the head of the Illecillewaet, which tumbles down the west slope of the Selkirks into the Columbia, now on the southward section of its Big Bend. The line, he decided, could descend the Columbia, cross it, ascend the Beaver, traverse the pass, then descend the Illecillewaet. It could then cross the Columbia a second time and stand at the eastern approach to the relatively unchallenging Eagle Pass, which would take it through the Monashees.

But again, as with the Kicking Horse, Rogers Pass posed daunting challenges. The pass itself lay nearly 2,000 feet above the Columbia, an elevation the trains would have to scale within 22 miles. On the western approach the situation was not quite as bad. Eastbound trains would have to crawl up nearly 3,000 feet, but would have 45 miles to do it, allowing a slightly better grade. But in the pass itself at the summit there was a far graver difficulty. Snow in the Rogers was unlike anything the railway had encountered anywhere and avalanches were distressingly common in winter. How could all this be overcome? The CPR would spend hundreds of millions of dollars and more than 250 lives would be lost before the answers were found.[5]

How Rogers delivered the news of his discoveries to the CPR's principals is part of CPR lore. He is said to have appeared at Hill's Minneapolis residence roughly clothed and unwashed, just as he was when he left the mountains a week or so before. Hill sent him by private car to Montreal where, still unkempt and filthy, he showed up at the door of Stephen's posh residence. The servants were dumbfounded to hear their master, in the midst of an elegant dinner party, order this ruffian bathed, dressed in formal attire and admitted to the banquet, where he regaled host and guests with the tale of his amazing finds. Rogers is said never to have cashed the $5,000 cheque he received for the job, but framed it instead. He didn't do it for the money, he said.

Meanwhile, everywhere else on the CPR enterprise, where things *were* being done for the money, it began to look as though the stockholders wouldn't make any. But others did. In Winnipeg officials from chief engineer Thomas Rosser down doctored the construction accounts to their own benefit and speculated spectacularly on the side in land because they, before anyone, knew where the line and therefore the towns were going to be. Fortune-seeking passengers clogged the supply lines and, along with bad weather and general inefficiency, impeded the track-laying job.

Hence flatcars loaded with rails jammed the SP&P, now the St. Paul, Minneapolis & Manitoba Railway, and Hill fumed to get them moved. Construction navvies griped, quit or took to stripping

[4] The west-travelling motorist on the Trans-Canada Highway follows the CPR route through the Kicking Horse and descends its valley west from the summit of the Rockies. As he approaches Golden he soon beholds a mountain barrier before him beyond the Columbia, running north to south, just as Rogers would have seen it. This barrier, however, is not the Selkirks but the declining line of another mountain system, the Purcells. These lie between the Selkirks and the Rockies in the southeast corner of British Columbia, and come to an end 28 miles to the north. The CPR did not have to contend with the Purcells. The track surveyors dodged north on the Columbia, then ascended the Beaver River which lies between the Selkirks and the Purcells. Bear Creek (now Connaught), which flows into the Beaver from the Selkirks, led them to Rogers Pass. (See map.)

[5] The question often arises: If transiting the Selkirks caused this much trouble, why would the CPR not have taken the 320-mile detour and followed the Columbia north and then south around the Big Bend? There are three answers: 1. The engineers did not fully appreciate the problems in Rogers Pass until they were already in it and it was too late. 2. Such a detour would have added a full day to the original transcontinental trip. 3. If they were going that far north, they might as well have gone back to the much less challenging Yellowhead whose western access is only 70 miles from the Big Bend.

the plush seats out of passenger coaches so as to sleep more comfortably on the job. By November of 1881 at the end of the first construction season, a mere 130 miles of track had been laid across the whole system.

In England the bond-peddling Stephen, finding investors little interested in the CPR, cursed the jeering newspapers, Jumbo and the Grand Trunk Railway. In Toronto the Grand Trunk was using two paid puppet columnists on the *Globe* to razz the whole CPR idea and discourage investors. The government money was draining away alarmingly, subcontractors began going unpaid, and the work bogged down further. It was about then that a towering figure with an imposing girth, an Edwardian beard, a fat cigar and a loud, confident voice burst into the office of J.J. Hill in St. Paul, threatening to build a railroad that would compete with the SPM&M for Canadian traffic.

Whether by stage, by mule or by ox, travel was arduous

Three-mile trains of bull carts were an important part of pre-railway transport; often stage customers had to push

Before the advent of steam the ox, the mule and the horse powered land transportation on the Prairies, never comfortably for the passengers. The most spectacular early conveyance was the bull train, the chief freighting system for goods coming north from Fort Benton in Montana, at the head of navigation on the Missouri River, to Fort Macleod and then up the trail to Calgary.

The individual unit consisted of six to eight pairs of oxen hitched to three wagons — known as the lead, the swing and the trail — with a little cart hitched on behind to carry the cooking and camping equipment. The load was typically about 15 tons, nine on the lead wagon, four on the swing and two on the trail. The heavily built boxes supported hoops over which canvas was stretched efficiently enough to keep goods dry in almost any weather.

Twenty or more of these three-wagon combinations would move together in a "train" up to three miles long. The oxen that powered them were broken in as four-year-old steers, worked to about the age of eight and then sold for beef. On a good day, they'd cover 10 miles or more. At river crossings the teams were led over first and then the wagons were hauled accross with long chains. On steep hills two or more teams were coupled up. When the ground became marshy the wagons were separated and hauled through one at a time.

North of Calgary, where the soil became too soft for the heavy bull trains, the Red River cart was favoured. Before the coming of steamboats and the railway, it supplied Edmonton over the Carlton Trail, which began at Fort Ellice, proceeded northwest to Fort Carlton (a 30-day trip), then west to Edmonton (another 30-day trip.)[a]

The man was William Cornelius Van Horne, 38, fresh from an impressive string of successful railway reorganizations in the midwestern states. Hill, anxious to divert him from his U.S. line's territory, suggested an even better job for him. Why not take over the faltering CPR in Canada? After an anonymous tour of the CPR project, Van Horne accepted, thus launching the most legendary career in Canadian railroading history.

Van Horne exploded upon the CPR scene at Winnipeg as the season began in 1882. He was, said railroad manager D.B. Hanna, "a dynamo run by dynamite." Within a week, he had fired Rosser and most of the CPR headquarters staff, replacing them with imported Americans whom he knew to be reliable.[6] Property speculation was halted by turning land disposal over to what amounted to a CPR subsidiary, the Canada North-West Land Company. If anyone was going to

[6] The departing chief engineer, Major-General Thomas Lafayette Rosser, a Confederate veteran of the Civil War, is said to have threatened Van Horne with a revolver outside the Manitoba Club, but was restrained before he could use it.

Red River carts consisted of a wooden box mounted on wooden axles between two wooden wheels — none of which was lubricated. This gave them their most memorable quality, an ear-piercing shriek from their axles that echoed across the Prairies. The effect was especially memorable when convoys of 200 or more travelled together.

However deafening, their arrival at a fort occasioned great excitement. Often a dance would be held in celebration. Their cargoes were amazing. They brought staples and luxuries alike: pianos and seed grain, clothing and farm implements, candy and window panes.

A bull train could not replace a Red River cart train, as I.G. Baker and Company had grievous occasion to discover in the spring of 1885. When the Riel Rebellion cut off the Carlton-Edmonton trail, supplies had to be sent in from Calgary. Rising to the emergency, the American company sent its heavy wagons north, carrying 630,000 pounds of provisions. The Baker drivers cursed and groaned as their vehicles bogged down on the sloppy northern trails. They eventually made it, but never tried again.

After the Canadian Pacific arrived in Calgary, a new vehicle appeared, the stagecoach. The coaches were far from the elegant carriages sometimes depicted in American western movies. Generally they were simply large spring wagons in which six people sat under canvas on two benches in the hindmost of three compartments. The centre compartment carried up to a half-ton of freight, and the driver's platform occupied the front third.

Between 1883 and 1885 three stagecoach companies competed for passengers and freight on the Calgary-Edmonton run. For $25 one way, a passenger could leave Calgary with 100 pounds of luggage and expect to arrive at Edmonton in five days, provided all went well. In many cases all did not. He might have to help push a mired wagon out of a mud hole, or find himself and his fellow passengers drifting downstream as the drivers attempted to ford a river.

Provincial Archives of Alberta, A-5414

A bull train at Lethbridge in 1885. North of Calgary the ground was too soft for their loads of 15 tons, and remained the preserve of the shrieking Red River cart.

The drivers, typically bush-smart Metis, also had to deal with sudden climatic phenomena like blizzards and chinooks. In February 1888 a stage from Calgary became lost in fog coming up Nose Creek valley, for instance, and spent an entire night just trying to find the trail. Then a snowfall further obscured the trail; it took two more days to find the nearest stopping house.[b] The stage fought blizzards and drifted trails the rest of the way to Edmonton, in a nine-day trip the *Edmonton Bulletin* described as "rather eventful." That same year a stage got lost in a blizzard between the present towns of Olds and Bowden. The driver walked round and round the vehicle all night to keep from freezing, only to find next morning that he was within shouting distance of the Lone Pine stopping house.

Bandits were one hazard that was almost unknown on the Canadian Prairies, although not entirely. In the summer of 1886, Alberta had its only known stagecoach robbery. Two bandits jumped the coach 15 miles outside Calgary, rifled through the mail and took the passengers' valuables at gunpoint. The pair then mounted and made good their escape, likely heading for the U.S.border.

When the rails reached Edmonton in 1891 and then extended across the province, wagon-freighting became limited chiefly to the as yet unopened north country. In the next century those trails would be used once again, however — as roads for the automobile. *B.C.*❦

[a] Fort Ellice was on the Assiniboine River, five miles downstream from the mouth of the Qu'Appelle, near the present town of St. Lazare, Manitoba. Fort Carlton is on the North Saskatchewan, 50 miles north of Saskatoon.

[b] So few were settlements on the Calgary-Edmonton stagecoach route that stopping houses, inns along the way, were an essential on a trip that could last a week or more. The accommodation they offered was typically spartan in the extreme, but passengers considered a night under a roof — any roof — much preferable to a night in a blizzard.

A Stoney Indian at Morley contemplates a dead navvy's trackside grave. A vanguard of 5,000 men had arrived, and were given to drinking, brawling, quitting and often dying on the job.

make a killing on town lots, Van Horne decided, it would be the company itself.

He would put down 500 miles of track in 1882, he boasted, an objective universally regarded as ridiculous. At first, the scepticism seemed well-founded. Even Van Horne seemed incapable of spurring the job to life. By July 1 the end of track had advanced only 70 miles. Van Horne, undaunted, appeared everywhere and at all times. It was said he could do any job on the road from engine wiper to track jockey to high financier. He would work all day, play poker, drink whisky and smoke cigars all night, then turn out for work at dawn.

He would strip off his clothes and ford rivers ahead of the grading crews, bawl men out mercilessly, fire them on the spot or reward them with uproarious laughter if they foiled his expectations by admitting to some misdemeanour or mistake.[7] He once took a locomotive across a rickety bridge when the nervous train crew refused. Another time, he fell in a river and spent the rest of the day stripped of his jacket and shirt and working in a nightshirt, his ill-concealed pants beneath it ripped up the centre and exposing the Van Hornian underwear. His appetite was awesome. He so despised what he considered the chintzy service of Pullman diners on the American railroads that he personally organized the CPR's own dining and sleeping car service. Even this he felt inadequate for himself and sometimes ordered diner crews to prepare three meals in one for him because otherwise he would go hungry.

By August his herculean efforts began to show results, and by the end of the year he had outperformed his boast, laying 420 miles on the main line, plus 100 miles of feeder lines, plus 28 miles of sidings. The following June 10, 1883, the track-layers had crossed the 110th meridian and reached the South Saskatchewan River. The Canadian Pacific had arrived in the future Alberta, had founded what was to become the city of Medicine Hat, and was moving towards Fort Calgary.

The CPR was the West's first megaproject. What arrived that day at Medicine Hat was the vanguard of about 5,000 men recruited from all over North America. They were given to drinking, brawling, quitting and often dying on the job which, particularly in the mountain regions, was very dangerous indeed. The North-West Mounted Police constantly monitored the construction camps, half-heartedly enforcing a rule against the sale of liquor on the job sites. That is, you could drink it, but not sell it. This rule was routinely ignored and bootleggers were everywhere.

But the process of prairie railroad construction was fast, and as much as six miles of track could be completed in a single day. An article in the *Edmonton Bulletin* of September 1, 1883, described in detail what happened after the surveyors and graders had done their part. A locomotive pushes loaded flatcars to the end of track, it explained, dropping telegraph poles as it goes, and depositing ties and rails when it stops. Horse or mule teams lug the ties forward, dropping them along the

Glenbow Archives, NA-782-11

Blasting a roadbed through the mountain section in 1884-85. Stephen's original CPR cost projection of $45 million proved low by more than half, mainly because of the mountains.

[7] More CPR lore. The navvies who had taken to borrowing passenger car seats as beds were handed a telegram in the middle of the night. It read: "Put back those seats — Van Horne." Seeming as it did like a voice from God, they hastened to comply.

In elegant splendour you could now behold a spectacular wilderness

Van Horne was first to realize that the vast and boundless mountains held vast and boundless tourist dollars

CPR President William Van Horne, whose own epicurean tastes were matched by an appetite that sometimes required three meals in one to be prepared for him, early realized the potential of the West, especially the Rockies, to attract first-class world travellers.

"May I not tempt you, kind reader," said a CPR advertisement possibly written by Van Horne himself, "to leave England for a few short weeks and journey with me across that broad land of mighty rivers, vast forests, boundless plains, stupendous mountains and wonders innumerable. You shall see all in comfort, nay, luxury."

Van Horne rejected as over-rated, over-priced and tacky the sleeping and dining car equipment that George Mortimer Pullman's company leased to American lines. The CPR should design its own bigger and better equipment, he decreed, to provide an unparalleled elegance across the continent. And dining car fare must be worthy too.

Hence a menu from an 1890 train travelling through Medicine Hat offered at 75 cents croquette of veal, roast beef or salmon in hollandaise sauce, various vegetables, champagnes and clarets, and a selection of fruit or a plate of Stilton cheese. Menus featured local specialities — here prairie game hen, there sockeye salmon. Havana cigars were 10 cents.

Sleeping cars were equally luxurious. "The seats are richly upholstered," says a brochure, "with high backs and arms, and the central sections are made into luxurious sofas during the day. The upper berths are provided with windows and ventilators, and have curtains separate from those of the berths below. The exteriors are of white mahogany and satinwood, elaborately carved..." Observation cars, initially without roofs, appeared before 1890. Tourist-class equipment soon followed, making transcontinental travel possible at lower prices.

But it was Van Horne's rapid realization that tourists require accommodation which would leave a permanent record on Alberta. An accomplished artist and amateur architect, he sketched a plan for an impressive baronial edifice to stand amidst the majestic mountains across the Bow from Mount Norquay. Completed in 1888, the $250,000 building was constructed of timber and boasted 250 beds. This was the first Banff Springs Hotel. Swiss-style hotels were opened at Lake Louise, Field, North Bend and Glacier in Rogers Pass.

In 1899 the CPR improved first-class service further still by introducing a new passenger express called the Imperial Limited. The exteriors of its cars were of polished red Honduras mahogany. Interiors were fitted with gold and ivory finishings in a Louis XV style. The Imperial's average speed was almost 30 miles an hour, cutting the Montreal-Vancouver time from 136 hours to about 100. Only 20 years earlier the Canadian transcontinental route could be travelled only by canoe, and took at least four months.

But even the Imperial sometimes carried third-class, non-luxurious colonist (or immigrant) cars. The backbone of the CPR's passenger traffic, these offered upper and lower sleeping berths without upholstery (as being easier to disinfect). Passengers supplied their own bedding, and brought food or bought it at scheduled stops. Soon the colonist cars would be carrying thousands of Irish, Ukrainian, Polish and German families — families that would create not only railway revenues, but the province of Alberta. *G.S.*❦

Glenbow Archives, NA-1753-38

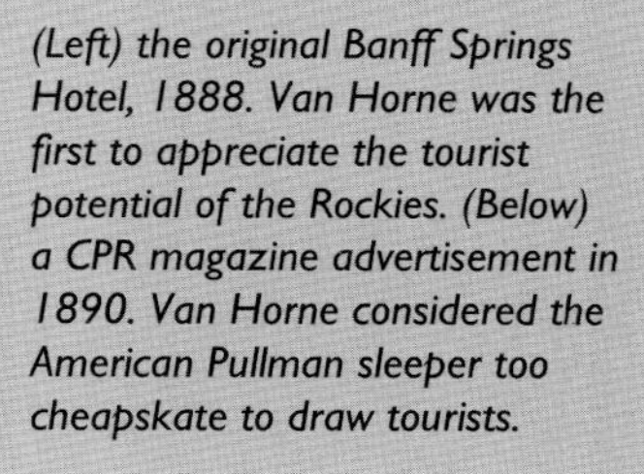

(Left) the original Banff Springs Hotel, 1888. Van Horne was the first to appreciate the tourist potential of the Rockies. (Below) a CPR magazine advertisement in 1890. Van Horne considered the American Pullman sleeper too cheapskate to draw tourists.

Glenbow Archives, NA-4474-25

FIRST-CLASS SLEEPING AND PARLOR CAR TARIFF.

FOR ONE LOWER OR ONE UPPER BERTH IN SLEEPING CAR BETWEEN

Halifax and Montreal - -	$4 00
Quebec and Montreal - - -	1 50
Montreal and Toronto - -	2 00
Montreal and Chicago - - -	5 00
Montreal and Winnipeg -	8 00
Montreal and Vancouver - -	20 00
Ottawa and Toronto - -	2 00
Ottawa and Vancouver - -	20 00
Fort William and Vancouver	15 00
Toronto and Chicago - - -	3 00
Toronto and Winnipeg -	8 00
Toronto and Vancouver - -	18 50
Boston and Montreal - -	2 00
New York and Montreal - -	2 00
Boston and St. Paul - -	7 00
Boston and Chicago - - -	5 50
Montreal and St. Paul -	6 00
St. Paul and Winnipeg - -	3 00
St. Paul and Vancouver -	13 50
Winnipeg and Vancouver -	12 00

Between other stations rates are in proportion.
Accommodation in First-class Sleeping Cars and in Parlor Cars will be sold only to holders of First-class transportation.

Provincial Archives of Alberta, E. Brown Collection, B-6128

Laying track in British Columbia in the early days. The toughest task in the toughest business, explained the Bulletin.

way. A gang of 10 men follows, placing the ties in position on the grade.

The rails are loaded on a cart by a gang of 12 men, all hands lifting each one. A horse drags the cart forward, the men sliding the rails off the end of it on top of the ties. Another gang follows, positioning the rails. As fast as the rails are laid, spikes are distributed and 20 men drive them in and bolt on the fish plates. Others meanwhile are raising and anchoring the telegraph poles. When the process is complete, the locomotive arrives again and pushes its flatcars down the new stretch of track. The men work dawn till dark. Railway building is the toughest job in Canada, the *Bulletin* concluded, and track-laying the toughest part of it.

P. Turner Bone, a Calgary engineer on the prairie and the mountain sections, recalled it all 62 years later in his book *When the Steel Went Through*. He remembered his first sight of Medicine Hat, when he rode in atop a load of rails a few weeks after the track had crossed the South Saskatchewan. It was little more than a collection of tents, but he met there some notable figures. His boss, chief engineer Herbert Holt, was destined to become Sir Herbert, one of Canada's leading financiers and for 26 years president of the Royal Bank. An office boy, known only as "George," was George Webster, later mayor of Calgary. A regular visitor who always ate in the CPR boarding house was lawyer James Lougheed, later a senator and founder of a political dynasty. What Bone remembered best, however, was the weather. One day his thermometer recorded 107 degrees Fahrenheit, the next plunged to 57, accompanied by a storm that blew down every tent in town and destroyed all the engineering drawings made in the previous week.

As the track-layers moved westward from what is now the Alberta border, the Canadian Pacific

8 Most of these mainline stations were at first identified only as numbered sidings. But George Stephen, working hard in Europe to find cash, lavishly named towns for important investors. Hence Suffield was named for Charles Harbord, 5th Lord Suffield. His brother-in-law was Edward Baring, 1st Lord Revelstoke, the man who took up a whole $15-million CPR bond issue and thereby had a B.C. divisional point, the town that grew up at the second crossing of the Columbia, named for him. Similarly the Marquis de Bassano, heir to a French dukedom, was a big stockholder. Tilley honoured Sir Leonard Tilley, finance minister in the Macdonald government when the railway's survival depended wholly on further government aid. Other names honoured CPR officials and associates. Brooks was for Noell Edgell Brooks, a divisional engineer. Shepard and Langdon got their names from the prairie contractors, who would doubtless have preferred an honour they were denied, namely a new contract for the mountain division. Exshaw honours Sir Sandford Fleming's son-in-law, William Exshaw, director of the cement company that established a plant there.

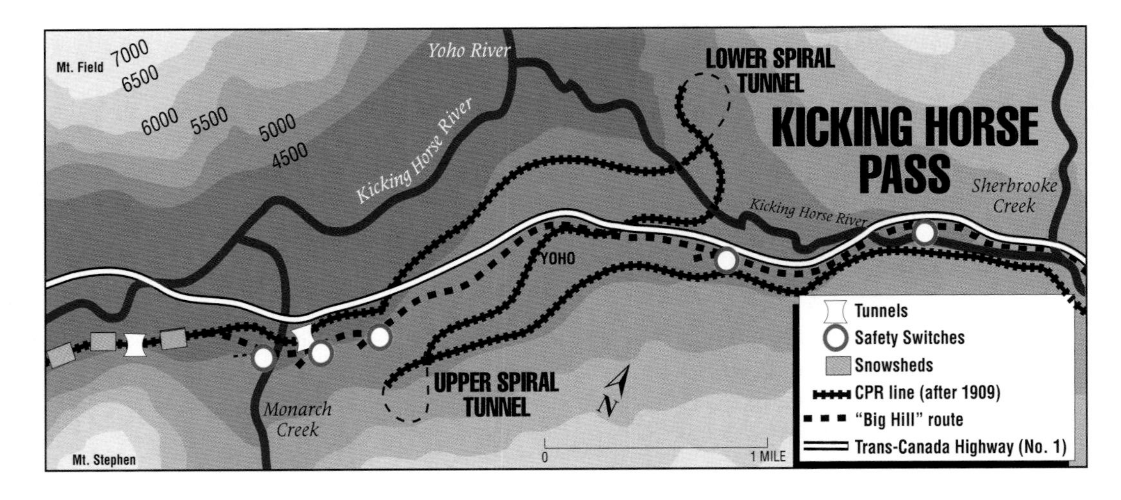

left its imprint forever upon some of the towns it established. Dunmore, Tilley, Brooks, Bassano, Shepard, Langdon and Exshaw, for instance, are all CPR-associated names.[8] Banff was so named by the railway because Donald Smith and George Stephen both came from Banff in Scotland. But the most curious tale of all is attached to the name Gleichen.[9]

Provincial Archives of Alberta, E. Brown Collection, B6016

Driving piles for a CPR bridge in 1885. Troubles climaxed in the spring, with unpaid contractors and the Mounties called back to the Prairies to deal with armed rebellion.

At Calgary the CPR had already caused some consternation before the track arrived. Speculators, certain the station would be located east of the Elbow, had bought up most of the property there before the Canada North-West Land Company began operations. By placing the station west of the Elbow on railway land, on the site of the future Palliser Hotel, the CPR instantly caused the collapse of real estate prices to the east. Canada North-West then held a sale of the lots to the west. Herbert Holt bought a whole block for himself and, after objections from company higher-ups, was made to give them up. Engineer Bone, however, was allowed to keep the two Holt had suggested he buy. The price was $300 for inside lots and $450 for corner lots. Many of these properties are now lined with highrise office buildings.

Whole buildings were lugged over from their former sites east of the Elbow, and within weeks what was essentially a construction camp began taking on the semblance of a town. On August 20, 1883, a newspaper called *The Weekly Herald* published its first issue. One of its prime editorial commitments, it declared, was to oppose the use of alcohol.

When the construction season of 1883 was over, the end of track lay near the summit of Kicking Horse Pass. Stephen had raised $30 million in Europe, and Van Horne had spent it all and then some. The company was in desperate straits. The market for CPR stock had crashed and a recession was beginning to seize the economy. Moreover, the costliest work still lay ahead. James Ross, the new chief engineer replacing Holt (who had decided to take on one of the mountain contracts), announced he would need 12,000 men in the mountains during 1884.

Still, the new season began with a promising discovery. An engineer named Charles Shaw found the first of a number of flaws in the proposed route through the Kicking Horse. Rogers had called for a tunnel through a mountain just east of Banff. By simply following the river valley to the north around the mountain, Shaw discerned, the railway could avoid enormous expense. The tunnel was never built, though Tunnel Mountain retains its name to this day.

[9] The simple explanation is that Gleichen was named for Victor, Count Gleichen, half-nephew of Queen Victoria. Ask why Queen Victoria had a half-nephew and the explanation is no longer simple. Victoria's father, Edward, Duke of Kent, spent much of his life as military commander or governor at overseas posts, living in Quebec and Halifax with a French mistress, Julie de St. Laurent. When it became clear his brother William IV would die without issue, Edward was enjoined to abandon his companion of 27 years and produce a legitimate heir to the throne. So he married the widow of the Prince of Leiningen. By her first husband she had a daughter, Feodora, who was thus Victoria's older half-sister. Feodora in due course married the Prince of Hohenlohe-Langenburg, whose principal secondary title was Count of Gleichen. Queen Victoria invited their son, her half-nephew, to live in England where he entered the Royal Navy as a lad. Gleichen became an advisor to the Prince of Wales and ultimately an admiral. George Stephen toured him across Canada, named an Alberta town for him and persuaded him to invest in the CPR.

Again and again the snowpack fell, burying 260 people

100-TON SNOWPLOWS AND MIGHTY TREES WERE THROWN LIKE FEATHERS AS THE CPR FOUGHT THE AVALANCHES OF ROGERS PASS

The dangers of early western railroading did not end when the track was laid. Bridge collapses, head-on collisions, derailments, prairie fires and above all avalanches continued to claim train crews and scores of passengers for years to come, as the railroad industry learned to run safely over prairies and through mountains.

The mountains were the worst, and the worst in the mountains was the 67-mile run through Rogers Pass in the Selkirks, starting about 78 miles west of the Alberta border. In a typical winter more than 30 feet of snow would fall there. Sudden melts would cause huge slabs of the mountainside snowpack to break away and hurtle down on the track. Trees with two-foot trunks would be snapped off and tossed aside like matchsticks. The track itself would be torn up, and any trains or buildings nearby would be smashed to pieces.

In the CPR's first winter, 1885-86, a slide buried 1,800 feet of track in a snowbank 60 feet wide and 30 feet deep. An eyewitness account of one avalanche gives a sense of how devastating and sudden they could be. C.G. Anderson, a commercial traveller from Toronto, was on a train stopped in the middle of the pass because an avalanche had just occurred ahead. "...Here close to Rogers Station great trees and boulders were torn up and hurled down from the mountain sides into this canyon (Bear Creek) upon the work train and the labourers without a moment's warning."

"I shall never forget the scene as I went down from our train to see them digging out the bodies of the unfortunate men," Anderson wrote, "while there seeing the brave fellows who were taking their lives in their hands at this work — for so great was the danger of another slide that the passengers were warned against going to the scene. I saw the bodies of three white men and several Japanese taken out cold and stiff in death...Like white and bronze statues, the whites and Orientals were recovered one by one."

Deaths from avalanches began the winter before the track crews arrived. In February 1885, a cook in an advance camp was killed by a snowslide. Soon afterwards three men in another camp were buried alive and never found. Then a man named Hill, who ran a little camp store, narrowly escaped when the edge of a slide hit the store and he got out through a window. A few days later a second slide wiped out the store, then another carried away a big equipment cache and six men were killed.

The CPR immediately began construction of 31 snowsheds, covering about five miles of the most dangerous sections in the pass. They did not work as well as was hoped. Avalanches continued to take their toll. Frank W. Anderson, in *The Incredible Rogers Pass*, relates some of the horrors that followed.

On the afternoon of January 30, 1899, a huge avalanche plunged down on the little Rogers Pass station. "Albert Cator, stationmaster, was talking to a young man at the station door. When they heard the slide coming, they rushed onto the platform. Just then the slide struck the building. Cator was swept away, but the young man dropped to the ground and was buried

Provincial Archives of Alberta, E. Brown Collection, B-6014

(Right) snowshed construction in Rogers Pass, undated. Many lived to tell about being struck – one man ended up in a tree – but 260 perished. (Above right) one of scores of trains derailed by avalanches in Rogers Pass, this one in 1897. Ten men died under snowslides before the first track was laid.

Glenbow Archives, NA-4428-25

up to his neck. Miraculously he survived. Not so fortunate were Mrs. Cator and her two children. They perished in the ruins of the station. Annie Berger, the waitress, survived with a broken leg. The night telegraph operator, Carson, was asleep in the bunkhouse. Rescuers found him in his bed suffocated. Frank Vago who coaled the locomotives was in his bunkhouse. He was picked up and jammed between the joists upside down. Vago survived.

"On the tracks section foreman Ridley was working inside a boxcar with a helper on top. The helper saw the slide coming, hollered a warning and jumped. He landed scant inches clear of the skirt of the avalanche, but his boss was swept away by the churning mass of ice and snow. In all, eight persons perished." That same day another slide came down on a snowshed and crushed it, killing a workman. The following day a blade flew from a rotary plough that was trying to clear the snow from another slide, and three workmen were injured.

Engineer George Williamson recalls another incident: "We were widening out what had been a previous slide. I was coupled onto the rotary plough, pulling out timbers from the slide. I saw some of the boys begin to run. I knew there was a slide coming and I started to back up. I got the engine inside the shed when, Bingo! Away goes the rotary. The engineer of the rotary, Jim Campbell, and his fireman had jumped and were hanging onto my pilot (cow catcher) as I backed in. Knocked the rotary away, oh say 75 to 100 feet. Smashed it all to pieces. It broke off my push casting.

"There must have been eight, ten, twelve men buried. When we dug out the men on the extra gang, I said to Tom Wilson, the foreman, 'Tom, do you think you got all the men out?' So he counted them. 'By Golly, George' he said, 'there's one missing.' Well, they dug around in the snow, and they touched this fellow. He was unconscious, but he lived."

The worst avalanche occurred on March 4, 1910. It began when a preliminary slide off Cheops Mountain buried a snowshed on Bear Creek, the tributary stream leading up into the pass from the Beaver River. Three crews were sent out with a 100-ton rotary plough to clear it. At about 11:30 p.m., atop Avalanche Mountain on the opposite side of the valley, a gigantic chunk of snow silently broke free, plunging 1,500 feet down the slope, gathering more snow as it came. It crossed the valley floor and swept up the opposite side, leaving 62 men buried alive.

So swiftly had it come that many of the men were found standing as they worked, picks and shovels in hand. One was discovered with a knife in one hand and a plug of tobacco in the other. The slide missed passenger train No. 97 by about 200 yards. The rotary plough was hurled 40 feet from the track and smashed beyond recognition. Its fireman, Billy Lachance, had strolled away from the plough and across a bridge over Bear Creek. He later recalled how he first felt the great wind that precedes an avalanche, just before it picked him up and threw him into the bush beyond. The snow thundered down upon him and stopped at his feet. He was the only survivor.

In 1911 and 1912, more than 100 slides would block the main line. At last, in 1916, the CPR opened the five-mile Connaught Tunnel that took the line under the mountain for the worst of the avalanche area. But there were more catastrophes to come. On the night of February 29, 1936, as engineer Percy Shafer took a cattle train out of the Connaught Tunnel and headed down to Revelstoke in pouring rain, he ran into an avalanche that had come down on the track. Before he could stop, his locomotive was derailed.

Another locomotive that had been working higher up the line dragged the cattle cars up to a siding, then returned with a work party to replace the ripped-out sections of the line. The locomotive crew jerry-rigged a coupling to the damaged locomotive tender and began pulling it back up the hill, while the work crew set about repairing the track. In mounting the slope, however, the second locomotive encountered another slide. The jolt detached the damaged tender, which silently rolled back down until, at tremendous speed, it hit the unsuspecting work crew. Eleven men were killed outright; another died en route to hospital. A 13th, trapped atop the runaway tender, finally jumped, hit a concrete wall and was killed.

A second tunnel, the 9.11-mile Mount Macdonald, the longest railway tunnel in the western hemisphere, was completed in December 1988, as part of the Beaver project to reduce the westbound grade in the Selkirks and reduce the bottleneck caused by the Connaught. It passes under Mount Macdonald, named for Sir John A. Budgeted at $600 million, the project was completed for about $500 million. This further eased the avalanche problem.

What helped most, however, was the stationing in the pass of artillerymen to protect the Trans-Canada Highway. Their shells bring avalanches down before they become lethal. In all, 260 people perished before the railwaymen mastered the Rogers Pass. *G.S.*❦

Higher up the Bow, an Indian had led CPR survey worker Tom Wilson up a little tributary to discover beautiful Lake Louise, which Van Horne, quicker than any to envision the tourist potential of the mountains, foresaw as a veritable bonanza. Immediately beyond, however, lay Wapta Lake, and here loomed one of the awesome engineering horrors posed by the Kicking Horse route.

Within its first 3.5 miles beside the Kicking Horse River, the right of way had to descend a stupendous 1,100 feet, from Wapta Lake down to the flat valley where the Kicking Horse unites with the Yoho River flowing in from the north. This would call for a terrifying 4.5% grade, more than double the maximum safety rules permitted. Thus if a train were 1,000 feet long, the locomotive would be 50 feet lower than the caboose, the height of a five-storey building. (In a modern train a mile long, the head end would be 225 feet below the tail, roughly a 22-storey building.)

The standard solution for such a situation would be a series of spiral tunnels, adding distance to the line by taking it in and out of the adjoining mountains so that the drop could be eased. But this would have held up construction for another year or more, and cost the company untold millions that it could never have raised. Van Horne made the decision immediately. Just over the summit of the Rockies, between Lake Louise and Field, British Columbia, the CPR main line would feature the "Big Hill," the steepest grade on any standard-gauge railway anywhere in the world. From the time the first locomotive ran down it, railroaders would curse the Big Hill and die on it.

At intervals along the line the railway installed what amounted to runaway lanes. If a train failed to give the agreed-upon signal of four whistle blasts, indicating it was under control, watchmen were to throw the switches and divert the train into the runaway tracks that mounted steeply up the mountain side, so its brakes could stop it. On August 2, 1884, shortly after the Big Hill line opened, engine No. 146 went out of control, the switchman threw the switch and the train roared onto the runaway track. The engineer somehow failed to apply the brakes, however. The train mounted the incline and smashed into a rock wall at the end of it. Seventy Swedish workmen on the cars behind jumped for their lives. Three members of the train crew and an uncounted number of Swedes were killed.

Crews became exceedingly cautious thereafter, stopping all trains at intervals as they came down. Even so, on a bitterly cold night in January 1889, engineer Jack Spencer, at the throttle of engine No. 314, was leading 14 cars of coal down the hill and found the brakes weren't holding them back. The man on the third safety switch thought he heard the four blasts and let the train run through. As the crew leapt from car to car trying to apply the hand brakes, the train jumped the rails on a curve and smashed into a rock face. A brakeman was killed. The fireman, his legs mangled, died en route to hospital. Spencer would never run the hill again and was transferred to the Swift Current-Medicine Hat subdivision.[10]

After nearly a quarter of a century of this, the CPR in 1909 opened the famous Spiral Tunnels which solved the Big Hill problem. The Trans-Canada Highway today follows precisely the route of the original line, fragments of which can still be seen beside the road.

Laying the track down the Kicking Horse was no easier than running trains down it. Tunnels were frequently necessary to ease the curves around the river's fish-tailing bends. This meant cutting through mud, which shifted and caved in and cost lives, as well as rock. The slopes were too steep for heavy drilling gear, so dynamite holes had to be drilled by hand. And the blasting shook out avalanches that thundered down the mountains while the construction crews below ran for their lives. During cold, damp weather, many men died of mountain fever, though no accurate tally was ever kept of how many. They were buried beside the right of way as the track moved on.

Beside or above the track ran the tote roads to haul in equipment, from which horses, mules and sometimes men plunged to death or grievous injury. One man was driving a horse along a tote road high above a raging cataract when the horse tripped on a stone and plunged over the edge, falling 70 feet into the river. The driver went with him, but somersaulted in the air and got caught on a tree trunk 28 feet down. He scrambled back to the top. Had that tree not been there, it might have changed Canadian financial history. The driver was Herbert Holt.

When the season was over, however, the track had not only reached the Columbia at Golden, but had moved 18 miles north to traverse it at First Crossing and had ascended the Beaver. It stood at the verge of Rogers Pass as winter approached. (First Crossing is now Donald, British Columbia, for Donald A., of course.) Meanwhile, the Onderdonk crews were building eastward from Kamloops and wintered on Shuswap Lake.

[10] After that wreck, engine No. 314 was repaired and returned to service as a "pusher" locomotive on the Big Hill, only to blow up, killing the engineer and fireman. The latter was found with the injector handle still clenched in his hand. Rebuilt again and renumbered, No. 314 served until 1917 and was scrapped. The dome of the original boiler is on display at the Spiral Tunnel viewpoint beside the Trans-Canada Highway.

Glenbow Archives, NA-303-92

An early prairie wreck near Fort Macleod on the Crow's Nest line, with a temporary track built around it.

On the prairie lines collapsing bridges posed the big peril

When the wind shook the whole structure and one big gust took it all down, the men on it didn't have a chance

The prairie lines were much safer than Rogers Pass, though here too, in the days before the century's turn, equipment and signal failures took a toll. The early wooden bridges — vulnerable to fire, pressure from ice break-up and even strong winds — were especially hazardous.

On April 13, 1898, for example, the *Lethbridge News* reported five men killed and six injured when a trestle bridge they were working on collapsed during a gale. It quoted a witness: "The wind which had been blowing pretty stiff from the south-west all forenoon was of a gusty nature and had shaken the bridge pretty severely, and an extra strong gust coming at this time and striking it head on, blew it over...Very few of the men had a chance to escape, the rest went down with the bridge, some of them falling a distance of 50 feet or more."

Prairie fires also caused concern. More than one train fell into a coulee or river after a bridge was burnt out by a grass fire. Many settlers blamed the railway for the fires, saying there was inadequate screening on the locomotive smoke stacks. This issue became the personal crusade of Major-General T. Bland Strange, back from his role in the 1885 Riel Rebellion and ranching near Gleichen. He argued that the CPR should plough six furrows along each side of the tracks as firebreaks where the railway passed near a town or ranch.

Strange even attempted to enlist the help of the governor-general, Lord Lansdowne, when the vice-regent visited the area. The CPR's William Van Horne took it personally and wrote to Ottawa: "General Strange is a sort of 'all-wise crank.' He has been following us in this matter for several years and has failed so far to prove that any one fire spread from the railway." The CPR's own theory on prairie fires was that they were deliberately set by buffalo bone hunters who wanted an easy way to locate buffalo skeletons on the Prairie.

Then there were the "miracles." On the night of November 10, 1897, an eastbound freight collided head-on with a west-bound near the centre of Calgary. The crews jumped before the trains hit. When the resulting fire was put out, several tons of dynamite were discovered in one of the derailed boxcars. "Fortunately for the trainmen, spectators and the whole city," said the *Calgary Herald*, "it did not explode. Had it done so, the consequences would certainly have been most terrible and many a Calgary home would have been desolate today." *G.S.*❦

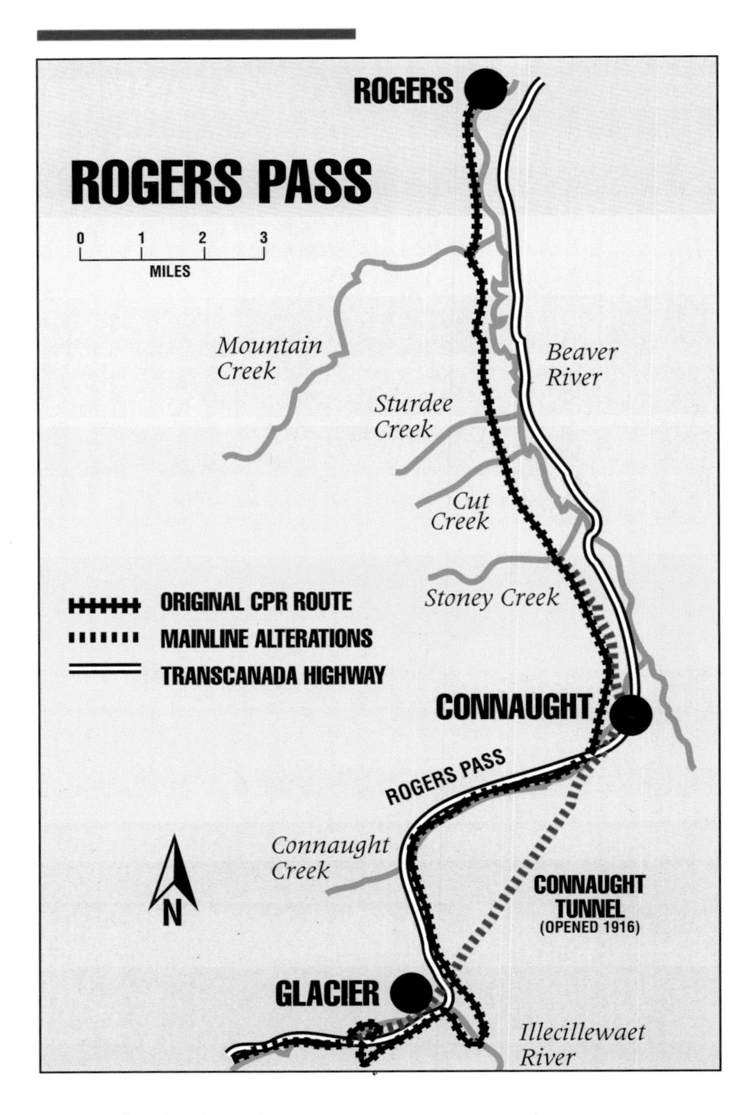

But back in Montreal Stephen realized that the Canadian Pacific was essentially bankrupt. It had squeezed every last possible nickel of capital from the private sector. The whole project, and with it any hope of a transcontinental Canada, would collapse unless the government came through with new loans. Along with his appeals ran Stephen's delicate use of what he called "bonifications," a polite word for bribes, offered to the right people at the right time. The bonification of a $45,000 necklace to Lady Macdonald undoubtedly helped,[11] though political developments of grievous dimension would also vindicate the railway's case. In any event, the funding came through and was there for the CPR's final western construction season, 1885.

This entailed the last, grim project in the mountains, the transit of Rogers Pass. By now patience had worn thin and behind the scenes the CPR's senior management was running on raw nerve and feuding bitterly. All this came to light many years later when historians examined their correspondence.[12] At one point, for instance, construction boss Ross became so exasperated with what he considered the bureaucratic incompetence of supply boss J.M. Egan back in Winnipeg that Ross threatened to walk off the job. Van Horne mollified him, then sent in a private detective to check on Egan's counter-charge that Ross was embezzling from the company. He wasn't.

In laying the track up to and through Rogers Pass, the CPR encountered three huge problems. Two of them it solved immediately; the third would require a full century of operation and hundreds of millions of dollars before it was finally overcome. The first was the succession of streams that flowed into the Beaver from the flanking Selkirks, splitting the wall of the valley with ravines as much as 200 feet deep. Each of these, with names like Mountain Creek, Stoney Creek and Surprise Creek, required a spectacularly high and intricate bridge, built at first from bolted timbers. While they supported the trains, they could be and were destroyed by forest fires until they were replaced by steel bridges within a year.

In Rogers Pass itself the builders encountered the second terror, a kind of blue clay too soft to blast when wet and too hard to dig when dry, that caved in with regularity. Rain and snow had bogged down progress towards the end of '84, so the company ordered work to be continued through the winter. This disclosed the third and worst problem. Average snowfall in the Selkirks is 30 feet a season. All winter enormous avalanches roar down the mountains — in March they could come several times a day — sweeping away tracks, buildings and trains, and burying them all in 50 to 100 feet of snow. The avalanche death toll would reach 260 before this problem was solved. The railway immediately built snowsheds to cover the track at crucial points. They helped, but not

[11] The origin of this story is obscure and slight variations exist. In the third volume of his history of the HBC, Peter Newman more than quadruples the price of the necklace to $200,000 (which would, however, be approximately the equivalent of £45,000) and says Smith gave it to Lady Macdonald.

[12] These feuds were disclosed in fascinating detail by University of Saskatchewan historian Ted Regehr at a seminar sponsored by the Glenbow Museum to mark the 100th anniversary of the CPR's arrival in Calgary. The Regehr presentation was published in Hugh Dempsey's *The CPR West*.

Provincial Archives of Alberta, A-3996

The famous Last Spike, driven by Donald A. Smith on November 7, 1885, in Eagle Pass, Van Horne immediately behind him to the left. The company was virtually insolvent, the workers unpaid, but the herculean task was finished.

enough. Not until the CPR had opened the five-mile Connaught Tunnel in 1916 and the nine-mile Mount Macdonald Tunnel in 1988 was the avalanche difficulty overcome.

Finally, liquor caused more trouble than ever before. In the territories, the ban on selling it had enabled the Mounties to maintain some semblance of control. But British Columbia was already a province and the provincial government liked the revenues it derived from the liquor trade. Within the construction districts there were more than 300 saloons, wrote an exasperated Sam Steele, the NWMP superintendent. By the spring of '85 all these troubles burst out at the end of track, as the great project neared completion.

The new money had not yet come through. Unpaid contractors were pulling out, unpaid labourers walking off the job. Some of them, in fact, were forced at gunpoint to stay. In March work was stopped by a general strike. Making matters worse, an emergency had summoned the indispensable Superintendent Steele and all available Mounties back to the Prairies. In the end, CPR management settled the strike by rushing some of the workers' back pay to the end of track. It then became a race for home. The track descended the Illecillewaet, crossed the Columbia again, and at Craigellachie in Eagle Pass met the east-moving Onderdonk crew. Here on November 7, 1885, Donald A. Smith drove in the last spike and the Canadian Pacific was complete.

But by then all the attention of Canada was elsewhere, directed in fact to the emergency that had sent Sam Steele rushing east the previous March. A contingent of armed Metis had ambushed the Mounties at Duck Lake in the District of Saskatchewan, killing 11 and wounding 12. Within a few months the 1885 Riel Rebellion had been suppressed, though it didn't reach its final conclusion on a scaffold in Regina until nine days after the last spike was driven home.❦

Until the shots rang out at Duck Lake, Riel had the angering West behind him

HIS DECLARATION FOR SEPARATISM COST HIM WIDE SUPPORT; AND AS TROOPS BY THE HUNDREDS BOARDED THE NEW CPR, THE WEST'S ARMED REBELLION AGAINST OTTAWA WAS DOOMED

Glenbow Archives, NA-343-1

Mountie Superintendent Crozier in 1880. 'Fire away, boys!' he shouted, and the rebellion was on.

It would be officially described later as an "impetuous" move, but when Superintendent L.N.F. Crozier led his long column of North-West Mounted Police and civilian volunteers out of Fort Carlton on the afternoon of Thursday, March 26, 1885, he felt he had cause enough.

Louis Riel's new "provisional government of the Saskatchewan" in the little Metis settlement of Batoche[1] had not only proclaimed itself the ruling authority in the central North West Territories, it had also formally demanded that Crozier's force in Fort Carlton surrender to it. Crozier of course refused. Instead he sent out a small squad to prevent supplies at nearby Duck Lake from falling into Riel's hands. Riel's men and some armed Indians met the little party of Mounties, blocked their way, taunted them to start shooting, and when they didn't, forced them to return to Carlton.

So what was Crozier to do now? True, it hadn't yet come to open war. No shots had been fired. True also, Colonel A.G. Irvine, commissioner of the NWMP, was advancing upon Fort Carlton with a contingent of reinforcements. He could wait for Irvine, thereby doubling the NWMP force, and then attack Riel with a much better chance of success. But that would mean two things. Riel would get further provisions. More significantly, the NWMP, which once already had refused to fight, would seem to be refusing again. The vaunted, almost mystical power of the Mounties, which the Indians respected and feared, would be undermined. And the Indians were what mattered. Riel had at most 1,000 men under arms. There were at least 20,000 Indians in the territories. If they joined him, this tiny insurrection at Batoche would become an Indian war across the entire prairie West.

Crozier decided. "Sound 'Boots and Saddles!' " he ordered. The Mounties would fight. He was soon leading his full troop out the fort gate: 56 Mounties, 41 Prince Albert volunteers and a little

[1] Batoche, on the right (i.e., right as you face downstream) bank of the South Saskatchewan, is 38 miles southwest of Prince Albert and 45 miles northeast of Saskatoon. The area, like most other venues of the Riel Rebellion, is a National Historic Site, which in 1991 was administered by the parks service of Environment Canada. The church and rectory used by Riel had been restored. Fort Carlton, 45 miles north of Saskatoon, sits in a clearing on a river flat on the right bank of the North Saskatchewan, surrounded by hills. By 1991, some of the fort buildings and the stockade had been restored and it was administered by the Saskatchewan parks service.

Saskatchewan Archives Board, R-A458

Winnipeg's 90th Battalion of militia men mustering at the CPR station. News of Duck Lake crossed the Prairies like a tornado.

seven-pounder artillery piece. Muffled against the March cold, they trotted up the trail. At a hilltop 12 miles short of Duck Lake the rolling prairie spread before them, a sea of crusted, mud-caked, late winter snow, broken only by the bluffs of bare poplars and the ravines of frozen creeks. The scouts took up their advance positions and the column crunched through the snow towards the rebellious Metis.

As they neared Duck Lake, their path lay up and down a series of three hills, poplar and brush encroaching on both sides. The main body had descended the first hill and was approaching the second when suddenly Crozier saw his scouts galloping back, Metis horsemen and a few Cree from the local band in hot pursuit. Immediately the Mounties formed their wagons into a barricade and sent their horses to the rear. No shot, however, had yet been fired.

In the lead of the pursuing party was a Metis the Mounties recognized as Isidore Dumont, brother of the Metis commander, accompanied by a Cree. Dumont was waving a white blanket, obviously seeking a parley. A Mountie interpreter stepped forward and discussions opened. But the Indian abruptly grabbed the interpreter's rifle, and a tussle began between the two. At the same time Crozier saw armed Metis creeping through the bush alongside the column. He was being surrounded. "Fire away, boys!" he shouted. Both the Indian and Dumont were shot down on the spot, as a hail of fire poured into the column from the surrounding trees.[2]

In the ensuing 40 minutes everything went wrong for the Mounties. They were wholly exposed while the Metis were concealed. Crozier ordered the cannon trained into the brush and trees, but by now the Prince Albert volunteers, under heavy fire and suffering many casualties, had worked their way into the bush and come between the Mounties and the Metis. Then someone rammed a shell into the cannon before the powder charge had been put in, jamming it and rendering it useless.

Crozier saw his men and the volunteers falling around him. Ten were dead, two were dying, 11 were wounded. Five horses had been killed or disabled. The Metis, apart from Dumont and the Indian, seemed to have suffered no casualties at all. He had no idea of their numbers, but they seemed like hundreds. (In fact, the Metis force consisted of 25 horsemen, later reinforced by 200 men on foot who arrived after the fighting was over.) Four Metis and the one Indian were killed at Duck Lake; among the several wounded was Gabriel Dumont, their commander. Crozier ordered a retreat. The wagons and horses were hitched up under fire, the wounded were loaded and the Mounties withdrew.

[2] At subsequent criminal trials, the Metis insisted they were not moving through the trees to surround the detachment, but were in fact trying to escape from it. They fired in self-defence, they said, after Crozier gave his command to fire on them.

The shrewd tactician of Riel's army was defeated by Riel

Gabriel Dumont amazed Middleton by his defence scheme at Batoche, yet Dumont was a Metis peacemaker

Superficially Gabriel Dumont seemed like someone out of a western novel — skilled horseman, crack shot, tireless in the saddle and equally famous as drinker and gambler. In fact he was deeply religious and was persuaded to the last that God talked to Louis Riel. But when Riel's last rebellion ended in disaster at Batoche, it was Dumont and not Riel who awed the Canadian conquerors.

Inspecting the carefully laid and buttressed rifle pits, so cleverly placed around the Metis capital, Major-General Frederick Middleton, a veteran of the Maori wars in New Zealand and the Indian Mutiny, pronounced them flawless. He publicly paid tribute to the skill of the Metis commander.

What Middleton did not then know was his own good fortune that Riel had countermanded almost everything Dumont had proposed. Had Dumont been given his way as the Canadian troops advanced upon Batoche, the outcome of the Middleton offensive would have been doubtful indeed.

When the rebellion broke out, Dumont wanted to pick off what was left of Crozier's Mountie detachment as it retreated to Carlton from Duck Lake. Riel said no. As the Canadian troops moved west on the railway, Dumont wanted to blow up the trains. Riel said no. As Middleton's men moved north on the town, his best cavalry securely and uselessly to the rear, Dumont wanted to harass the infantry like buffalo, and attack by night so that they couldn't sleep. Riel said no.

These tactics, standard practice in guerrilla warfare, would have greatly impressed the Indians who were watching everything. That they would have lured the Indians east to the defence of Batoche seems altogether likely, and that would have gravely endangered Middleton's force. But always Riel said no.

Among the Canadian troops, meanwhile, propaganda was circulated to inflame them against Dumont. He beat and tortured prisoners, they were told, and when one poor wounded captive pleaded for his life because he had a wife and children, Dumont had laughed viciously and blown the man's brains out.

There is no record of such things ever having happened, however. As the truth came out, a very different sort of Dumont appeared. He was a thoroughly experienced hunter and had chased buffalo from Red River to the foothills of the Rockies. But he was best known as the peacemaker of the Metis, the man always summoned to settle internal disputes or to negotiate with the Indians. He had in fact been the author of a crucial treaty the Metis secured with their rivals and enemies, the Blackfoot. "One might travel the plains from one end to the other,"said the famous Sam Steele of the NWMP,"and never hear an unkind word said of Dumont. When in trouble the cry of all was for Gabriel."

But Dumont believed in Riel. He saw that at Red River rebellion had accomplished provincehood for what was then chiefly a Metis area. Riel had done it. Riel spoke English; Dumont could not. Riel was learned; Dumont was not. Riel

The wounded Gabriel Dumont now knew what to do. His force could attack the retreating Mounties all the way back to Carlton. With luck, not a single one would make it. If prisoners could be taken, they would become bargaining chips. "No," said Louis Riel, who had observed the fighting, crucifix in hand. "For the love of God, no more killing. There has already been too much blood shed." Bitterly Dumont obeyed. Louis, after all, talked to God. Louis knew. The bloodied survivors were allowed to retreat unmolested from what came to be known as the Battle of Duck Lake.

News of the battle ripped across the Prairies like a tornado. The Mounties had been defeated. The old chiefs remained wary, the young hot bloods were eager to fight. If the white invasion was not stopped now, they said, then the land was lost forever. Around Calgary, the Blackfoot became noticeably surly and hostile. The Bloods and the Peigan were thought to be arming in the vicinity of Fort Macleod, the Cree in the area of Edmonton, Fort Pitt and Battleford. The Stoney around Battleford had joined the Cree. All of these stories ticked eastward on the Canadian Pacific telegraph line, setting off in Ontario the greatest call to arms since the War of 1812.

The Royal Grenadiers were called out immediately at Toronto. The sergeants couldn't find them all on such short notice, but 300 men reported for duty and more were expected. The Queen's Own Rifles mustered next. "There is the wildest excitement among them all," reported the *Globe*. The 7th Battalion was summoned to arms at London, Ontario, the 66th Battalion of the Princess Louise Fusiliers at Halifax, with the 63rd Rifles to hold in readiness. Much closer to the scene, the 90th Winnipeg Battalion of Rifles was ordered out at 10 o'clock on the night of the battle and the next day had 334 men and officers ready to move.

knew the politicians; Dumont did not. Most important, God talked to Riel as He talked to no one else. Louis must therefore lead the people. Gabriel would lead the army.

In organizing his 300 buffalo hunters for war, the Metis general followed the system they knew so well. Captains of scouts were appointed to patrol the area and 10 captains of fighting companies were also selected. But not until the Canadian force was within 17 miles of Batoche did Riel permit Dumont to move against them. Then, at Fish Creek, the vastly outnumbered Metis laid their ambush, lost the element of surprise by firing too soon, but even so held off the army for a whole day. This stalled Middleton for two weeks and enabled Riel to make a final appeal to the Indian chiefs. With the Metis performance so inconclusive, however, they failed to respond in time.

Once the Battle of Batoche was lost, Dumont escaped to Montana. But Riel, in prison, admiringly told reporters that Dumont had made his way into the Canadian camp the very next night and stolen the horses with which he would make his escape. It was great stuff for cowboy novels. Ever since he played his losing role in the North West Rebellion, Gabriel Dumont has been increasingly cherished as a Canadian hero.

Dumont wandered the United States, eventually starring as "The Hero of the Half-breed Rebellion" in Buffalo Bill's Wild West show, where he would stand and snarl appropriately at the paying customers. But he quickly grew disillusioned with life as a sideshow attraction and continued wandering the continent until an amnesty, granted in 1890, allowed him to return to his beloved Prairies. He lived in quiet seclusion in the little settlement of Gabriel's Crossing near Batoche until his death, of natural causes, in 1906.

He could not capture the Canadian artillery, it was said. But he did capture the Canadian heart. *G.S.*❦

Glenbow Archives, NA-1063-1

Gabriel Dumont in the 1880s. A tough, skilled Plains fighter controlled by a visionary.

"Never before in the memory of the oldest inhabitant," reported the Toronto *Mail*, "did this city present so warlike an appearance as yesterday." It described the grey coats of the Queen's Own and the scarlet tunics of the Royal Grenadiers, who had been up all night polishing equipment.

How were all these men going to get to the North West Territories fast enough to make a difference, people wondered. The answer came in two words: Canadian Pacific. The line was now complete through the Prairies, except for four unfinished sections on the north shore of Lake Superior, totalling about 70 miles, around which the troops could be carried by sled. But lost in all the fear and excitement was the question: What had caused this? Why had the Metis taken up arms?

In fact, the Metis were only one of four groups in the North West that had deep grievances against Canada and the government of Sir John A. Macdonald. The Indians, their lands gone, their food rations cut back, their women and children starving, were likewise on the verge of revolt. (Their desperation has been described in an earlier chapter.) The "half-breeds" or "mixed-bloods," distinguished from the French-Indian Metis because they spoke the English of their HBC fathers and grandfathers, were also supporting Riel, up to but not including the point of rebellion. Most surprising of all, many of the settlers similarly supported him and they had no Indian blood whatever. It was not, in other words, merely a question of Metis unrest. Most of "Canada's Colony" was in much the same ferment.

The Metis and half-breed grievances were twofold. Following the Red River Rebellion in 1869, the Manitoba Act of 1870 promised a land grant of 1.4 million acres to be distributed among all those of mixed Indian and white blood. Since neither Riel nor his provisional government had

Provincial Archives of Alberta

Louis Riel. Before the fighting broke out, even many white settlers identified with the Metis frustration with Ottawa.

asked for this, its appearance in the act has been something of a mystery. University of Calgary historian Thomas Flanagan, in *Metis Lands in Manitoba*, supports a suggestion made 20 years later by Archbishop A.A. Taché of St. Boniface. According to this theory, Abbé J.N. Ritchot, curé at St. Norbert and Riel's closest adviser during the rebellion, negotiated the Metis grant as compensation for Manitoba being denied control over its own land.

Not for three years after the Red River Rebellion did the dominion government begin to distribute the land, however, and it took another six years to complete the process. Meanwhile the Metis and half-breeds of the North West Territories spent years on petitions, delegations and fruitless discussion of a similar land grant for them. This was finally settled at 240 acres per adult — or, failing that, a form of scrip, redeemable in cash. (Most would choose scrip.) By February 1885 the government seemed ready to pay, but still hadn't done so when the Battle of Duck Lake occurred. The scrip was then rushed west on the next train.

Equally distressing to all settlers on the northern Prairies — Metis, half-breeds and newcomers alike — was the fact that none of them could prove they owned the land they had chosen to live on, since the government had not surveyed it. Following the 1869 rebellion, most Metis had simply moved farther west on the Prairies, their nomadic Catholic communities based upon highly organized and disciplined buffalo hunts. Each had its own priest who conducted mass and ran a school as the group moved from place to place across the Prairies. But as the settlers arrived and the buffalo vanished, the Metis reluctantly took up farming, as the half-breeds had already done.

They often adopted municipal constitutions of notable sophistication, a sedentary adaptation of the mobile governments developed on the open Prairies. Thus considerable Metis settlements arose at St. Albert outside Edmonton, at Lac la Biche and Lac Ste. Anne in the future Alberta, and at St. Laurent, Duck Lake and Batoche in the future Saskatchewan. There were similar half-breed settlements at Prince Albert, at Whitefish Lake and at Victoria Mission east of Edmonton.

These, together with other fledgling communities — at Edmonton, at Saskatoon where the Temperance Colonization Company founded a successful village,[3] at Battleford which had served as headquarters for the trans-prairie telegraph line, at the NWMP posts Fort Walsh and Fort Macleod, and at the surviving HBC posts of Forts Pitt[4] and Carlton on the North Saskatchewan — composed the major settlements on the Prairies before the arrival of the CPR.

In every one of them the lack of property title was causing endless trouble. Disputes over who owned what were everywhere raging. Squatters could settle on a farm where a family had lived for years, and there was no legal way to evict them. The Dominion Land Survey, with its townships and 640-acre sections, was itself provoking further acrimony as it proceeded west across the country, by ignoring the strip lots back from the river into which both Metis and half-breed settlements had been divided. Some found that under the DLS system, they were living on school land or HBC land. What were they to do?

Their answer had been to send petitions and make representations to Ottawa, but for more than 10 years Ottawa had done nothing. It then appointed a man to make what was supposed to be a "preliminary" survey. But he called it the permanent one; land was bought and sold on the basis of it. William Pearce, later a central figure in the rancher vs. farmer fight at Calgary, had to be dispatched to straighten it all out. By 1885, amidst much confusion and litigation, Ottawa had finally confirmed the river lot system in the half-breed settlement at Prince Albert, but not at St. Laurent, Duck Lake and Batoche.

In Manitoba, meanwhile, settlers lured to the West by enticing federal promises of abundance and prosperity found themselves in an impossible position, their savings gone, their crops lost

[3] Saskatoon represented the sole success in a program that became one of the Macdonald government's many dismal immigration failures. Under it, private settlement companies paid $2 an acre for designated tracts not located on railways, the payment rebated when they were successfully settled. The program attracted much speculation and almost no settlers. But it further alarmed the Metis, some of whom had long occupied lands turned over to these companies.

[4] Fort Pitt was located on the North Saskatchewan, 10 miles east of the future Alberta-Saskatchewan provincial boundary, and 35 miles northeast of Lloydminster.

The murder of the Frog Lake white men, from a contemporary sketch. First Duck Lake, then Frog Lake roused the dominion as nothing had before.

Glenbow Archives, NA-1193-2

Thomas Quinn, the Indian agent. He was killed by Wandering Spirit, precipitating the Frog Lake massacre.

through early frost and all profit impossible because of extremely high freight rates on everything they brought in and shipped out. The province was dotted with abandoned farms. At a great protest rally in 1883, the Manitoba and North-West Farmers' Union was founded. Many from the territorial settlements attended.

Hence a rebellious mood had seized the West, summed up by the *Prince Albert Times* in one memorable editorial:

> The people of Manitoba and the North West Territories have for a long time been struggling by every legitimate means in their power to impress upon the eastern provinces the fact they have been treated with deliberate and gross injustice, and that however anxious they may be to avoid extreme measures, they will not shrink, should the worst come to the worst, from taking any steps absolutely necessary for the vindication of their rights....The Dominion Government, possibly compelled by the people of the East to act against its better judgement, occupies the contemptible position of a greedy, grasping, overbearing bully, who has, however, totally misjudged the fighting power of the subject it has chosen to oppress.

As though that language were not forceful enough, the *Times* concluded by taking the gloves right off:

> Where they get the information which induces them to believe the people are likely to submit much longer, we do not know; but we can answer them that they need not look for their friends among the Canadians, half-breeds or Indians, as they are likely soon to be made aware of in a manner at once startling and unpleasant.

That editorial ran on May 10, 1884. During the previous three months, settlers, half-breeds and Metis, working together, had developed a list of grievances and demands and forwarded these as a petition to Ottawa. As usual they were ignored. But 25 days after the editorial appeared, a French and English delegation arrived at St. Peter's Mission in Montana to ask the help of the local school teacher in solving the problems of the Canadian North West. His name was Louis Riel.

Riel had fled to the United States after his government at Red River was frightened away by the

Provincial Archives of Alberta, E. Brown Collection, B-2026

(Above) General Middleton in 1885. His odd march against Batoche has mystified military analysts. He kept his cavalry in the rear, and then needlessly split his force in two.

(Right) Major-General Thomas Bland Strange in 1871. He led the Calgary contingent north to Edmonton, then down the North Saskatchewan to defeat Big Bear.

arrival of Canadian troops. In two successive elections, his faithful followers in the Manitoba constituency of Provencher had elected him to parliament, but he could not take his seat because he was wanted for the murder of Thomas Scott, the Orange militant his provisional government had executed. The Ontario government offered a $5,000 reward for his arrest.[5] "Where is Riel? God knows," Prime Minister Macdonald had declared. "I wish I could lay my hands on him." It was later disclosed that he not only knew where Riel was, but had arranged a cash payment for him to stay out of Canada, since his return and trial would have hopelessly split Catholic Quebec from Protestant Ontario and possibly wrecked Confederation. The Commons later granted Riel amnesty provided he remain outside the country for five years.

During the five years, Riel wandered through the United States, his letters reflecting a religious mania in which he saw himself as a "prophet" with a "mission" to change the world. He was later admitted to the insane asylum at Longue Pointe in Montreal and spent 20 months in the provincial asylum at Beauport. Thereafter he became a teacher in Montana, but kept in careful touch with events in the North West Territories. He accepted the proposal of the June 1884 delegation and returned to Canada forthwith.

Glenbow Archives, NA-1847-2

At the Metis settlements of St. Laurent and Batoche his leadership was accepted without question. Then, to his astonishment, he found himself equally sought after by the English half-breeds and settlers at Prince Albert. At first he feared to accept their invitation to come and visit them. But reassured that the "Scott affair" would not be held against him, he addressed a packed rally of English settlers on July 19, impressed them with the moderation of his ideas, and said that "responsible government" and provincehood were at the heart of his program.

The meeting could not have been more successful. His chief supporter in Prince Albert, a Catholic convert named William H. Jackson who would become one of the few Prince Albert citizens to join him in rebellion, issued a manifesto enunciating a case that would continue to echo from the West for a hundred years: "The Ottawa legislators are responsible to Eastern constituents, not to us, and are therefore impelled to legislate with a view to eastern interests, rather than our own." Jackson's manifesto called for "provincial legislatures with full control over our resources." The legislatures would not be conferred for another 20 years, control over resources for another 45.

By September the Riel movement and others allied with it were spreading throughout the territories. At Qu'Appelle on the CPR line, the Settlers Rights' Association was formed. The North-West Farmers' Union sent fiery missives to Ottawa. In Edmonton, Frank Oliver's *Bulletin* spoke out in loud support, though he questioned Riel's leadership, perhaps knowing something of Riel's mental condition, and would denounce his cause vehemently when it became separatist. Other newspapers, controlled as they were by the eastern-based Conservative party, condemned the movement from the start.

Meanwhile Indian agents, Mounties and other federal officials in the field increasingly prevailed upon Ottawa to act — to complete the surveys, to send the

[5] In one of Canadian history's dramatic vignettes, Riel actually showed up at the side entrance of the Parliament Buildings in January 1874 and signed the parliamentary register. Before the startled clerk could do anything about it, Riel had vanished into the afternoon snows. The Commons later passed a motion expelling him as a man wanted for murder.

[6] Before making this fated decision, Riel consulted his friend and supporter Charles Nolin, who persuaded him to make a novena (nine days of prayer) before acting. Riel so pledged. Apparently persuaded that his people were losing the resolve to fight, however, he made his declaration on March 18, the eighth day of the novena.

scrip, to restore the Indian food ration, to reduce the freight rates. But nothing moved Ottawa.

(Above) Prince Albert, a vulnerable town on the North Saskatchewan only one day's march north of Batoche.

The following March, in 1885, Riel made the reckless move that instantly cost him the support of the English half-breeds and settlers everywhere, and left the Indian chiefs with serious doubts about his capability. He suddenly abandoned all constitutional process and declared the Metis settlements on the Saskatchewan a provisional republic. The Catholic clergy, long aware of his strange visions and stranger theology, immediately opposed him, refusing him the sacraments. It was, says George F.G. Stanley, foremost of the Riel historians, "the act of a madman."[6] He had forgotten that two things had changed since he employed the same tactic 16 years before at Red River. One was that Canada now unquestionably owned the North West. The other was the Canadian Pacific.

Acting swiftly, Riel named his government, made Gabriel Dumont commander of his army, declared the Catholic priests the agents of the NWMP, took over the Batoche church and rectory as his headquarters, began seizing the contents of all stores and supplies in the vicinity, arrested two dominion government agents, and would have arrested an NWMP inspector had the Metis not misidentified him and picked up the wrong man.

But the NWMP moved quickly too, tripling its strength in the Saskatchewan District, setting up militia units at Battleford and Prince Albert, and prevailing upon the English half-breeds and settlers not to join Riel. When Riel's appeal to them came, they held aloof. But the increasingly urgent NWMP warnings to Ottawa still went unheeded. Even when the first bulletin of the Battle of Duck Lake came in, it was received by many influential people with complacent disbelief. The Tory *Gazette* in Montreal described as "absolutely false" the reports of an uprising in the North West Territories. "There is not the remotest symptom of trouble," it assured its readers. In Kingston, Ontario, the *Whig* reassuringly quoted a speech the prime minister made two days before Duck Lake. "I do not believe there is the slightest danger from the half-breeds," Macdonald declared, "unless they are joined by the Indians."

But this was already happening. When word of the Duck Lake incident spread across the Prairies, the old chiefs could restrain their starving followers no longer. What followed was not so much slaughter as pillage. The starving natives broke into HBC stores and the homes of white settlers and grabbed everything they could carry off, especially food. The bloody exceptions occurred around two Cree reserves: at Big Bear's Frog Lake camp in present-day Alberta, 30 miles northwest of Fort Pitt; and

Chiefs of the Blackfoot Confederacy in Ottawa after the rebellion, with Lacombe (left) and translator Jean L'Heureux. Indians (from left) North Axe of the Peigan, Three Bulls and Crowfoot of the Blackfoot, and Red Crow and One Spot of the Bloods.

Provincial Archives of Alberta, H. Pollard Collection, P-200

Public Archives of Canada

Montana Historical Society

(Above) Wandering Spirit, as sketched by one of his captives, Theresa Gowanlock. (Right) a later photograph of Big Bear's son Imasees, who fled to the United States after the uprising.

among the Assiniboine and Cree bands, the latter led by Poundmaker, in the Eagle Hills near Battleford.

Word of the defeat of the redcoats at Duck Lake reached the Frog Lake Cree on April 1 and at first many thought it was a prank. (The Indians had taken delightedly to the notion of April Fool's Day, calling it Big Lie Day and amusing themselves by playing tricks on each other.) Big Bear himself was hunting moose in the bush. The Cree had seen their local three-man detachment depart the previous day for Fort Pitt after a messenger arrived with urgent news for the Frog Lake Indian sub-agent, Thomas Trueman Quinn, one of a dozen resident and visiting whites. But Quinn, a tough, unpopular man who as a boy had survived the 1860 Sioux uprisings in Minnesota by hiding in a barrel, was not unnerved by the possibility of a Cree uprising nor were the other whites. All had elected to stay.

When Big Bear returned later on Big Lie Day, he found his son Imasees, the band War Chief Wandering Spirit and all the young men very excited. That night Wandering Spirit led the fighters of the Rattlers society to the far side of Frog Lake for a war dance, where he twice challenged them to "eat two-legged meat" with him upon the morrow. After dawn, a score of them entered the settlement fully armed and decked in their scalps, battle insignia and war feathers, their faces painted solid crimson, some with yellow daubs and heavy black stripes under their eyes.

At first they confined themselves to rounding up the whites and half-breeds and pillaging the stores and farm buildings for livestock and ammunition. Big Bear burst into the mêlée and demanded angrily that they leave the HBC store alone. After he left to see to the protection of the prisoners, however, the warriors found two cases of Perry Davis Pain Killer, which was 90% alcohol, and the fate of the Frog Lake whites was sealed.

Later that morning the whites attended a mass, at which Wandering Spirit knelt in the aisle of the mission church with his Winchester while his drunken followers roared in and out laughing, howling, beating drums and prancing around in stolen underwear and other articles of clothing. Big Bear, now quite frantic, sent a runner to Chief Kehiwin's nearby camp of peaceful Woods Cree to come and help contain the warriors. But within an hour it was too late.

The Indians ordered the prisoners to the Cree lodges and Quinn ("Sioux-speaker" to the Cree) refused. "You have a hard head," declared Wandering Spirit. "If you love your life you will do as I tell you." Quinn, perhaps unaware that Big Bear's authority had vanished the moment the warriors initiated hostilities, replied, "Big Bear has not asked me to leave. I will not go." Wandering Spirit raised his rifle. "I tell you — go!" he shouted, and thereupon shot and killed Quinn. That sent the warriors into a frenzy. Within minutes, seven more whites (two of them Oblate priests) and one Metis lay dead. Two white widows and the HBC clerk William Cameron fled to the nearby Woods Cree camp. (Cameron, who recounted his experience in his book *Blood Red the Sun*, lived another 66 years, dying in 1951.)

The fact that Big Bear himself had done everything humanly possible to prevent the butchery and then spent the next month securing the lives of the white prisoners and trying to evade further armed confrontation, did not come to light until the band's prisoners testified at his subsequent trial. Even then the evidence was widely ignored. All that the outside world heard immediately was that Big Bear had slaughtered many at Frog Lake.[7] Henry Quinn, the slain sub-agent's nephew and the settlement's blacksmith, had jumped between two houses when the firing broke out, fled through the bush and carried the news to Fort Pitt.

When it ticked back east on the telegraph, the fury of mobilization escalated everywhere, even in Quebec where more than half the men who joined up were French-speaking.[8] More significantly, however, it was learned that some 50 people had attended a "Riel sympathy meeting" at

[7] At Frog Lake in the 1990s there was a store, a school, and the hall and band office of the adjacent Indian reserve. The pit foundations of the 1885 church, school and farm manager's house could still be seen. A monument there had long commemorated the nine victims of the Frog Lake massacre, some of whom were buried in the nearby cemetery. Massacre was not a term appreciated by the residents of the reserve, however, who thought their side of the story should be acknowledged. After the remains of Big Bear's camp were discovered a mile away (complete with musket barrels and trade axes) during a survey for a Husky Oil pipeline, the pipeline was rerouted and efforts were begun to have the whole area declared a National Historic Site.

[8] Of five Quebec units called up, two were French-speaking: the 65th Rifles and the 9th Voltigeurs, which together contributed 545 men of Quebec's total of 1,012. Ontario sent 1,929 soldiers and Nova Scotia 383. Western Canada contributed 2,011, exclusive of the NWMP. Counting support troops, the total number of military personnel involved on the Canadian side was 7,982 in the army plus about 500 in the NWMP.

Rivard's Hotel in Montreal, an omen of the convulsive political consequences that would follow.

Elsewhere across the northern Prairies, from Buffalo Lake to Lac la Biche, Indians in warpaint confronted HBC and government officials, and seized food and ammunition. Big Bear's Cree, joined by several neighbouring bands and oblivious to the mustering of some 8,000 troops, police, militia and volunteers across the dominion, spent the next 10 days slaughtering cattle and feasting while the warrior faction wrangled with the older chiefs about whether to continue the depredations. In for a penny, in for a pound, argued the warriors, their ears filled by Metis messengers with bogus reports of rebel victories.

Eventually Big Bear's band moved against the Mounties at nearby Fort Pitt. The post was indefensible and when Wandering Spirit showed up on April 13 with 250 men, Big Bear insisted that they negotiate the evacuation of noncombatant whites. But midway through their parley with HBC trader William McLean outside the post, the Indians sighted three Mountie scouts returning from reconnaissance, riding hellbent for the gate. They shot one dead and ripped the body to shreds, and wounded another, who made it to safety with the third. McLean then agreed that the 44 white civilians would surrender to Wandering Spirit upon Big Bear's assurance of their safety, and in exchange the handful of redcoats would be allowed to retreat down the North Saskatchewan. Only upon the civilians' insistence did the detachment consent. They took what arms they could carry, destroyed the rest and spent the next seven cold and wet days in a leaky scow floating down to Battleford.

William McLean, the HBC factor who negotiated the surrender of 44 Fort Pitt whites to Wandering Spirit.

Battleford, meanwhile, had been in an uproar since the beginning of April. Before any word of Duck Lake reached the Cree and Assiniboine reserves scattered throughout the vicinity, Poundmaker, a handsome and level-headed man recently acknowledged as head Cree chief in that area, had decided to bring his whole band — women and children included — into the settlement. They only wanted to collect their regular rations, since the agents responsible for issuing them had fled the reserve. Word of the rebellion reached Poundmaker's band en route on March 30.

Glenbow Archives, NA-1315-18

The Battleford Cree Chief Poundmaker. After a day of pillage, his band returned to the reserve at Cut Knife Hill to await events, which were not long in arriving.

Their approach also unluckily coincided with the dual murder of an unpopular farm instructor, James Payne, on the Mosquito Assiniboine reserve south of town, and of a neighbouring white farmer, Barney Tremont, who refused to give horses to the Assiniboine killers. Poundmaker's approach was therefore assumed to be hostile. Some 500 Battleford settlers immediately fled to the town's NWMP barracks, and Indian agent J.M. Rae refused to come out and parley. The Battleford HBC trader, named McKay, and another man ventured forth instead, and agreed to surrender food from the HBC store. As they returned, they were shot at by some roving Metis but weren't hit.

While these negotiations were proceeding, some Assiniboine and Cree began looting the empty houses, and it was only by the next day that Poundmaker and other chiefs prevailed upon them to stop. The Indians then returned to Poundmaker's reserve to await a response from Ottawa to their urgent appeal for more food. Robert Jefferson, a government farm instructor on the Poundmaker reserve who was married (simultaneously) to two of the chief's daughters, says in his memoirs (*Fifty Years on the Saskatchewan*) that the returning Indians helped several departmental officials cross the Battle River on their way to safety, and that most of the looting was perpetrated by whites after the Indians were gone. In similar fashion, the government cook survived Poundmaker's "attack" by serving meals to anyone who came into his kitchen. The settlers, however, remained cramped behind the NWMP palisade for the next three uneventful weeks, sending out a stream of telegrams expressing their conviction that Poundmaker was on the warpath.

During the crucial weeks that Riel's doubtful Cree allies feasted and powwowed farther west, there was a similar stalemate downstream at Fort Carlton, where the whole thing had started. NWMP Commissioner Irvine deemed the fort indefensible. He evacuated the Mountie force and the wounded from Duck Lake to Prince Albert, a hazardous endeavour since it meant moving through Metis-held territory. Again Dumont urged an attack on the vulnerable Mounties, and again Riel restrained him. But Prince Albert now could be defended; it would pose a constant threat to Riel from the north when Canadian troops would later move upon him from the south.

With the Mounties holed up at Prince Albert and Battleford, Riel's power had reached its peak; panic spread throughout the future province of Alberta. At Lac la Biche, 90 miles northwest of Frog Lake, the people became terrified at the rumour Big Bear was headed there next. Both Metis and whites met to decide what to do. "All these gentlemen were terrified," wrote Bishop H.J. Faraud, "their faces distorted with fear."

Here, too, the Indians were starving and had already been considering an attack on the local HBC fort. H.S. Young, the HBC manager, was sent to Edmonton where a pack train was furnished with supplies for the Indians and sent back north. When word of the Frog Lake slaughter reached the freighters, however, they refused to continue and turned back. Young carried on home and to his horror found his store stripped of all its goods and the other buildings wrecked.

The scene at Lac la Biche had repeated the one at Battleford. The Indians had first asked for goods. Upon refusal, they moved in and took them. "There followed," Bishop Faraud wrote to his Oblate superior, "an indescribable scene, men, women and children charging into the store, and

A condensed schematic of the Battle of Fish Creek, as sketched by an officer in Middleton's column. The general (at centre, pointing) is directing fire from a nine-pounder into the bluff below, occupied by Dumont's snipers in rifle pits. Thus ensconced, 150 rebels held the Canadian force of 800 at bay for the day. The smoke in the left rear is rising from a Metis farmyard bombarded by Canadian artillery; the smoke at right results from an unsuccessful Metis grass fire aimed at disorganizing the army. The ambush cost the Canadians 10 dead and 40 wounded, compared to four dead and fewer wounded among the Metis and Indians.

Illustrated London News

invading the houses. After less than 15 minutes, scarcely a pin was left. Merchandise, provisions of all descriptions, furs, everything had disappeared. At the instigation of the Metis rebels, they smashed the windows, doors, tables, and chopped the chairs to pieces with axes. Books of every description were torn up and carried away by the wind. The women amused themselves by tearing up the carpets, and ripping apart Mrs. Young's clothes, and slicing them up with scissors. They had orders not to burn anything and they did not. But everyone who saw the place beheld a beautiful little fort reduced to a scene of utter desolation."

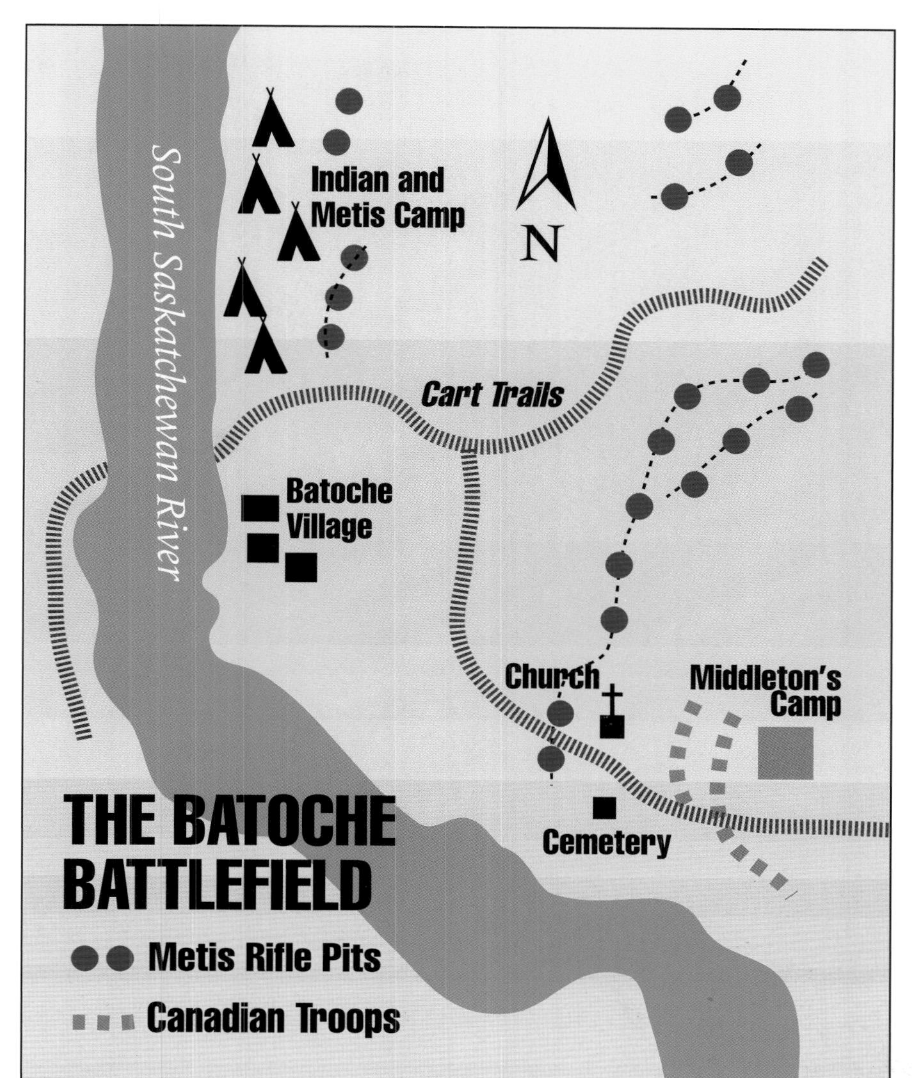

The Lac la Biche citizenry, mostly Metis, fled in terror into the bush and later took refuge in the nearby Oblate mission. An emissary from Wandering Spirit arrived and demanded they join the rebellion. When they refused, he warned he would be back, but he never reappeared. At Lac Ste. Anne and Rivière Qui Barre northwest of Edmonton, the Indians pledged their support for the rebellion. The Indian agents fled for Edmonton. At Battle River Crossing, near the future Ponoka, the whites fled and the Indians took over the HBC store and their possessions.

Panic accounts meanwhile poured out from the papers of Ontario. The Belleville *Intelligencer* reported that Fort Carlton was under bombardment. (Actually, some of the buildings had been burned by accident when Irvine's force withdrew.) The *Kingston Daily News* reported an Indian agent murdered at File Hills near Fort Qu'Appelle. (He wasn't.) Seven thousand Indians under Chief Piapot were rising in the Treaty 4 region, said the *Globe* (they weren't), and the mayor of Calgary had telegraphed urgently to send troops (he had). An emissary of Riel had reached the Sioux around Portage la Prairie, Manitoba, and they were ready to rise, said the *Globe*. (He had, and they weren't.) The Fenians[9] were preparing to invade Manitoba, said the *Kingston Daily News*. (They weren't.) A newspaper in St. Paul reported 40 Cree in full warpaint besieging Swift Current, the settlers huddling in the CPR station, and a paper in Winnipeg denied it, adding that you couldn't believe anything you read in the newspaper in St. Paul, which was using the rebellion to divert settlers into Minnesota.

The *Globe* poured a stream of invective upon "Old Tomorrow," its accustomed appellation for Prime Minister Macdonald who, it said, had caused the rebellion by putting off the Metis problems. "If the advice of the *Globe* had been taken," it added, in the sanctimonious style its critics would complain about for the next hundred years and more, "all this trouble and all this loss of life would have been avoided."

But as everyone on the southern Prairies, especially in Calgary, knew, the key question remained to be answered. What would the Blackfoot do? They had been the most fearsome warriors on the plains. All eyes were turned on their great chief, Crowfoot.

Here Macdonald had moved already. As soon as the rebellion began, he telegraphed a message to Father Albert Lacombe who he knew had the confidence of the Blackfoot. Persuade them to stay out of it, he urged. Lacombe obliged and wired back Crowfoot's assurance of neutrality. Crowfoot himself confirmed this, assuring the prime minister, "We will be loyal to the Queen whatever happens." But as Lacombe later observed, Crowfoot used the rebellion as a device to gain further con-

9 A group of dissidents in the Fenian Brotherhood, an Irish independence society organized in New York City, defied its own superiors and organized military raids on Canada in the 1860s. All were quickly repulsed. Another abortive raid was made during the Red River insurrection. Rumours of further Fenian raids unsettled Canada for two more decades, though none occurred.

Saskatchewan Archives Board, S-A42

Big Bear (centre) under arrest in Prince Albert. The others (from left) are Sergeant Smart, Const. Colebrook, Const. Nichols and Const. Sullivan.

cessions from the government, and sure enough, new food supplies were rushed to his camps. A few weeks later Crowfoot found another reason to stay put, when he saw hundreds of soldiers passing through Blackfoot country on the CPR. The troops from Canada were arriving and they looked formidable indeed.

What Crowfoot observed were the 65th Rifles of Montreal, the Winnipeg Light Infantry and the 9th Voltigeurs of Quebec, which were reinforcing two mounted scout units recruited locally, and numerous local militia units.[10] These were all placed under the command of Major-General T.B. Strange, a retired artillery officer who had taken up ranching and was now recalled to service. Beside the general rode the NWMP's Sam Steele, precipitately called away from his liquor control efforts in British Columbia.

Strange was to head one of three attacks northward from the CPR main line. He was to advance on Edmonton, then proceed down the North Saskatchewan and relieve Fort Pitt. The presence of his force was also intended to discourage the Indians of the western plains from joining those in rebellion, precisely the effect it had on Crowfoot. A second force under Colonel W.D. Otter was to advance north from Swift Current and relieve Battleford. The main force under Major-General Frederick Middleton, the commander in chief, was to drive north from Qu'Appelle and take the Metis stronghold at Batoche.

The plan, says historian George Stanley, was well conceived but badly executed. It might indeed have been a disaster except for the actions of Riel himself. Dumont implored Riel to sanction the kind of guerrilla tactics the Metis position obviously demanded. Blow up the CPR line and kill the troops en route, he urged. Riel overruled him. That was no way to fight a war, he said. Harry them at night, proposed Dumont, so they get no sleep and their morale cracks. Good soldiers do not attack at night, responded Riel.

And as Middleton moved north he kept his best cavalry in the rear, the Metis observed, exposing his infantry to frontal assault by skilled riders. The front could be turned and made to stampede just like the buffalo, said Dumont. These are not buffalo, Riel countered, they are human beings. Dumont seethed yet obeyed, and waited for an outcome that seemed increasingly hopeless — a few hundred poorly armed Metis, using mostly shotguns for which they had very little ammunition, against troops equipped with artillery, rifles, and worst of all, a Gatling gun[11] (an early version of the machine gun) that they had acquired from the Americans.

The Canadians had their problems too, chief among them Middleton, who distrusted his troops because they were colonials. Some of them, he noted in exasperation, had never before fired a gun. He therefore advanced with a caution that exasperated his men, while a Metis spy who served as a freight-hand in his column dutifully reported daily to Dumont. Then, when Middleton reached the

[10] From Calgary, Fort Macleod and Medicine Hat came the Rocky Mountain Rangers and Steele's Scouts. St. Albert, a Metis community that opposed the rebellion, contributed the St. Albert Mounted Riflemen. In addition nearly every community had its home guards.

[11] The Gatling gun, named for its inventor, Richard Jordan Gatling, consisted of six, eight or 10 rifle barrels enclosed in a case and revolving on a pivot. The cartridges were fed through a hopper down concentric grooves, dropping into each breech and discharging the shell casing as the bundle of barrels revolved. Its manufacturers made spectacular claims for it, declaring it could discharge 2,100 cartridges a minute.

South Saskatchewan at Clarke's Crossing, he ordered a move that has mystified historians ever since. He divided his force, sending half of it down the river's left bank, half down the right (left and right, that is, as you face downstream). Thus he would have to meet any attack with precisely half his force. Noting this, Dumont was finally able to persuade Riel to allow an attack on the enemy before they reached Batoche where the outcome would be certain Metis defeat.

Dumont hid about 150 men in Fish Creek ravine, 17 miles south of Batoche, directly in the path of Middleton's right-bank force of about 800. Although Dumont's men opened fire too soon to effect surprise, his main tactic worked. As the Canadians appeared silhouetted against the sky over the edge of the ravine, the sharp-shooting buffalo hunters picked them off. After some hours of this, Middleton's artillery finally got the range of the ravine. Many of the Metis fled, although some 50 held the position until nightfall, then withdrew in the darkness. The Battle of Fish Creek was a draw, but its effect was to delay Middleton by two weeks, giving Riel time to play his last card.

This consisted of an appeal to Poundmaker and Big Bear to join him at Batoche and inflict a major defeat upon Middleton. Neither chief was in control, however; they were unable to gain consensus among their followers. In Big Bear's camp, the Plains Cree wanted to move to Batoche, the much more passive Woods Cree to stay put. In Poundmaker's, the Stoney and some of his own young warriors were for action, the older chiefs for staying put. This procrastination removed the last hope of rebel success.

At Swift Current the first concern of Otter's mounted column was the relief of Battleford. Meeting no resistance, he moved rapidly north and took just 10 days to reach the jubilant settlers on April 24. Middleton's orders were that Otter stay there, but his troops were eager for action. Otter therefore wired for, and received, the approval of Indian Commissioner Edgar Dewdney to "punish" (in Otter's words) Poundmaker's band for its "great depredations" by launching a surprise attack by the greater part of his 550-man force against the Cree reserve. He set out the night of April 28 with 325 men, 48 wagons, two seven-pound pieces of artillery and a Gatling gun.

The Cree were camped 25 miles to the west on their reserve at Cut Knife Hill,[12] named after a Sarcee whom the Cree had defeated there in years gone by. Poundmaker had been containing his own young hothead faction, along with sundry Assiniboine warriors and Metis agitators, for the past several weeks. Just before dawn on April 29, an old Cree named Jacob With the Long Hair came yelling through the camp that soldiers were coming up the hill.

As men, women and children fled in confusion from their tepees, a volley of rifle-fire struck the lodges, knocking several over. No one was injured, however, and in short order some 50 warriors were shooting back. Otter's men soon gained the abandoned camp, but found themselves exposed and being picked off by Cree in the surrounding brush. This went on for most of the day, the Cree losing five men and the Canadians eight. With darkness approaching, Otter saw that his position was already dangerous and growing worse. He ordered a retreat to the next hill. At that point, says historian Stanley, Poundmaker could have cut Otter's force to pieces but he held his men in check.

Otter's aim had been to teach the Cree a lesson. At the Battle of Cut Knife Hill they had learned one, though not

[12] Poundmaker's body was reburied beneath a monument that commemorates him at Cut Knife Hill. A cairn marks the battle site.

The fortified Northcote, *sent against Batoche. The Metis lowered their ferry cable and sheared off both funnels, putting it out of action.*

Glenbow Archives, NA-363-50

Captain James Peters, photographer, Glenbow Archives, NA-363-41

The Batoche battlefield. After three days of cautious skirmishing with defenders in rifle pits along the brow of a slope behind the church, Canadian militia ignored orders and charged from their left flank around the cemetery. Short of ammunition and badly outnumbered, the Metis defenders broke and ran. The Canadians rapidly captured the village, and then returned sniper fire from a few Metis in the woods along the river. The rebels soon dispersed, however, and the battle was over, with eight Canadians dead.

the lesson he intended. They had discovered that, though outnumbered three to two, they could defeat the Canadians. Bolstered by this reassurance, they began moving to reinforce Riel at Batoche. They had barely begun, however, when the news arrived that Batoche had fallen and Riel was captured.

Reinforcement for Middleton had been sent with the steamer *Northcote*, on loan to the army and equipped with cannon. Its attack on Batoche from the river was meant to coincide with Middleton's land attack, but it got there early. What followed, the first "naval" action in prairie history, was a fiasco. The Metis lowered their ferry cable across the river. It sheared off the *Northcote*'s two funnels, leaving ship and crew drifting helplessly downstream.

Middleton meanwhile had retrieved his force from the left bank of the river and his army was moving upon Batoche. He was greatly discomfited to find the town ingeniously defended, however, with well-constructed rifle pits along the river bank and around the town. Thus the defenders were able to fire from a thoroughly protected position on very vulnerable attackers. Repeated assaults scarcely touched the defenders, let alone dislodged them, and only under the constant protective fire of the Gatling gun or artillery could Middleton's men move forward at all. He kept up these assaults for three days, his casualties mounting and his troops getting more and more disillusioned. The tactic had only one great merit; the Metis were running out of ammunition.

On the fourth day, May 12, Middleton changed the plan. He sent a diversionary force of 150 to a flank of the town hitherto unassailed, in order to execute a dual assault from both sides. This too misfired in execution. One side attacked and the other didn't. Furious, he ordered his troops back to their original positions. But the militia units, now thoroughly fed up, simply disobeyed him, and with loud whoops suddenly launched a frontal assault upon the town. The Metis, overwhelmed, fled for the woods, Riel among them.[13] Within about 15 minutes the Canadians entered Batoche and captured it, the victory secured by their disobedience.

A Metis rifle pit at Batoche.

Riel hovered in the woods four miles north of Batoche for three days, before he was discovered by two scouts. He surrendered willingly upon assurance that he would not be tried by a military court. Dumont replied with defiance to a summons to surrender. He had 90 cartridges left, he said, to fire at anybody who wanted to come and get him. He escaped to Montana. Middleton sailed on the hastily repaired *Northcote* to Prince Albert where Irvine's Mounties had been kept inactive ever since they'd evacuated

Glenbow Archives, NA-363-47

Daniel Ross, one of 12 Metis and Indians slain in the final charge. According to Dumont, one of the dead was 93 years old, another 75. Ross was also very old, but his exact age is not known.

Carlton — much to the scorn of the Canadian soldiers who called them "gophers" (because they allegedly disappeared at the first sign of trouble). Then he moved up the river and received the surrender of Poundmaker. The chief demanded terms. Middleton replied that Riel's surrender had been unconditional and so must his be. Poundmaker's bedraggled followers, hungry and despairing, excited only pity as they appeared at Battleford and laid down their arms.

Strange's force in the meantime had moved without opposition from Calgary to Edmonton, then by barge down the North Saskatchewan to the abandoned Fort Pitt. He now turned upon the only enemy left, Big Bear, and discovered his camp near a hill called Frenchman's Butte, on the river 25 miles northeast of present-day Lloydminster. As the women and children dug pits to shelter themselves, the warriors defended the hill, beating back several assaults by Strange's force. When the artillery shrapnel rained down upon them, however, they prepared to surrender. But suddenly Strange, believing the attack a failure, called it off.

The Cree, encumbered by women, children and a collection of exhausted white prisoners, stumbled north through mud and rain and swollen waist-deep streams. Strange, fearing a trap and remembering Custer's disastrous "last stand" on the Little Bighorn in Montana, did not immediately follow. Steele's Scouts caught up to Big Bear, skirmished with him at Steele Narrows, and withdrew.

For the next three weeks both Strange's force and Middleton's lugged their heavy equipment through the muskeg of northern Saskatchewan in pursuit of Big Bear, moving slower even than the old chief, his women, children and prisoners. But the Indian leader, who had opposed the war from the beginning, could not hold together the coalition of Plains and Woods Cree that the war chiefs had contrived. The former wanted to continue the fight, the latter gradually vanished into the bush. Big Bear, furnishing his prisoners with new moccasins and supplies, sent them south in the care of an HBC officer. They reached Fort Pitt on June 24 after 62 days as captives. Big Bear himself darted first north, then south, dodging the troops until he reached Fort Carlton. There he surrendered to his friend Sergeant Smart of the North-West Mounted Police.

Thanks chiefly to the Canadian Pacific Railway, the North West Rebellion was over. But its consequences had not yet begun. They were about to cause the biggest reversal ever suffered in Canadian politics.❦

[13] Riel's discussions with his council during the siege of Batoche, it was later revealed, had not been concerned with the attack at all, but with what the days of the week would be called under the new heaven-directed regime he was establishing.

Glenbow Archives, NA-1081-3

Riel standing in the dock, addressing the jury. Judge Richardson, wearing spectacles, is seated to Riel's immediate left, behind the bench.

The hanging of Riel changed our politics for a whole century

'Deliver us...' he said, and the trap was sprung – Quebec Torydom perished with him

When Louis Riel raised the Metis in revolt at Batoche in 1885, the Conservative party had been the ruling force in Quebec for the entire 18 years of the confederated Canada's life. Ontario might and did waver into Liberalism. Not Quebec. It was both small-c and capital-C conservative, provincially and federally, its clergy standing in unswerving support of Sir John A. Macdonald's government.

Two years later, the Conservative power in the province had been so thoroughly demolished that throughout the 20th century no provincial Conservative administration ever existed there again and — apart from a single short-lived interval in the 1950s — the Conservatives would have no hope of gaining the province federally until the rise of Brian Mulroney precisely 99 years after the rebellion broke out.

The unquestionable cause of this, the greatest political reversal in Canadian history, was the trial and execution of Louis Riel. It began in April 1885 as what seemed a mere tremble of support for him at a Riel sympathy meeting in Montreal, attended by about 50 people. It had mounted by the year's end into an earthquake that shook down the central bastion of Tory power in Canada.

At the heart of the quarrel was religion. The ultra-Protestant Orange Order,[a] the most powerful force in Ontario, demanded that Riel be executed as a French Catholic traitor and murderer. The Quebec response was *la voix du sang,* literally the "voice of blood." Quebeckers defended him as a French Catholic compatriot. The irony was that Riel had been ousted by the church for heresy from the day the rebellion broke out.

From his surrender at Batoche onward he cut an increasingly pathetic and compelling figure, one that has inspired novelists, poets, even an opera. His insanity, expressed in his extravagant religious pronouncements, far from damaging this appeal, served only to strengthen interest in him. So did the growing realization that however strange his theology, his cause had great merit, was essentially just, and commanded increasing support all over the world as the press followed him to his doom.

Riel was transferred to the North-West Mounted Police jail in Regina and kept under heavy guard. By then a Riel Defence Committee had been organized in Quebec and funds raised to send west four eminent counsel — François Lemieux, Charles Fitzpatrick, J.N. Greenshields and T.C. Johnstone — to defend him. Discovering when they arrived that all Regina's hotels, such as they were, were full, they spent their first night on the floor of the courtroom in the town's land titles office.

Riel had begun giving interviews to the press immediately upon his arrest, disclosing that he had been appointed by God

Judge Hugh Richardson. The defendant must hold his peace or dismiss his lawyers

"to occupy the greatest position in the dominion." The charge was high treason and the trial judge was a stipendiary magistrate, Hugh Richardson, the retired lieutenant-colonel of an Ontario militia regiment, a bank manager who had become a lawyer, practised in Woodstock, Ontario, and served briefly with the Department of Justice. He had a reputation for balance and fairness.

The trial opened in July, four months after the rebellion broke out. Riel, confident of acquittal, appeared in court in a light tweed suit with a huge white sombrero he habitually doffed in a sweeping bow. His lawyers questioned the jurisdiction of the Regina court. The objection was summarily dismissed. In the dock Riel scoffed aloud. (No appeal was ever permitted.) The judge asked him how he pleaded. "I have the honour to answer that I am not guilty," he replied. The jury panel consisted of 30 farmers, four merchants, a hotelkeeper and a contractor, of whom six, all English-speaking, were selected to hear the case.

Meanwhile 10,000 people turned out to cheer the returning troops as they began arriving at Winnipeg on 20 CPR coaches. Their British general paid lavish tribute to Canada and "the bravery of her sons." The lieutenant-governor of Manitoba declared how fortunate Canada was to have such a soldier to lead them. All of this engendered increasing disgust in Quebec. What these men had defeated with rifles, cannons and machine guns, it was muttered, was at most a thousand half-armed, largely illiterate farmers whom they outnumbered eight to one (a contention that ignored, however, the 20,000 Indians, many of whom may have stood ready to join the rebellion).

Saskatchewan Archives Board, R-B278

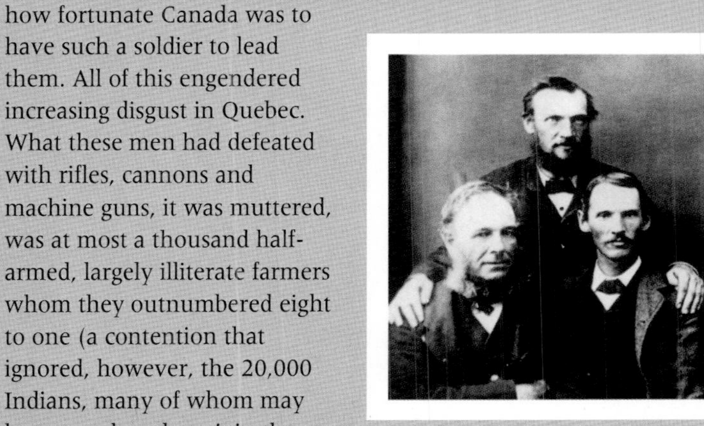

The six anglophone jurors who urged mercy, (from left) Francis Cosgrove, Walter Merryfield, Edwin Brooks, Ped Deane, Henry Painter and Ed Evett. Brooks later said that they wished they had a federal cabinet minister in the dock alongside Riel.

At Regina, Riel himself and his lawyers submitted affidavits declaring that the witnesses who could establish Riel's innocence had all escaped to Montana. Would the Crown grant them immunity to return and testify? The Crown would not. The lawyers then read another affidavit declaring Riel not guilty by reason of insanity. In the midst of this Riel jumped to his feet. "Insane?" he shouted. "If I am insane, I want to know it. Perhaps I am, but it would be satisfactory to know my mental condition." He asked to address the court, but was not allowed to.

At Winnipeg that day an effigy of Riel was suspended across Main Street in front of the Brunswick Hotel. Beneath it was a gallows and under that were Roman candles. At a signal, the figure dropped into the fireworks which went off and consumed it in flame. "A large crowd seemed to gather a good deal of amusement from the display," said one newspaper report.

As the Crown's case unfolded, witness after witness from Batoche was called. One testified that Riel had declared "a war of extermination." He had said, "We want blood, blood, blood! Nothing but blood will do us." Another said Riel seemed to be conducting a "revenge" against Sir John A. Macdonald. The defence succeeded in deriving from almost every witness assertions attributed to Riel which seemed to establish his insanity. When mention was made of his "Republic of the Saskatchewan" there were roars of laughter from spectators. The *Montreal Star* reported: "Riel does not appreciate this merriment, and with an expression of mingled rage and despair, gazes about the court. He shakes his head."

Finally the Crown called Riel's old friend, cousin and supporter, Charles Nolin, a key member of his "cabinet," to testify against him. Nolin spoke of Riel showing him a book, written in blood, in which his plans for a new world government were described. Riel swayed back and forth in the dock, sitting down, then springing to his feet. He finally broke down. "Your honour," he exclaimed, "this case is getting extraordinary. My counsel are men of great talent, gentlemen of ability, and while endeavouring to acquit me of the serious charges of high treason, are endeavouring to show that I am insane...I deem it my duty in defending myself to ask the witness a number of questions."

The judge replied that only his lawyers could question witnesses. Riel fell back in his seat. "I obey your call," he said, then turned to the jury and remarked: "Oh but then its effect will be lost on the jury, and the testimony cannot be destroyed."

The judge said Riel must either dismiss his counsel and conduct his own defence or let his lawyers do it. He couldn't do both. "My cause is in their hands," Riel replied despairingly. "Kind and unforgetful friends, known in better days, have sent them here to defend me."

Again Riel sought to speak and again the judge refused him, his lawyers adding that they could not continue to defend him if he did not remain silent. Riel, still distressed with the insanity plea, seemed exasperated. He shook with emotion as he said, "I cannot abandon my dignity. I realize to the fullest extent what confinement in an insane asylum is [he had spent more than two years in Quebec asylums]. No, I don't care for an animal existence unless it is accompanied by the neutral dignity of an intelligent being." Then, turning to the reporters, he added: "Take that down."

Two Oblate priests were called in his defence, and said they considered Riel insane. A fellow jail inmate was called and said the same, mentioning Riel's prayers which kept him awake all night. Two doctors described Riel's insanity as "ambitious mania."

Glenbow Archives, NA-433-1

Glenbow Archives, NA-4140-1

21 of august,
Some one will write to
Charles Nolin to make him
ashame of himself, for
having given a testimony
of imagination, of contra
dictions, of revenge, of
falsehoods.
I hope that through our
Saviour's help, that will
be written after my
acquittal.

Charles Nolin, who testified against Riel, and a memo Riel wrote about Nolin's 'testimony of imagination, of contradictions, of revenge, of falsehoods.'

The jury returned a guilty verdict and recommended mercy, but Riel was sentenced to be hanged in September. Across the country the conflict became increasingly nasty. A Quebec clerical paper declared that French troops had been sent "against their own brothers," and that every soldier who belonged to the Orange Order carried in his pocket a little piece of rope to hang Riel. A Tory paper in Toronto attacked the conduct of the French troops when in action. All over Quebec rallies demanded that Riel's life be spared, 3,000 braving a Quebec City blizzard to register their outrage. Riel's lawyers, back from the trial, addressed another crowd estimated at 5,000, Fitzpatrick declaring Riel's cause just, whatever Riel's condition.

The superior of the Oblate Order, which had opposed the rebellion, observed that its real cause lay in an Ottawa government indifferent to the country it had taken over. He cast the first doubts on the Canadian troops who, he said, had "disgraced themselves in the most shameful fashion by the wholesale plundering of half-breed property." Even their commander had "personally appropriated" a fine horse and wagon.[b]

Continuing press interviews with Riel gained him more sympathy. His behaviour was courteous; he bowed to his guards; he found it "no trouble at all" to provide all visitors with autographs. "Humanly speaking," he said, "nothing can save me," though he was confident he would be "preserved from death through the divine and saving influence of our Lord Jesus Christ." At St. Vital outside Winnipeg, it was reported that his aging mother, who had become "crazed" during the rebellion, was now "able to realize the dreadful position in which her son is placed." His brother Joseph, a "respected" man, was "in a dreadful state of mind." His wife, who had endured the rebellion with him, was "nearly heart-broken."

In November the anti-Macdonald *Globe* made another disclosure. Some of the lands upon which the Metis lived had been given over to the Prince Albert Colonization Company. Tory MP John White was a blind shareholder in this company, the *Globe* revealed. So was a man the newspaper identified as Mr. Jamieson, son-in-law of Mackenzie Bowell, a Macdonald cabinet minister.[c]

On November 15, after three postponements, word arrived at the Regina jail. Riel was to be hanged in 20 hours. Two companies of troops now guarded the jail, amid rumours that the Indians were about to rise in rebellion again. "Well," said Riel as the sombre sheriff approached him, "and so you have come with the great announcement. I am glad." The sheriff then told him its contents. "I am glad," Riel continued, "that at last I am to be released from my sufferings."

He thanked the sheriff for his "personal consideration" while he had been in jail, and asked to be buried in St. Boniface, Manitoba, the province created as a result of his rebellion. The sheriff asked what should be done with his personal estate and effects. "Mon cher," replied Riel, touching his breast, "I have only this. This I gave to my country fifteen years ago and it is all I have to give now."

Pandemonium broke out in French Canada. Telegrams descended upon the offices of Macdonald's Quebec ministers. Riots were expected in Montreal if the execution went ahead. There were rumours of an impending insurrection in St. Boniface. The British government privately advised Macdonald to call it off. All over the world, newspapers were coming out on Riel's side. "He shall hang," vowed Macdonald, "though every dog in Quebec bark in his favour." The quotation was to haunt the Tory party in Quebec for decades to come.

Riel had a last meal of eggs and toast, and now, reconciled at last with the church, took the advice of Father Alexis André and publicly blessed Macdonald. "I pray that God will bless Sir John and give him grace and wisdom to manage the affairs of Canada well," he said.

He was neither sad nor gloomy on his last night, said Father André. Riel spoke of the execution of Thomas Scott, which he had ordered, and recalled that when the firing squad failed, he had ordered a final shot to put the man out of his misery. He hoped his hangman would be equally efficient.[d] Had he not executed Scott, he said, the Red River colony would have been torn by rebellion, and many more lives lost.

He recited in Latin the *Laetatus Sum*, the 122nd Psalm:

> I was glad when they said unto me,
> We will go unto the house of the Lord,
> My feet shall stand
> Within thy gates, O Jerusalem.

He was then told the time had come. He seemed to faint momentarily, but recovered himself, walked resolutely to the scaffold, prayed for 20 minutes, responded clearly and resolutely to the ritual prayers for the dying, declined to make any final statement, bowed to the *Globe* reporter (one of four persons allowed as witnesses) and recited the Lord's Prayer with a priest as the hood was adjusted. At the words, "deliver us," the trap as prearranged fell from beneath his feet and, said the *Globe*, "Louis 'David' Riel was launched into eternity." He died within two minutes. He was 41.

Gone with him were the fortunes of the Conservative Party in Quebec. Thousands turned out in Montreal after *La Patrie* called for "voices that might be heard, from the shores of the Atlantic to those of the Pacific, in protestation of the execution of Riel." Macdonald was fighting fiercely to hold his caucus and cabinet together. His cabinet was a curious mix, ranging from Bowell, the Orange grand master, to Sir Hector Langevin, the head of the ultramontane Catholic party. Sixteen Quebec MPs quit the caucus, and it took all the skills Macdonald had acquired in a lifetime of politics to hold the cabinet together. But hold he did, playing one French member off against another and repeatedly warning that if Canadian politics split along strictly French vs. English lines, the country could not survive.

The Liberals moved swiftly in Quebec, their brightest young star, Wilfrid Laurier, declaring: "If I had lived on the shores of the Saskatchewan I would have taken up a rifle myself to defend my property." To underline his support for the Metis, he contested and won the Saskatchewan seat in the Commons when he led the party to its great upset victory in 1896. His was one of the four seats whose establishment in the territories is widely regarded as an accomplishment of Riel's.

If the Conservative cause suffered in Quebec, the Liberal one fared no better in Ontario. The championing of Riel split the federal Liberal caucus just as gravely, and the wily Macdonald quietly had a French Conservative put forward the motion that deplored the execution. This gave the Tories the chance to speak first on the question every day and prevent the Liberals from moving an amendment. In the end the motion was defeated 146-52, with 17 Conservatives voting for it, and 24 Liberals against.

Glenbow Archives, NA-3012-9

A RIEL UGLY POSITION.

But political adroitness could save the Quebec Tories only so long. The next provincial election left them as a minority government. When the new Nationalist party, created by the Riel furore, united with the Liberals, this brought down the government. A Liberal-Nationalist coalition formed an administration, the Nationalist party soon disappeared, and Quebec's long Liberal era began. Federally, Macdonald, strengthened by the achievement the Canadian Pacific represented, won one more election. But Laurier triumphed in '96, burying Quebec's federal Tories for years — until in another age and another century Quebec nationalism would sweep aside its Catholicism, and a new set of political imperatives would take control. *T.B.*❦

[a] The Orange Order was created in late 18th-century Ireland to maintain the country's "Protestant constitution." Its name commemorates William of Orange's victory at the Battle of the Boyne. Loyal Orange Lodges spread throughout the world and were especially active in Toronto.

[b] Margaret R. Stobie in *The Other Side of Rebellion* tells how valuable furs were also stolen from Charles Bremner, a prosperous Scottish halfbreed who was trapping, trading and farming near Poundmaker's reserve. Bremner and his family were taken prisoner by Poundmaker's people, and when the army found him among them he was charged with treason. While he was being tried and acquitted, his stock of fur was seized on Middleton's orders — and not, it seemed, for the benefit of the dominion government either. A long legal battle finally ended with the declaration that Middleton's action had been "unwarrantable and illegal." Western members kept bitterly raising the Bremner question in the House of Commons, but not until 1899, by which time Bremner was impoverished, did he get compensation for his fur: $5,364.50.

[c] Future prime minister Mackenzie Bowell was also grand master of the Grand Lodge of Ontario East, and later grand master and sovereign of the Orange Association of British America. As an MP he moved for the expulsion of Riel from parliament, thereby winning a grateful testimonial from the Orange organization.

[d] The hangman, Jack Henderson, had been Riel's prisoner at Red River 16 years before. Part of Riel's hair, his suit buttons, his moccasins, even his suspenders were removed from the body and cut up as mementos.

CHAPTER THREE

The West pays for a sea-to-sea Canada, but the Americans force a new deal

CENTRAL B.C. WAS BECOMING AN AMERICAN STATE, SO THE CPR WAS ALLOWED TO CROSS THE CROW'S NEST IF IT CUT THE GRAIN RATES, AS DEATH AND DISEASE IN ITS CAMPS BECAME A NATIONAL SCANDAL

The fewer towns along a railway line, the less money the line will make. That is the rule of railway economics. For Canada it posed a dilemma. Either Canada must connect east to west through American territory or defy the economics of the railroad industry.

The government of Sir John A. Macdonald chose the latter. If Canada was to be a sea-to-sea nation, it must set aside mere economics. Populating its enormous new western territory required a railway. The same boxcars could ship Quebec and Ontario manufactured goods west and grain east.[1] But where should this railway run? Economically, there could only be one answer. Already railroads were crossing the American West. The cheapest avenue for western Canadian grain was through St. Paul and Chicago. That way, the rail system would be supported not only by the Canadian prairie towns it served but by the American towns along its route as well.

But the implications for Canadian nationalism would be fatal. Canada's entire communication with its western region would be subject to the control and prices charged by the American railroads. Worse still, western Canadians would have to travel through St. Paul and Chicago before they got to Toronto or Montreal. Their Canadian connection would be something that lay far beyond their American one. How long before the American became the real one, their "Canadianism" purely hypothetical? Not very long, Macdonald concluded.

But an all-Canada route would mean building a line across the immense, desolate forests of northern Ontario, blasting through the granite of Lake Superior's north shore, then through interminable ridges of rock and miles of muskeg swamp between the Lakehead and the open Prairie. And what traffic would pay for all this? Where were the towns? There weren't any, and none could be expected to appear. Apart from fur traders, Indian bands and a few sawmills, there was nothing between southern Ontario and the Red River, and in all that distance there was little possibility of agricultural development. In short, an all-Canada route would be a financial disaster.

[1] When the CPR was built there was as yet no case for shipping the grain west. The Panama Canal was not opened until 1914, meaning that grain bound for European ports would have to round Cape Horn. Rice-eating Asia then provided no market for Canadian wheat, oats and barley.

Provincial Archives of Alberta, A-9163

When Canadian Pacific financier George Stephen and others sounded out the London money markets to finance such a venture, they at first met only with scorn. A railway around the north shore of Superior? Nonsense! It would be closed four months of the year, sneered one New York newspaper. So Stephen reached a conclusion. Only if there were an absolute guarantee that no traffic from the Canadian West could move south through the United States could the capital be raised, and even then it was dicy. Macdonald reluctantly accepted. It was either a monopoly railway in the West, or no coast-to-coast Canada, he decided. After a furious debate in the Commons, the contract, with the monopoly clause in it, was approved.

But the price of this monopoly — the price, that is, of sustaining a railway through more than 1,000 miles of nowhere — would fall squarely upon the farmers who sold the grain and bought the goods the railway shipped out and in. It would be they who supported the coast-to-coast national aspirations of eastern Canada. Would they be prepared to do this? And even if they were, was it economically possible?

Glenbow Archives, NA-3012-24

As the CPR neared completion in 1885, and western protest over the CPR monopoly began to swell, Grip magazine ran this cartoon likening the railway to a fattened pig.

The first returns were not at all reassuring. By 1885, much of the Manitoba countryside along the three-year-old main line was already a wilderness of abandoned farms, each a broken dream. Early frosts had made short work of the Red Fife wheat upon which so many hopes had been placed. And even if a crop were taken off, the price of everything from men's boots to horse harness was crazily beyond prices in Toronto and Montreal, or even across the border in the Dakotas, simply because of the CPR's freight rates.

Worse still was the price the farmer received for his wheat. International markets determined grain prices. You took that price, subtracted from it shipping costs, and the farmer got whatever was left. It was such a pittance, he couldn't live. So he pulled up stakes and left for the United States. That had been the common experience.

The survivors meanwhile raged against the CPR monopoly. Their neighbours across the border, they said, were charged far less to ship their grain. Why couldn't Canadian farmers use the American lines? Manitoba determined to fight it out. The result was a terrible showdown, one that threatened to produce another armed rebellion.

The province, enraged at the CPR's rates, had incorporated a rival railway under provincial charter. Macdonald called provincial railway charters illegal and ordered it revoked. Manitoba refused, forcing Macdonald to concede that he had no legal grounds. But, he declared, if that Manitoba railway "invades" the CPR's protected territory, the 15-mile strip along the U.S. border in which, under the monopoly clause, no other railway may operate,[2] then Ottawa would enforce the law.

By 1888 a provincially owned track was being built south towards Emerson at the U.S. border to connect with the Northern Pacific, which paralleled the CPR on the U.S. side. It was aimed smack at the protected CPR territory. The CPR met the challenge by building a branch line directly across the path of the provincial railway.

What followed is known as the "Battle of Fort Whyte." (The name was a joke. There never was a battle and there never was a Fort Whyte. But William Whyte was general superintendent of the CPR's western division at the time.) In his official history, *The Canadian National Railways,* Colonel G.R. Stevens recounts the incident. Tory Premier John Norquay of Manitoba[3] said he would, if need be, force the provincial line through "at the point of a bayonet." He ordered his construction crews to work at night, and in darkness they laid the "diamond" (a railway term for the level crossing of two sets of tracks) into the CPR line and kept on going. The next day a CPR crew ripped out the diamond and carried it whooping back to their yards.

Soon a mob of farmers turned out, put back the diamond and stood guard over it with pitchforks. A CPR locomotive arrived, threatening the farmers with a dose of live steam. Then a locomotive drew up on the provincial line, similarly threatening the CPR crew. Neither followed up the

[2] An exception was naturally made for the CPR's associate line, the old SP&P that Jim Hill, George Stephen and Donald Smith had so skilfully purloined from its Dutch backers to get themselves into the railway business. After the CPR was completed, Hill took control of the SP&P (by then called the SPM&M) and incorporated it into his Great Northern system. But it moved nothing to or from Canadian ports.

[3] Provincial and national governments of the same party would split recurrently throughout the entire history of the West, as the national governments found themselves having to put the interests of the populous central provinces ahead of the much less populous Atlantic and western provinces because the big vote always resided in the centre of the country. The Americans had mitigated this condition by establishing a powerful Senate in which the states were equally represented.

Provincial Archives of Alberta, A-3956

A grading contractor's camp on the Crow's Nest line in 1897. The southern route into the mountains led to the famous grain shipping agreement with Ottawa which set a fixed rate for the next nine decades.

threat; and for two weeks the rivals faced each other. A fight broke out at one stage and a farmer got a black eye. Otherwise there were no casualties. But the police and army wisely stayed out of it. Nobody wanted another rebellion. Even so, demanded the farmers, why must they pay the cost of "holding Canada together?"

By now the issue had become national. The interests of five million Canadians, declared the CPR's president, William Van Horne, are being subordinated to those of 10,000 Manitobans. (In fact, observes historian Stevens, the Canadian population was well under five million at the time, and there were 150,000 Manitobans.) If the provincial line continued, said Van Horne, he'd move the CPR shops out of Winnipeg. The prime minister lost his temper, declared that Manitoba was acting as a "front for foreign railroads," and threatened to do anything he could to shake confidence in Manitoba on the world's bond markets because the province was being run by "impecunious politicians who think only of office." Roared the *Manitoba Free Press* in reply: "We will not submit to being told that we are not to build a railway with our own money on our own soil. On with the road, injunction or no injunction!"

Macdonald relented and allowed Manitoba to proceed. The new road was built, connected with the Northern Pacific and proved an immediate disappointment. The rates scarcely dropped at all. The Dakota farmers, who were the NP's chief customers, made sure it charged the Manitobans enough that Manitoba grain couldn't compete with Dakota grain.

So Manitobans, soon joined by the settlers who were filtering along the CPR's main and spur lines in the North West Territories, continued to seethe and go broke. By 1896, though world food markets had begun to recover and Wilfrid Laurier's Liberals had taken office at Ottawa, animosity towards the CPR had grown so severe that word of it had reached London and was affecting the price of CPR securities. But a new source of western wealth had appeared, and the CPR's management decided it must gain access to it if the company was to survive.

The new hope lay in the Kootenay country of British Columbia. From the 1860s onward, American prospectors had been pushing north from the Idaho and Washington territories. By 1890 the Silver King mine was in operation at Toad Mountain near Nelson, silver and copper had been found at Trail Creek, and five other major claims had been established. All of these had seemed like logical pickings for the Northern Pacific, which ran from St. Paul to Portland through the old HBC post of Spokane. A mining and rail promoter named Daniel C. Corbin incorporated the Spokane Falls and Northern in 1888; it had pushed far enough north on the Columbia to pick up ore barged down from Canada. By 1892 he had acquired the rights of a defunct Canadian railroad, and had a line into Nelson that picked up ore shipped down from ports farther north on Kootenay Lake.

In the meantime Jim Hill, now utterly alienated from the Canadian Pacific, although he had helped to create it, had amalgamated his American railroads into the Great Northern, which crossed the northern states from St. Paul to Everett, Washington, on Puget Sound. He planned a spur up from his main line at Bonners Ferry, Idaho, to the south end of Kootenay Lake.

Provincial Archives of Alberta, A-2957

The CPR's Macleod station in 1898. Ottawa put up a cash subsidy of $5,000 per mile and a loan guarantee of $20,000 per mile, to keep south-central British Columbia from joining the United States.

Then 50 miles west in the Kootenays came another threat. A flamboyant mining promoter named F. Augustus Heinze of Butte, Montana, had acquired some rich base metal deposits at Rossland, British Columbia, and built a narrow-gauge line that plunged round hairpin curves and switchbacks for 13 miles down the 2,000-foot drop between there and the Columbia. Here at Trail Creek, later called Trail, he had built a smelter, barging its output down into Washington State.

In short, a rich mineral industry of the B.C. interior was rapidly becoming American. When Thomas Shaughnessy, vice-president of the CPR, toured the area he found endless evidence of this. Goods were flowing north duty free. Local business was almost entirely American-owned. The Rossland mine and Trail smelter were manned and managed by Americans. All the mining equipment and food was being supplied from the United States. Even the appearance of the towns was American. How long would it be before an American "provisional government" was established and the area voted to join the United States? The Kootenays must be "Canadianized" quickly, he urged.

And he just happened to know how to do it. The Canadian Pacific must run into the region, and the cheapest access (though far from the shortest) was not from the CPR divisional point of Revelstoke on the Columbia to the north. It was from Lethbridge in the District of Alberta to the east, following the Crow's Nest Pass route through the Rockies. Which in turn, he added, would require a major dominion government subsidy for the CPR of, say, $5,000 a mile in cash, plus $20,000 a mile in low-interest government loans.

Van Horne and Shaughnessy had persuaded the dying Tory government to go along with this scheme but could not induce the warring Tory ministers to actually do anything about it. They had also been deftly developing connections in the Laurier Liberal camp, however, in particular James D. Edgar, railway critic in the opposition and Laurier's close adviser, and John S. Willison whom Edgar had connived to be made editor of the Liberal *Globe*. Willison was a champion of the West and had boldly proposed that CPR freight rates on grain should be controlled. Curiously, in private discussions, Van Horne and Shaughnessy had not discounted the idea, though the original contract had exempted CPR rates from government control until the company paid a 10% dividend on its common stock, something it had never done.

When Laurier took office, however, the CPR suffered a major shock. Their man among the

[4] Blair and another Maritimer, William Pugsley, make an odd appearance in the history of Edmonton as the big-money eastern backers of the Edmonton District Railway, one of numerous schemes to bridge the North Saskatchewan. The name of the EDR was changed in 1897 to the Edmonton, Yukon & Pacific when a line was projected to the coast via the Stikine River. But in 1900 the company was still, by painful stages, building Edmonton's Low Level Bridge.

Liberals, Edgar, didn't make the cabinet, but became speaker of the House. Appointed railways minister was Andrew G. Blair, former premier of New Brunswick and a man with very definite ideas on western railway development.[4] Blair felt the government should build and pay for the Crow's Nest line, then lease it to all railways that wanted to use it, much as highways are used today. That way, he said, competition would hold the rates down. This scheme did not at all please the CPR because, since the showdown in Manitoba, other railway operators were now appearing in the West and making money at it.

Complicating the Crow's Nest situation even further was the government of British Columbia. The Kootenays, after all, were part of that province, and the contest seemed to lie between the American roads that wanted to take all the Kootenay business south and the CPR, which wanted to take it all east. British Columbia wanted it taken west to Vancouver and Victoria, and had furnished

The C&E Railway: 9 years getting it and 20 cursing it

Well at least the line from Calgary won't belong to the CPR, they said – but then came another bad surprise

Thunderstruck by the news that the CPR would bypass them, Edmontonians were sure of the consequences. Gone would be the visions of impending metropolitan status. Edmonton for a century had been the major centre of the western Prairie. Now, unless at least a spur line connected it to Calgary, it could decline with the fur trade that created it. Their response was to bring into existence the Calgary and Edmonton Railway, an institution they spent nine years promoting, and the next 20 condemning and deploring.

To the CPR, such a spur line presented three obstacles. Edmonton was 200 miles north of the main line. Getting to it meant crossing the 150-foot-deep valley of the North Saskatchewan River. And Edmonton voted Liberal. All of these difficulties, particularly the third, were considered insurmountable.

After several local attempts to build the line, all of them aborted by bad planning or lack of capital, a credible group incorporated the C&E in 1890, nine years after the CPR's southern route was announced and seven after the main line reached Calgary. Its directorate was stellar, including rail promoters William Mackenzie and Donald Mann, financiers Edmund B. Osler and Herbert C. Hammond, and mainline contractors James Ross and Herbert S. Holt. They had such impeccable Ottawa connections that they won for the C&E the status of "colonization railway," eligible for a 6,400-acre Crown land grant for each mile built. As well, they won a cash grant of $1.6 million for carrying government personnel, supplies and mail for 20 years.

The work went swiftly, requiring only 13 months of the 41 the contract allowed. It was said to have been guided by the recollections of Father Albert Lacombe, whose memories

Glenbow Archives, NA-237-8

Territorial Lieutenant-Governor Edgar Dewdney turning the first sod in Calgary in 1890. Edmonton would get a rail connection at last.

of the old bull train trail proved so accurate the surveyors came to rely on them.

The C&E group had another popular merit. They were independent, not part of the detested CPR whose monopoly was now being denounced and challenged all over the West. Or rather, apparently not. Scarcely had the last spike been driven on the afternoon of July 27, 1891, just across the North Saskatchewan from Edmonton, when it was abruptly announced that the line had been leased to the Canadian Pacific, plainly the plan from the start. (Hadn't anyone noticed? C&E director E.B. Osler had been a member of the CPR board since 1885.)

This deception began the C&E's troubles, and they mounted into the next century. When, demanded Edmonton, would the company bridge the North Saskatchewan? The answer became evident: Never. So Edmonton discerned the C&E's message: You build the bridge and we'll use it. Edmontonians were furious.

a charter and massive land grant to an as yet unfulfilled project called the British Columbia Southern Railway, which it empowered to serve southern British Columbia as far east as the Crow's Nest. Its purpose, of course, was to channel Kootenay traffic westward, though two great mountain ranges, the Monashees and the Cascades, stood in the way.[5]

Van Horne and Shaughnessy had seen this proposal not as a threat but as an opportunity. They forthwith opened negotiations to buy the Southern, seeking running rights on the west side of the Crow's Nest to Kootenay Lake. As to the idea of continuing west to Vancouver, well that might come later. On these vague terms the Southern was ready to sell.

The CPR strategists had also scored another coup. At Trail they acquired Heinze's smelter with its crazy narrow-gauge line down from Rossland. They also laid plans for another, standard-gauge line west to the Grand Forks district where even richer ore had been found, all of it exiting on the

[5] **The promoters of the B.C. Southern were William Fernie, for whom the B.C. town was named, and Colonel James Baker. Fernie was an ex-seaman and ex-miner who discovered the Crow's Nest coal deposits and later became gold commissioner for B.C. Baker was provincial secretary, minister of mines, a Cranbrook real estate developer and the brother of two notable Victorian figures: the explorer Sir Samuel Baker and Baker Pasha of Middle East military fame.**

Worse still, economic development stalled in Edmonton and blossomed instead on the south bank, so that New Edmonton was soon rivalling Old. "Nothing has been done in the Northwest which has had a greater effect in retarding its development than this course of action," snarled *Bulletin* publisher Frank Oliver, never a man to understate a case.

Rail service, however, began well: Two trains a week, fare about $8, time about 12 hours for the 191-mile trip. Two years later, however, this deteriorated. The line was extended south to Macleod, but the equipment wasn't extended. The same train just had to run farther. The result was increasing unreliability and breakdowns, and a rising chorus of complaint, much of it printed in the newspapers. "The railroad from Calgary to Edmonton," wrote a Nova Scotia clergyman, "is almost as bad as the old corduroy...The cars are always crowded on the outbound trip, and the train is always a long one, and it is never on time, and the fare of travel is four cents per mile." Some vituperation even broke into popular verse:

Ho! let her go – she's off at last,
We aren't so late tonight.
An hour and forty all you say?
By God! That's out of sight.

And here she goes, and there she rolls,
A-playing pitch and toss.
While Luggin by the track rides on,
And keeps up with his hoss.

Edmonton's outrage would not explode, however, until another railway bridged the river, and the CPR tried to block its trains. But that showdown was to occur beyond this volume in the next century. *G.S.*❦

The first train into South Edmonton station, 1891. It turned out to be the detested CPR after all.

City of Edmonton Archives, EA-10-2760

Provincial Archives of Alberta, E. Brown Collection, B-6022

Chinese labourers at work for the CPR in the Kootenays. In 1882 alone, 2,200 died, mainly from the wretched conditions in their camps.

American side.

In January 1897 Van Horne and Shaughnessy took their Crow's Nest Pass proposal to the Laurier government, essentially the same one they had made to the Tories. They then discovered that the man they really had to deal with was not Blair at all, but Laurier's senior lieutenant for the West, Clifford Sifton. This, as it turned out, was not good news.

Yes, said Sifton, the government would put up the money for the Crow's Nest line, just as the Tories had promised. Unlike the Tories, however, this government wanted a number of things in return, namely: a three-cent-a-hundredweight cut in grain shipping rates everywhere on the CPR system; government control of all rates both ways on the Pass line; the return at a moderate price of all CPR lands east of the Third Meridian;[6] and the surrender gratis of all lands the CPR was acquiring through the B.C. Southern.

John A. Eagle in his CPR history, *The Canadian Pacific Railway and the Development of Western Canada*, quotes an eye witness's reminiscence of Van Horne's reaction: He "almost jumped to the ceiling" when he heard what Sifton was asking. Feelers were sent out immediately. To whom could they appeal beyond Sifton? To Blair? To Laurier? The response came back: The prime minister "would be guided largely by Mr. Sifton's views" on any policy affecting the West.

The following day, after consulting his executive committee, Van Horne replied. The CPR would accept all the terms but those on land. The properties east of the Third were "the cream of our grant." The railway must have $2.50 an acre for them, and an "adequate" price for the B.C. Southern land. As to the grain rate cut, it would agree. It would equalize rates across the Prairies so everybody paid the same, but the aggregate benefit would be three cents.

Although a tentative deal was made, the issue was not yet resolved. Blair took his case for government ownership of the line to the Liberal caucus, which split grievously on the issue. The western members, in particular Edmonton's Frank Oliver, wanted the line publicly owned and leased to competing railways. He simply did not trust the CPR.

Sifton prevailed, however, and on June 3, 1897, the deal was signed that would become the Magna Carta of western agriculture. Known as the Crow's Nest Pass Agreement, it required that the line run through Macleod (the CPR wanted to bypass it), that the cabinet must approve all rates on the Crow line, that rates on all grain and flour shipped to the Lakehead be cut by three cents a hundredweight, that certain rate reductions be made on specified items — fresh fruit, coal oil and agricultural implements — that other railways could use the Crow's Nest line, and that 50,000 acres of coal lands in the East Kootenays be turned over to the dominion government.

What mattered most to farmers was not simply that the rate was cut — though that three cents would mean the difference between staying and leaving for thousands of people — but that the

[6] The north-south lines in the Dominion Land Survey that sectioned the West began at the First (or Principal) Meridian, which was arbitrarily established about 10 miles west of Winnipeg, far enough out not to interfere with the Red River strip lots. Every fourth degree of longitude thereafter, the DLS called another "meridian." The Second fell approximately on the future Manitoba-Saskatchewan border, the Third in mid-Saskatchewan and the Fourth on the Alberta-Saskatchewan border. The Fifth passes through Stony Plain and Calgary, and the Sixth comes down through Jasper. The northern part of the Alberta-B.C. boundary is on Longitude 120, two degrees west of the Sixth.

precedent was established that grain rates could be controlled by statute. So firmly did they embrace the agreement that repealing an amended version of it 86 years later occasioned a 10-year fight in Ottawa. The original bill gained third reading on June 29, Liberal Frank Oliver voting against the government.[7] It received all three Senate readings and royal assent on the same day.

The Crow's Nest Pass Agreement established a spirit of accord between the Laurier government and the CPR, but it was short-lived. Sifton saw railway construction as a means of stimulating immigration. Settlers could use work on the track, he reasoned, to get themselves started. The government therefore prohibited the import of transient labour. This distressed the CPR, whose contractors routinely hired foreign labour for the dangerous and gruelling work at the end of steel. The toll in lost lives on the B.C. sections of the main line, mostly through scurvy and cholera and mostly Chinese, was a national embarrassment and scandal.[8] But would Canadians, or settlers, be willing and able to stand the conditions?

The work had scarcely started west from Macleod when trouble began, though it wasn't with Canadians. A thousand Welsh farmers and labourers had been recruited to work on the line, no doubt with the idea that they could afterwards find jobs in the coal mines which were already beginning to appear in the Crow's Nest area. The Welshmen were not happy with the conditions, the pay or the life in the camps. It was not long before their complaints began appearing in the British press. Immigration recruiters wrote frantically to Ottawa, protesting that the publicity was gravely damaging their campaign to find settlers.

Glenbow Archives, NA-3082-2

CPR president Thomas Shaughnessy in 1910. Feather beds and bathtubs, he thundered, did not go with railroad construction; Canadian workers were soft.

Meanwhile hundreds of Canadians from Toronto and Montreal flooded west to work on the new line, expecting the railway to pay their fare, then learning it was to be deducted from their wages of $1.50 a day less $4 a week for board. Finding the work far too hard and conditions unbearable, many quit and were promptly arrested for defrauding the contractors of the fare. The NWMP magistrate who tried them, sentencing them lightly, quickly became exasperated. The problem, he said, was created by agents for the contractors who promised these men far more than they got. Many had signed contracts they couldn't read.

Then stories began appearing in the prairie papers about the working conditions. In Calgary the *Weekly Herald* noted that accidental deaths were occurring frequently on the Crow's Nest line and were never investigated. The *Macleod Gazette* cited rumours of dreadful conditions in the camps, including one report that 150 men, all suffering from diphtheria, had been transported for 150 miles in open gravel cars.

The result of these reports and persistent NWMP representations was an inquiry by a three-man royal commission. The commissioners heard appalling complaints: of men being forced to sleep in the open without blankets, or in unheated boxcars or leaky tents; of being cold and damp and unable to get dry anywhere at any time or even to wash; of rampant colds and diphtheria; of inedible food; of bad medical care; and of frequent deaths, either from disease or accident. The commissioners decided unanimously that all these reports were true and made assorted recommendations.

Shaughnessy, now the CPR's president, exploded. The commission report was "one-sided and unfair," he said. No attempt had been made "to understand the conditions that must attach to frontier life." He blamed the all-Canada hiring policy. Canadians, he said, expect "to get high wages, a feather bed and a bathtub." That was not the way railways could be built under Canadian circumstances, he declared.

But by now the CPR was no longer the only company building railways in the West. It had a competitor.❦

[7] Historian John Eagle recalls that more than 30 years later Clifford Sifton acknowledged that Blair and Oliver, not he, represented popular opinion on the Crow's Nest Agreement. "We acted against the public sentiment of two-thirds of the people of Canada" who wanted competition on the Crow's Nest line, he said. But the government, Sifton added, had to contend with the fact the CPR was "on the verge of bankruptcy." Others deny the CPR's state was that precarious in 1897.

[8] Historian Hugh Dempsey's *The CPR West*, a report of the Glenbow Museum's centennial forum on the CPR, includes a paper by Patricia Roy that details the horrors endured by the Chinese in building the main line in British Columbia. She quotes Chinese merchants in Victoria who said 2,200 died on railway construction in 1882 alone.

The hazards of early railroading were legion

TRAIN WRECKS AND OTHER RAIL ACCIDENTS WERE A REGULAR NEWSPAPER FEATURE IN THE YEARS BEFORE THE CENTURY CLOSED; HERE ARE A FEW OF THEM

Fort Macleod Gazette, **April 26, 1897:** Collision on the C&E near Macleod. One person killed, one injured.

Same paper, same edition: Bridge over the Oldman River collapses; three cars fall in; brakeman killed; ice pile-up blamed.

Medicine Hat News, **December 2, 1897:** Freight slams into the rear of a stopped train on the Crow's Nest line; one killed.

Same paper, same edition: Bridge collapses; five or six cars roll into the Oldman River; one dead.

Fort Macleod Gazette, **April 15, 1898:** Wind blows down a coulee bridge under construction nine miles from Lethbridge; five workers killed; six injured.

Medicine Hat News, **May 19, 1898:** Bridge burns out east of Medicine Hat; 40 cars pile up; engineer and fireman killed.

Fort Macleod Gazette, **July 8, 1898:** Engine No. 361 struck by nine runaway lumber cars on the Crow's Nest line near Pincher; engineer and fireman killed.

Glenbow Archives, NA-2520

***Fort Macleod Gazette,* August 5, 1898:** Rail worker Joseph Herietha dies on the Crow's Nest line when he falls asleep dead drunk on the tracks and the shouts of the approaching train crew can't awaken him.

***Fort Macleod Gazette,* September 2, 1898:** Train strikes a flatcar with four men on it working on the Crow's Nest line; three killed.

***Weekly Herald,* January 12, 1899:** Brakeman accidentally falls off the end of a train; is dragged 200 yards, train running over his arm; he then falls off a bridge; arm must be amputated; he refuses anaesthetic. "Saw away, doc," he says. He survives the operation in good condition.

***Medicine Hat News,* February 2, 1899:** Brakes fail to hold freight crossing bridge; it rear-ends another train; locomotive and tender plunge into river; three killed.❦

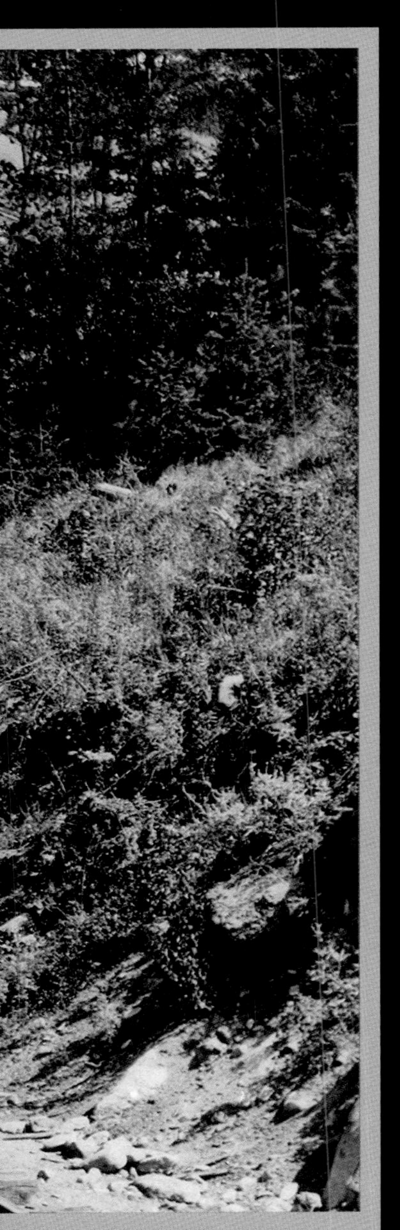

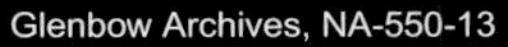

Glenbow Archives, NA-550-13

A derailed passenger train (left) with its engine and coal car off the track and the crew awaiting rescue. (Above) a wintertime CPR wreck on the north shore of Lake Superior in 1890.

collapses buckled a passenger train south of Strathcona, May 29, 1899 (below) and smashed freight cars at Medicine Hat (opposite page).

Provincial Archives of Alberta, A-2979

Medicine Hat Museum, PC8.1

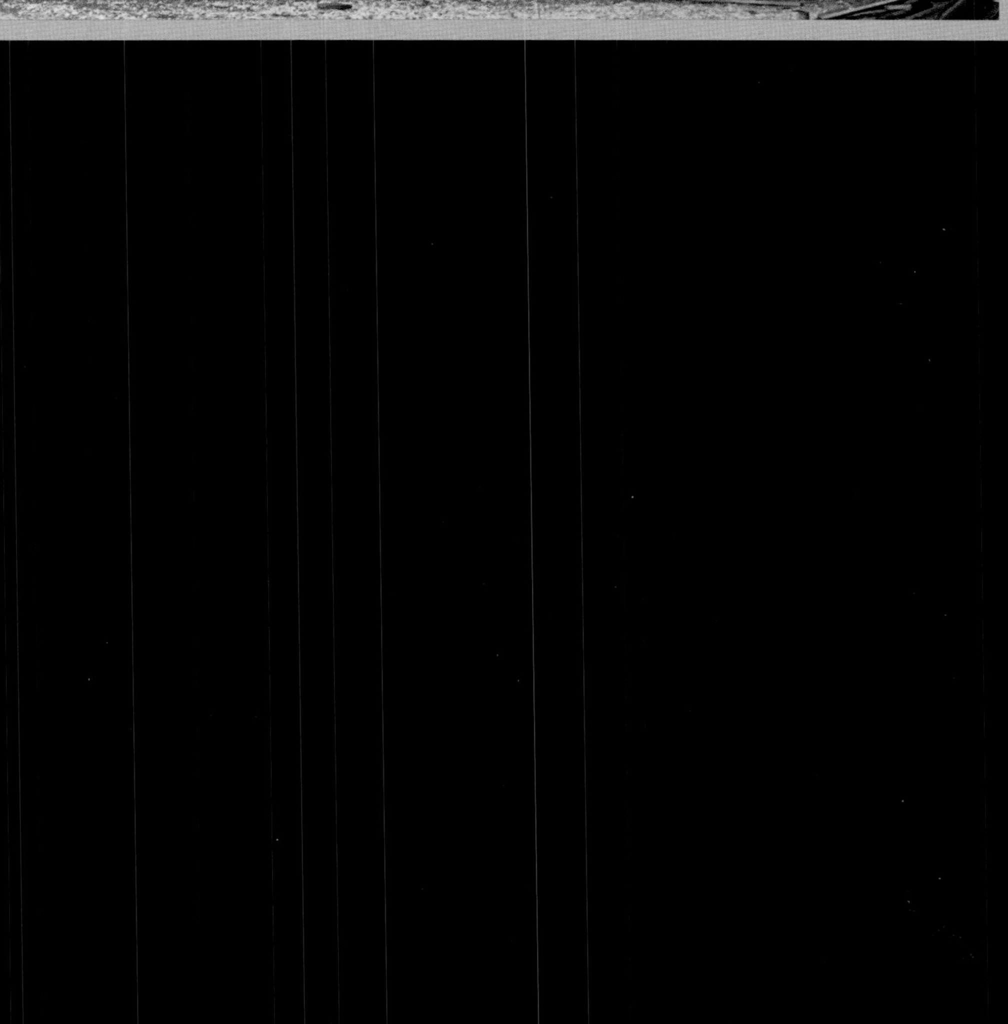

Glenbow Archives, NA-2420-13

Provincial Archives of Alberta, E. Brown Collection, B-6225

Provincial Archives of Alberta, E. Brown Collection, B-6223

Workmen struggle to extricate derailed trains on the C&E line near Leduc (above and lower far left) and in southern Alberta (top far left).

CHAPTER FOUR

A cigar-chewing, prayer-saying duo promises to put rails into Edmonton at last

BUT SIR WILFRID DIDN'T LIKE THEIR ROUGH-HOUSE DEMEANOUR, AND HE FAVOURED THE PLAN FOR A MORE 'SUBSTANTIAL' RAILWAY – GOOD HEAVENS, ALARMISTS SAID, SUPPOSE THEY *BOTH* WERE BUILT!

When Sir Wilfrid Laurier became prime minister in 1896, sitting as member of parliament for Saskatchewan, the prairie railway system seemed to him absurd. West of Manitoba, the best soil and the best land for settlement lay on the northern prairie, along the North Saskatchewan Valley and even in the distant Peace River region. Yet the only railway, the Canadian Pacific, ran through the south, not the north. It reached the north only through spurs off its main line, like its much-reviled subsidiary, the Calgary and Edmonton, which his newly elected Alberta MP, publisher Frank Oliver of the *Edmonton Bulletin*, had been cursing in print since the day it opened. If the West was to be settled, and settled it must be, there must be a new railway to serve the north.

Donald Mann of the Canadian Northern. 'Very well,' said he to the German officer. 'We'll fight with axes.'

CN Archives, 15013

The obvious solution would be a CPR northern line, but the mere mention of this made westerners almost foam at the mouth. The CPR's monopoly, most agreed, was the cause of many of the West's problems, and even though Manitoba had successfully broken it eight years ago, it still remained a fact of life nearly everywhere on the Prairies.

And so, concluded Laurier, a competing Canadian line must be built. But by whom? By the government? Heaven forbid! Past governments had built the Intercolonial to the Maritimes. Its waste, poor service and interminable losses had become a national disgrace. The public didn't want any more government railways. Besides, full development of the West's arable land would entail $300 million in railway construction, triple the price of the CPR. The dominion government's annual revenues totalled only $36 million, and its taxes already had reached a staggering $5.42 per capita. How could even higher taxes possibly be justified?

Then could the new railway be built by a private company? But how could it find capital? All over the world investor confidence in railways was vanishing. The British-owned Grand Trunk, main line of central Canada, had lost money for 40 years. Even the CPR, with strong government backing, had only barely made it. What private syndicate would undertake another line to the Canadian West?

Over the next two years, an answer to this question started to emerge, though Laurier didn't much like it. It would mean doing business with two men of a type the suave and elegant

CN Archives, x48056

prime minister found most distasteful. Donald Mann was now in his early 40s, a beefy, cocky, bragging, cigar-chewing roughhouse of a man, born at Acton, Ontario, on the Grand Trunk main line, who had given up plans to enter the ministry, headed west and learned construction from the pick-and-shovel level up. He had become foreman, then superintendent, then railway contractor. He was as adept at drawing up his own legal contracts as he was at telling stories about himself and everything else, stories that were as delightful as they were in many instances fictional.

Was it true, for example, that when he undertook a railway construction contract in Hong Kong he offended a haughty German army officer who challenged him to a duel? "You may choose the weapons, sir," said the officer. "Very well," replied Mann, and after some thought he chose a weapon he'd been using since boyhood. "I choose axes," he said. "We'll fight with axes." The German asked for a translation to make sure he had heard correctly, then dismissed Mann as a lunatic.

There was no doubt whatever about Mann's religious proclivities, however. Despite the coarse construction camp language he was plainly a mystic, given to taking long, solitary walks in the wilderness, always convinced that every problem could be solved by prayer. But the work gangs loved him, and in 1883, when he got a subcontract on the Kicking Horse section of the CPR, he met the man who would become his lifetime partner.

Will Mackenzie was one of a horde of children in a Scottish immigrant family that had settled at Kirkfield, northeast of Toronto. The neighbours said he was a drifter. He tried running a store, then took a contract cutting railway ties, even tried teaching school. Each time he'd given up and pushed on. He was slight, wiry, quick-witted, restless and imaginative, and his piercing eyes seemed to see instantly through people and problems, so that he reached rapid solutions and carried them out while others still pondered.

(Above) co-founder William Mackenzie. Like Mann, he was too rough-hewn for Laurier's refined sensibilities. (Below) Mann (extreme right) with a CPR engineering party in British Columbia, 1885.

People either loathed Mackenzie or loved him. Though he was a militant Presbyterian, the nuns at the convent attended as a school girl by his Catholic wife, Margaret Merry, were among those who loved him. They lent him the $5,000 it took to get him into the railway construction business. (Bitter critics would one day point out that borrowing was something Will Mackenzie knew how to do best. He would borrow a staggering $300 million from the government of Canada

Glenbow Archives, NA-4428-7(b)

The four workhorses of the CPR's 19th-century western engine fleet

The 'Mountain Mule' beat Rogers Pass, while the 'Mogul' proved a failure and the little 4-4-0s outlasted all

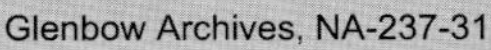

A steel-cabbed 2-8-0 engine in 1893. More dependable than the Mogul.

Provincial Archives of Alberta, E. Brown Collection, B-

The 4-6-0, or Ten-Wheeler, the most versatile CPR steam engine ever.

By the late 19th century steam locomotives were available in numerous shapes, sizes and wheel configurations. What the Canadian Pacific required was not a variety of them, but versatility in the same unit. Fuels ran from cordwood to lignite to anthracite. Water could be acid or alkaline and heavily mineralized. Grades in the mountains were appalling. The CPR needed tough, simple designs, and not very many of them, so that maintenance could be standardized.

Its workhorse on the Prairies from the start in 1881 was what railroaders call, from the wheel configuration, the 4-4-0.[a] They were simple, rugged and clean, and the CPR began with 41 of them and would buy nearly 400 before they went out of use. A 4-4-0 could haul 10 40-ton cars at about 45 miles an hour. The first was the *Countess of Dufferin*,[b] built in 1872 by the Baldwin Locomotive Works in Pennsylvania, and barged down the Red River to Winnipeg to serve on the Pembina line to the border, the first CPR operation. Two 4-4-0s lasted in working order until the end of CP's steam era in 1960.

Over the next 20 years, three other types were to see extensive service in the West. When the CPR head of steel passed Calgary, "the mountain mule" appeared. This was the enormous 2-8-0, picked especially for the Big Hill, the brutal 4.5% grade in Kicking Horse Pass just west of the future Alberta border. Its eight small (49-inch) wheels sacrificed speed for pulling power, and placed maximum weight on the drive wheels, a critical factor for uphill work. The 2-8-0s quickly proved their worth and became the standard mountain freight unit for three decades.

What didn't work was the Mogul, a 2-6-0 introduced in 1888 for service in Rogers Pass. The Mogul wasn't powerful enough. Its two-wheeled truck permitted too much pressure to come onto the flange of the front driving wheels on the curves, causing rapid wear and high costs. Although the CPR was to buy or build 47 Moguls, the design soon yielded to the more dependable 2-8-0s.

Provincial Archives of Alberta, E. Brown Collection, B-6002

A 2-6-0 with snow plough. A small early workhorse.

But the standard all-round locomotive of the 1890s, and the most successful CPR unit of all time, was the 4-6-0. Many variants were to appear over the coming decades, as CP built nearly 1,000 so-called Ten-Wheelers. The big, heavy 4-6-0s were the first CPR locomotives with a metal cab, a vast improvement over the earlier wooden structures. These machines did everything, from hauling freight and passengers over mountain passes and across prairie expanses to shunting cars around the yards.

Meanwhile the prairie experience rapidly added to technological change. The most immediately recognizable was the pilot, known throughout North America as the cow-catcher, a wedge-shaped framework designed to sweep livestock and detritus out of the way to prevent derailments.

Smokestacks had to create a good draft for the firebox while cooling red-hot wood embers enough to reduce fire hazard. The early solution was the distinctive diamond stack, which contained a grating to catch large chunks, as well as a conical internal baffle to delay the exit of embers. When coal replaced wood, the huge stacks were no longer necessary.

Another early feature was the sand dome mounted atop the boiler. By spilling sand through a pipe onto the tracks, this enabled crews to obtain extra traction when starting out or climbing hills in icy conditions. Some Kicking Horse Pass 2-8-0s mounted two sand domes. Then came the large, single headlight and the externally mounted cylinders, soon to become standard for easy maintenance. By 1900 the CPR locomotive fleet totalled 781. Before the steam era expired, the company would acquire some 3,200 steam engines.

Most major improvements in railway technology, however, had to await the 20th century, like superheaters that greatly increased a steam engine's efficiency, and the Miller coupling that ended the bone-jarring jerk each time a train left a station. In the 1890s brakemen still had to couple and uncouple manually what was known as the Lincoln Pin.

Early cabs were open in the rear to winter's 40-below temperatures. Stoking had to be done by hand. Signals were primitive, made by hands, whistles or swinging lights, and written orders were picked up "on the fly" from wooden hoops.

Braking could be exceedingly hazardous. Each car had its own manually actuated brake. Before each downhill grade or station, brakemen had to jump from car to car to engage brake levers. In winter, this exercise could be nearly suicidal. In all seasons, overheating brakes and runaway trains were common.

Although Canada would not exist without the CPR and the technology that made the enterprise possible, strikingly little remains of that extraordinary pre-1900 era. Many written records have been lost. Few railway histories emphasizing the actual machinery have been written. Photo collections languish in archives and only a few of the original locomotives survive, often lying neglected in sheds across the land.[c] *G.K.* ❦

[a] A locomotive's wheel configuration is indicated by a three-numeral code. The first gives the number of wheels in the locomotive's leading "truck," which guides the unit around curves, the second the number of main drive wheels, which propel the engine and bear most of its weight, the third the trailing wheels, if any, which further distribute the weight.

[b] The *Countess of Dufferin* stood in stately distinction for years outside Winnipeg's CPR station, then was retired ignominiously to a warehouse. In 1991 a fund was being gathered to provide it with a more fitting location.

[c] The Canadian who has done most to remedy this neglect is Omer Lavallee, an economist, historian, inveterate railway buff and long the archivist of the CPR. He is the author of *Van Horne's Road*, an account of the CPR's construction, as well as *Canadian Steam Locomotives*. With its hundreds of photos, detailed descriptions and roster of all 3,200 CP steam units ever built, this is the authoritative work on the subject.

Glenbow Archives, NA-4967-29

A wood-fired 4-4-0 engine at the Canmore roundhouse in 1886.

before he and Donald Mann were finally stopped.)

Mackenzie, too, was a popular boss, though the workers found his piety a bit much. For instance, he had a piano hauled into his campsite and encouraged his men to gather to sing Presbyterian hymns rather than gather to drink bad whisky. In any event, by 1884 he had discredited the earlier scepticism and scored notable success, landing a subcontract on the Kicking Horse job where he encountered Mann, four years his junior. They found they were a team. Mackenzie could get brilliant ideas and Mann knew how to carry them out.

They also found a mentor. James Ross, who superintended the CPR's whole horrible mountain construction job, liked them both and taught them things about railway building they could learn nowhere else. In fact, they were at the time a foursome. Herbert Holt, another contractor, completed the circle. When the main line was finished, all four worked on the CPR's spur lines and took on the construction of the Calgary and Edmonton. But then they split up. Ross took Mackenzie east to build street railways. Holt went into finance and was long the president of the country's biggest bank, the Royal.

Mann stayed in the West, dabbling in small construction jobs and keeping his eye on something called the Winnipeg and Hudson Bay Railway, a scheme to run a line from Winnipeg to the Bay, eliminating the long haul the grain must make through northern Ontario by reviving the old Hudson's Bay Company route. Mann, Ross and Holt had built 40 miles of the W&HB before it went broke, owing them money, because Ottawa withheld the usual railway grants. Uncertain navigation in the Bay meant the scheme would fail, Macdonald had argued. Manitobans suspected what he really feared was its success. If western grain could reach the world on the short route through the Bay, where did that leave Montreal, Toronto and the CPR?

Then in 1893 another project fell through because it couldn't get financing. Called the Lake Manitoba Railway and Canal Company, it envisioned joining the Manitoba lakes and Saskatchewan valley by a canal system, and linking them by rail to Portage la Prairie on the CPR. But the Manitoba government desperately wanted this scheme to work, and approached Mann to take it on. Could he somehow save it?

The latter sought out Mackenzie and together they formulated a plan. They would take over the defunct W&HB for the money it owed them, and join it to the canal company. They would abandon the Hudson Bay route and instead get the right to run a line west to Prince Albert on the North Saskatchewan, thereby penetrating the promising lands of the northern Prairies. They would also gain control of three defunct and bankrupt railroads that together had the right to run southeast from Winnipeg, through Minnesota, then back into Canada again and on to Port Arthur on Lake Superior. That way they would be able to transport grain to the Great Lakes and the sea. Since Manitoba so desperately wanted a competing railroad, it could be prevailed upon to guarantee bonds. Land grants already available under existing legislation would provide enough to complete capitalization.

The scheme seemed wild, yet where exactly would it fail? The Manitoba government embraced it, and Mackenzie and Mann began piecing their fragments together into a system. Along with the canal company, they made the key acquisition of its part-time auditor, David Blythe Hanna[1], the humorous, exuberantly ingenious Scot who became their first superintendent and top executive through the amazing adventure that was about to unfold.

Hanna described in his autobiography how their first line was run: "Service was our motto; we had more stopping places to the ten miles I think than any railway in the world. Only a few of them were on the timetable. We put down and took passengers to suit our pleasure."

The new railway, Hanna recalled, presented something rare in the industry's history, a railway everybody loved. So glad were settlers to see it, they volunteered their help with the grading. In response Mackenzie and Mann donated to them 3,000 bushels of seed grain, cleaned and sacked. When an engine hit a heifer, Hanna, who happened to be aboard, had the brakeman (an ex-butcher) cut the animal into beef, sell it to the passengers, and pay the farmer full price. Nothing like this had happened for a long time on the CPR.

Around the continent the partners scrounged equipment, much of it second-hand: two locomotives and 50 new freight cars from Cobourg, Ontario; two second-hand passenger cars from the Grand Trunk; a collection of old flatcars that were never inventoried.[2]

Finally, on January 13, 1899, when all the pieces were put together and operating, they gave their collection of fragmented lines a name. It would be called the Canadian Northern Railway, said Donald Mann. Then that June he made another announcement: "We are now asking parliament for permission to extend our line to Edmonton." This was the announcement that Alberta's future capital had been awaiting for 18 years.

"We have no plans at present for a transcontinental line," Mann added, but nobody believed him, least of all in Edmonton. If the Canadian Northern reaches here, they said, then only 250 miles west is the easiest pass possible through the Rockies: the Yellowhead. Beyond that, there's a straight run along water-level grades to the North Thompson and another relatively easy run down to Kamloops. That would put them within shooting distance of the coast. "Watch the Canadian Northern. Mackenzie and Mann will take the Yellowhead." That was the talk at Edmonton.

Laurier didn't like that talk, however, any better than he liked Mackenzie and Mann. They were uncouth men; they were salesmen, trimmers, shortcutters. While nobody could say their dealings with government were actually dishonest, they were, well, slippery. Laurier wanted people of a more "substantial" background, who could fit better into the Montreal and Ottawa social scene. By the century's end, he thought he had found just the man. In fact, that man had found him. His name was Charles Melville Hays.

Next to the Intercolonial, the Grand Trunk had been the Canadian rail industry's most notable financial disaster. It had been financed entirely in Britain and scarcely ever paid a dividend. Its longtime president had been the charmingly witty Sir Henry Tyler. But in 1895, the year before Laurier took office, the Grand Trunk's stockholders rebelled. They ousted Tyler and in his place introduced a respected British civil servant who had helped run the Suez Canal and reorganize the finances of Egypt. He was Sir Charles Rivers Wilson, who just knew that the secret of successful railway management in Canada was to hire the right American to do it.

The CPR had found William Van Horne. In the general manager's office of the Wabash, St. Louis and Pacific, Wilson found Hays and offered him spectacularly more money than anything the moribund Grand Trunk had ever paid before. In a whirlwind of reorganization, Hays made the Grand Trunk profitable. He then turned his mind westward and began unfolding to Laurier's ministers and the prime minister himself a grand scheme that would, admittedly, require substantial government assistance. It would be called the Grand Trunk Pacific, and it would run from Winnipeg to the coast. By what route? Why, by Edmonton and Yellowhead Pass, of course.

But were not Mackenzie and Mann proposing to do just that, in fact already had their Canadian Northern headed across the Prairies? Well, yes, but could that be taken seriously? Those two had certainly built railways, of course. But were they not simply fly-by-nighters? The Grand Trunk Pacific, by contrast, would be a substantial railroad. Laurier liked the sound of this man Hays. If a second transcontinental line was to be built, here obviously was the person to do it.

But just suppose, said alarmists, that *both* northern railroads should actually come to pass — one might then destroy the other. And on that uncertain note, the 19th century closed upon Canadian railway development.❦

[1] D.B. Hanna provided the name for Hanna, Alberta, which a Mackenzie and Mann branch from Calgary to Saskatoon would reach in 1911. He would also become the first president of the Canadian National in 1917, and quit in 1922 because of political interference in its administration. His autobiography, *Trains of Recollection*, is a classic in railway history.

[2] The Canadian Northern used to "borrow" flatcars from the CPR when it needed them for carrying cordwood, according to a Mackenzie and Mann conductor mentioned in Hanna's autobiography.

Gentlemen ranchers near Calgary in 1883.
Provincial Archives of Alberta, E. Brown Collection, B-114

Section Five
The Ranchers

Chapters by Mike Byfield
Sidebars by Mike Byfield and Gregg Shilliday

Glenbow Archives, NA-1047-1

Cattle fording the Bow River east of Calgary around 1900. The disappearance of the buffalo left an eerie ecological vacuum on the grasslands. The first big cattle drive from Montana crossed the Bow in 1881, two years after the last Canadian buffalo were wiped out.

The bison gone and the grass rich, Alberta offers a ranchers' bonanza

An industry founded on Spanish culture and U.S. technology invaded from the south as the Kansas Pacific reached Abilene and thousands of cattle began roaming free on the Prairies

The great buffalo herds began to diminish even before the mournful wail of the steam locomotive first echoed across the Prairies, leaving an eerie ecological vacuum on the wild pastures that had supported up to 50 million migratory buffalo. Cattlemen were not slow to recognize these plains as near-ideal grazing land.

Across the sprawling basins drained by the South Saskatchewan and Milk rivers grew "prairie wool," a drought-yellowed blend of blue grama, june, spear, bluejoint and other buffalo grasses. Westward and north lay slightly damper districts dominated by wheat grass and the dark, flag-like heads of grama. Chinook winds, a natural phenomenon that seemed like a miracle, not only melted the snow cover periodically but also cured the plants on the stalk, locking in their exceptional nutrition. And even when the "blue northers" howled, river bottoms could provide range animals with some refuge. So too could the steep-sided, twisting coulees that would come to bear names like Whisky Gap, Verdigris, Chin and Lonely Valley.

To the west loomed the foothills of the Rockies, crowned with lodgepole pine and white spruce. More sheltered and better watered, this belt was blessed with flower-strewn bunch grasses. The tufts, typically 12 to 18 inches high, consisted mainly of fescues and wheat grass, so wiry that a horse could be tethered to its clumps. Isolated outcrops elsewhere on the Prairies — the Porcupine and Cypress hills, and the Milk River Ridge — likewise afforded protection from the wind. But wind or no wind, early cattlemen favoured the open Prairies. They claimed prairie wool made the better forage, with a steer fattening out 100 pounds heavier than it would grazing in the hill country.

Glenbow Archives, NA-857-1

An early view of A.E. Cross's A7 ranch near Nanton. The rolling hills of the Blackfoot held a romantic and financial fascination for British and eastern Canadian capitalists and adventurers. All they needed was a railway.

Early on, hostile Indians and the sheer mass of the buffalo had prevented ranchers from venturing into this territory. But elsewhere in the Americas the beef industry had already developed a history and a mythology. Perhaps the most horse-addicted range man of all was the *gaucho*, a long-haired, bearded frontiersman who began herding wild cattle of Spanish origin in the mid-17th century in Argentina, Paraguay, Uruguay and Brazil. He was an archetypal cowboy and his needs were simple: horse, knife, poncho, tobacco and open-toed boots made from the legskins of a colt. He disdained work done afoot, indeed could scarcely walk, his legs bowed from years on horseback, his big toes deformed into talon-like claws from clutching his small wooden stirrups.

The gentry of Buenos Aires resented the fierce independence of the *gaucho*. Similarly, in Mexico the mixed-blood *vaquero* learned the skills and freedom of the trade, and thereby offended that country's race-proud Spanish aristocrats who had regarded horsemanship as an upper-class privilege. Once refrigeration ships were developed in 1879, however, and Europe's markets opened to beef from the Americas, the big landowners moved in, taming the *gauchos* and the *vaqueros* into peons and taming cattle-raising into a high profit industry. All across the open plains of the Americas the story was the same. The persistent ideal of the free-riding frontier cowboy would repeatedly shatter against the hard realities of money, class and race.

Mexican cattle were trailed northward, penetrating Texas and California, where the animals were permitted to run wild by the million on the open range, a practice unprecedented in Europe. By 1850 breakaway movements and the U.S. war with Mexico had made both these states American. By the early '60s their cattle were being driven north into British Columbia's interior

The single reason the Canadian West wasn't so wild

The Mountie patrols upheld the law, yet Const. Herron's terrible death showed that the cost could be high

The North-West Mounted Police constantly increased their posts and patrols to keep pace with the breakneck expansion of the ranching industry through the 1880s. "On no other frontier was the cattleman afforded such protection as he established his herds," writes University of Alberta historian David Breen in his authoritative *The Canadian Prairie West and the Ranching Frontier 1874-1924*. "The vigilante committee was consequently practically unknown on the Canadian range."

By 1889, five NWMP divisions operated a surveillance network from deep in the Rockies to Swift Current. That year more than 2,000 mounted patrols were carried out by "E" Division alone from its base in Calgary. Regular and less predictable flying patrols from "A" Division, headquartered at Maple Creek in the District of Assiniboia, linked up near the Willow Creek outpost with "K" Division out of Lethbridge.

Medicine Hat, as an example, was one of 10 outlying detachments in "A" Division, with one officer, four non-commissioned officers and 16 constables. The two divisions from Fort Macleod, "D" and "H", interlocked with Lethbridge and Calgary; patrols from Macleod and Calgary met at High River.

It was gruelling, dangerous work. L.V. Kelly, whose colourful masterpiece *The Range Men* stands as the classic account of early ranching in Alberta, told a particularly grim tale about Constable James Herron, on patrol out of Lethbridge in 1891. The sun, glaring on the snow day after day, induced snow blindness. "He lost his horse, and in the bitter weather of March 2 started out to find help, wandering aimlessly over the wide prairies, sightless, frozen by the cold winds, staggering along until about a mile from the Brown Ranch and succour, where he finally gave up in exhaustion and despair. With his remaining strength he placed his revolver to his head and killed himself to end his sufferings."

The NWMP checked the coming and going of all strangers. They visited ranchers and settlers. At times patrols along the border turned back Montana cattlemen hoping to let their (sometimes diseased) steers pass from the unregulated and hence overgrazed American range onto the better-managed Canadian grasslands. The Mounties' mere presence was a potent discouragement to theft of livestock, always a primary duty of the force. The four largest ranches each enjoyed the protection of a nearby police detachment.

The NWMP, though justly famed throughout the world for their perseverance and personal honesty, were not quite perfect, however. *The Range Men* recounts, for example, the story of Sydney Burgoyne, a police sergeant dispatched by the officer in charge at Macleod to help out at Claresholm. The rail line had just reached Macleod. Burgoyne, passing a hotel at the railhead, felt a little thirsty. He stopped in to imbibe. On his way to the hotel cellar to obtain a little more illegal liquor, the Mountie tripped over an Indian lying on the stairs. The Indian made a fuss, whereupon the Mountie cracked him across the skull with his pistol.

The Indian's companions immediately complained to Burgoyne's superior at Macleod. Would he tolerate a sergeant who drank on duty and assaulted an unarmed man? A police investigation followed, but Burgoyne easily "proved" that his arrival time at Claresholm could not possibly have allowed for a stopover at a bar along the route. The hotelkeeper, for his part, swore the Mountie had not been on his premises.

What Burgoyne's superiors did not realize was that their man's rapid arrival in Claresholm was not a matter of dedicated riding. A sympathetic railway work crew had stuck him and his horse on a rail car and sent the locomotive on a special trip northward to his destination. The NWMP never did discover his secret; his exoneration held. *M.B.*❦

Provincial Archives of Alberta, E. Brown Collection, B-1838

valleys to supply meat for the Cariboo gold rush.

But American railway promoters knew that the "Great American Desert" (as early geographers called the plains between Mexico and central Alberta) had a far greater beef potential. They knew that a cow worth $4 in Texas would fetch $40 back east. Thus in 1867, while British North Americans concluded three years of bickering over terms for confederating four of Britain's Atlantic and Great Lakes colonies, an event of far greater economic advantage to the future Alberta occurred at Abilene, Kansas.

This village had just been reached by the track gangs of the Kansas Pacific Railway. Longhorns from Texas were immediately driven up the Chisholm Trail and the Abilene Trail to Abilene. The bellowing herds totalled 35,000 head in 1867, booming to 700,000 by 1871. There, where steel rails intersected the most famous of all cattle trails, the first cowtown was born. A string of others would follow as the railheads moved westward, one of them to be known as Calgary.

Capital, both American and British, poured into Texas. Why, a man could just gather these wild critters and let 'em feed on virtually free grass. No barns, no fences and almost no care. Just collect the cattle occasionally and take them to market. Newspapers headlined tales of easy profits. Investors, caught up in a frenzied "beef bonanza," pushed into Wyoming and other western territories.

Before steers could start grazing the ranges to the north at equally handsome returns, however, three distinct obstacles had to be removed: the buffalo, the Sioux and the Blackfoot. These did not prove insurmountable. As early as 1870 the buffalo herds were recognized as in serious decline, succumbing to the new technology acquired by Metis and Indian hunters. And though General George Custer and a force of 266 U.S. cavalrymen died at the hands of the Sioux along Montana's Little Bighorn River in June of 1876, the Sioux surrendered to the U.S. Cavalry four months later. The year after that, Canada concluded Treaty No. 7 with the Blackfoot.

Among the first ranchers were the North-West Mounted Police. In the summer of 1875 they

A cowboy lexicon reveals ranching's Spanish origins

The Spanish influence dominated and shaped the western cattle frontier, says Richard Slatta in his social history *Cowboys of the Americas*. "The Anglo-American cowboy learned his trade from the *vaquero*. Spanish terminology, equipment and technique spread from Texas and California throughout the western United States." Certainly the Spanish impact on the lingo of Alberta's ranches and rodeos, including of course the Calgary Stampede, is evident. Some examples:

- *Lingo* itself comes from *lengua*, meaning "language."
- *Ranch* derives from *rancho*.
- *Stampede* is little changed from *estampida* (whose 'i' is pronounced 'ee').
- *Rodeo* is pronounced "raw-DAY-o" in Spanish but the spelling is the same. *Rodear*, meaning to "go around," refers to the seasonal roundups that would also occur later in the north. The end of the roundup was a natural time for *vaqueros* to compete sportingly at riding, roping and other skills.
- *Buckaroo*, an early American word for cowboy, is a corruption of *vaquero*, which is pronounced "bak-AYR-oh."
- *Wrangler* derives from the Spanish *caballerorango*, which the Spaniards abbreviated to "rango."
- *Lariat* descends from *la reata*, the same implement.
- *Lasso* goes back to *lazo*.
- *Bronco* is the same in both languages.
- *Chaps*, the leather leggings worn by cowboys, is shortened from *chaparejos*.
- *Dally*, an English-sounding term that means the practice of deftly looping a lariat's free end around the saddle horn, rather than tying it, comes from *dar la vuelta*, Spanish for "give a turn."

But little love was lost between Mexican cowboys, a few of whom ventured into Alberta, and their English-speaking counterparts. The latter were imbued with the racial disdain common to virtually all Anglo-Americans and most Europeans of the period.* In the United States, Mexican hands typically earned half the wages of an American, though observers like the cowboy-loving President Theodore Roosevelt grudgingly acknowledged that *vaqueros* generally "do the actual work well enough."

Although some historians have high praise for the Mexican cowhand, he had the reputation on the northern range of being cruel (or crueller) to animals, as well as highly superstitious. On the other hand, he disdained the Colt "equalizer" and other handguns as a coward's tool in a fight. He preferred the knife. *M.B.*❦

*Anglo superiority had of necessity to make one exception for Jesus Navarro, manager of the famous Cochrane Ranche in the 1880s. The Spanish pronunciation of his given name was customarily subverted to "Say-SOOS."

had moved out of Fort Macleod and established a second post, Fort Calgary, at the forks of the Bow and the Elbow. Another detachment, scouting west of Macleod, is said to have lost a pair of difficult-to-replace pincers (pliers) at a campsite. They couldn't find them and called the place Pincher Creek. (There are variants of this story, one of which is that the Mounties *found* a pair of pincers there, lost perhaps by prospectors in the 1860s.) Over the next six years Pincher, Fort Macleod, and Fort Calgary became the region's three chief ranching centres.

The Mounties established a dominion cattle herd in 1879, following the example of small independent operators who were already trailing animals into the foothills. Two years later the Conservative government of Sir John A. Macdonald established a new rangeland policy, permitting a person or company to lease up to 100,000 acres for 21 years, at one cent an acre annually. Rich, Conservative easterners and Britons, Quebec's wealthy Senator Matthew Cochrane a front-runner among them, were able and eager to acquire giant leases of Alberta range.

While its herding technology was essentially Mexican and its shipping technology American (i.e., by rail), the Canadian industry very soon began developing one definite distinction. It was law-abiding — thanks entirely to the prior presence of the NWMP. The ordinary constable commanded wide respect and created an environment much in contrast to the armed lawlessness of Wyoming and Montana, where Civil War veterans terrorized the plains with banditry.

NWMP constables were typically the sons of Ontario farmers, tradesmen or clerical workers. Officers often came from the same upper-class families that stocked the professions, the church, the military and the civil service in central Canada and the Maritimes. Conservative party patronage played a major role in selecting the officer cadre, just as it did in selecting lessees for the large, very valuable tracts of western range. Hence a cosy but tough-minded alliance between police and ranchers was forged from class solidarity, and many Mounties became early ranchers and ranch managers themselves after their NWMP service.

Sheilagh Jameson, long the chief archivist with the Glenbow Museum in Calgary, credits the Methodist missionaries, the McDougall family, with bringing the very first breeding stock onto the southern Alberta range — not without difficulty. In the autumn of 1873, the Reverend John McDougall and his trader brother, David, drove 11 cows and a bull down from Fort Edmonton to their mission among the Assiniboine at Morley. The little herd was swept away by buffalo on the trail, but later recovered. The bull reportedly tried to join the bison herd but was gored for his unwelcome enthusiasm. When the McDougalls later brought about 100 head north from Montana, some of the herd escaped and headed homeward. In a neighbourly act typical of the time, an ex-trader named Fred Kanouse rounded up the fugitives. Realizing they belonged to the McDougalls, he took the trouble to return the cattle back north.

During 1876 and 1877 George Emerson and other traders trailed in hundreds of animals — both horses and cattle — from Montana. Among the buyers were onetime police officers experimenting with herds of their own. Emerson himself would become a grand old man among the independent Alberta ranchers. Born in 1841 and raised at Danville, Quebec, the frontiersman had homesteaded in Iowa, prospected for gold in Montana, and then crisscrossed the northern Prairies as a freighter with the Hudson's Bay Company's Red River cart trains. After years as an independent trader, he started a spread along the Highwood River.

The slightly unworldly nature of some early settlers shows up in a tale about Emerson in Edward Brado's *Cattle Kingdom*. William Fares, a big cattle buyer, had paid $60,000 (a sum worth more than $1 million today) to the pioneer. The cheque remained uncashed after six months. Curious, Fares journeyed out to the Emerson ranch. He found the rancher watching a couple of his cowboys playing Seven Up, a popular card game, while a Chinese cook nagged them all to eat before their dinner got cold. Emerson, who kept all his accounts in his head, was surprised to hear the cheque hadn't cleared the bank. After hunting around, he discovered it stuffed in the pocket of an old vest hanging on a nearby nail.

The credit for establishing the first true range herd, however, often goes to Fred Kanouse, the man who rescued the McDougall herd. This whisky trader, son of a Fort Benton judge, arrived at the mouth of the Elbow River by way of Fort Whoop-up, years before the Mounties. Whisky trading was rendered precarious, he found, by the occasional fatal shootout with his customers, the Blackfoot. With the arrival of the police, Kanouse went into buffalo hunting and then cattle. According to respected lore, the ex-trader turned 21 cows and a bull loose on the open range near

The white she-wolf that so long foiled the prairie hunters

A prairie wolf slashes with its razor sharp fangs as if its teeth were knives. This carnivore, despite its immensely powerful jaws, does not usually bite into the flesh of its victim and lock on. Rather, in hunting a grazing prey, the wolf will dart in and cut the ham strings on the hind legs. Down falls the crippled quarry, and within moments one of the pack will slice its jugular vein. In this fashion, prairie wolves in their thousands culled the bison herds for thousands of years. After the buffalo were all but exterminated from the plains the grey spectres retreated into the western foothills, only to reappear when cattle came in the buffalo's stead.

In 1886, rancher A.E. Cross reported that he was losing 10 to 25 colts a year from his 200- to 250-horse herd on Mosquito Creek. It was a typical toll. Smaller ranchers were occasionally driven right out of business by the predators. Big operators, since the territorial government long refused persistent requests for a public bounty on wolves, often offered private bounties. Unemployed cowboys frequently became winter wolf-hunters, with varied success. Range riders could pick off coyotes with rifles and even six-shooters, but the great wolves proved too cautious.

In 1889 ranchers in the Porcupine Hills, west of Nanton, were especially irate over years of marauding by a large female wolf, entirely white but for the black tip of her tail. Any full-grown wolf was considered capable of destroying $1,000 worth of cattle annually, females with cubs much more. The parent would be more active while she instructed her young in the fine art of killing. This white specimen, known to haunt a particular coulee, was considered especially cunning and destructive. Every spring, according to the stories, she would emerge with six or eight pups in search of colts and calves.

Finally cattlemen in the Porcupine Hills pooled their resources to offer a special $75 premium for the hide of the white female. Two cowboys, Joe McIntosh and Charlie Brown, managed to run her to ground and rope her, dragging her over the Prairie until she was dead. But only Stanley Pinhorn, manager of the Oxley Ranche, proved willing to honour his share of the bounty: $25.

The wolf problem diminished after 1896, when the newly formed Western Stock Growers' Association offered a bounty that rose as high as $15 for females. From 1897 to 1902 the association paid out on 2,254 wolves, and the packs were under severe pressure from homesteading farmers as well. Early in the new century they disappeared from the plains entirely. *M.B.*❦

Glenbow Archives, NA-2157-3

Cowboys near Brooks with a dead wolf. After the stockmen put a bounty on them, wolves vanished from the plains in less than 10 years.

Fort Macleod in the fall of 1877. Unlike the cattle of the police and the McDougalls, these animals went untended through the winter. Next spring Kanouse rounded up his entire herd along with 21 calves.

In 1879 Emerson and a partner, Tom Lynch, drove 1,000 head up from Montana to establish their ranch near High River. That year George Maunsell obtained a discharge from the NWMP and, with his brother Edward, put cattle on the range. But troubles plagued these and most other fledgling operators. Their buffalo gone, the Indians were at times reduced to eating gophers. The police received almost daily complaints about livestock theft. Ranchers demanded protection or compensation from the government for stolen animals.

NWMP commander Colonel James Macleod gave them no comfort. Any rancher who killed an Indian, he declared, even in defence of his cattle, would be hanged. Not only was this the legally and morally correct position, the Mounties were far from any reinforcements and did not relish the thought of an Indian war. Furthermore, Macleod asserted, the uncared-for cattle were often wandering back to Montana, perishing on the range from natural causes or being rustled by other

Winter-killed cattle on the Bow River in 1903. The first deadly winter occurred in 1886-87, in which some ranch districts lost half their livestock.

The hideous winter that nearly killed the whole industry

Catching the ranchers unprepared, it left thousands of cattle frozen as they stood and entire herds dead

Cowboys paid in pain for their place in the newly opened West, but their suffering was far surpassed by the trials inflicted on their animals. The worst winter endured by the cattle herds during the 19th century struck in late 1886. The following account of that terrible season, reported in 1913 by L.V. Kelly in The Range Men *on the basis of eye witnesses' memories, constitutes a remarkable passage in the history of western Canada's ranching industry:*

Deep snows had fallen and drifted, crusting so heavily that no steer could "muzzle" through to the hidden grasses, though the wiser horses managed to make pretty good shift with their hoofs. Very little hay had been put up, owing to the ranchers' belief that it was unnecessary and also to the fact that so much good hay-land had been grazed over during the summer and fall. John Herron of Pincher Creek had a few stacks of millet and other tame hay, the first grown in the district, but as a rule every rancher was woefully short on feed. Ten years had passed since Fred Kanouse turned the first range cattle loose to rustle on the plains around Macleod, and during all that 10 years there had been no general, heavy loss, so the ranchmen naturally figured there was no likelihood of one coming.

Consequently the storms and drifted, crusted snow were a terrible blow, especially among the new or "pilgrim" stock that had been brought into the ranges in vast herds, totalling 30,000 head north of the Old Man's alone when winter started. These were the first "stocker" herds in Alberta, and they suffered tremendously, much more than the native stock, though the

whites. His force, he said, would not "act as herders over a country about one hundred miles wide, and over two hundred miles long, as the ranchmen who have squatted through that section are scattered over a country of that extent." So 16 cattlemen, including four former Mounties, conducted Alberta's first roundup, then retreated with their stock to the Marias River range in Montana.

By then the NWMP were establishing their own herds, one near Macleod, another near Calgary. The police proved better at maintaining the law than at maintaining the herds, and the dominion government had to continue buying beef elsewhere as well. Nevertheless, the Mountie endeavour somewhat eased the Indians' desperation. Between 200 and 300 natives were fed through the winter of 1880-81 at Macleod, a year when 200 small operators grazed modest herds on free grass between the U.S. boundary and the Bow.

Though these former traders and policemen demonstrated the industry viable in Alberta, their latter died in thousands. When the bitter weather was at its worst, there were 40,000 starving horned creatures within a radius of 25 miles of Macleod.

The rabbits died, the lynx left, the herds of antelope starved in hundreds, the poor brutes wandering into the very settlements, where they were often killed in the streets. The I.G. Baker Company's cattle, the first "beef" herds in Alberta, were scattered widely through the south and suffered frightful loss. A beef herd is one made up of cattle that are being fattened for market, such as the present herds of P. Burns & Company and J.H. Wallace, who do no breeding, but simply buy young or mature stock and round them into prime shape. Sixty per cent of this first beef herd was wiped out in the winter of 1886-1887.

Yarding like moose, the cattle in the great country north of the Old Man's River died like flies, bitter winds, no food, and a continuing extreme cold soon huddling the stock in suffering bands, unable to travel far because of the mighty drifts.

Ezra Pearson, manager of the 'MHR' at Medicine Hat, left that town on the early morning of February 4th to drive the 23 miles to the ranch, the snow two feet deep on the level, with great drifts here and there and the thermometer 54 degrees below zero. Driving four horses to a light sleigh, it took Pearson three long days to make the distance.

This ranch had put up hay for their stock, but even they suffered considerable loss, chiefly among the last bunch of stock they had taken in that fall. All over the ranch country the price of hay soared to phenomenal prices, ranchers standing willing to pay forty dollars a ton for all they could get and being unable to secure a single wisp. Those fortunate enough to possess a few stacks hoarded it like gold, and stood ready to fight to save a single forkful.

Clustering in the coulees or huddling on the open, the animals suffered and died in enormous numbers. Some, breast-high in packed and crusted banks, died as they stood; some who were sheltered somewhat by bluffs or coulees starved pitifully, ravenously searching for food until the frost had reached their vitals.

The bodies of great steers were found in the spring, heaps of them, with their throats and stomachs punctured and torn by sharp splinters from dried and frozen branches and chunks of wood which they had swallowed in their anguish. The coulees showed the most bodies in the spring, for naturally the animals sought their shelter, crowding close together for the warmth of each other's bodies. One would succumb, others would crowd in on that body, others would drop, and when the winter broke the bodies lay piled six and eight deep all up the bottoms of the ravines. Hundreds of animals, helplessly endeavouring to find sustenance, sucked the hair from the hides of their dead comrades, dying finally with their throats, mouths, and stomachs lined with it.

Throughout, the ranchers and the cowboys performed prodigies of endurance, riding wide and far and hard in their supreme efforts to save such of the herds as they could. They did little good, being only able to watch their stock perish and hope for a break in the weather that never came until nearly the first of March.

John Quirk of High River, in his efforts to save his herds, drove and dragged some of the most exhausted ones to his ranch house, where he and his wife attempted to rejuvenate the exhausted creatures by pouring warm water on their frozen limbs.

Kelly noted that "well-conditioned beeves" west of Calgary died after three weeks in the frigid temperatures, even though snowfall was light and food abundant in that district. A sudden chinook in mid-March instantly melted all the snow to the south, flooding river valleys and drowning yet more cattle. As near as can be judged, the average losses were about 25% around Calgary, 50% to 60% from High River to the Oldman, 20% to 25% in the Pincher Creek district, and 50% around Medicine Hat where horse herds suffered considerable loss as well.

Thereafter ranchmen put up hay with religious consistency, a chore cowboys loathed. Shelter was provided for calves and weaker cows during the coldest weather, in contradiction to earlier assertions by ranch operators that winter care for their herds would be uneconomic. The brutal experience of 1886-1887 was the industry's first major setback. It drove some ranchers out of business. The industry as a whole, however, learned a lesson and kept on. M.B.❦

animals would not have impressed the fine breeders of the East or of Europe. Most were descended from Longhorns, offspring of the Spanish Retinto breed that had wandered the Texas *praderas* for nearly 400 years, whose horns, tip to tip, measured up to eight feet. They were tough, long-legged animals, immune to tick fever but too thin through the loins and rump to be a good beef specimen. Colour varied from dull yellow through red and black.

The Longhorn descendants had lately been crossed with Shorthorns, Herefords and Angus in Wyoming and Montana, however, and these meatier scrubs began arriving in quantity in Alberta by 1881. That was the year the CPR contract was signed, promising direct access to eastern markets. Canada's own beef bonanza was about to occur.❦

CHAPTER TWO

British peers and eastern tycoons plunge into ranching and fail at it

IN ONE OF ALBERTA'S STRANGEST ERAS, LORDS AND HOUNDS PRANCED OVER THE PRAIRIES HUNTING COYOTES, BUT LIKE THE SPRAWLING DISASTER CALLED THE COCHRANE RANCHE, THE EPOCH SOON ENDED

When Captain William Winder returned to his home at Lennoxville, Quebec, in 1879, on leave from the North-West Mounted Police, he may have suspected that the vision he brought with him would launch a new age on the Canadian Prairies — what could be called "The Era of the Great Ranches." It was destined to last little more than 20 years, but it would provide an intriguing and flamboyant epoch in the history of Alberta. Elegant British peers would be improbably partnered with tobacco-spitting cowhands, while sophisticated English ladies tried to teach Indian women, fresh off the plains, the correct place-settings for formal dining.

Winder's scheme was straightforward. He would raise capital among the wealthy English-speaking breeders of purebred cattle in Quebec's Eastern Townships. He would buy an enormous herd of Longhorns in Montana, drive them north to the boundless expanse of superb grazing land around Fort Calgary and market the steers back in Montana. Already the Northern Pacific was building its way across North Dakota and had plans to keep on west.

A roundup crew near High River in 1895. As a way to make money it seemed simple enough; and with the Cochrane land grant in 1881, the era of the big, absentee-owned ranches had begun.

Winder found the money, but then couldn't find the land. It was there all right, but the dominion government as yet had no plan under which the cattlemen could use it. However, he accomplished one thing more that was to prove decisive. His talk of big-time cattle-ranching in Canada caught the ear of an Eastern Township industrialist who had a great deal of money, much of which he made in cattle hides[1], who had a consuming interest in cattle-breeding and who had superb connections in the Macdonald government. This was Senator Matthew Henry Cochrane, and what followed was the Cochrane Ranche: first, biggest and financially most disastrous of the four great ranches of Alberta's great ranching era.

Matthew Cochrane was a self-made man. He was born at Compton, near Lennoxville, in 1823, the son of an immigrant Ulsterman who had become a prosperous farmer and merchant. He left school at Grade 8 because his father needed him on the farm, and at 18 went down to Boston and got into the leather business. In 1854 he moved the business to Montreal, where his 300 employees were generating an impressive $500,000 in annual sales by the mid-1880s.

Yet livestock remained his first love. Among British and American breeders, Shorthorns were the most prized purebreds of the period. In 1868 Cochrane bought Duchess 97 for 1,000 guineas (roughly $5,000 Canadian at the time), the highest price ever fetched by a British Shorthorn cow. The gamble paid off. His Hillhurst Farm sold its own Fifth Duchess for $17,900 in 1877. But a ranch in the West, that would be really something. Cochrane put together a plan to establish a herd of 2,000 to 3,000 animals, including 75 purebred bulls. It would need a big spread of land somewhere in the foothills country. His friend and neighbour John Pope, Macdonald's minister of Agriculture, laid the scheme before cabinet.

What emerged the following year, 1881, was a program under which huge tracts of prairie land could be leased for 21 years, cancellable on two years' notice if the land were required for settlement. To ensure ownership of his buildings and the core of his operation, a rancher could buy acreage equal to 5% of his total lease at $2 an acre. The scheme, it was urged, had definite merits. Land use was controlled, unlike the practice in the territories to the south where everybody's cattle ran everywhere, where land disputes might be settled by shootout, and where overgrazing became inevitable. With a more permanent hold on the land, it would not pay the lessee to overgraze it.

That fall Cochrane committed himself. Historian Sheilagh Jameson of the Glenbow Institute

[1] **Before the invention of vulcanized rubber by Charles Goodyear in the 1840s, machine belting was made of leather. As Matthew Cochrane and other businessmen discovered, buffalo hide was tougher and therefore more effective than cattle hide, a circumstance which contributed to that animal's near-extinction.**

Glenbow Archives, NA-118-4

Glenbow Archives, NA-239-25

Senator Matthew Cochrane of Montreal. Of the four great early ranches, his was the first, biggest and most financially disastrous. (Below) interior of the Cochrane ranch house in 1886. Ernest Cochrane, the senator's third son, is reading on the couch.

estimates his first herd at double his initial intention: just over 6,800 head, purchased for about $125,000 in Montana. The drive, the first big operation of its kind into Alberta, took the animals to the senator's 100,000-acre lease on the Bow River upstream of Calgary.[2] Cochrane had secured the release of Major James Walker from the NWMP and hired him as resident ranch manager. The former Mountie stumbled through mistake after mistake for two years while learning the hard way about big-scale ranching in the new land.

"This drive [from Montana] has remained the criterion for hard driving, as no such great numbers of animals have ever since been moved so rapidly by trail," reported L.V. Kelly, longtime Calgary and Vancouver newsman, in his book *The Range Men*. Thirty cowboys and 300 horses moved the cattle at 15 to 18 miles a day, working from dawn until dark. Even at night the beasts were too crowded to eat properly. Calves could not keep up. The cowboys traded many a foundling for a cup of tea or, by preference, whisky. After being counted where the Canadian Pacific's Calgary station would later rise, the herd was pushed across the Bow at the future site of the 14th Street bridge and on to the ranch. An October storm struck almost immediately, the weary beasts still unrecovered from their gruelling trek. As many as 1,000 head died before they'd learned to locate shelter and water on the unfamiliar range.

Trouble with local settlers also began almost immediately. That winter the Cochrane cattle carried only "hair" brands, a big C scratched temporarily in the hide, which disappeared when the animals shed their winter coats. In the spring of 1882 Walker was ordered by his Montreal-based management to round up and brand all unbranded animals on the lease. He obeyed the instruction with military thoroughness, his cowboys scooping up cattle belonging to local homesteaders as well, down to a pet cow and calf. The settlers retaliated, using their more intimate knowledge of the terrain to locate and rustle cattle from distant coulees before they were branded by the Cochrane hands. The big ranch was regarded bitterly by many neighbours from that point on.

Later in 1882, Walker went shopping in Montana again, buying about 2,600 head. A snowstorm struck before the herd reached Fish Creek (now a park in south Calgary). The American trail boss recommended that the cattle be left in the sheltered valley for a month or so to recuperate. Walker, acting under orders from Montreal, insisted that the journey to Big Hill — the name of his ranch's headquarters — be completed as contracted. The final leg of the drive through heavy drifts wreaked havoc. Worse was to follow. No chinook came. The steers tried to shift southeastward toward better grazing but the cowboys, again following strict orders from the east to keep the ani-

[2] The original Cochrane Ranche headquarters was designated a provincial historic site in 1977, although no building had survived except a bunkhouse from the British American Ranch Co.'s sheep-raising years there. The property became an interpretive site in 1979, and in the 1990s there were plans to reconstruct at least one of the original buildings.

Glenbow Archives, NA-239-2

mals on Cochrane land, hazed them back.

Irritated residents would sell little of their scarce feed to relieve the suffering beasts. Dead cattle piled up in the coulees. By spring, it was said, a man could walk across some gullies, or even along their entire length, without stepping off the carcases. Cochrane had probably lost more than half of all the livestock acquired in Montana. Walker resigned. (Thereafter, he purchased timber rights from the Cochrane company, did well with a sawmill, and became mayor of Calgary and one of its founding citizens.)

But Matthew Cochrane wouldn't give up. The Cochrane Ranche Company acquired a further 170,000 acres well to the south near the Oldman and Waterton rivers, where the winters should be milder. The Bow River lease was transferred to a newly formed Cochrane subsidiary, the British American Ranch Co. To the horror of other ranchers, British American immediately lobbied the Macdonald government for permission to place sheep on its Bow ranges. Until then, federal officials had banned sheep from leases in the Canadian West. Cowboys traditionally loathe shepherds along with sodbusting cultivators. Confrontations in the American West had already become literally murderous.

Glenbow Archives, NA-2003-1

Yarding sheep at the 76 Ranch in the Etzikom Coulee country of southeast Alberta. In 1884 Cochrane moved his cattle south and, to the horror of neighbouring ranchers, devoted his vast northern lease west of Calgary to sheep.

U.S. cattlemen usually grazed their open ranges to the point of complete destruction within seven years. Sheep could survive a little longer on the abused land and thus earned the blame for the entire catastrophe. (Sheep, unlike cows, have front incisor teeth that allow them to crop pasture closer to the roots.) In drought-prone districts, the forage might not recover for half a century. Canadian officials, conservative by instinct, had accepted anti-sheep arguments from the likes of Matthew Cochrane, but now the most politically potent rancher of all had thrown his weight the other way. In its more northerly climes, Cochrane suggested, Alberta should be mutton country.

Since Cochrane had the connections, Cochrane carried the argument.[3] His Big Hill operation nevertheless lost another bundle of money. In 1884 the Cochrane company brought in more than 7,000 sheep, mainly from Wyoming and Montana. The winter was mild but hundreds of animals died anyhow, from lambing and prairie fires, and during one blizzard a large flock walked out of its corral on snowdrifts and onto a frozen slough. When a melt followed, many drowned. Worse yet, Australia's burgeoning wool production was driving prices down. British American sold its sheep in Alberta, taking losses in the severely limited market. Over the next two decades the Bow lands were eventually taken over in smaller chunks by homesteaders, or purchased outright by cattlemen.

Even off the range, moreover, Cochrane had his losses. For instance William Kerfoot, a Virginian who managed the Big Hill sheep operation, successfully sued the company in 1885. Kerfoot had stubbornly defended a herder, though his Montreal bosses wanted the man fired after a number of sheep died in his care. Kerfoot, who argued the herder was not at fault under the circumstances, was fired himself. His lawyer, James Lougheed, won a settlement of $1,650 plus costs and interest when the case was heard by a Calgary court. Kerfoot's son later recorded his father's assessment of Cochrane's absentee eastern managers. They had, he said, "the knack of getting together a lot of good men and then ignoring their recommendations, usually with heavy loss to themselves."

Senator Cochrane was very much the absentee landlord. His eldest son James Arthur was a

[3] Continuing protests from other ranchers eventually forced Ottawa to prohibit sheep in the south country. Sheep were allowed to roam anywhere north of a stream rising in the Rockies and meandering eastward along a course about 30 miles south of Calgary. Though dignified on maps with the name "river," this stream was more accurately known among local folk thereafter as Sheep Creek.

Remittance men: Tales and truths and outright lies

EXILED BY THEIR BLUEBLOOD FAMILIES, THEY DRIFTED INTO PIONEER ALBERTA AND MASKED TRAGEDY WITH ANECDOTE

Many a 19th-century English rake who overindulged in alcohol or women or other reprehensible behaviour found himself exiled by his embarrassed family to his nation's overseas colonies. As recompense a regular allowance would be mailed (remitted) to him. Some of these "remittance men," in their Ascot ties, monocles, and vivid waistcoats and caps, gravitated to Alberta. A few actually mended their ways. But most did not, and cultivating tales about them became a local amusement, often indulged at the expense of truth. These yarns, however dubious, have survived the years.

Provincial Archives of Alberta, H. Pollard Collection, P-475

A remittance man's shack northwest of Cochrane about 1900. Their English manners charmed women, but rarely into marriage.

There is the one about the Englishman drinking with a group of cowboys in a hotel, for example. The bar closed. A cowboy recalled he had a bottle in his room. "I'll fetch it straightaway," said the remittance man. Mischievously, the cowboy gave him the number of the room next door, occupied by a bride and her husky groom, the latter now enjoying a drink himself. The remittance man calmly plucked the bottle from the groom's hand, and moments later found himself being hurled back into the bar, bottle-less. "I caught that bloody bounder," said the remittance man as he picked himself up. "He was in your room drinking your whisky. I tried to rescue it and he became quite violent." No one told him why.

Another remittance man, temporarily out of funds, hired on as a cowboy. He was fired two days later, so the tale went, when he couldn't remember whether he was supposed to round up 11 two-year-old steers or two 11-year-olds. (No steer would be on the range until age 11.)

A few remittees actually started ranching. Some of these, legend would have it, rode their horses right into the bars and drank in the saddle. In *Gentlemen Emigrants,* Patrick Dunae tells of a High River character allegedly called Sir John the Astronomer because he discovered a fourth star on the label of Hennessy's three-star cognac. There was also the drunken "Lord Dutton" whose sister lost patience and stopped sending the quarterly cheque. So he wired home in the guise of a friend announcing Lord Dutton's death and asking for cash to cover his funeral. She sent it. What happened next is not recorded.

In letters home, remittance men would often lie about their accomplishments to boost the flow of funds. One said he had a ranch stocked with 700 full-blooded gophers, and he needed an extra $1,000 to keep them fit for the spring market.

There was always the danger that the British "connection" might pay a visit, however. As recounted in Hugh Dempsey's *The Best of Bob Edwards,* remittance man James Rossiter, who lived in a shack, persuaded a neighbour to lend him his substantial ranch house and cattle spread to impress his father. The entire crew co-operated, with the owner playing the part of foreman and the rest obligingly taking orders from young Rossiter. Rossiter *père,* by the time he left, was so impressed he gave his son another £500.

The reality behind these stories was often far from humorous — a man who literally rolled in a gutter, an alcoholic shrieking in delirium tremens, or the graduate of a fine private school reduced to street begging. Why did they drink? Some blamed the shortage of wives. White women were scarce and the few eligibles were more likely to choose a husband with property and stability. (And sad to say, an Englishman who took up life with a native girl was held in deeper contempt than an irresponsible remittance man.)

Even remittance men had their good points, however. Rarely did they whine about their treatment. Their exquisite manners charmed women, though rarely into marriage. And most of them enlisted for the First World War. The West's final judgement was summed up in an observation quoted by folklorist Robert E. Gard in *Johnny Chinook*: "Those fellows were green, but by God they're not yellow." *M.B.*❦

Glenbow Archives, NA-644-28

The British influence brought panache if not always practicality. Complete with hounds, this was the annual 'Sons of England Benevolent Society Coyote Hunt' of 1895.

director of the Cochrane Ranche and made numerous visits to the West (the first in 1882 to deliver a prize bull), but was headquartered in Quebec. Son William F. did come out in the 1880s and ran the Cardston operation for many years, however, and about 1900 third son Ernest B. began to share in the work of the ranch.

Yet another Cochrane disaster was barely staved off on the Waterton Lakes range during a blizzard in the winter of 1885-86. The cattle, unable to reach grass under the heavy drifts, appeared doomed. Frank Strong, a veteran ranch foreman from Fort Macleod, offered to save the animals for a fee of $1,000. The deal was quickly cut. Strong rounded up approximately 500 horses from local Indian reserves. For two days he drove the horses through the snow towards the trapped cattle. Once the trail was broken, Strong simply let the horses pound back to their home pastures. The starving cattle followed them, finding plentiful forage on the Peigan Reserve. For Strong, success tasted all the sweeter because he was the man who had headed up, when he was 23, that first disastrous drive northward in 1881.

Cochrane's southern property, then totalling 67,000 acres, was sold to the Mormon Church in 1906, three years after the senator's death. Church managers in the Salt Lake City office decided to leave about 30,000 acres in grass. In 1968 the Mormons in turn sold out for $3 million to Morris Palmer, an American oilman living in Calgary. (It's still a very large spread for the beef industry; a modern ranch commonly takes in 5,000 acres.) But the Cochranes retained the mineral rights on their southern range. This would one day prove valuable.

During 1882, the year after leasing regulations were established by the dominion government, 75 leases covering four million acres of land were approved by Ottawa. Ranch holdings soon formed a compact block along the foothills from the international border to the Bow valley. By 1883 some 25,000 cattle roamed this area. Three years later the cattle population had more than quadrupled and horses numbered 11,000.

While nearly all this stock was owned by the four big ranches — the Cochrane, the Oxley, the Walrond and North-West Cattle — there were many smaller operations. Some of these were run by an assortment of British expatriates and absentee landowners whose names rippled across the Prairies like a breeze through rough fescue, although they proved even less enduring.

The High River Hunt Club, an ex-Indian Army officer's initiative, specialized in raising steeds for crack British regiments such as the 13th Hussars. Major-General Thomas Bland Strange dreamed up the Military Colonization Company Ranche for his fellow army officers from Britain and India.[4] He located it on the Bow downstream from Calgary, whose male citizens he despised for their "cowardly" concern over the city's safety during the 1885 Riel Rebellion. Strange accused Indians, neighbours and the CPR of burning his range. In his mind, the Canadian Pacific crews

[4] Generally speaking, the spelling "ranche" was preferred by British and British-influenced owners. Those more acclimatized to North American and western ways tended to spell the word less pretentiously as "ranch." One rueful Briton suggested a different distinction, however. A ranch was likely to make money, he quipped, and a ranche was not.

Walter Gordon Cumming, a Quorn Ranche shareholder, pictured here in Calgary in 1893. He brought in a herd of Polled Angus cattle from Scotland.

Glenbow Archives, NA-2307-17

were riddled with treacherous Irish Fenians. After he had fought with most of his neighbours, his enterprise collapsed.

John Stewart started the Stewart Ranch near Pincher Creek, named for his prominent Ottawa lumber family, and he also formed the Rocky Mountain Rangers during the 1885 Riel Rebellion. The ranch was sold off in 1888. The Quorn Ranche, between Sheep and Tongue creeks, was established by members of a hunt in Leicestershire, England. Its efforts to raise highly bred horses proved ill-advised. The remounts couldn't endure the rough and tumble of Mountie work, and the ranch never did break into the British military market. Its fine animals were reduced to local construction work, an inappropriate and uneconomic outcome. A further financial drain on the operation was the need to entertain a stream of owners, their sons and friends. These enthusiastic fox hunters scampered after coyotes with the Quorn's specially imported, long-legged hounds.

There were others: Lord Castletown's Mont Head Ranche Company;[5] the Canadian Agricultural, Coal and Colonization Company of Sir John Lister-Kaye; the Circle; the Cypress Cattle Company; the Mount Royal; the Chipman (a Halifax-financed initiative whose lease lay within Calgary's present city limits); the Bow River Horse Ranch; the Medicine Hat Ranching Company; and many more.

It seems evident that the rough (though not sweat-labour rough) quality of the southern Alberta frontier appealed to British and eastern Canadian gentlemen. According to one tale, during the initial western tour of the governor-general, the Marquis of Lorne, his party pulled up at a stopping house on the trail between Calgary and Fort Macleod. An aide to Lord Lorne inquired as to the menu for the day. There's soup, he was told. What kind of soup, asked the aide. "Damn *good* soup," came the reply. (Precisely the same story is told of the Earl of Lathom, Lord Chamberlain to Queen Victoria, who stopped at Kamoose Taylor's hotel in Macleod when visiting his Oxley Ranche. Author Kelly also said that ex-whisky trader Taylor did the honours as waiter, complete with a dirty towel carefully draped over one arm.) Shortly afterwards, Lord Lorne invested in the Alberta Ranche Company in a consortium with his former aide, Sir Francis de Winton, and Sir F.F. Mackenzie.[6]

But Ottawa clearly favoured the four major firms of the cattle industry. In 1884 two-thirds of all stocked land in southwest Alberta was controlled by 10 companies. Almost half of that was held by the big four, whose leases often extended from the front range of the Rockies to the adjacent Prairie, benefiting from both sheltered terrain and open grazing.

The Oxley Ranche syndicate was formed in March 1882, its birth wrapped in the personal oddities that would entangle much of its early existence. John Craig, a veteran livestock operator from Ontario and one of the finest cattle judges in the country, had marshalled about $200,000 among his Canadian friends for a western ranch. He then journeyed to London, where he fell in with Alexander Staveley Hill, QC, PC, DCL, JP, recorder of Banbury, deputy high steward of Oxford University, judge advocate of the fleet and member of parliament for Staffordshire West. Hill said

[5] The great scale of Alberta ranches came naturally to some of the British gentry who invested in them. Lord Castletown, for example, held 22,241 acres in Ireland according to an 1878 listing, and that was small in comparison to the estates of, say, the Marquis of Waterford, totalling 117,218 acres. The Waterford holdings included those of other members of the Beresford family, who numbered among them Lord Delaval Beresford, owner of the Mexico Ranch on the Red Deer River and companion of Florida Wolfe, a black woman he had met in Mexico.

[6] Historian David Breen, in his study of the ranching frontier, comments that the list of ranching syndicate directors "reads like a 'who's who' of the Canadian parliamentary and financial worlds." Aristocrats mixed on these boards with the merely rich, and high-born fellows began appearing in the West. Fort Macleod memoir-writer John Higinbotham recalled how the three Garnett brothers, Jack, Arthur and Lewis, always insisted upon dining in evening dress. Few expatriates would go that far to "keep from reverting to savagery," says Breen, or require delivery of a piano while the railway was still several hundred miles distant. Such eccentricities were nevertheless indicative of a certain social order.

Glenbow Archives, NA-237-11

Nestled against the foothills, the upper Walrond Ranche in 1893. It earned annual dividends of 30% in the 1880s.

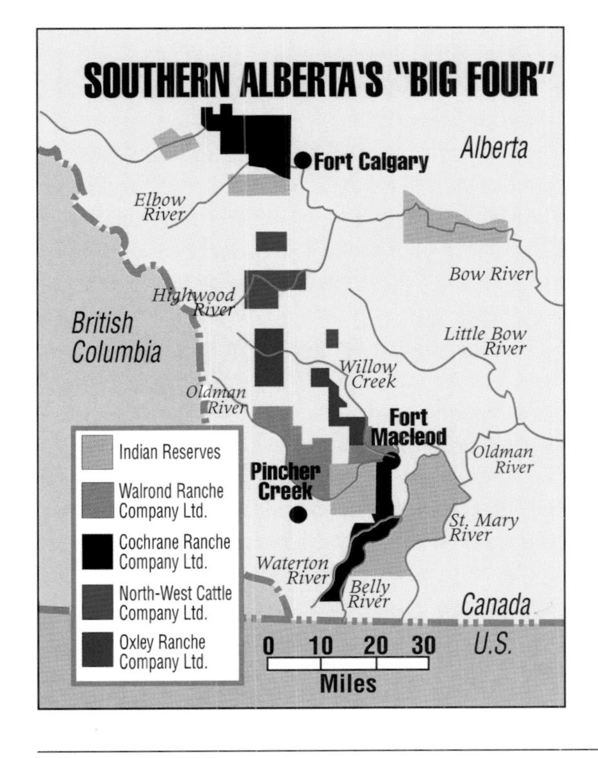

he could raise a much larger sum, but only if Craig agreed to restrict the consortium to English gentlemen.

Craig was tempted. Bigger herds were thought likely to earn higher rates of return. As he himself wrote, "...the larger the herd the less proportionate expense, and therefore the greater profit in proportion to capital..." His Canadian friends agreed to step aside, and Hill then inexplicably failed to come up with much sterling. But Craig was able to enlist Lord Lathom,[7] Kamoose Taylor's distinguished onetime guest and himself a prominent British breeder, and the venture got off the ground. A large lease was acquired which turned out to be front range territory, described by the *Macleod Gazette* as "admirably adapted to the raising of grizzly bears, mountain sheep and goats." Then the group managed to obtain further leases of excellent grazing along Willow Creek.

[7] The Earl of Lathom, for whom a station west of Calgary was named, was the head of a family called Wilburgham or Wilbraham in Lancashire and Cheshire, which traces its origin to the sheriff of County Chester in the reign of Henry III (1216-1272). Lathom owned 11,000 acres in Britain. (The earldom became extinct in 1930.)

Walrond ranch hands on a chuckwagon in 1901 during the June roundup.

Glenbow Archives, NA-1035-4

But Hill frequently failed to pay the Oxley's bills from his perch in London. After a visit to the ranch, Lathom reportedly raged at Hill for forcing Craig to borrow money from "shopkeepers to carry on our ranching." His protest did not improve matters. At one point Oxley cattle were seized in Montana and sold to cover bad debts. Frank Farmer, a young American rancher owed money by the Oxley, froze to death in 1885 while travelling north to collect. Later that year Hill's nephew Stanley Pinhorne fired Craig and took over as manager. In 1892 Pinhorne was found dead in his bed with a bullet through his head, an apparent suicide. When Craig published his angry reminiscences in 1903, British ranch owners and some of their Alberta managers resented his contemptuous treatment of their blueblooded colleagues. During the 1920s the Oxley operation found its way into the hands of local owners.

The Walrond Ranche was organized in 1883 by Duncan McEachern, then dominion veterinarian, who came west as its general manager. Most of the capital came from Sir John Walrond[8] and other British investors. The company assembled leases totalling 260,000 acres along the Oldman River and into the Porcupine Hills. It earned annual dividends of 30% on invested capital through the 1880s.

Jim Patterson, who drove the first Walrond herd north from Montana and later became ranch foreman, was deadly accurate with a sixshooter. Out riding one Sunday, McEachern challenged him to shoot a blue grouse in the pine branches. Patterson fired twice and the bird fell, its head neatly sheared off. But he'd needed two shots, chided McEachern. The first, explained Patterson, was to clear away a branch that obscured the bird's head. A shot in the body would have spoiled it for lunch.

McEachern was himself the target of an unknown gunman one night in 1893, although the

[8] The Walrond name seemed to lend itself to creative spelling. It came from the name of the Walrond family of Devon. Sir John Walrond was High Sheriff of Devon and MP for Tiverton. His son William Hood Walrond was raised to the peerage as Lord Waleran.

[9] The outlaw Harry Longbaugh, sometimes spelled Longabaugh, was nicknamed the Sundance Kid after the little town where he served his only jail sentence, for stealing a horse. After leaving the District of Alberta he joined the notorious "Wild Bunch" in Wyoming and was reputedly their best shot. But in the rapidly civilizing West, crime increasingly didn't pay. With Butch Cassidy and a girl named Etta Place, Longbaugh took his banditry to South America, where he was mortally wounded by the Bolivian cavalry and Cassidy shot himself rather than face jail. By other accounts, Sundance escaped and lived a quiet life as Harry Long in Casper, Wyoming, until he died, either in the 1930s or as late as 1957.

potshots missed. All southern Alberta assumed his assailant was an irate farmer. Ranchers firmly threw all "squatters" off their leases. Farmers, they knew, would spoil the range. The farmers, all small-timers, resented the ranchers' influence in Ottawa, where the government inevitably backed them, using the Mounties to do it. McEachern's hard line on eviction pitted him against editor Charles Wood whose *Macleod Gazette* was militantly pro-homesteader. The *Gazette*'s charges were picked up by the eastern news media, and the fight grew long, mean and ugly, with Wood raging against the "clique" that ran the country, and the ranchers protesting that their side was never given, namely that the land was too dry to farm and if tilled would become desert.

Finally McEachern, lawyer James Lougheed and other ranchers took over Calgary's *Weekly Herald* in 1888, switched their advertising there and forced Wood out of his editorship. The *Gazette*'s new editors proclaimed southern Alberta as ranching country, humbly vowing to promote the interests of that industry. The stockmen's advertisements returned, but Fort Macleod's glory days had faded for good. Eventually the Walrond too suffered an undignified fate. In 1908 its leases passed to beef packer William Roper Hull and later to Calgary meat packer Pat Burns. Today some of the original ranch lands have been reassembled as the Waldron Grazing Co-op.

The best-managed of the big four was North-West Cattle, known by its brand as the Bar U Ranch. Captain Winder, the NWMP officer who started it all, had a brother-in-law, Fred Stimson, who recruited the steamship magnates Sir Hugh and Andrew Allan of Montreal (the former still notorious from the Pacific railway scandal) as financial backers for the venture. Riding the southern Alberta range in early 1882, Stimson selected a site along the Highwood River at Spitzie Crossing. He imported 21 purebred bulls from Chicago, then brought 3,000 cattle over from Idaho's Lost River country, pulling off a model drive that allowed the ranch to avoid escalating cattle prices in Montana.

Eight days of heavy snow struck in September (the same storm that savaged the second Cochrane drive on its way from Fish Creek to Big Hill). The Idaho cattle drifted south before the north wind, moving as far as Fort Macleod. Stimson left the animals on the southern range, though it wasn't his lease, and the strategy paid off. Bar U losses were minor compared to the catastrophe that devastated the Cochrane herd penned up on its home territory. Eventually North-West herds rose as high as 30,000 head of cattle.

Stimson was something of a wit. A train once killed one of his horses, for instance. If a horse couldn't outrun the CPR, he drily observed, it didn't deserve to live. A big man with a carefully cultivated western drawl, the Bar U manager had a bent for filching other people's property. Driving home from High River one day, he couldn't resist stealing the double trees from a wagon left by the trail. Later he found a Bar U cowboy swearing because the trees from a Bar U wagon had been pinched. Stimson had robbed himself. But he also had a happy knack of collecting good hands. Among his men were the famed black cowboy John Ware and, for a brief period, a fine range rider named Harry Longbaugh. Longbaugh soon returned the United States, however, where he would become known as "the Sundance Kid."[9]

Another promising recruit was George Lane, who arrived from the United States in 1884 with a stake of $100. Stimson made him ranch foreman. Eventually Lane started ranching and cattle buying in his own right, forming a syndicate that bought the Bar U itself in 1902 for $250,000. At the time, this was an industry record for a single transaction. This ranch also was sold to the omnipresent Pat Burns in 1926, and broken up into parcels for its final sale in 1950.

But there were survivors. One was the Glengarry, a jewel nestled deep in the Porcupine Hills west of Claresholm. Another was the McIntyre, crowning the Milk River Ridge east of Cardston. The Glengarry was the work of Allan Ban Macdonald, a railway supplier and merchant from Ontario. William McIntyre, a Mormon born in Texas, had previous ranching experience in Utah. Perhaps coincidentally, neither entrepreneur could boast a British title or an eastern Canadian fortune.

In addition to these, there sprang up hundreds of smaller spreads where herds were counted by dozens of head rather than hundreds or thousands. Owners often employed one or two hands only. Such people homesteaded rather than leased their land. Alberta historian Lewis G. Thomas, who grew up on a small ranch (480 acres) eight miles west of Okotoks, describes the modest dimensions of his boyhood home: "The frame house, originally consisting of two ground floor rooms each about 16 feet square, with bedrooms above, is T-shaped and each part has a steeply sloping roof." A

Glenbow Archives, NA-789-19

John Norrish.
Range—High river.
Address—High River, N. W. T.
Ear Marks—Half under crop left ear.
Also owner of cattle branded H on left hip.
Horse brand—Same on left shoulder. 42 1y

Sayers Bros.
Address—Macleod, N.W.T.
Range—Macleod.
Horse brand—H on left jaw. 21-11-4

Military Colonization Co. of Canada,
(LIMITED.)
Range—North bank of Bow river, west of Blackfoot Reserve to mouth of High river
Cattle brand—House brand on right hip.
Horse brand—Same, or inverted on left shoulder.
Horses for sale. 19-9-4
Apply to T. B. Strange, Managing Director, Gleichen, P. O., N. W. T.

JOHN WAIR.
Address—High River, N. W. T.
Range—High River.
Cattle brand—???? on left hip.
Horse brand—2 on left hip.
Marks—Wattle on right side of neck; Swallow fork in left, under and over slope in right ear. 10-10-4

James D. Murray.
Address—Fort Macleod, N. W. T
Range—Stand Off, Belly River.
Cattle brand—5 on right hip.
Horse brand—5 on right shoulder. 12-9-84-1y

North-West Coal and Navigation Co.
Range—Porcupine Hills and Coal Banks.
Address—Fort Macleod, N. W. T
Mule brand—C N on left hip.
Work Cattle brand—C N on horn and left hip. 13-11-4

Jerry Potts.
Range—Peigan Reserve.
Address—Fort Macleod, N. W. T. 4-8-4

A. U. G. M. Thomas.
Range — Forks of Fish Creek.
Address—Fish Creek, N. W. T.
Cattle brand—6666 on left flank. 5-1-5

Colin Genge.
Range—Willow Creek.
Address — Macleod, N. W. T. 16-2-5

Joseph Carr.
Range—From Macleod to Kipp.
Address — Macleod, N. W. T. 7-11-4

Morris & Shaw.
Range—St. Mary's river.
Address—Macleod, N. W. T.
Cattle brand—Same on left side. 18-7-5

Frank Strong.
Range—Belly River.
Address — Macleod, N. W. T. 14-11-4

C. E. Denny.
Range—Willow Creek.
Address—Fort Macleod, N. W. T.
Cattle brand — CD on right hip. 31-10-4

Andrew Bell.
Range—High River.
Address—High River, N. W. T. 6-8-4

D Wanamaugher
Range—Willow Creek.
Address—Fort Macleod, N. W. T. 30-10-4

T. Banbury.
Address—Fort Macleod, N. W. T. 21-5-5

James S. Norris.
Address—Fort Macleod, N. W. T.
Range — Fort Macleod and Willow Creek. 10-10-3

R. J. H. Christie.
Range — Between Old Man's river and Willow Creek.
Address — Fort Macleod, N. W. T. 28-10-4

British American Ranche Co.
(LIMITED.)
Range—Bow River, N. W. T.
Address — Calgary, Alta.
Vent—Inverted on left hip.
Well broken horses of all classes constantly on hand. The undersigned will attend at the Calgary House every Monday to meet parties desiring to purchase horses.
A number of good pack horses for sale. 20-4-4
W. D. KERFOOT, Manager.

Levasseur & Stedman.
Range—Fort Macleod.
Address—Fort Macleod, N. W. T.
Vent—Same on left hip. 13-6-4

F. S Westropp.
Range — Between Old Man's River and Willow Creek.
Address—Fort Macleod, N. W. T. 9-10-3

R. M. Patterson.
Range—Slide Out, Belly River.
Address—Macleod, N.W.T.
Horse brand—Same as cut on left shoulder 31-10-4

B. M. Godsal.
Range—Pine Creek.
Address—Calgary, N. W.T.
Horse brand—Same as cut on the left shoulder.
Vent—Cattle, brand sideways on right hip; horses, same on left hip. 14-11-5

James Bell.
Range—Slide Out, Belly river.
Address—Macleod, N.W.T.
Horse brand—Same as cut on left shoulder. 7-11-4

S. Livingston.
Range—Elbow river.
Address — Calgary, Alberta, N. W. T.
Horse brand—Same on left thigh. 43-1y

Maunsell Bros.
Range—Between Old Man's river and Willow Creek.
Address—Macleod, N.W.T
Horse brand—IV on left hip. 9-10-4

Jos. Monte.
Range—Old Man's river near Macleod.
Address—Macleod, N.W.T. 9-10-4

J. WALTER INGS. FREDERICK W. INGS.
Ings Bros.
Range—North fork High River.
Address—High River, Alberta, N. W. T.
Horse brand—OH on left shoulder. 24-10-5

John Quirk.
Range—High River.
Address—High River, N. W. T.
Marks—Dewlap on right hip of this year's calves.
Horse brand—J on left shoulder. 24-5-5
Vent—Q on right shoulder horses on left hip.

Quinn & Campbell.
Address—Fort Macleod, N. W. T.
Range—Middle fork of Willow Creek.
Horse brand—Q on left shoulder.
Vent—Cattle, Q on shoulder, and horses on hip. 4-9-5

M. Gallagher.
Range—Between Belly and Old Man's river, near Macleod
Address—Macleod, N.W.T.
Horse brand 15 on near shoulder. 9-10-4

F. W. Craig.
Range—Willow Creek.
Address—Oxley Ranche.
Horse brand—Same on left shoulder. 24-8-5

S. Brouard.
Range—Slide Out, Belly River.
Address—Macleod, N.W.T.
Horse brand same on left hip. 27-11-4

J. Dougherty.
Range—Limekiln Bottom.
Address—Macleod, N.W.T. 84-9-4

D. Grier & Bro.
Range—Between Old Man's river and Willow Creek.
Address—Macleod, N.W.T.
Horse brand—20 on near shoulder. 9-10-4

J. D. Geddes.
Range—Bow river, near Calgary.
Address—Calgary, N. W.T.
Horse brand—Small heart on left shoulder.
Calves branded with horse brand on left hip.

Trefoil Ranche Co.
Range—Between Old Man's river and Willow Creek.
Address—Fort Macleod, N. W. T.
Horse brand—Z on left shoulder.
Vent—Z on left hip. 9-10-4

Cornish Cattle Company.
Range—Willow Creek.
Address—N. Bryant, Manager, Macleod, N. T.W.
Horse brand—B on right shoulder.
Vent—Same on left shoulder. 9-10-4

Some of the founding brands of the southern Alberta district, as published in the Macleod Gazette *in 1884.*

Dave Cochrane, legendary pilferer of early Alberta

He even stole a stove from the NWMP, and then cooked the Superintendent's dinner on it

Southern Alberta's most infamous squatter was the rascally Dave Cochrane, no relation to Quebec Senator Matthew Cochrane, Alberta's first big-time rancher, their common surname notwithstanding. Dave Cochrane mustered out of the North-West Mounted Police and squatted on the Blood Reserve in the late 1870s, claiming he was there before the Bloods. He refused to move until an arbitration board appointed by the Indian Commissioner awarded him $3,500 and a free homestead. He sold the homestead for a few hundred dollars, then defiantly squatted on range leased by the Walrond Ranche.

A skilled pilferer, Cochrane once noticed a fine new kitchen stove in the NWMP yard at Fort Macleod. He quietly removed it piece by piece, first a leg, then a lid, then the door, as opportunity offered. Eventually nothing but the heavy frame remained. He poured water over that and waited until it was red with rust, then approached the NWMP superintendent and, pleading as a veteran of the force, asked if he could have that old wreck of a stove. The officer inspected the stove and wondered where it came from, but readily agreed to give it away as worthless.

Later the same Mountie officer stopped by Cochrane's homestead for a meal. There in all its shining glory stood the refurbished stove. Now where did you get that fine stove? the policeman inquired. "Why, you gave it to me yourself," came the reply. "I just polished her up some." Local tradition holds that the superintendent did no more than stroke his chin reflectively, saying nothing.

Duncan McEachern, the veterinarian who managed the Walrond Ranche, routinely drove squatters off his leases. He cottoned even less to the presence of Cochrane, already notorious. But Cochrane agreed to leave only if he was paid $5,000 for the "improvements" he had made to his homestead. It was a substantial sum. McEachern angrily refused. So the story goes that Cochrane, lighting his pipe at the time, held up the match and asked if the Walrond manager had ever pondered how a tiny flame could burn off a large range. Yes indeed, McEachern had noted that phenomenon. He finally agreed to pay $2,700.

Cochrane inevitably went into the whisky smuggling business. In 1890, according to a much-told story, a NWMP corporal discovered a cache of hidden whisky and waited for the smugglers to appear. At last Dave Cochrane and a youthful companion showed up, and a few minutes later Cochrane led a pack train laden with kerosene tins towards the St. Mary River. Such tins were a container favoured by whisky runners. Spotting the Mountie, Cochrane whipped his animals forward through the ford. The policeman gave chase, catching up with his quarry on the other side of the river, arresting him and escorting him to Fort Macleod. On inspection, however, his kerosene tins were found empty. The illegal booze had been in the possession of the companion, and that overlooked lad was by then long gone. *M.B.* ❦

kitchen was added later.

Thomas remembers a plethora of homes along the Sheep — log structures of many and individual designs. Frame construction became more common after 1885. Water was drawn from the creek; there might be a pump. Furniture, brought along from the East or England, might offer Victorian comfort but was far from lavish. Table settings were good-quality earthenware rather than porcelain. But even a rancher of little wealth typically enjoyed a gorgeous view of the winding valley and the Rockies.

Economically, the big cattle barons formed a very distinct stratum. Their sumptuous ranch houses, sometimes built from sandstone, frequently boasted tiled bathrooms and intricate plasterwork — interior decors similar to country houses of the wealthy back in Britain. They might enjoy furnaces rather than mere stoves and were, of course, first to install plumbing. These residences were the scene of grand entertainments and formal dinners. The best London periodicals were at hand. Members of the cattle compact, together with their wives, joined exclusive clubs and artistic societies. The semi-feudal tone of their lives was enhanced by the existence of numerous hired hands.

Countering differences in wealth within the industry, though, was a remarkably homogeneous set of social attitudes shared by most ranchers. Politically Conservative, they mostly attended the Anglican Church and (whether English or Canadian) their loyalty to the British Empire was indelible. Cowboys were amazed at how little physical work was done by many of them, especially the British contingent. The entire ranching caste was almost mad about sports and games, however. "At

[10] English hunts (like the Quorn, which derived its name from a village in Leicestershire and was one of the most prestigious) were an expensive pastime. In the late 19th century it was not uncommon for a hunt member to keep a dozen or so 500-guinea hunters, along with the necessary grooms and other support staff. Chasing coyotes in Alberta was a good deal less costly.

Glenbow Archives, NA-118-3

Willow Creek roundup crew near Nanton in 1895. George Lane, at right, eventually bought the huge Bar U, one of the original big four. The large leases were breaking up by the turn of the century, as the smaller operations gained in numbers.

Pincher Creek, for example, it was the smaller stockmen who introduced polo to North America in 1884; homesteaders, not wealthy lease-holders, inaugurated the celebrated racing meets at Mosquito Creek the following year. Similarly, the smaller ranch owners brought the first hunt clubs[10] to Alberta in 1886," recounts University of Alberta historian Patrick Dunae in his book *Gentlemen Emigrants.*

The spectacle of grown men in packs pointlessly pursuing hounds and coyotes through the coulees must have amused the western hands. Nor would all have been impressed that Major George Ross, son of the officer who founded the High River Horse Ranch, was celebrated as a world-class polo player adept at hammering a ball around the Prairie. Cowboys and ranchers got along surprisingly well nonetheless, each group apparently so convinced of its own innate superiority to the other as to feel no need to be hostile about it.

Relations with the Indians went less well, particularly the attempts of some ranch wives to turn Indian women, lately off the plains, into domestic servants. In 1889 Mary Ella Inderwick, daughter of a wealthy family in Perth, Ontario, and wife of a British-born former aide to Governor-General Lord Lansdowne, wrote a letter describing her experiences on the North Fork Ranche near Pincher Creek. "...We are the grand owners of a dear ugly discriminating bull terrier who does not allow an Indian near the place, but I have tried to make use of a squaw who is the nominal wife of a white man near us, to do the washing, but had to give her up, as she stolidly went on rubbing a table napkin all the time I was away from her side one morning and when I returned hoping to see a tubpile of washed clothes I found one table napkin in holes, the result of an hour's work. At scrubbing the floor she was equally hopeless as she sat in the middle and slopped all round her — aimlessly. Poor Shomacki — or some such name — and poor, poor John Fisher (her husband)! Who was once I believe a missionary."

Mrs. Inderwick was in no doubt that these failures were entirely due to the Indian woman's stupidity, of course, never for a moment considering her own comic inability to explain alien tasks to her would-be servant. She further remarked that "Indian squaws" were forbidden for the first time to attend a police ball at Fort Macleod that year; several "half-breeds" were nevertheless permitted entry. Then she went on to complain that England-born people often looked down on the Canadian English, a prejudice that "makes my Canadian blood boil!" But Mrs. Inderwick did love her new country: "We are in the foothills — no plains here — but the most glorious ranges of hills and rolling prairie — which all seems so near that one starts to ride to a certain landmark but finds oneself no nearer at the end of an hour."

Provincial Archives of Alberta, E. Brown Collection, B-127

Typical of small homestead ranches is this one in the hills west of Calgary in 1886.
Although the less prosperous stockmen did not join the Ranchmen's Club, most were Anglican and thoroughly Conservative.

The Ranchmen's: From boxcar to 6th St. elegance

Club rules banned political and religious discussion, and also dogs – but one Indian war dance was okay

Glenbow Archives, NA-3795-1

Calgary's Ranchmen's Club first occupied leased rooms above the Restaurant Mariaggi on the north side of Stephen Avenue between what are now Centre and 1st Street West.

In a time-honoured tradition, British ranchers in 19th-century Calgary did whatever they could to recreate in Alberta the institutions they had left behind in Britain. Besides good schools and churches for their families, the ranchers naturally felt they required a proper club. The result, in 1891, was Calgary's exclusive Ranchmen's Club. It was followed by the High River Club, the Cypress Club at Medicine Hat and the Chinook Club at Lethbridge, all dominated by the ranching fraternity.

Modelled on the famous gentlemen's clubs of Victorian England, the Ranchmen's quickly became *the* gathering place for Calgary's ranching and business

Women like her often felt very much alone, however. The Inderwicks' nearest female neighbour lived 22 miles away, although the air was so pure, they claimed, that their rooftops were visible in the distance. In 1884 one rancher wistfully counted just four marriageable white women between High River and Montana. Men would survey incoming stages with field glasses to spot the brightly coloured parasols that indicated female passengers. Few single girls retained their solitary status for long.

Nesta Skrine, who lived on the Bar S Ranch along Mosquito Creek, wrote: "I made the usual mistake of bringing out a maid from home; but when in the course of time the mistake rectified itself, and she went the way of all womankind in the West, I took to the broom and duster, and was surprised to find what a calmness descended on my spirit with release from the task of supervision [of household help]." Also descending on the spirit of this Irish poet was the far more egalitarian spirit of the North American west.

Mrs. Skrine, who published under the name Moira O'Neill, called Alberta "emphatically the land of the Younger Son." Her own husband, Walter, was the youngest son of a landed family in Somerset. In an article titled, "A Lady's Life on a Ranche," printed by *Blackwood's Edinburgh Magazine* in 1898, she pointed out that life on a small income was very restricted in Britain. There sport and social life were expensive. "Shooting, fishing, and hunting, just the things that would bring you to the verge of bankruptcy at home, you can enjoy here practically for nothing. You can have all the horses you want to ride or drive ... the panels of your democrat [wagon] will not be adorned with your worshipful crest and motto. But then — solacing thought — neither will anyone else's..."❦

Glenbow Archives, NA-1365-2

Mary Ella Inderwick, mistress of the North Fork Ranche near Pincher Creek. Indian women, she found, made hopeless domestics.

elite. Among the original members, according to a list published in 1953 by the club, were well-known cattlemen like A.E. Cross, Fred Stimson and William F. Cochrane. Some prominent men in law, banking and the military (e.g., lawyer and politician James Lougheed) were also invited to join.

Club members first met in rooms leased above an Italian restaurant on Stephen Avenue, where a dumbwaiter was used to bring up food and drink from the kitchen below. Rules were based on the British model except for an explicit restriction against conversation dealing with "politics and religious questions of every description." Dogs were not allowed on the premises either.

Temporary accommodations were later set up in a converted railway boxcar, but as membership grew there was a desire for something more permanent, and more suitable. After the club's incorporation in 1892 new quarters were built on McIntyre (now 7th) Avenue. In 1896 a financial crisis, severe enough that serious discussion was given to shutting down, provoked members into raising a bond issue and increasing dues. Membership grew fairly quickly after that. By 1904 the club boasted 92 full-time members, and it wasn't long before the executive decided to build an even larger facility on 6th Street S.W. The new premises opened in 1914 and endured through the 20th century.

Glenbow Archives

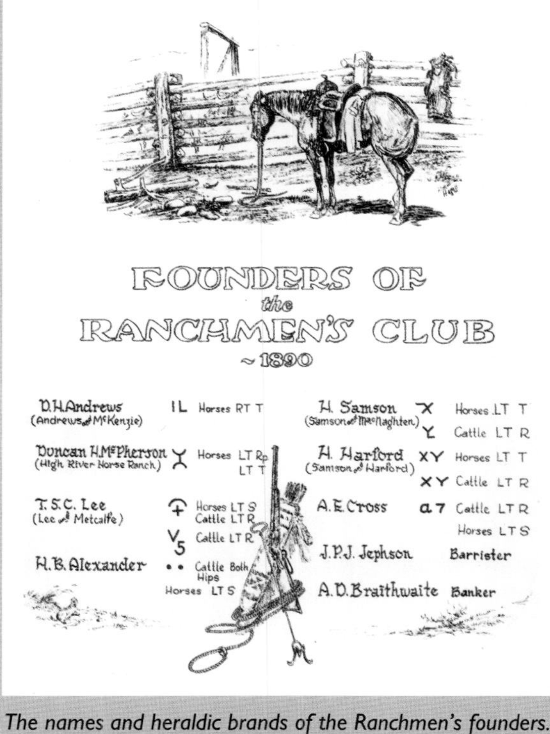

The names and heraldic brands of the Ranchmen's founders.

The north lounge was the preserve of senior members. A junior member of several years' standing might be invited into it for a brief moment to exchange a few pleasantries — a highly significant ritual that could be initiated by a senior member only. Women were allowed as guests of members, but they had to come in through the side door and certain rooms —like the billiard and poker rooms — were strictly off limits.

Behaviour was sedate by and large, but not always. Edward, Prince of Wales (who owned a ranch in the foothills) dropped in for dinner one night in 1919. To celebrate the fact that the prince had been made an honorary chief of the Stoney tribe, his hosts decided to have a war dance. So the inebriated revellers built a bonfire in the foyer by the giant oak staircase, dabbed on warpaint, and danced and hollered their way into club lore. *G.S.*❦

Provincial Archives of Alberta, E. Brown Collection, B-66

Only his expertise with horses and cattle gave the cowboy his credentials, but legend has invested his job with enduring glamour. This one posed in southern Alberta in 1886.

The real cowboy behind the legend finds freedom but at a high price

HE WORKED DAWN TO DUSK, HIS HOME IN SUMMER WAS A SOD SHACK, DANGER WAS HIS CONSTANT COMPANION AND GUTS A JOB NECESSITY ❦ HE OFTEN DIED OF DRINK OR V.D. – BUT HE REMAINS A CAPTIVATING IMAGE

A cowboy's work was dangerous, dirty and physically uncomfortable. He was a hired man, not particularly well paid as a rule, enjoying no job security, and with the odds stacked against his becoming a rancher himself. The cowpuncher generally serenaded his cows, not pretty girls, and he was not usually in a position to support a wife and children. Venereal disease and the ravages of alcohol were common causes of death among these men in frontier times. Yet the range rider stuck to his way of life more stubbornly than most rich ranch owners hung onto their land, and the public clung equally tenaciously to the legend of the free-roaming paladin of the plains.

At dead centre of a cowboy's life lay work. His trade was no different in principle from plumbing or medicine — just another set of economically useful technical tasks. A ranch hand might relish his whisky or a spectacular vermilion sunset, but so could ordinary mortals, even the despised sodbuster and sheepherder. Only his expertise with cattle classified a man as a cowboy, in daily work that has never been widely understood outside the beef business because it makes dull film fare.

The skill of Canadian range riders was not "Canadian" in any working sense. The techniques of their craft evolved, detail by detail, skill by skill, as the herds spread north from Old Mexico via the American West into Alberta, the B.C. Interior and southwestern Saskatchewan. British and eastern Canadian cattle companies investing in ranches out west depended on Americans and American-trained western Canadians to run their operations. Their troubles frequently began when they didn't listen to their local managers.

Unlike Europe's feudal knights or 19th-century grandees, cowboys did not usually sentimentalize about individual horses.[I] Animals were tools; on a trail drive or roundup, each rider would be supplied with about six mounts. Besides range-riding and trail-riding, specific horses were trained for cutting a steer out of the herd, swimming or night work. They were handled by a wrangler, often a youth (there were no female hands, though wives and daughters might handle animals on a small ranch). Some ranchers preferred not to hire cowboys who owned their own horses, on the grounds that they tended to baby them. But according to pioneer Alberta pharmacist John Higinbotham in his reminiscences, *When the West Was Young*, western Canadian riders were thought to be gentler with their steeds than Americans.

Roundups occurred twice yearly: a big one in the spring to brand calves, and a smaller operation in autumn to collect cattle for shipment. These provided the most strenuous work of the cowboy's year. During the era of unfenced grasslands, southern Alberta herds mingled over the winter across a territory about the size of Belgium. Ranchers would pool their cowboys, sending hands in proportion to the estimated size of their own herds and agreeing on a single foreman.

One of the biggest roundups in Alberta, which took place in 1885, followed the classic pattern. That spring about 100 cowboys supplied by 15 chuckwagons swept up 60,000 cattle across 10,000 square miles. The men were in the field for a couple of months. At night, shifts of riders working in pairs circled the growing herd, moving in opposite directions and gentling the animals by softly singing or whistling. Stampedes could occur in the dark, triggered by the stray flash of a match, the unseen presence of a wolf or some inexplicable bovine nightmare. Range men got little sleep at this

[I] There were exceptional instances of deep affection for an individual mount, as pioneer Saskatchewan cowboy R.D. Symons recounts in his autobiography, *Where the Wagon Led*, of his horse Roany: "Never did he lose a trail on the darkest night. Never did he push at me, nor step on my foot while being saddled. Never did he refuse a steep place or a boggy patch. Never once did he put a foot in a badger hole; and some of the knolls on that range were pocked like the lid of a pepper pot. To feel him change feet in the black dark to avoid a hole was to wonder how God made such an animal....He could locate cattle by their smell. He could bite the tailbone of a steer that wouldn't turn to suit him. Yet bringing up a small calf, he was like a nursemaid, maybe just giving its behind a gentle shove with his knee....And you couldn't spoil him. He was as stand-offish as only a good horse can be. He no more cared for my petting than he cared to push me with his nose. Like two good men who think the world of each other and work together for years without showing it outwardly, never interfering with each other's privacy, so Roany and I were a team."

Branding on the Bow River horse ranch, near Cochrane in the 1890s. Hard work in a magnificent setting.

Glenbow Archives, NA-5035-1

Glenbow Archives, NA-237-15

An interior view of a ranch bunkhouse in 1894. A pot-bellied stove and kerosene lighting added to the aroma of sweat and tobacco.

time of year.

After the early days, rustling posed a relatively minor problem — the vigilant Mounties saw to that — but a persistent difficulty surfaced at the big spring roundups. Mavericks (calves whose mothers, and hence owners, could not be identified) were claimed automatically by the South-Western Stock Association during the 1880s. This self-regulating ranch industry group partially financed its efforts on behalf of the common good by selling the maverick calves. But smaller ranchers resented the loss of even a few calves. Small operators who couldn't afford to send anyone to the spring roundups suspected that their calves were being arbitrarily seized, and constantly challenged the maverick policy of the association, which was dominated by larger stockmen. Though the regional roundup was abandoned after 1885 in favour of district roundups, the maverick issue continued to divide ranchers until the advent of barbed wire and individual ranges.

Seasonal trail drives in Alberta did not take on the epic quality of their American counterparts. Distances were shorter. (However, Jerome Harper of British Columbia's celebrated Gang Ranch drove 1,200 cattle from the Chilcotin down the Okanagan Trail and all the way to San Francisco, arriving in 18 months with his stock in good condition. That is still accounted one of the West's great drives, though Harper was bankrupt by the end of the journey.) Calgarians would cheer as a herd passed through town on its way to the stockyards hard by the railway. The "point" or lead steers were guided by swing riders on the shoulders of a herd. Behind them rode flank riders at the hips of the roiling mass of cattle. More cowboys, bandannas over their noses and mouths in bandit fashion, ate dust in the "drag" or rear of the drive. One rider could manage an average of 250 to 350 head.

Larger drives occurred, of course, when the big ranchers imported their first herds. In *Ranching with Lords and Commons*, Oxley Ranche manager John Craig described the challenge of the St. Mary River, 12 miles north of the American boundary, in July 1883:

> It was an interesting sight to see a herd of three or four thousand cattle swimming those rivers in high water. The greatest difficulty is overcome when the lead of the herd takes the water and strikes across. The drag end is now crowded up, cows with their young calves in the rear, the little fellows struggling nobly with their heads only in sight, at first with pleading 'baas' as they strike into the ice-cold water, but which they soon give up when they discover that it takes all their wind for the effort. How close they keep their little heads to their mother's. The whole herd is crossing, strung out. Now the leaders are landing on the opposite shore, and a forest of heads and horns only is visible in the foaming waters ...
>
> The moment they are over, the steers and dry stock take to quietly grazing, but the cows are all excitement after their calves — eight hundred to nine hundred mothers bawling for their young ones and the same number of calves crying for their mothers has a rather disquieting effect. The cows soon find their own, and then peace and quietness are restored.

For the riders, the end of the trail to market brought temptation. During the 1880s a cowboy

[2] Women in general appreciated the cowboys' typical courtesy toward them. Ranch wife Mary Ella Inderwick wrote: "We have a cow-camp — a shack for the cowboys — and they have their own cook, so we only get an occasional one for meals if he happens to be riding nearer the house than the camp. They are a nice lot of men. I love their attempts to help me to appear civilized. Though they ride in flannel shirts, they never come to the table in shirt sleeves. There is a black alpaca (!) coat which hangs in the shack attached to the house for the cowboys' use — and each one struggles into it to live up to the new regime, which began with a bride at the ranche, and this is done so enthusiastically and with such good will that I have no qualms of conscience that I am a nuisance ..."

Glenbow Archives, NA-777-21

Open-air shaving in the Milk River area. Bunkhouses were palaces compared to line camps and patrol accommodation.

made $40 to $60 a month, his foreman $100 to $120. Prostitutes charged $2 to $5. Many a man trying to accumulate capital for his own small ranch impetuously invested his savings in female companionship and liquor instead. With women so scarce, plenty of westerners visited brothels with little or no sense of shame. A house of ill repute was generally a tidy affair, luxurious compared to a bunkhouse, and offering a cosy sense of home that appealed to men starved for emotional and physical affection. They were a feature of every cowtown, and the fancy ladies of Lethbridge (the town's "soiled doves" as one clergyman called them) reputedly preferred the freer-spending cowboys[2] to the local coal miners.

Food probably topped the list of a range rider's pleasures back at the ranch. As for cowboys throughout the Americas, beef provided plentiful and much-appreciated provender. Coffee and tobacco were tastes that bordered on necessities. Canadian ranches roasted their own coffee beans.[3] A good ranch cook could produce much the same grub from his carefully organized chuckwagon on the trail as from his cookhouse. Fred Ings, owner of the Rio Alto Ranch on the Highwood River, wrote: "Breakfast at daybreak was eaten in the mess tent, a hot substantial meal of meat, potatoes, bread, jam, with strong black coffee. Our dishes were

[3] The following six-month supply list for the Cochrane Ranche, was ordered on February 21, 1885: "20 sacks best flour, 30 lbs raisins, 10 sks coffee sugar, 3 boxes Price's Baking Powder, 2 sks oatmeal, 100 lbs rice, 2 sks cornmeal, 200 lbs coarse salt, 500 lbs bacon, 100 lbs table salt, 500 lbs apples, 50 lbs soda, 6 boxes dried prunes, 10 gals vinegar, 200 lbs green coffee, 20 lbs mustard, 20 lbs best green tea (small), 6 lbs cinnamon (grd), 6 cases Leaf lard (360 lbs), 5 lbs all-spice, 15 boxes canned corn, 20 lbs pepper (whole), 10 boxes canned tomatoes, 1 lb ginger (grd), 3 boxes electric soap, 10 gals best syrup, 1 box candles (about 20 lbs)." The supplier was further advised to include two or three gallons of good, plain cucumber pickles if available but on no account to send "expensive bottled stuff like Chow-chow."

How the brands put a crimp in cattle thievery

Like the Texans before them, Alberta's first ranchers let their cattle roam the open range. They therefore needed a way to establish ownership, and to help prevent rustling by homesteaders. Hence a permanent form of livestock identification, branding, was introduced.

Branded steers were first seen on the Prairies in the 1870s, and range associations began pressuring the territorial government to institute recorded brands at a central registry. The first was registered in 1880. Within 20 years the territorial total was 3,000, and in 1991 there were 55,000 brands in Alberta.

The brands themselves had to be simple enough to identify quickly but difficult for rustlers to alter. A branding iron bore the shape of a registered brand, usually a couple of letters or numbers or a combination of the two. In some parts of the American range it became a hanging offence to be caught with any running iron that was not cast as a registered brand. The oldest Alberta brand continually held by one family is the A7 mark used by the Cross family since 1886.

During the roundup a cowboy would ride through the herd, roping unmarked calves by their hind legs and dragging them to the branding fire. Two other hands, known as wrestlers, manhandled the calf down. Brands were usually applied on the left ribs or hip of the animal. Because cattle always mill to the right in a corral, the left flank is more visible from the fence.

Heating the branding irons was a specialty in itself. If applied too cold, the iron would not penetrate the hide deeply enough to leave a permanent mark. If the metal was too hot, the brand might blotch or the animal could be injured. Although still in use a century later, branding had been giving way to less painful methods — magnetic implants, computer collars and ear tags. *G.S.*❦

How three renowned bronc riders got their first jobs

Franklin, Ricks and 'Nigger John' all broke in the impossible horse and joined ranching mythology

Glenbow Archives, NA-3046-4

Bronco-buster and rancher Frank Ricks. He borrowed an outlaw – and confounded his tormentors.

Johnny Franklin, a young Texan who had ridden up the Chisholm Trail from his home state to Kansas, drifted into Alberta during the autumn of 1888 and was hired by the Strong Ranch on the Belly River as an ordinary hand. Come spring, ranch manager Steve Cleveland was looking for someone to break wild horses as saddle animals. The pay was $75 a month, nearly double the average cowboy's wage. According to L.V. Kelly in *The Range Men*, Franklin's soft-spoken response to Cleveland was almost turned down out of hand.

"Can you ride?" asked the ranch boss.

"I guess so."

"Well, I'm not going to take a chance with a man who can't," declared Cleveland. "I want these horses broken right, for they are to go to the Mounted Police."

Franklin still wanted to try, so Cleveland produced an old roan outlaw, an infamously mean critter. To everyone's astonishment, the young Texan gave them a performance of the most tenaciously graceful riding they had ever seen. He kept that job as a bronco-buster for nine years. The post was considered a soft touch at the time, though few Albertans today would call it easy work. On a busy day, Franklin would rope, saddle and ride 15 raw horses.

Two other contenders for the palm as best bronc rider in the Canadian West were Frank Ricks and the most famous Alberta cowboy of all, a black man known as "Nigger John" Ware. In 1878 Ricks had won a saddle and $100 in gold as the champion rough-rider at the California state fair in Sacramento. He arrived in Alberta five years later, in charge of driving 250 horses from Oregon. At that time the Cochrane Ranche kept one of the nastiest horses ever to enter the territory, a dark chestnut beast that had remained an outlaw for 10 years, and ranch manager William Kerfoot enjoyed a joke as much as any of his hands. When Ricks arrived on foot one day in September 1883 and asked to borrow a horse, Kerfoot offered him the chestnut.

Ricks roped the wild horse. The Cochrane crew watched, aware that their brute was a savage man-killer bent on not merely throwing but also battering a rider. Ricks mounted. The horse crawfished, jackknifed, pitched, came apart, sunfished, rainbowed and tried to chin the moon — but the cowboy stayed on the outlaw, raking it from tail-stump to ears with his spurs

tin and we ate sitting around on bed rolls or a box if one was handy, or on the ground." (One cowboy wag suggested that if a horseshoe sank in the coffee brew, it wasn't strong enough yet.)

R.D. Symons in his memoirs described how a field cook would bake yeast bread if he had a stove, or "good Dutch-oven soda bread if he cooked on a campfire." His own outfit was fond of "finger-lickin' syrup and canned tomatoes." The central place of food on the range shows up in the way cowboys remembered their jobs; a rider would refer to working "with the Spencer [chuck] Wagon in '13" the way that another man might recall living on King Street in Regina.

Cowboys wore wool or buckskin shirts when the weather turned cooler. Trousers were corduroy or butternut-coloured cloth. Pant legs might be worn inside or outside the spurred boots, with leather or sheepskin chaps for riding. A sixgun was carried if needed to shoot snakes and other and beating it half-senseless with his quirt, until the animal could barely stand. His reputation made, the bronco-buster got work on the Mount Royal Ranche. (Incidentally, the chestnut continued as mean as ever, 1,000 pounds of dangerous horse-flesh.)

In 1882 John Ware met Tom Lynch, trail boss of the drive that brought in the first herd from Idaho for the North-West Cattle Company's Bar U. About one in six cowboys in the United States was black, but few entered Canada. Lynch, who shared the racist feeling that was all but universal at the time, agreed under pressure from another hand to give Ware a job as cook's helper and night herder. He was issued an old plug for a horse and a dilapidated saddle. As the herd trailed north from American Falls, Ware asked his boss for "a little better saddle and a little worse horse." The cowboys, always ready for fun, searched out their worst demon and saddled it. The animal exploded into action but Ware remained in control, wearing the beast into submission. Promoted to day rider, he later managed to rope two rustlers who had stolen Bar U cattle from the drive. Contrary to Montana custom at that time, Lynch did not hang the thieves from a tree, but released them with a mere tongue-lashing.

Who was the best rider of the trio? Franklin and Ware were said to have never been thrown, a rare distinction. But the big black man rode awkwardly, laughing as he bounced and rocked all over the horse's back; he stayed on through the strength in his clenching knees. Ricks and Franklin rode with grace rather than brute force. Author Kelly's informants leaned to Franklin as the most skilled. The Texan-turned-Albertan could outguess his horse before it jumped, swinging instinctively into position to withstand each jolt before it came. He relied on balance, never using any more muscle than absolutely necessary. In this way, he didn't get "churned" in the guts after a few years of "twisting" and he continued horse-breaking much longer than most of his colleagues in that demanding business.

Glenbow Archives, NA-263-1

Legendary cowboy rancher John Ware, with his wife and children (Robert and Nettie) in 1896. He wanted 'a little better saddle and a little worse horse.'

Franklin was chosen to judge the bucking at the first Calgary Stampede in 1912. A friend asked how he'd determine the winner in the event of a tie. Although he was a good deal older by then, the buster replied with complete sincerity: "I'll just ride both them horses myself. That's the only way to find out which bucks hardest."

Time was kind to all three of Alberta's great early rough-riders. Franklin operated a slaughterhouse out of Fort Macleod. Ricks started his own ranch. So did Ware, whose white friends — and they were legion — took a perverse pride in their black buddy's irrefutably fine character. *M.B.*❦

range varmints, but weapons tended to get in the way of work and weren't a regular feature. Cowboy hats in Alberta came smaller than the Texan standard, due to the difference in weather. The Stetson company's Calgary model featured a seven-inch crown with a 4.5-inch brim. A bandanna, frequently red, was standard dust protection. In *Cattle Kingdom,* Edward Brado says the bandanna might also be used to strain out the wigglier creatures when drinking from a prairie puddle.

Ranch bunkhouses were spartan affairs where clothes and equipment hung from pegs; a pail or two of water, along with a basin, served for washing. A pot-bellied stove and kerosene lighting added to the stink of sweat and tobacco. Like men in camps everywhere, cowboys occupied their spare time with cards, books and yarning. But in no sense was the bunkhouse considered a real

[4] Not all cowboys trembled at the prospect of social disapproval. In 1896 cowboy Frank Crean asked an NWMP inspector whether he could collect half the fine if he named the culprit responsible for a fire near Fort Macleod. The policeman agreed; fines were commonly split between the Crown and an informant, in order to encourage such reporting. Crean, who later became a civil engineer, promptly confessed that he himself was responsible for the blaze. He did indeed recover half his own fine.

home. Many hands found themselves laid off in winter, one reason the job was considered poorly paid.

Crude though the bunkhouses may have been, they were palaces compared to the line camps where many cowboys spent most of the summer. It was impossible to patrol a large range from the vicinity of the ranch house; hence line shacks had to be constructed, generally of sod or rough logs. From this base a man could risk his life crossing streams (most cowboys couldn't swim), dragging panic-stricken steers from mud wallows and chasing off wolves. Here he would commune with flies, snakes and his bovine charges until autumn's marketing drive took him to town.

Fire was an ever-looming menace on the range, particularly in early spring and late fall when the tinder-dry grass was free of snow. A front of flames could sweep over the Prairie at the speed of a galloping horse. Stock associations demanded that any rancher living within riding distance of a fire report immediately to help fight it, or face censure by his colleagues.[4] A match carelessly dropped by a pipe-puffing cowboy was known to have started one blaze. A cook with a hunting party near Pincher Creek was fined $50 in 1887 after the fire he triggered almost incinerated Fort Macleod. That inferno burned range 68 miles long and up to 15 miles wide.

But the most persistent suspects in prairie fires were the Canadian Pacific's spark-flinging locomotives. In 1885 almost the entire Blackfoot Reserve was burned off thanks to the railway, an accident that left the Indians short of food that winter. Another fire started by a CPR engine burned for three days on the Circle Ranch between the Bow and Little Bow rivers. Howell Harris, its manager, resorted to slaughtering cattle and dragging their dripping bodies over the flames. Even when the surface fire was extinguished by the Circle cowboys, it smouldered in the grass roots, springing up anew in a breath of wind. The peril of catastrophic conflagrations abated only when homesteaders eventually broke up the grasslands with their cultivated fields.

Richard Slatta in *Cowboys of the Americas* maintains that all cattle hands were brothers under the skin. "[Mexican] *vaqueros* admired their fellows who were long-suffering, patient, uncomplaining, and persevering, just as Anglo cowboys esteemed men who worked in bad weather or with

Ranch cook Charlie Lehr and the grub tent of the High River roundup in 1896. On a range rider's list of pleasures, food ranked high, and the cook was a VIP.

Glenbow Archives, NA-466-

pain, went without food, and tracked down stray animals at all costs. Courage — riding into the midst of a milling herd, for example — represented another *vaquero* virtue. The *vaquero* and cowboy expected and valued these qualities. Virtuous action would not bring praise, but failing to measure up to the *vaquero* standard could bring criticism, censure, or ridicule." Confirmed the *Texas Live Stock Journal* in an 1882 article: "A man wanting in courage would be as much out of place in a cow-camp as a fish would be on dry land...We are certain that no more faithful employee ever breathed than he [the cowboy]...we know that we will be sustained by every man who has had experience in this matter."[5]

Glenbow Archives, NA-207-108

Mexican John, a Montana cook, working at his chuckwagon in the 1880s. Meat and potatoes, bread, jam and pies – and plenty of strong black coffee.

Rarely did a cowpoke stay in the saddle much past the age of 40. Some men did manage to finance their own spreads. And ex-ranch hands were natural employees for livery stables in town, an inglorious but more comfortable existence. But even in their own day, ranchers would wonder what happened to all the old cowboys. The pre-homesteading heyday of the beef industry was so short — about a quarter of a century in western Canada — that many of its veterans must have leaked almost invisibly into numerous other occupations.

The legend lives on, though the number of cowboys at work today is small. While few urban westerners nowadays have ever met a range rider, they may still sense a haunting familiarity in the traditional Code of the Range:

- Be independent, but always ready to help your neighbour.
- Ask nothing of the government boys, or you'll find yourself in the rat race.
- Feed the stranger and his hoss; ask no questions.
- Say little, talk soft and keep your eyes skinned.
- Don't argue with the wagon boss. If he's wrong, he'll find out.
- Don't stare at the brand on a stranger's hoss. But make a note.
- Deal with the other fellow's stock as you would your own. Feed the stray, help the bogged. He's doing the same for you.
- If paper and pen aren't handy, back up your word as you would your signature.
- Don't stick a plough in the land. It's catching.
- Women come in two breeds; the ones like your mother, and the one behind the lace curtains. And you don't talk about either kind.

It may be virtues like these that account for the cowboy's place in North American mythology, for everything from Hollywood's western film fantasies to country music crooners. Another factor, some say, lies even closer to the core of the legend: the nearly mystical link among professional riders of horses, a primal joy that has invariably sprung up wherever mounted males have worked or fought. Finally, there was the freedom of the open Prairie. Another ranch down the trail would always be willing to hire a veteran worker, with few questions asked. No family responsibilities, just the liberty to roam at will. It is a dream shared by many, but few have ever been able to live it.❦

5 World-famous cowboy artist Charlie Russell wrangled horses in Montana's Judith Basin for 11 years, an accomplishment he apparently valued at least as highly as his painting and sculpting. The range men rode tall in many people's eyes, not least their own.

CHAPTER FOUR

In the furious battle of the '90s the settlers doom the big ranches

WAS BUREAUCRAT WILLIAM PEARCE RIGHT IN OPPOSING SETTLEMENT? THE QUESTION IS STILL DISPUTED, BUT WHEN THE GRANDEES LEFT, SELF-MADE RANCHERS TOOK OVER AND THEIR HEARTS LAY IN ALBERTA

Glenbow Archives, NA-339-1

William Pearce in the 1880s. To the big ranchers he was a clear-headed ally – to squatters an implacable foe.

To the aristocratic British and central Canadian dignitaries who established the western cattle industry in the 1880s, the homesteaders squatting on their leased lands were at first little more than a nuisance. By the early '90s they constituted a real problem, however, and by the mid-90s an active menace. Finally, by the turn of the century, homesteaders predominated. The Era of the Great Ranches was fading, nearly all the grandees were gone, and a new figure — the small, tough, commercial rancher, often trained by the big corporate ranches and now on his own — dominated the cattle business in the District of Alberta. This transition was rough, nasty and very political.

For all but the last four years of the two-decade struggle, the big ranches had an unwavering ally. William Pearce was the quintessential civil servant, embodying both the best and worst that bureaucracy can represent: the best because he had deeply considered convictions about the terms upon which western Canada should be developed; the worst because he imposed these convictions with scant regard for "uninformed" local opinion.

Pearce had already turned up in the centre of other territorial controversies. He had been responsible for surveying the Metis river lots, the bureaucratic procrastination over which had helped start the 1885 Riel Rebellion (although the delays had been no fault of Pearce's). He had been responsible also for the dominion survey at Fort Edmonton, which embroiled him and Tory Ottawa in a conflict with the Edmonton business community that would endure in the courts well into the 20th century. He then moved on to Calgary where he became the point man in the rancher-homesteader controversy.

To farmers everywhere, particularly in the North Saskatchewan River country, he stood for everything that was bad — for the Tory Macdonald government and its western henchman, the sometime territorial governor and sometime Interior minister, Edgar "Dirty" Dewdney. He was also the aide-in-residence to the arrogant A.M. Burgess, Macdonald's deputy Interior minister, who considered himself above and beyond mere elected politicians. In addition, Pearce stood for the riding club set that ran the big ranches and burnt the little hovels of any homesteaders found squatting on their leases.

Pearce's defenders, at the time and later, saw him very differently: as a civil servant with guts enough to declare much of the southern Prairie unfit for grain cultivation, something that would be unmistakably evident 40 years later in the dirty thirties. Far from opposing farming, he actively encouraged irrigation works on the lower Bow. Finally, he was to become one of the founders of the National Parks. Since Pearce was identified with the Macdonald era, his apologists say, he became the victim of a Liberal smear that the facts do not vindicate. Whether saint or sinner, however, Pearce "was regarded as the ruling power in the West" in the Tory era, wrote one of his former colleagues years later in the *Calgary Herald*. "We regarded him with fear and trembling, and he was undoubtedly a czar in all western affairs which came under the jurisdiction of the Department of the Interior." Ranchers revered him; settlers railed against him as the harsh and arbitrary toady of the cattlemen.

The arrival of the CPR in 1883 brought good news and bad news for the ranchers. It provided them with far better transportation to eastern markets for their cattle, but it also began funnelling people into the District of Alberta. Many of the immigrants looked over the vast, trackless Prairie and simply squatted on it at random, erecting homes, fencing off water access, cultivating land, raising their own stock, and ignoring the grazing leases. The grazing law of 1881 had already declared that established farmers could stay. This muddied the issue, since there was no record of who was there when the law was passed. Moreover, some squatters took this exemption as giving tacit permission for others to settle too, although it did not.

The ranchers naturally complained. Not only were the squatters hindering their operations, in the long run they were endangering their whole industry. They suspected other motives, too. They thought some squatters were not farmers at all, but would-be ranchers trying to establish themselves with rustled stock. They further suspected that some were trying to establish a bogus land claim, and would then blackmail the rancher into paying them to leave. Duncan McEachern, manager of the Walrond Ranche, complained in 1891 to Interior Minister Dewdney that he had paid squatters to vacate his property "to prevent ill feeling, but we cannot continue paying and it would be but fair for the law to be so amended as to give us protection. My fear of a collision between them and our men prompts me to thus appeal to you."

The cattlemen could always count on a sympathetic hearing from the dominion government, and from Pearce. Ottawa believed there was virtually unlimited land elsewhere on the Prairies to settle, and better land for crop farming at that. They recognized that the beef industry had opened up the region to commerce at considerable financial risk. And after all, the ranchers had the law on

Squatters John and Richard Copithorne evolved their homestead on Jumping Pound Creek, west of Calgary, into a mixed farm and then the Lazy J Ranch. This is the first ranch house, about 1900.

Glenbow Archives, NA 3017-5

their side. Burgess, the imperious deputy minister, toured the West in 1884 and reported that "antagonism between ranchers and settlers is purely theoretical, such antagonism being forced by small, independent speculators forcing themselves upon the lease of the ranchers and entering into competition with them, and then demanding restitution for being forced to move, or refusing to pay government rent."

The antagonism was anything but theoretical, however. Forcible evictions were commonplace. Ranch hands routinely ripped down settlers' fences, and pulled down or burned their cabins. After one such eviction, Walrond Ranche worker J. Lamar reported, "The whole tribe of them are boiling over with wrath." When the settlers responded in kind, the ranchers accused them of theft and arson. A letter to his superiors from Ernest Cochrane, manager of the British American Ranch Company and a son of the senator, dated May 14, 1887, told of a ranch hand who went to some squatters under the pretence that he was thinking of squatting himself: "He asked one man if the B.A.R. Co'y would not run him off if he settled on their lease and the fellow's answer was 'Oh, just show them a box of matches and they will leave you alone' and then proceeded to tell how he was on one of the townships lately thrown open, but if he had not gotten his way before long he would have done some burning."

The settlers could make a case too. They had been enticed to a frontier by talk of "freedom" only to find it ruled by what they considered exclusionary autocrats. On top of that, they frequently saw their stock disappear when the cattle drives of the big ranches moved through their area, sweeping up every animal as they went along. They vowed to fight back. On April 5, 1885, at the farm of John Glenn on Fish Creek, the Alberta Settlers' Rights Association was formed. It demanded representation for the District of Alberta in the House of Commons, and that the land be thrown open to homesteading. The settlers even alluded to the possibility of taking up arms alongside Riel.

The *Calgary Herald* account of that first meeting quotes association chairman Sam Livingston, known as the first Calgarian since he was living on the townsite before the NWMP arrived, as declaring that "a settler was worse off than a wild animal, as a wild animal had a closed season in which he could not be hunted but that the settler was chased at all seasons of the year. As long as the lands are under leases, the country was no use for settlers as they might as well settle in the Pacific Ocean." Livingston then threw down another challenge: "For the present, I defend my claim as my neighbours do, behind my Winchester."

William Pearce had no sympathy at all with that point of view. "If squatters are permitted to

Provincial Archives of Alberta, E. Brown Collection, B-124

A Calgary area ranch in 1886. Only 40% of the ranch country could produce a decent grain crop, argued western czar Pearce, and that only 75% of the time.

take up land where they please," he wrote to Dewdney, "the water and hay will be taken, and the rest left, and taken, too, by a class who have not the capital to utilize the domain to the capacity it should be." The appreciative ranchers offered him an award in Montreal in 1899, which he refused. Historian David Breen thinks Pearce was acting out of conviction: "What appeared to the pro-settlement group to be partisanship was in reality an unwavering conviction that full and open settlement could not be morally or economically justified in all parts of the prairies, and the drought-driven refugees of later years are witness to the validity of his assessment."

Years later Pearce himself sought to substantiate that assessment. In 1913, reviewing 40 years of prairie life in a letter to W.J. Roche, then Interior minister, he concluded that only 40% of what he called the "grazing area" produced a decent grain or fodder crop, and then only did so 75% of the time. This was not enough, in his opinion, to justify widespread settlement. His bureaucrats were telling him the same thing. As late as 1897, the surveys branch of the Department of the Interior said settlement in the dry region should be controlled for the "ultimate good of the country as a whole." The realistic capabilities of the land were always his first concern, Pearce said.

The dominion government had other worries, however. The CPR had been expected to trigger a rush for land in the West. It was not happening, and political pressure mounted for a more aggressive colonization program. Meanwhile stories of downtrodden squatters, bravely battling ruthless ranching elites, increasingly swayed eastern public opinion. Thus in 1886 the settlers scored their first major triumph. Noting that some of the lease-holders were turning out to be little more than land speculators, an annoyed Macdonald cancelled the leases of those who had not stocked their land sufficiently, and announced that no future leases would prohibit settlement. This was a major blow to the ranchers, not because it was unfair but because it meant the Tories were beginning to look the other way.

Then in 1892 came another blow. The government must provide land grants for the Calgary-Edmonton railway line, opened the previous year. This gave it occasion to re-examine the lease system further, without seeming to be caving in to the squatters or to the opposition Liberals. As the review proceeded, leases closed to settlement were cancelled one by one. To compensate, ranchers had the option of purchasing one-tenth of their leases at \$2 an acre (a price later reduced to \$1.25), and "water reserves" were established to assure ranchers access to rivers and streams. But squatters just settled on the water reserves anyhow, and Pearce found his power to evict them rapidly diminishing.

In 1896 came the biggest reversal of all. The long Tory regime, which had ruled Ottawa since

Provincial Archives of Alberta, E. Brown Collection, B-145

An Alberta ranch hand in 1884. Politics and weather would turn against the affluent absentee lease-holders, but cattle could still be raised on the plains, and crops too. The new ranchers and farmers who followed them were there to stay.

Confederation except for one five-year interval, was ousted by the Liberals under Wilfrid Laurier. An entirely new regime took over the Department of the Interior, and the new minister, Manitoba's Clifford Sifton, was a powerful advocate of settlement. Burgess was gone. Frank Oliver, publisher of the *Edmonton Bulletin*, friend of the squatters and relentless foe of both Pearce and Burgess, was Alberta's Liberal MP. This in itself had profound significance. It meant that Alberta's political demographics had changed. The northern part of the territory, a mixed farming area peopled by settlers, had already become more populous than the ranching district in the south. So the district had gone Liberal, a fact that would have pivotal implications for the decade ahead.

Pearce was saved for a time by his experience and sincerity, but he was abrasive and uncompromising and had many foes. Sifton soon moved against him, first stripping him of his secretarial staff. When Pearce still wouldn't quit, Sifton ordered him to Ottawa where he intended to shift his area of responsibility to mining. Pearce refused to leave Calgary, and was demoted to inspector of surveys in 1901. (His career was far from over, however. He would live three decades into the new century and die in Calgary in 1930.)

Even the weather seemed to turn against the big ranchers. Between 1896 and 1903 rainfall averaged 15 inches annually, up from 10 inches a year in the preceding decade. How could it be argued the area was too dry for grain? In 1898 G.H.V. Bulyea, the new Liberal commissioner of agriculture for the North West Territories (who seven years later would become first lieutenant-governor of the new Province of Alberta), decided the leasing system and its water reserves displayed "a very narrow view of the situation." Newer bureaucrats in the Department of the Interior were less inclined to view the area south of Calgary as too dry for grain. In 1901 the ranchers' water reserves were withdrawn, and the land thrown open for public sale. The Era of the Great Ranches had come to an end.

The curious social stratum of aristocratic elegance largely disappeared with it. But the plains were still there and cattle could still be raised on them, and in the place of the grandee rancher the cattleman-entrepreneur almost immediately appeared. This man's fortunes did not lie in England, Ireland or central Canada. They lay in his homestead and his ranch, typically smaller and less grandiose than those of the earlier day, and his dreams were rooted in the West. Here he would create something permanent. Here he would build his life and become part of the bedrock foundation of the new province.❦

The founders of Alberta's ranching dynasties

The grandees who opened the cattle industry in the 19th century were not destined to rule the Alberta range over the 20th. That arduous honour would fall, for the most part, to smaller ranchers who managed to co-exist alongside the homesteaders. Many of the West's second-generation cattle entrepreneurs, men like A.E. Cross, Frank Ricks and John Ware, began as managers and foremen with the Cochrane, Oxley, Walrond and other outsider-owned spreads. As these monoliths slowly disintegrated during the late 1890s and early 1900s, chunks of their lands were picked off by their own employees and others with a keen eye and a small bankroll.

Ranching proved a tough business. Besides the Crosses, a mere half-dozen clans have survived in Alberta as substantial beef operators since the 19th century. These durable cattlemen include the Burtons west of Claresholm, the Hargraves hard by the Saskatchewan border north of Walsh, the Lynch-Stauntons north of Pincher Creek, the McKinnons east of Calgary, the Rosses in the south, and the Copithornes in the Cochrane area. Other ranching dynasties and careers there would certainly be, notably that of the spectacular Pat Burns, most renowned of Alberta business figures, but only these few pre-date the 20th century.

The following pages tell how some of them began.

A.E. Cross of the A7 – a fortune in beef and beer

Alfred Ernest Cross was the archetype of the new entrepreneurial rancher who would rise in the place of the aristocrats. Unlike many of the others, he was born to wealth. But the fortune he amassed and the mark he left on the province were far beyond anything he arrived with on that day in 1884 when he stepped off the train at Calgary.

His father, Alexander Cross, was a Court of Queen's Bench judge in Montreal and an adviser on economic and linguistic policy to successive dominion governments. A.E. was his fourth son, born in 1861. He received his early schooling in England, then attended business college in Montreal. Summers spent at his uncle's Quebec farm piqued his interest in agriculture and he became a veterinarian, establishing at McGill University a valuable contact — Duncan McEachern, later dominion veterinarian and manager of the Walrond Ranche.

From boyhood Cross was fascinated by the West. His older brother Harry was ranching in Colorado, and his letters home were filled with tales of danger and adventure. Alfred's own chance came when he landed the post of bookkeeper and assistant manager on the Cochrane Ranche. New on the job, he had to treat a horse that had been spurred raw from ear to tail. He lured the frenzied beast into a squeeze gate by jumping in himself and provoking it to charge him, at which point he scrambled out. There was much applause. This boy had guts.

Glenbow Archives, NA-2307-21

Rancher A.E. Cross, pictured in Calgary's 'Wolf Den' in 1893. He knew he had to diversify.

He also had initiative. Two years later he took up his own quarter section on Mosquito Creek west of Nanton. He ran smack into the disastrous winter of 1886-87, losing 60% of his stock. But he persevered and soon had established what became known as the "A7" Ranche.* With financial help from his father and two of his brothers he ultimately managed to corral a 60,000-acre grazing lease.

He already knew enough about agriculture, however, to realize he should diversify. He joined lawyer James Lougheed in Calgary real estate investments, and was soon lending his father's

Glenbow Archives, NA-2536-4

Helen Macleod Cross as a bride in 1899. Three Montreal socialites lost out.

money to developers. He also spent $3,000 of his brother Willie's money on 80 acres of land inside the city limits. Today it is the site of the Calgary Stampede.

In 1891 circumstance intervened to inspire another enterprise. Suffering from a stomach injury caused by an unfriendly horse and an unfortunately placed saddle horn, he went east to convalesce. While there, as a diversion, he studied the art of brewing. Counting on the end of prohibition in the North West Territories, which came the next year, and the taste of western ranchers and farmers for something other than bad whisky, he borrowed $50,000 from the bank and $1,500 from his father, and raised another $50,000 through a share issue (bought mostly by his friends). With this capital he founded the Calgary Brewing and Malting Company. His shareholders included W.R. Hull, W.F. Cochrane and Duncan MacPherson. The first brew frothed forth on St. Patrick's Day 1893.

In its early years the brewery went through a succession of brewmasters with too much fondness for their own product. So Cross, ever the hands-on manager, took advanced brewing courses in New York and Chicago, and spent many a 12-hour day running the brewery himself. He continually pursued new opportunities, wangled a virtual monopoly on beer sales to CPR construction crews in the Crow's Nest, and sank his profits into coal and other mining ventures in the Kootenays.

He developed certain business rules, like "Never borrow money from a bank" (though he did it on occasion) and "Never sell ranchland to raise capital." "Grass is the forgiveness of nature," he once wrote. "...Should it fail for a single year, famine would depopulate the world."

Another apparent Cross rule, although he never quite stated it, dismayed his shareholders: "Never pay a dividend." He financed the expansion of his business empire from the brewery's receipts. In Sherrill MacLaren's *Braehead: Three Founding Families in Nineteenth Century Canada*, one disgruntled backer is quoted as complaining: "Damn it, Cross! Things are never going to be in perfect running order because you'll never be satisfied with the present!"

It was indeed on the future that A.E.'s mind seemed riveted. Before the First World War he assured his brewery a market by buying 50 hotels across the West. In 1912, along with James Lougheed, R.B. Bennett and prominent dominion civil servant William Pearce, Cross formed Calgary Petroleum Products Ltd., which brought in a well the next year. He held shares in the Calgary Gas and Water Works Company, which built a pipeline from its initial strike east of the city to the brewery, making the Calgary Brewing and Malting Company the first industrial consumer of natural gas in western Canada.

But Cross never pushed too hard; caution prevented him from amassing the unmanageable debt loads that drove other Alberta entrepreneurs under in the uncertain times of the late 19th and early 20th centuries. Even prohibition in Alberta (1916 to 1924) could not sink him; his brewery continued to turn out 3,600 bottles an hour.

The entrepreneur was as much a social and political animal as a businessman. He had, he said, a "restless, roving craze over women" and broke three engagements with Montreal socialites before marrying Helen Rothney Macleod in 1899. The daughter of former NWMP commissioner James Macleod, Mrs. Cross became the first president of the Women's Canadian Club and a founder of the Women's Hospital Aid group. A.E. Cross himself was a founding member of the Western Stock Growers' Association, twice serving as its vice-president, and a founding member and president of the Calgary Board of Trade. With a $25,000 guarantee he helped create, with Pat Burns, Archie McLean and George Lane, the Calgary Stampede.

He was also a politician who, like others after him, made a radical transition from unquestioning nationalist to champion of western rights. In 1899 he was elected to the territorial assembly in Calgary East. Sitting as an independent, he began as an outspoken advocate of strong central government but soon became appalled by what he considered Clifford Sifton's chaotic immigration and settlement policies. His final speech in the assembly argued for provincial status for Alberta and Saskatchewan. Each could support a population larger than any other in the country, he insisted: "I have that much confidence in the West, gentlemen. The outcome of this reconstruction will be the formation of the nation's greatest and most powerful provinces. Most importantly, the people will be in the front rank."

A.E. Cross died of pneumonia in 1932, leaving his business interests in the hands of his eldest son. The Depression forced Jim Cross to retrench back to the brewing and ranching industries, liquidating many of the family's other holdings. In 1962, facing increasingly intrusive and restrictive government policies, he sold the brewery to E.P. Taylor's Canadian Breweries Ltd. for $18 million and put all his energies into his Bar Pipe Ranch west of Okotoks.

Jim Cross died in 1990, predeceased by his sister Margaret, called Marmo, who with her husband, Vancouver lawyer Jack Shakespeare, was killed in a car accident in 1980. The youngest son, John Cross, who spent his life running the A7 ranch at Nanton, died in 1991. Alexander (Sandy) Cross was retired and living in the Millarville area in 1991, as was A.E.'s daughter Mary Dover, an officer in the Canadian Women's Army in the Second World War and a former Calgary alderman. *M.B.*❦

*Cross wanted his brand to read "A1" to reflect the quality of his cattle, but inspectors told him the A1 brand could be altered too easily by rustlers. So instead he adopted the brand A7, seven being the number of sons in the Cross family.

Richard Lynch-Staunton — a 50-cent start

Glenbow Archives, NA-184-73

A.H. Lynch-Staunton (at right), who began ranching with his brother Richard on Pincher Creek, pictured with the Canadian polo team in 1899.

One branch from a remittance sprig remains alive and well in Alberta's ranching industry, albeit altered beyond recognition. Family tradition has it that Francis Hardwick Lynch-Staunton, born in 1828, was far too fond of partying and was exiled from Ireland for (it was said) the good of Ireland. Among the brood of 12 children he raised in Dundas, Ontario, only one managed to obtain much of an education, and that at his own expense.

But that one wasn't Richard Lynch-Staunton, who arrived in Alberta in 1885 at the age of 18, with a horse, a saddle and 50 cents. He and his brother Alfred, who had just left the North-West Mounted Police, started ranching on Pincher Creek. They prospered, continually buying more land and starting four butcher shops in neighbouring towns to retail some of their produce.

In 1901 Richard married Isabelle May Wilson, a nurse whose two brothers ran the Starlight Ranch. Not long afterwards, as their son Frank Lynch-Staunton recalled in his memoirs *Greener Pastures*, the new bride was lying in bed one early morning when she overheard the following conversation between her husband and several Assiniboine Indian women who had come to call:

"Dick, you get squaw?"

"Yes, I get squaw — white squaw."

"Where is she?"

"In bed."

"No good. You should have red squaw. White squaw always in bed. Red squaws work."

The Lynch-Stauntons did work, though. They were known to play polo, true enough. But not only did they descend to shopkeeping — much disdained by the bluebloods — but they were not afraid to get on the business end of a pitchfork.

Few descendants of Alberta's immigrant gentlefolk long continued to run herds, even on the smallest scale. But Frank Lynch-Staunton, born in 1905, succeeded his father at Antelope Butte Ranch and also made his mark in other respects. In 1979 he became Alberta's 11th lieutenant-governor, representing the Queen in his province with minimal pomp. A true Alberta cattleman in his social attitudes, he never donned the gold-braided uniform worn by his predecessors in the vice-regal office. That, he said, was not the Alberta way.

He died in 1990. His son, Hugh Lynch-Staunton, inherited Antelope Butte Ranch. *M.B.*❦

Lachlin McKinnon – a lost wallet led to the LK

Glenbow Archives, NA-2198-1

Lachlin and Sarah McKinnon in 1893. After a hard-luck start, prosperity.

Lachlin McKinnon arrived in Calgary on March 10, 1886, with $7.50. He was 21. He could read and do arithmetic, and not much more in the academic line. His Scottish parents, pioneers in the hardwood bushland of Ontario's Grey County, could afford to provide him with little education. But what he had heard of the West enthralled him, so that's where he headed.

After months of living hand to mouth in Calgary, the young man landed a job as personal attendant and chore boy to Major-General Thomas Bland Strange at the Military Colonization Company Ranche. He was soon promoted to wrangling 250 brood mares at $40 a month, then went line-riding near Cheadle. But as the green hand, he was repeatedly laid off before he'd learned his job fully. One winter he swamped with an Eau Claire lumber crew west of Banff at $25 a month.

During 1888-89 McKinnon line-rode all winter by himself, often shouting so the echo would keep him company. For several days he was snow blind. Riding into Calgary in the spring with his back pay of $228 in his hip pocket, he spotted smoke near Shepard. He alerted local ranchers and helped save nearby buildings, but his wallet slipped from his pocket during the firefighting, and he was flat broke again. Shortly after that he broke his collarbone, and then his left leg. To top up his cup of misfortune, he lost another month's pay from his pocket.

But his luck eventually turned. His foreman found the month's pay, his employer paid him for the time laid up with broken bones and, wonder of wonders, McKinnon spotted his own wallet in some of the grass saved by his efforts during the previous year's fire. Though the gophers had chewed up a few bills, the young man wound up just $20 short. And by 1892 he was foreman on the Canadian Coal and Colonization Company's 76 Ranch.

A year later Lachlin McKinnon married Sarah Whitney, and by 1895 was constructing log buildings on his own homestead and caring for 60 head of cattle. He had saved more than $2,500 from wages and a little livestock trading. When their first son, Charlie, was born in 1897, the father immediately began planning how the boy would help him with the never-ending work of a small ranch. The McKinnons were flooded out twice by the Bow, tried to sell their land, changed their minds, and rebuilt their home on higher ground. Trying to cope with haying and harvest machinery, McKinnon vowed that his second son, John Angus, born in 1898, would be trained as a farmer.

Eventually the McKinnons' LK Ranch prospered mightily. Subsequent generations would encounter new difficulties while branching into the oil industry (LK Resources Ltd.) and packing industries (XL Foods Ltd.) But after almost a century, five McKinnon heirs were operating in the beef industry, one was raising horses and yet another of Lachlin's descendants was a farmer. Keith McKinnon, who feeds cattle at his Kenwynn Farms Ltd. near Carseland, was president of the Calgary Stampede in 1991. *M.B.*❦

James Hargrave – a Cree's good advice paid off

In late 1882 a fur trader named James Hargrave arrived via train at what is now Maple Creek, Saskatchewan, then the end of steel for the Canadian Pacific.

Hargrave had begun his career with the Hudson's Bay Company at York Factory under the supervision of his uncle, chief factor at the post on the bay's bleak shoreline. But the shrewd nephew recognized that the coming of the railroad would both diminish the fur trade and generate new opportunities in western Canada. He trudged on foot from Maple Creek to the point where the CPR was to cross the South Saskatchewan and set up a store in a tent on the banks of the river. Thus he was already in business when the track crews got there in the spring, and the tent town that became Medicine Hat appeared.

Soon Hargrave was building up a small cattle herd. Fire swept through his accustomed range in the fall of 1888. A Cree acquaintance suggested he winter his animals near the Lake of the Many Islands with Grass Up to the Horses' Bellies, east of Medicine Hat. The Indians had long hunted buffalo on the flood plain formed by creeks flowing into what is now called Many Islands Lake. The soil, its fertility regularly replenished by inundation, supported an exceptionally lush cover of prairie wool.

Hargrave trailed his herd into this pasture that same winter. At the end of the 20th century, his family was still there, and was operating two big blocks of range in Alberta and Saskatchewan through Hargrave Ranching Co. Inc.*

Glenbow Archives, NA-4061-3

The James Hargrave family circa 1888. The original prairie wool still covered the Hargrave range in 1991.

Bert Hargrave, a grandson of the founder and a four-term Conservative MP, observed in 1991 that the original prairie wool still covered his range. "It's never been cultivated. This country is too rugged for grain, but the outcrops and coulees provide ideal shelter for cattle in winter. The regenerative power of the original short-grass prairie is truly astonishing. We had three seasons of drought up to this year, but with some rain at last, the grass is better than I've seen it in 60 years." *M.B.*❦

*How big is the Hargrave spread? Ranchers tend to avoid questions concerning the extent of their ranges and herds. A farmer will usually say how many sections he cultivates as readily as a city dweller might reveal the square footage of his house. But a rancher is liable to react to the same inquiries much as an urban citizen would to a query about the size of his bank account.

Walter Ross's clan still ranches the dry Milk River country

Walter I. Ross, eldest son of a Presbyterian minister in Quebec, got his start as a railroad contractor in Texas and at Rat Portage (now Kenora, Ontario). In 1885, however, he and a partner bought 400 Shorthorn heifers in Ontario, shipped them by boat to Fort William and by train to Medicine Hat, and established a ranch near present-day Magrath. One hundred years later the Ross family remained strongly represented in the southern Alberta cattle industry.

The Ross ranches expanded, contracted and expanded again, encompassing at their peak 12,000 head of cattle on half a million acres in southern Alberta, southwestern Saskatchewan and Montana. Walter I. Ross's son George Graham Ross carried on the business. So did his three sons: George G. Jr., John C. (Jack), and Walter (Stubb). In 1991 four of Walter I.'s great-grandchildren were active in three family ranches, and a great-great-grandson was about to join them.

Long before taxes and subsidies and benevolent governments, George G. Jr. wrote in 1967 in the *Free Press Weekly* farm paper, his grandfather "started out broke and ended up broke, but helped a lot to blaze the trail for all of us who have followed." The Ross herd suffered tremendous losses in the hard winter of 1906-07, for example, when some survivors were recovered fully 400 miles south in Montana. George G. Sr. served in the First World War, and returned to buy back his father's original spread, Lost River Ranch, 80 miles south of Medicine Hat on the U.S. border, in 1920. Then the hard winter of 1919-20 killed some 3,000 head, and was followed by a market collapse. That "broke the outfit," his son wrote, "but they weren't looking for any government assistance, they settled their own affairs..."

Settle them they did. Through bad times and good the hat-shaped Ross brand (registered in 1909) came to represent sound business management and good conservation practice. George G. Sr., who held U.S. private pilot's licence number 50, also started the family flying tradition by patrolling his range in a Curtis-Wright plane. His three sons all became flyers too and, when George G. Jr. finished his stint with the Royal Canadian Air Force in the Second World War, they began again to rebuild the family ranch holdings.

By 1949 they had reassembled 167,000 acres in southeastern Alberta. Lost River Ranch once more became their headquarters, and by the 1960s they were running 6,000 head on 283,000 acres of rangeland. George G. Jr. had also begun to write a regular column for the *Free Press Weekly*. Youngest brother Stubb had founded an airline in Lethbridge with a borrowed $52,000 and a nine-passenger plane. When it was fully acquired by PWA Corp. in 1991, Time Air was worth about $60 million.

George G. Ross Jr. died in 1972, Stubb Ross in 1987. But in 1991 Jack Ross and his sons John and David were operating the Milk River Cattle Co., in the Aden area 60 miles south of Lethbridge, still using the hat brand. George G. Ross III (called Graham) and his wife Marilyn had the Flying R Ranches, just south of the Cypress Hills. And at Lost River Ranches his sister Mary Jane and her husband Leonard Piotrowski, soon to be joined by their son Tim, were running a cow-calf operation and supplying rodeo stock. *M.B.*❦

Glenbow Archives, NA-3914-4

Patriarch Walter I. Ross (seated at right) about 1904.
One grandson started an airline, but most Rosses kept on ranching.

FRED BURTON STARTED AS A SQUATTER IN THE PORCUPINE HILLS

Glenbow Archives, NA-1435-4

Frederick A. Burton in 1900. Five sons took up rodeo competition, agricultural economics – and ranching.

Frederick Alfred Burton, a younger son in a big family on small farm at Guelph, Ontario, came to Alberta by rail in 1886. He was 18, and according to his own youngest son Gordon, writing for the Claresholm History Book Club 88 years later, he had a stake of $5. So he first got a job on the Winder ranch west of Claresholm, operating a walking plough — something he knew how to do. Then he hired on at the Cochrane and other ranches where he learned to handle a saddle horse and work cattle. In 1889 he registered a brand (R on the left ribs), and in 1896 squatted on the south fork of Trout Creek at the edge of the Porcupine Hills, 20 miles west of Claresholm.

That brought an indignant letter from the superintendent of mines, who had charge of such matters. If settlers were allowed to squat just anywhere they liked, that official informed Burton, the public interest "would be sadly interfered with." Burton, a strong, steady man who developed a deep love for the Porcupine Hills, managed nevertheless to get title to his quarter section. He then proceeded to add more property piece by piece, until by the 1930s he and his sons were running some 1,500 head of cattle and 700 horses.

Eighteen ninety-six was also the year Fred Burton married Minnie Furman, whose family had trekked into Montana by covered wagon from eastern Oregon in 1886 when she was 13, and moved into Alberta two years later. The Burtons made the 40-mile drive from their Trout Creek homestead to Macleod only two or three times a year to buy staples. But three sons were born to them there: Fred C. (1898); Ed (1899); and Alfred, called Toots (1905). John F., called Pat, was born in 1907, after they bought more land and a better house on Burke Creek in the next valley south, and Gordon L. in 1916.

Besides cattle, Fred Burton Sr. ran sheep for a while, and bred work and saddle horses until about 1930. Fred Jr. used to look after the horse herd on open range north of the Bow River in summer, sometimes riding the 100 miles there from the Burton homestead in a single day. Despite prairie fires, dry summers and bitter winters, the Burtons kept up their modest expansion. Other settlers arrived; some departed. By 1902 Claresholm began to develop on the new Macleod-to-Calgary railway.

When Fred Sr. died in 1951 he left two good ranches totalling some 20,000 acres. Fred Jr. and his wife, Bessie Bell Burton, continued to live and work on one, followed by their son Frederick George. Ed, Toots and Pat had bought spreads of their own. All four older brothers were notable rodeo competitors, Pat Burton winning the Canadian and North American roping championships in 1933. Gordon Burton, who had earned a PhD in agricultural economics and taught at McGill University and the University of Saskatchewan, took over the original family ranch. Fred and Minnie Burton had established a durable tradition. *M.B.*❦

THE BROTHERS COPITHORNE STARTED SMALL AT COCHRANE

The Copithorne spreads around Cochrane originated with three sons of an Irish dairy farmer who raised 15 children on 120 acres in County Cork.

First to reach Canada was John, who had been expelled from school for cheating on an examination. He mule-skinned and bull-freighted in Manitoba and Saskatchewan, and served as a volunteer during the Riel Rebellion of 1885, before squatting along Jumping Pound Creek west of Calgary in 1887. His brother Richard had arrived by then. As eldest son, he had worked with his father until he was 27. The brothers built a sod-roofed cabin; later one family lived just up the hill from the other.

John's wife Susan brought up nine children, traded butter and eggs at the I.G. Baker store in Calgary, worked off the occasional bout of temper punching a pan of bread dough, and competed with growing numbers of neighbours for the local wild berry harvests. The homestead evolved into a mixed farm, then the Lazy J Ranch.

Glenbow Archives, NA-3017-1

Richard and Sophia Copithorne in 1895. They raised children, Herefords and Clydesdales on Jumping Pound Creek.

Richard married Sophia Wills, an Ontario lass just 16 years old, in 1895. She bore seven children along that beautiful but isolated creek, finding recreation in her beloved piano. In 1914 the couple moved to Vancouver Island for a year, where John and Susan had already retired. But Richard chafed for Jumping Pound and they returned there for good. Sophia died in 1923. Richard's holdings, where he ran a big herd of Herefords and more than 300 Clydesdale horses, eventually grew to 26 square miles. Affluence did not change his lifestyle, though; his chief diversion was hunting coyotes on horseback.

Third brother Sam Copithorne taught school in Ireland before emigrating in 1904. He built a cabin atop a hill on the Lone Star Ranch, worked with his brother Richard for a time, then built up his own Hereford ranch in the Springbank area. In 1915 Sam married Beatrice Blanche, daughter of another rancher.

They had two sons and two daughters. Bea Copithorne, while constantly cooking for employees and guests, cut a fine figure riding sidesaddle through the district. Sam was by reputation a hard man, whose stern face could look as sour as a crock full of salted cabbage. Neighbours used to say he always had three crews — one coming, one working and one going. But he grew great quantities of flowers and potatoes, and continued to break horses until he was 75.

The Copithornes still cluster near Cochrane, their lands divided and expanded many times. The town's telephone directory lists 18 family members; most descend from Richard and Sam. Richard's son Clarence became an MLA in the 1970s, sitting first as an independent and later as a Conservative. He served on the provincially appointed Citizens' Advisory Committee on the Constitution, which inspired the campaign for a Triple-E Senate.

"We'll probably still be around these parts in another century," allows Ken Copithorne, grandson of Sam and a district leader of the Reform party. *M.B.*❦

Homesteaders leaving Edmonton to break land at the turn of the century
Provincial Archives of Alberta, E. Brown Collection, B-669

Section Six

The Sodbusters

Chapters by Mark Stevenson
Sidebars by Celeste McGovern and Mark Stevenson

OF PLENTY
OUTFIT.

CHAPTER ONE

The West opens with a big failure — The CPR arrives, but not the settlers

PALLISER'S TALK OF A PRAIRIE DESERT BEGAN TO LOOK RIGHT ❦ THE RAILWAY MONOPOLY, THE TARIFF AND DROUGHT SPELLED DOOM ❦ EVEN THE *MEDICINE HAT TIMES* HAD TO ADMIT TO DOUBTS

Glenbow Archives, NA-588-1

Captain Palliser (left) and Dr. Hector. Some suspected it would be a buffalo-hunting adventure at government expense.

The strongest evidence the cattlemen could cite in their confrontation with the sod-busters was the report of Captain John Palliser, made some 40 years before in 1862. Throughout the early 19th century the British had watched the American advance across the West. If the area north of the 49th parallel was not settled under the Union Jack, they feared, the Stars and Stripes would soon be flying over it. But could the huge Hudson's Bay Company territory of Rupert's Land be settled at all? That is, could it support agriculture? No one seemed to know for certain, and there were strong opinions both ways.

Sir Archibald Alison, a Scottish lawyer and historian, wrote that the region was "doomed to eternal sterility from the excessive severity of the climate, which yields only a scant herbage to the reindeer, the elk and the muskox." Sir John Richardson, on the other hand, who saw some of Rupert's Land as a member of a party searching for the lost Franklin expedition, reported in 1852 that "from Fort Edmonton down to [Fort] Carlton, and far below, a range of five hundred miles, the country and climate invite the husbandman and the plough."

Thoroughly confused by conflicting reports, the British in 1857 set up a select committee of the Commons to study the evidence. Contradictions continued. In his *Illustrated History of Western Canadian Agriculture*, Grant MacEwan quotes the testimony of the HBC governor, Sir George Simpson: "I do not think that any part of the Hudson's Bay Company's territories is well adapted for settlement. The crops are very uncertain." Others agreed with him. Colonel John Henry Lefroy, who had travelled extensively in the northern part of Rupert's Land, said the region was "almost entirely denuded of soil," with winters "so intense that over a very large portion the soil is permanently frozen. The seasons are so short and so uncertain that crops are likely to be cut off."

Of course, Simpson had a vested interest in keeping settlers out of his fur trading empire. Some of the company's own men contradicted him on the West's farming potential. Alexander Isbister, a former HBC clerk born at Cumberland House on the

Provincial Archives of Alberta, E. Brown Collection, B-5880

A CPR survey crew in the western territory. They helped prepare for a land rush that took 30 years to happen.

Saskatchewan River, told the committee that "agriculture can be carried on in all the country intervening between the Great Lakes and the Rocky Mountains."[1]

Only on-the-spot investigation could resolve the question, the Commons committee decided. In consequence its chairman, Henry Labouchere, wrote to Captain Palliser, thereby launching an expedition that would provide much fuel for the cattlemen's fire.

Palliser's qualifications were not entirely self-evident — apart perhaps from his valuable London connections, his fluency in four languages and a demonstrated love of adventure. A 40-year-old bachelor heir to a wealthy Irish estate, he was a globetrotter, big-game hunter, all-round man of means and action, and an intimate friend of John Ball, under-secretary of state for the Colonies. But Palliser was also a fellow of the Royal Geographical Society, had spent the winter of 1847-48 hunting buffalo in the upper reaches of the Missouri River, and in 1853 had written a book, *Solitary Rambles and Adventures of a Hunter in the Prairies.*

The Palliser appointment raised certain qualms in HBC circles. This was not to be a buffalo hunt at government expense, warned Edward Ellice, longtime HBC investor and a former director. It was to be a comprehensive survey of the Prairies, complete with an assessment of the region's soil, agricultural potential, mineral reserves and timber resources. Reassuringly, Palliser's team included James Hector, a doctor turned geologist and biologist; John W. Sullivan, astronomer; Eugene Bourgeau, botanist; and Lieutenant Thomas Blakiston, surveyor.

The expedition — 20 men, two wagons, six Red River carts and 29 horses — set out from Fort Garry, already coming to be called Winnipeg, in July 1857. They spent three years criss-crossing the Prairies, digging holes to test soil conditions, and making notes of the flora, fauna and weather. Adventure befell them unsought.

The following March, for instance, as Irene Spry recounts in *The Palliser Expedition,* Hector found himself and his five-man party hopelessly lost half way between Edmonton and Fort Pitt (which was about 30 miles north of present-day Lloydminster). The doctor

[1] A.S. Morton of the University of Saskatchewan uncovered HBC records from 1674 which suggest that the company routinely expected subsistence farming at its posts. Each was to be provided with "a bushel of wheat and rye, barley and oats, or a barrel of each in casks, and such sorts of garden seeds as the Governor shall advise" (along with a Bible and the Church of England's Book of Common Prayer). Alexander Mackenzie declared in 1787 that trader Peter Pond's garden on the Athabasca River was as fine "as I ever saw in Canada."

Canadian Pacific Limited, 16354

A CPR promotion car advertising the West's agricultural potential (right). Only British stock desired. (Below) Palliser's 'Fertile Belt' and semi-desert triangle.

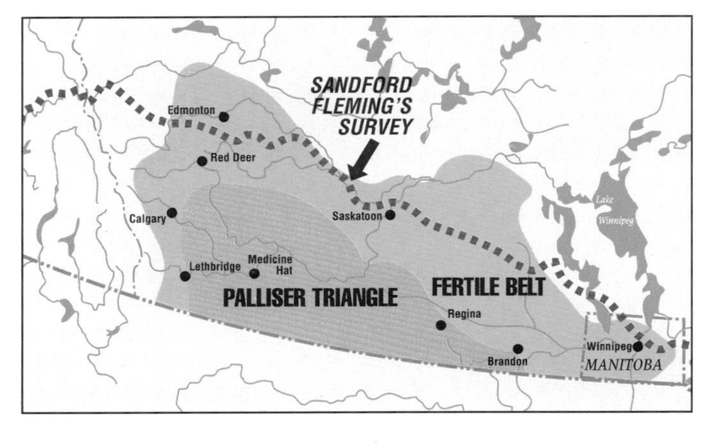

had forgotten his compass. A snowstorm wiped out any trace of a trail and every rolling hill looked the same as the last. After two days of frantic travel in no particular direction, they stumbled upon an Indian camp.

"On hearing where we were bound for, the Indians would hardly believe us," wrote Hector, "for we had turned completely round...we were already half way back to our starting place. We at once turned right about, and, as the weather cleared up, we reached Fort Pitt in two days...well starved, and some of us quite snow-blind."

The next summer, other Indians proved less obliging. In the Cypress Hills of what is now southern Alberta and Saskatchewan, Palliser's account records a dramatic standoff. A party of Bloods showed up at his encampment and announced they intended to kill one of his Stoney guides. "Olivier Munroe, brother to Felix, whom we had all looked on previous to this as a fool, now began to talk to them in their own language," wrote Palliser, "saying...'You want to kill the Stoney: well, kill him; but think well! for you will have to kill every one of us; and as to him (meaning me), he will be the first to fire.'" The Indians left.

Hector's most harrowing experience, however, was to leave a more permanent mark on western history. Pushing upstream into the Rockies on one of the east-flowing rivers, he came upon an upland meadow beyond which, over a sharp drop, another river plunged down westward — in other words, a pass. Expedition guide Peter Erasmus, in his book *Buffalo Days and Nights,* described what happened next. One of the packhorses stumbled, slid into the stream and had to be hauled out. Then Hector moved to remount his own horse, but as soon as he reached for the reins it "whirled and kicked him with both feet in the chest." Erasmus estimated that the doctor was unconscious for fully two hours, while his companions watched anxiously over him. Thus was the name "Kicking Horse Pass" added to the map of Canada. Less than a quarter century later this improbable defile in the Rockies would provide the passage for the country's first transcontinental railway.

Close escapes notwithstanding, Palliser presented his report to the Colonial Office on April 4, 1862. His expedition's findings were decisive, and the report is still admired as long on detail and short on hyperbole — a refreshing change from the customary grandiloquence of the times.

Palliser called a crescent-shaped band of territory arcing from the Red River settlement to the Peace River country the "Fertile Belt." It had rich soil, abundant grass and rain, and trees for timber. In other words, it was entirely suitable for settlement. He was lavish in his praise for this area: "The richness of the natural pasture in many places on the prairies of the second level along the North Saskatchewan and its tributary, Battle River, can hardly be exaggerated...Almost everywhere along the course of the North Saskatchewan are to be found eligible situations for agricultural settlement, a sufficiency of good soil is everywhere to be found, nor are these advantages merely confined to the neighbourhood of the river..."

But south of the Fertile Belt he found a wedge of short-grass land he called "an extension of the Great American Desert." This was precisely the area the cattlemen claimed. The base of the Palliser Triangle, as it soon became known, runs along the U.S. border (then un-surveyed) from southwestern Manitoba to the Rockies; its apex is just south of Lloydminster where the Battle River crosses the Alberta-Saskatchewan border. This area he considered unfit for cultivation: "[It] is desert or semi-desert in character...[and] can never be expected to become occupied by settlers...Although there are fertile spots throughout its extent it can never be of much advantage to us as a possession."

Palliser in short would have left the southern grasslands to the cattlemen. Nevertheless, his report fundamentally changed the perception of the Prairies. No longer a vast, homogeneous and forbidding wasteland, cut by a few fertile river valleys, it came to be seen as a varied and promising territory. Thus his work led to the eventual settlement of Alberta and the Canadian West, although this was to prove a far from spontaneous occurrence.[2]

Five years later came Confederation, and three years after that the new Dominion of Canada completed the purchase of Rupert's Land from the Hudson's Bay Company for £300,000 and assorted other benefits. "I would be quite willing, personally, to leave that whole country a wilderness for the next half century," wrote John A. Macdonald, "but I fear if Englishmen do not go there, Yankees will."

Thus challenged, the Department of Public Works dispatched Lieutenant-Colonel John Stoughton Dennis to the Red River district in 1871 to begin a massive survey of the whole prairie region. A uniform grid was imposed upon the land. Moving west from longitude 98° (a point west of Winnipeg later commemorated by a stone marker beside the Trans-Canada Highway) and north from the 49th parallel, the Dominion Land Survey divided the territory into square-mile sections designated by iron spikes.

[2] Westerners had to work long and hard to provide definite evidence substantiating Palliser's largely favourable report. In 1884, for example, the Calgary and District Agricultural Society persuaded the CPR to let them mount in a railway car an exhibit of grain and vegetables grown in central Alberta. The car toured eastern Canada all the way to Halifax that winter. Easterners were reportedly so impressed with the produce that they suspected fraud.

Ploughing the brown soil near Calgary in 1884. Macdonald would as soon have left 'that whole country a wilderness for the next half century' but for the Yankee threat.

Provincial Archives of Alberta, E. Brown Collection, B-78

Loneliness became the vast Prairies' great terror

It led some into 'prairie madness' but it produced a 'mystical' people who would mark the sparrow's fall

The great ocean itself does not present more infinite variety than does the prairie ocean. In winter, a dazzling surface of purest snow; in early summer, a vast expanse of grass and pale pink roses; in autumn, too often a wild sea of raging fire. No ocean of water in the world can vie with its gorgeous sunsets; no solitude can equal the loneliness of a night-shadowed prairie; one still feels the stillness and hears the silence, the wail of the prowling wolf makes the voice of solitude audible, the stars look down through infinite silence upon a silence almost as intense. This ocean has no past — time has been nought to it; and men have come and gone, leaving behind them no track, no vestige, of their presence.

Thus did William Francis Butler, the British officer whose special report contributed to the formation of the North-West Mounted Police, describe the Canadian Prairies. His book, *The Great Lone Land,* published in 1872, enchanted the English-speaking world, luring men and women west to see and dwell within this boundless sea of waving grass.

They in turn recorded their reactions in letters, novels, poems, newspaper accounts and essays that streamed from this land over the next half century.* These amply confirmed Butler's impression, sometimes in rapture, often in what seemed a haunting terror.

"Just why I fear that some one of us will get lost on the prairie, I don't know," Sarah Ellen Roberts wrote in her diary (published in 1968 as *Of Us and the Oxen*) after settling near Stettler with her husband and three sons at the turn of the century. "But whatever the reason, the fact remains that if one of the family is out after dark I am perfectly frantic with anxiety; and while the rest laugh at me, I notice that none of them want to take any chances of having to spend the night alone on the prairie, even in summertime. There is, of course, no real danger, except in winter, and that there is danger then, no one can deny."

Certainly John Donkin, a Mountie writing in the late 1880s, would not have denied it. In *Trooper and Redskin in the Far North-West* he gives a graphic account of a prairie blizzard: "It is almost indescribable in its deathly power. It is the most terrible wind that rages upon earth; a cloud burst of powdered ice, accompa-

nied by a violent hurricane, with the thermometer away below zero. I am utterly impotent to describe the cold....in these terrible tempests, settlers have been known to have gone to feed their oxen in the stables, just a few yards from their door; and have been seen no more alive. Some have been discovered when spring has lifted the shroud of winter; their bones picked clean by coyotes."

If the Prairies proved hard for a man, it was often worse for his wife. In *Alberta: A New History,* Howard and Tamara Palmer recount the opposed reactions of Mormon settlers Richard and Millie Harvey. To Richard the land was "paradise indeed," but Millie never stopped longing to return to Utah. Miles from medical help, food supplies and even neighbours, she found the lonely Prairie an endless trial. Even the tall grass was a threat; she dressed her young daughters in red sunbonnets so as not to lose them in the fields.

Like Butler, Sarah Roberts was engulfed by the loneliness: "I think that during the first few weeks of our stay here I never went to the door of the tent without scanning the horizon...to see if I could discover anywhere upon the seemingly boundless prairie, any living, moving, thing. For there were times when the loneliness was so oppressive that to see even a herd of cattle moving toward a little meadow where the grass looked greener gave me a distinct sense of relief and companionship."

"It is a country to breed mystical people, egocentric people, perhaps poetic people. But not humble ones," wrote the novelist Wallace Stegner in *Wolf Willow.* "At noon the total sun pours down on your single head; at sunrise or sunset you throw a shadow a hundred yards long. It was not prairie dwellers who invented the indifferent universe or impotent man. Puny you may feel there, and vulnerable, but not unnoticed. This is a land to mark the sparrow's fall."

But Elizabeth Mitchell, travelling the North West after the turn of the century, recounted in her log (*In Western Canada Before the War*) how an old woman told her of the severe depression known as "prairie madness." It could afflict women (and bachelors) facing loneliness in ship-like sod huts on the sea of plains. "A woman alone in the house all day may find the silence deadly; in the wheat-farming stage there may not even be a beast about the place...she may grow shy and diffident, and not care to make the effort to tidy herself up and go to see a neighbour — any neighbour, just to break the monotony. Then fancies come, and suspicions, and queer ways, and at last the young Mounted Policeman comes to the door, and carries her away to the terrible vast 'Sanatorium' that hangs above the Saskatchewan."

The other great theme of early accounts, however, is the triumph of courage and determination. In *The Pioneer Years 1895-1914,* Barry Broadfoot presents a Taber pioneer's recollection of one dramatic incident: "One day when the men were away and Mother had just returned to the shack she saw fire and smoke in the distance and she had the pails of water. She dipped gunny sacks in the water and ran to meet it...As the fire got close to the house, Mother fought it, beating at the high flames with the two wet potato sacks...until she was exhausted...When [the men] came back and saw where the fire had been they ran to the house and there they found Mother, very dirty, very smoky, very tired, but she had saved the children's prairie home and enough grass for their horse."

Through countless such hard-won individual victories, the settlers who made their homes on Butler's great trackless ocean would finally prevail. *C.M.*❦

* Among other important books on the pioneer West are: *Fruits of the Earth,* Frederick Philip Grove, 1933; *New and Naked Land,* Ronald Rees, 1988; *Land of Pain, Land of Promise,* Harry Piniuta, 1978; *The Promised Land,* Pierre Berton, 1984; *The Last Best West: Women on the Alberta Frontier, 1880-1930,* E.L. Silverman, 1984; *Images of the West,* R. Douglas Francis, 1989.

Fresh logs, fresh mud, fresh sod, and not a fellow human being for miles upon an ocean of grass.

Provincial Archives of Alberta, E. Brown Collection, B-711

Thirty-six such sections formed each township. Each section was further subdivided into 160-acre quarter-sections, the base unit for settlement. This could prepare the way, it was thought, for the same kind of land rush that was already occurring in the vast American West.[3]

The Dominion Lands Act came next. Passed in 1872, it followed the pattern of the 10-year-old U.S. Homestead Act, offering settlers quarter-sections in return for a $10 filing fee. Anyone 18 or older, or any head of a family, could apply, regardless of citizenship. To gain clear title, a settler was obliged to construct a habitable home, break a specified acreage on his land, and live there at least six months a year for three years.

Significant chunks of prairie remained out of reach, however. Besides the CPR's 25 million acres along its rail line, a further seven million acres were reserved for future railway development. The HBC kept 50,000 acres around its posts (3,000 acres each), plus one-twentieth of the Fertile Belt (roughly 6.6 million acres). Two sections of each township, usually numbers 11 and 29, were declared school lands, to be sold to defray the costs of education in the area. Finally, Ottawa kept five million acres to grant or sell to former soldiers and NWMP men.

Pioneers were encouraged to think long-term, writes Gerald Friesen in *The Canadian Prairies: A History*. Between 1872 and 1894, a settler could file an interim claim upon the quarter-section next to his, reserving it for purchase once he obtained clear title on his first allotment.

Ottawa was confident there would be a tremendous rush to the West, based on the resounding success at Red River. Farming there had also seemed dubious initially. Its first winter wheat crop, cultivated without oxen or ploughs, failed completely in 1812. By mid-century, however, Winnipeg was a thriving agricultural community. On October 21, 1876, it sent its first shipment of wheat for export — 857 bushels to Toronto at 80 cents a bushel. The wheat was Red Fife, the variety that had turned southern Ontario into a breadbasket. The next year, eastern buyers came to Winnipeg looking for 20,000 bushels, Grant MacEwan records in *Between the Red and the Rockies*. If this was possible in Manitoba, why not on the Prairies to the West?[4]

Helping the agrarian settlement along was the development of the purifier. First introduced to North America from France in 1870, it was a new milling device that separated bran and middlings from flour. Until then, hard spring wheat was in little demand because, despite its superior strength, it lacked the desired whiteness. The purifier changed all that. "This...rendered valuable the crops of Minnesota, the Dakotas, and western Canada," writes William Edgar in *The Story of a Grain of Wheat*, "and led to the agricultural development of that

[3] **Surveying could prove incendiary, as Ottawa had learned two years earlier. The first attempt to survey Rupert's Land, in anticipation of the land transfer, provided the final factor that precipitated the first Riel Rebellion. The Dominion Land Survey would become a factor in the West's second rebellion 15 years later.**

[4] **Albertans accused Manitobans of actually trying to divert the immigrant flow. The *Calgary Tribune* in May 1889 lashed out at Manitoba "agents" for boarding trains to dissuade settlers from proceeding farther. These subversives, the paper claimed, "urged them very strongly against coming to such a terrible place as Calgary, which they represented as having a climate so severe that it was impossible in winter to bear with it."**

Glenbow Archives, NA-1472-7

FREE HOMES FOR ALL.

Government Lands in the Canadian Northwest,

HOW TO OBTAIN THEM.

HOMESTEADS PRE-EMPTIONS AND WOOD LOTS.

GOVERNMENT LANDS.

HOMESTEADS, PRE-EMPTIONS AND WOOD LOTS.

A "homestead" not exceeding one-quarter section, or 160 acres, is a free grant from the Government. Any person, male or female, who is the sole head of a family, or any male who has attained the age of eighteen years, is entitled to a homestead. The condition under which the grant is made is that the homesteader shall reside on and cultivate the land for three years. The person receiving a homestead entry is entitled at the same time—*but not at a later date*—to a pre-emption entry for an adjoining unoccupied 160 acre tract. The settler will not be called upon to pay for the pre-emption until the expiration of the three years that entitles him to receive a deed from the Government for his homestead. The price charged for pre-emptions within the Railway belt is $2.50 (10*s.*) per acre.

A settler is allowed a period of six months after date of entry for entering upon and taking possession of the land, but he must not be absent from his homestead for more than six months at any one time without special leave from the Minister of the Interior. *Only the even numbered sections of a township are open for homestead and pre-emption entries.*

Should the settler find that he cannot comply with the conditions of the three years' residence, he is allowed to purchase his homestead by paying $2.50 per acre therefor, provided that he has resided on the land for twelve months from date of entry, and has brought under cultivation at least thirty acres thereof.

Any person who has obtained a deed for his homestead after three years' residence may obtain another homestead and pre-emption entry.

Settlers that have not sufficient wood growing on their homesteads can purchase from the Government wood lots not exceeding twenty acres in size at $5.00 per acre. In addition to this, settlers are allowed, free of charge, a permit to cut timber on vacant Government lands—a sufficient quantity of wood, house logs and fence timber to meet all their requirements during the first year of homesteading. They are forbidden to dispose of wood from their homesteads, pre-emptions, wood lots, or what they may obtain under free permit, to saw-mill proprietors, or to any person other than an actual settler, for his own use. A breach of this condition. or non-fulfilment of homestead conditions, renders the entries of homestead, pre-emption and wood lot subject to cancellation. Should such concellation be made, all improvements become forfeited to the Government, and the settler is not allowed to make a second homestead entry.

The attention of intending emigrants is drawn to the fact that the privilege of obtaining a pre-emption will be discontinued after January 1st, 1885. For those who wish to obtain large farms at a cheap rate, the coming spring will therefore be the most desirable time to emigrate. The title of the lands previously referred to remains vested in the Crown until after the Patent is issued; unpatented lands cannot be seized for debt. In case a settler dies, the law allows his executors to fulfil the homestead conditions, thus securing the estate to his heirs.

The fees charged are as follows: Homestead, $10; pre-emption, $10; permit fee, 50 cents.

LIBERALITY OF CANADIAN LAND REGULATIONS

CONTRASTED WITH THOSE OF THE UNITED STATES.

The fee for taking up a homestead or pre-emption entry is only $10, whereas it is $26, and in some cases $34, in the States.

The privilege of receiving a pre-emption entry at the same time as that for a homestead is granted is denied to the settler in the United States.

The settler must reside *five years* on his homestead in the United States, as against *three years* under the liberal regulations of Canada.

The taking of a homestead in Canada does not prevent a settler from purchasing other Government lands.

The following liberal allowance of timber is given to the settler on prairie lands free of charge: 1,800 feet of house timber, 400 roof rails, 30 cords of wood, and 2,000 fence rails—equal in value to about $60. No such grant can be obtained under the land regulations of the United States.

Particular attention is drawn to the fact that settlers, on completing their homestead conditions, are allowed the right to obtain a second homestead and pre-emption. This concession on the part of the Government has only lately been allowed, and this fact alone places the Canadian regulations, in the matter of liberal treatment of the settlers, far ahead of those of the United States.

section of the western continent."

Bolstered by such confident expectations, Ottawa could afford to be choosy. It wanted not just any settlers, but British settlers. As the *Lethbridge News* would later put it: "To the tenant farmer of Great Britain, the West offers free homesteads, good markets, civil and religious liberty under the protection of the same old flag which has sheltered them in the past...No class or creed distinctions exist, and merit alone is the stepping stone to promotion and positions of trust and responsibility."

The federal Department of Agriculture concurred. A British immigrant, said a departmental bulletin in 1879, "would have the satisfaction of feeling that he is assisting to build up a great British Empire, having for its seat the northern half of the continent of North America." Coupled with this view was another preference, namely for wheat, already viewed as the West's most promising cash crop.

Douglas Owram of the University of Alberta, in *Promise of Eden: The Canadian Expansionist Movement and the Idea of the West,* provides graphic contemporary examples. Wheat, wrote Thomas Spence, clerk of the legislative assembly of Manitoba and immigration pamphleteer, is the "engine of empire." It is "pre-eminently the food of civilized nations...The nice adjustment of its vital properties supports brain, and blood and muscle, in just proportion requisite for the highest type of manhood. Refinement, fortitude and enterprise most distinguish those nations which most consume wheat. Beef-eating and wheat-consuming races at once dominate and elevate the rice and pork consumers with whom they come into contact." Ontario poet Charles Mair thought so too. "Wheat," he declared, "is Empire."

With all arrangements complete — the land surveyed and legislation in place, railway connections soon to be made through Minnesota and a Canadian route planned —

A homestead near Edmonton in 1891. Only 2,000 new homesteaders per year came into the vast North West Territory.

Provincial Archives of Alberta, E. Brown Collection, B-217

Ottawa settled back and waited for the rush to begin. It didn't. The year 1874 saw only 1,376 applications filed in the entire territory; in 1875 the number dropped to 499. For nearly three full decades, in fact, the land rush failed to materialize. Until the late 1890s, the flow of people remained a trickle. Only about 1,000 per year came to the territory of Alberta between 1885 and 1890, and only about 2,000 per year in the five following that.

Historians and economists have long argued about the explanation for what they call "the lull." Some note that international conditions were not conducive to emigration. Eastern Europeans, not yet welcome anyway, were not pushed off their land until late in the century. The political and religious persecution that forced them to look overseas had not yet fully manifested itself. Furthermore, an international depression hampered the movement of people in the 1880s, and low wheat prices dulled the lustre of farming, even in a potential breadbasket.

In an essay in *The Prairie West: Historical Readings*, University of Alberta economist Kenneth Norrie argues that the lull was inevitable for more basic reasons. Any rush to the "semi-arid" lands of the Canadian Prairies had to wait until the more farming-friendly "sub-humid" lands of the United States had been filled, he contends. Another view holds that the National Policy of the Macdonald government, with its high tariffs to protect Ontario and Quebec industry, kept people out because the duty on farm machinery dis-

John Macoun gave the lie to Palliser, but was he right?

His exuberant study of the Prairies greatly encouraged settlers – but was deplored as fraud and falsehood

John Macoun was a man of exuberant energy, and equipped with a short fuse. As staff botanist on Sandford Fleming's Canadian Pacific Survey in 1872 he earned the nickname "Haypicker," for his habit of leaping from boats or wagons to seize prize specimens. And when a senior Ottawa official questioned his conclusions on western agriculture, Macoun recounts in his autobiography, "I told my interlocutor that my statements were convincing to an intelligent man, and that, if they did not convince him, I was sorry for his intelligence."

That particular encounter was part of a flaming controversy over the extensive chunk of southern Prairie known as the Palliser Triangle, classified as desert and semi-desert by Captain John Palliser in 1862. John Macoun, the Irish-born chairman of natural history at Albert College in Belleville, Ontario, was convinced that Palliser was dead wrong and was determined to prove it.

Having journeyed as far as Edmonton with Fleming, he had proceeded to the Pacific coast on his own, making observations all the way. Then he returned east with another expedition in 1875. In 1882 he was appointed botanist to the Geological Survey of Canada and became its assistant director and naturalist in 1887. Meanwhile he had begun an intense anti-Palliser campaign, publishing his own conclusions in a massive tome, *Manitoba and the Great North West,* in 1882.

On the potential of the so-called Fertile Belt of the Prairies, Macoun agreed with Palliser and then some. Where Ontario averaged 15 bushels per acre of wheat and Manitoba could produce 23, he predicted the Edmonton yield would be more than 30 bushels and Peace River 40. "No man can doubt this, for a glance at the map will tell him that there is actually no limit but the want for a market to the wheat crop of the North West."

But Macoun emphatically disagreed with Palliser's description of the southern Prairie as desert. "It was all equally good land," he declared. Even in the traditionally parched country surrounding the Cypress Hills he found that "none of the land was poor pasture and much of it had a good fertile soil well suited to agriculture." On the potential for western settlement he was just as positive: "What in the spring of 1880 was a vast prairie covered with waving grass, will in the spring of 1882 be alive with settlers and its solitude and loneliness gone forever."

He had plenty of opposition. Among his detractors was Henry Hind, a geologist sent to the West by the dominion government in 1857. Hind believed that Palliser's division of the Prairies into fertile and arid zones was well founded, and said so. In 1883 he condemned Macoun's work as "manufactured falsehood and fraud," designed to "distort and magnify the physical features of Manitoba and the North West Territory for the purpose of inducing immigration." Even Lindsey Russell, then deputy minister of couraged agriculture. The National Policy certainly sparked outrage in the West and helped build the Patrons of Industry, the first prairie protest party. In a speech in Saltcoats, Assiniboia, reported in *The Patrons Advocate* on February 13, 1895, the Reverend J.M. Douglas[5] vented his frustration: "The cry, of course is 'protect our infant industries,' but these infants have been too long at the breast. Shame on them, children fifteen years old, and unable yet to stand alone."

Then, too, there was the fury against the CPR, its early monopoly, its refusal to build a line through what Palliser had called the Fertile Belt, and above all its freight rates. In 1883, it cost 30.6 cents to ship a bushel of wheat from Moose Jaw to Thunder Bay, almost half the amount a farmer could hope to sell it for. "Our freight rates are oppressive," complained clergyman-farmer Douglas. "Don't mistake me. I have a great admiration for the CPR; as a nation we are proud of that railway but it has had great privileges and it is not treating us fairly."

Just as important, no doubt, was the news filtering out of the West. Bad weather, insects, prairie fires and primitive farming methods all made agriculture a hazardous business. Even the marvellous Red Fife could not guarantee success. Early frost destroyed the crop, particularly in 1884, 1885 and 1888. Drought was common too through the 1880s, and again from 1892 to 1894. "Many prairie farms were abandoned," writes Grant

[5] James Moffat Douglas (no immediate relation to future Saskatchewan premier and dominion parliamentarian T.C. Douglas) was elected MP for Assiniboia East in 1896, with Liberal and Patrons support. He had a hand in establishing the first royal commission on the grain trade, also in 1896.

the Interior, called Macoun a "superficial scientist, though a clever knave."

The naturalist became notoriously edgy and aggressive under fire. When Colonel G.A. French of the North-West Mounted Police challenged his opinions, Macoun wrote to Fleming: "I think I see my way to annihilate French. I will touch him on his want of knowledge and also on his want of honesty." When Liberal Alexander Mackenzie failed to accord him what Macoun felt was his due credit in a House of Commons speech, the botanist began cursing him and screaming from the gallery until the security guards dragged him out.

Public Archives of Canada, 33784

Botanist Macoun. He screamed from the Commons gallery until the guards dragged him out.

Yet Macoun's optimism was to prove highly influential upon a government which at that point was anxious to maximize western farming potential. York University geographer John Warkentin ("Steppe, Desert and Empire" in *Prairie Perspectives* 2) writes that the Dominion Lands Branch relied heavily on his work. The "portion of the so-called American Desert which extends northerly into Canadian Territory, is proved to have no existence as such," said one 1880 branch publication.

Another fan was the governor-general, the Marquis of Lorne, to whom *Manitoba and the Great North West* was dedicated. Visiting the Assiniboia area south of Battleford in 1881, he too agreed that this was no desert. "The newer maps, especially those containing the explorations of Prof. Macoun," he said, "have corrected the wholly erroneous idea....[The region could] not be excelled for agricultural purposes."

Douglas Owram of the Univer-sity of Alberta suggests that Macoun also influenced the CPR's choice of the southern route and hence the subsequent patterns of settlement. But historians are not inclined to condemn him outright for ill-founded boosterism. The U of A's Lewis H. Thomas points out, in his essay "A History of Agriculture on the Prairies to 1914," that Palliser was in the West in the dry years of the late 1850s. Macoun was there in the 1870s, when the Prairies were unusually lush.

Many a dust-devastated prairie farmer might not have felt so forgiving, though, half a century after Macoun's report. For in the prolonged drought of the 1930s, the "dirty thirties," it seemed horribly certain that Palliser had been right all along. *M.S.*❦

Provincial Archives of Alberta, H. Pollard Collection, P-459

Opening the northern Prairie near Lloydminster around 1900. Some said it was 'almost criminal to bring settlers here...'

MacEwan. "In some districts 50% of the settlers removed the barbed wire from their fences and left."

On May 14, 1896, *South Edmonton News* editor R.P. Pettipiece contributed his own explanation for farm failure and abandonment. People nowadays just weren't up to the standards of their predecessors — especially the women. "The New Woman," he wrote, lacks the fortitude and stamina of her early pioneer forebear in Ontario who "stayed at home and piled brush, aye, and sometimes took an axe and felled trees that the New Man of today would tire to look at." The New Woman demanded creature comforts, impossible in the West. "A school and church are expected at every quarter section; log houses are 'pesky things' and a cold day starts them talking of 'home'...their ideas are too swift for the times, especially when times are not good, as at present."

But western journals for the most part long sustained a note of defiant optimism. Letters, editorials and propaganda disguised as news all lauded the vast agricultural potential of the country. There was no booster more indefatigable than the *Medicine Hat Times*. It took to calling the area "the Banana Belt," on account of the mild winters. "Snow seldom lies on the ground more than a few days and is quickly removed by the warm dry Chinook wind," the paper soliloquized on December 11, 1890. "The sky is usually cloudless and the sun steeped air pure."

The following February, however, even the *Times* was confessing disillusionment: "It has been the fashion in the past to try to induce farmers to come here by telling them that the country was peculiarly adapted for their industry...But in view of the almost total failure of the grain crop last year and the partial failure the previous year, it would be almost criminal to bring settlers here to try to make a living out of straight farming."

By the mid-1890s pessimism had become common. The major breakthroughs were still to come, the major reinforcements yet to arrive.❦

CHAPTER TWO

Despite hail, drought and heartbreak, the westward trickle becomes a flow

A STARVING MOTHER AND HER CHILDREN WALKED NINE WEEKS TO FIND FOOD ❦ A FAMILY SAW ITS WHOLE YEAR'S WORK DESTROYED IN 10 MINUTES ❦ A WOMAN TRUDGED 15 MILES TO HAVE A BABY ❦ THAT WAS ALBERTA

Drought, crop failure, hail, early frosts, prairie fires, grasshoppers and a hundred other calamities took an unremitting toll on prairie agriculture through the 1890s. Nine out of 10 emigrants from Europe went to the United States, and of every 10 who did come to Canada, four left for the United States soon after. Nevertheless three major factors promised change.

One was economic. Agricultural prices all over the world ended a long decline in 1896 and were climbing. So land was in demand, and land in the United States was running out. The second was technological. Farm methods were improving. The first grain elevators had appeared. Irrigation had been tried out on the southern prairie and was working.[1] The third was purely human. No trial, it seemed, could long thwart the settlement urge. Albeit fitfully, a trickle of settlers flowed onto the farmlands of the future Alberta. From their efforts emerged stories of tragedy, heartbreak, raw courage, desperate determination and inextinguishable hope that became the foundation of the province's history.

One such story comes from the pages of the *Edmonton Bulletin*, June 8, 1899:

> A Galician woman, half starved and thoroughly exhausted, with three small children, applied at the police barracks on Tuesday for food and shelter...after having spent nine weeks on the trail. The youngest child, a baby of 12 months, she had hauled the entire distance in a primitive home-made hand cart which also contained the slim

[1] Another technological factor, and not a negligible one, was the new, cheaper sulphite process in paper manufacture. Periodicals with news of the world became available to isolated prairie homesteads. So did mail order catalogues proffering goods that promised to relieve the spartan lives of farm folk.

Provincial Archives of Alberta, 67-143-1

No. A.

DOMINION LANDS.

INTERIM HOMESTEAD RECEIPT.

Office of Dominion Lands, Edmonton District.

19th Nov 1889

I Certify that I have received from Giles Hayward Rowswell by his Agent Elisha Rowswell the sum of Ten Dollars, being the office fee for Homestead Entry for ... Quarter of Section 14 Township 52 Range 24 West of 4th Meridian, and that the said G. H. Rowswell is, in consequence of such entry and payment, vested with the rights conferred in such cases by the provisions of "The Dominion Lands Act," respecting Homestead rights.

Local Agent.

The holder of this receipt is required to give six months' notice in writing to the Commissioner of Dominion Lands, Winnipeg, before making his application for patent.

(OVER.)

Provincial Archives of Alberta, E. Brown Collection, B-727

Homesteading in the Edmonton area: the Stafford farm at Beaver Creek. It was a land indescribably beautiful, but utterly unforgiving.

> supply of rags which did duty for their covering when sleeping out at night.
>
> The other children were eleven and three years of age...Through the medium of an interpreter the woman then told that her husband had left her about three months ago to go to Calgary and get work on the railroad. They had not heard of him since and not having a cent of money or anything to eat had to get out to avoid starvation. The unfortunates were given shelter for the night in the police barracks and taken over to the immigration shed in Strathcona yesterday, where they will be cared for while the police endeavour to find the whereabouts of the missing husband.

It was upon women more than men that "the burden of Empire-making most truly rests, and she is often worn and old before her time," wrote Elizabeth B. Mitchell, a young Scotswoman who visited the West during the later frontier days, in *Western Canada Before the War*. "She has little ease — but she has great honour, she is really a queen ruling in her domain. The words suggest cant and exaggeration, but there is none."

For both men and women the new land was at once indescribably beautiful and utterly unforgiving, promising prosperity but often delivering bitter disappointment. In *The Pioneer Years 1895-1914*, newspaperman and author Barry Broadfoot chronicles experiences recounted by the settlers themselves. Here is one of them:

> A hailstorm on the prairies. It was a thing we had never experienced before, not from where we had come from, and we just couldn't believe it...It was in 1898. You could look out over that field and it was the most beautiful sight in the world. As far

Provincial Archives of Alberta, E. Brown Collection, B-255

as the eye could see that field was waving with glorious golden grain and just ready for the harvest and we were getting ready to cut it, getting ready to stack it.

It was just about noon and the men were coming in for dinner before starting on that field and during dinnertime the sky darkened and the storm clouds rolled up and there was flashes of lightning everywhere. Tremendous rolls of thunder warned us we were in for a storm, but I don't think anybody thought all that much of it. It would delay the harvest, that was all.

We took shelter when the storm rolled over us, and when we came out 10 minutes later our beautiful waving fields of wheat were a blackened, battered mess of mud and straw...Huge hailstones lying everywhere.

Our farmyard was strewn with the dead bodies of Mother's chickens, and the swollen river had swept away the geese and ducks that had been feeding on it. In our pasture were, everywhere, the bodies of our young cattle and calves that had been pounded to death by hailstones the size of walnuts.

All in 10 minutes, without knowing what was going on as we huddled in the shelter, all the work of a year had gone for nothing. Just nothing. Just battered, blackened crops in the mud, good for nothing at all.

Western and Canada Its Great Resources

The Testimony of Settlers Farmer Delegates and High Authorities.

Glenbow Archives, NA-3684-4

(Top) binding oats on the Corberan farm at Horse Hills, 1891. A year's work could be pounded out of existence by one 10-minute hail storm.

Then too, settlers often lacked the most elemental agricultural skills. In *South Edmonton Saga: A History of Strathcona County*, a descendant describes how Walter Heathcote, 41, a London library clerk, and his wife, Nan, 32, who had worked in a millinery shop, arrived at Strathcona with their four daughters, aged three to eight, to begin life on their selected homestead, 15 miles southeast of the station on the Hay Lakes Trail:

All their worldly goods including a piano were loaded onto a wagon with the girls piled on top and the trip into the wilds began. On the way to the homestead, the wagon became stuck in a slough and had to be left there all night. Nan and the girls had to be carried to dry land. Their first shelter was a lean-to type of shack made of logs and a sod roof which was woefully inadequate when it rained. Nan

Charles Ora Card fled jail and led the Mormons north

'THIS IS HOME NOW,' A MOTHER TOLD HER WEEPING FOUR-YEAR-OLD, AND THRIVING FARMS SOON VINDICATED HER CONFIDENCE

Charles Ora Card drew his companions around him. "Brethren, I have an inspiration that the Buffalo Plains is where we want to go," he said. "If the buffalo can live there, so can the Mormons."

It was October 1886; the three men were standing in British Columbia's Mission Valley, looking east towards the mountains. Members of the Church of Jesus Christ of Latter-day Saints in Utah, they had been sent by church president John Taylor to find an "asylum" for their people under "British justice."

The U.S. government had dissolved the 56-year-old Mormon church as a corporate body for practising polygamy. More than 1,300 of its members had been imprisoned, according to *A History of the Mormon Church in Canada,* published by the *Lethbridge Herald* in 1968. Children of polygamous marriages were declared illegitimate. Jailed for cohabiting with three women was Card, head of the Cache Stake (diocese) of northern Utah and son-in-law of Brigham Young, the man who led the Latter-day Saints to Utah in 1847.

But Card escaped and with two colleagues, James W. Hendricks and Isaac E.D. Zundell, went by train to Spokane Falls, Washington, to carry out the president's assignment. Trekking north, they decided the best B.C. land had already been taken. Wrote Card in his journal: "Our prayer is constantly, Father direct us by revelation that we may seek the right place."

Revelation came through an old mountaineer from Montana, who told the Mormon scouts about the Buffalo Plains of southern Alberta. Back to the east they travelled, to the Belly and St. Mary River country. Where Lee's Creek joins the St. Mary (14 miles from the U.S. border) water, coal and timber were plentiful. The nearby Blood Indian Reserve offered an opportunity for missionary work.

Glenbow Archives, NA-1759-1

Refuge seeker Card. 'Brethren, I have an inspiration that the Buffalo Plains is where we want to go.'

Zina Card, one of his wives, later recorded what followed: "With their heads bowed in reverent inspiration, they knelt before the Lord and asked his blessing to rest upon them for a decision that would meet all the requirements that were asked. His Spirit was with them in great abundance... and he, Charles O. Card, turned to them and said, 'Brethren, this is the place.'"

Mormon tradition also tells how three "Nephites," (immortal beings believed to aid Mormon missionaries) guided him to the place, and how Card dreamed of bees swarming to a hive, the saints gathering at the Lee's Creek site. However it was chosen, the town of Cardston would grow there, becoming the most widely known Mormon centre in Canada.

Card went back to Utah, narrowly escaped being jailed again, and recruited 41 settlers in eight families, curiously titling his list of them "Names of Missionaries for the Land of Desolation." In the spring of 1887 he returned to Canada, having shaved off his beard and adopted a pipe and an Irish brogue to disguise himself from American authorities along the way.

Glenbow Archives, NA-143-3

Cardston after 10 years, looking northwest. 'As settlers they are desirable; as Mormons, most undesirable.'

With him came covered wagons laden with oats, vegetables, trunks of clothing, tools, teakettles, rocking chairs and much more. Among the party was Jane Woolf Bates, 13 at the time, who later recalled evenings around the campfire: "We listened to the sweet strains of the mouth organ played by Will Rigby and Brother John. One of the favourite songs was, 'Hard Times Come Again No More.'"

One day Card, forging ahead, was heard bellowing. They found him standing over an international boundary cairn, his bald head "glistening in the sun." They had reached Canada. "The men threw up their hats and joined him, yelling: 'Three cheers for our liberty as exiles for our religion!'" Then each member of the cavalcade added a stone to the cairn.

As they approached Lee's Creek, wrote Jane Bates, "there was talk of home. 'We'll be home tonight.' 'How good it will seem to be home.' 'Just wait 'til we get home...' They arrived in the rain, the long, sodden grass laying flat, the trees drooping and dripping...Wilford, aged four, clasped his arms about mother and looking into her face, said woefully, 'Ma, you said we'd be home tonight.' 'Yes, dear,' she said, 'this is home from now on.' With quivering lips and brimming eyes he asked, 'If this is home, where's all the houses?' Mother gazed around too. Who can tell with what longing, but bravely and cheerfully, she reassured him?"

By the next morning six inches of snow had fallen. "Is this the kind of place you've brought us to?" one of the women called out to Card. "Isn't it beautiful?" he replied, and wrote in his journal: "Truly I feel that we have a faithful band of exiles here who are bound to make a mark in the land that will weigh on the credit side for the Saints."

Canadian reaction to the Mormons was mixed. Said the *Lethbridge News*: "At Lee's Creek we found a large and thriving Mormon settlement. Considering the short time that this settlement has been established, the progress made is wonderful, and stamps those who compose it as people of more than ordinary energy." The *Edmonton Bulletin*, however, was horrified: "For their religion they have taken to the desert, for it they exist...As settlers they are desirable; as Mormons most undesirable."

Such criticisms were muted somewhat after the church officially abandoned polygamy in 1890. A steady stream of Mormons was soon arriving from Utah, and they won wide praise for pioneering irrigation farming. "These people," noted the *Lethbridge News* in 1893, "are industrious and law abiding and are doing much in the way of development." The forecasts of Charles Ora Card were becoming a reality. *C.M.*❦

Provincial Archives of Alberta, E. Brown Collection, B-273

A steam-driven threshing machine in 1898. Technology was reducing the back-breaking toil and speeding the harvest. As early as the 1880s, four- and five-horse ploughs and mechanical seed drills were common.

and Walter sat up all night holding umbrellas over the girls' heads to try to keep them dry.

Water was very scarce near the lean-to. One had to go down into the tall timber, burrow among the moss and dead leaves until one had a little hole, then wait for the water to seep in, dipper it into a pail and then boil it before it could be used for drinking.

They had a few chickens in a little wired-off place next to the lean-to, and the ashes from the stove had been put there where there was no dry grass or other inflammable material. Somehow, there remained live sparks among the ashes and the chickens scratched them to the lean-to and it caught fire. Nan and the precious water saved the lean-to. With all her strength Nan dragged the big double-topped wagon out of the line of fire and thus saved all their belongings.

Eventually their log house was built. The first room was quite large, with a roof of three large peeled poplar poles laid from end to end of the house, covered by split poplar logs and tar paper. Over this was placed turf which became heavy when wet. It grew a good crop of weeds and grass, giving it a most comical appearance.

They bought a sow which was named Maud after the song, Come into the Garden, Maud. It was quite appropriate as she was always trying to get into the garden to root up the vegetables. A horse was purchased for $10 and $2 worth of butter. He became tangled in some barbed wire. He was cut very badly across the chest between the forelegs. So Nan became a surgeon, sewing up his wounds with a needle and a thread. She shuddered at every stitch but it had to be done.

During the second winter, the minister called and of course had to be invited to stay for dinner, although all they had to offer him was frozen potatoes. There was no butter as they sold all they had to buy flour. Walter could not afford warm shoes, so he tied sacks around his feet, stuffed with straw, and earned the name, 'Hayseed.'

In December, 1895, Nan walked 15 miles into Strathcona to be delivered of another daughter in the Strathcona Hotel.

The Heathcotes eventually gave up the farm and moved to Edmonton where Walter worked for the Imperial Bank until he retired 30 years later at 78.

Calamity and hardship notwithstanding, the trickle of settlers continued, emanating at first as two rival streams from Ontario and Quebec. The former assumed that the West would develop the British character to which they were accustomed, while offering new opportunities. The latter were determined that Catholic influence and the French language should prevail. The French effort failed, but not without a valiant struggle.

The first French settlement (as distinguished from Metis) was begun by two Quebec brothers named Lamoureux, who in 1872 started farming in the heavily wooded region close to the mouth of the Sturgeon River. The hamlet of Lamoureux (population 66 in 1991) perpetuates the name. More settlements followed in the 1890s, primarily through the tireless perseverance of Father Jean-Baptiste Morin, a priest who shared with the bishops of Quebec the vision of a Catholic and French-speaking West. The Alberta weekly publication *L'Ouest Canadien* reported in 1898 that 2,256 French settlers were living in and around the communities of Edmonton, St. Albert, Morinville, Fort Saskatchewan, Saint-Pierre, Beaumont, Stony Plain, Rivière-qui-Barre and Vegreville.

There the limit seemed to be reached, however. Quebeckers did not respond to the call in great numbers. Like so many others, they preferred the warmer climes of the United States. It was New Hampshire and Massachusetts, rather than the North West Territories, that lured them away.

Far more settlers arrived from Ontario, causing some to dub the territories "Rural Ontario West." They were primarily British in origin and their familiarity with the language, social structure and politics made them immediate pillars of prairie society. Doctors, lawyers and politicians tended to be ex-Ontarians like the Haultains, the Olivers and the Lougheeds.

Since Ontarians usually arrived alone or as single families, they are not so easy to trace as the group migrations. As Grant MacEwan recounts in *Harvest of Bread,* however, a few did come in groups. Methodists from London, Ontario, set down roots in Red Deer in the 1880s and were notably successful. A contingent of 298 Parry Sounders (so called because they had first tried to farm on the Canadian Shield near Georgian Bay, and derisively nicknamed "the Sorry Pounders") settled on land northeast of Edmonton in 1892, with mixed results.

The Parry Sounders had come west under the leadership of one Thomas G. Pearce, with the cheery slogan "All for the West. All aboard. If you can't get a board get a slab. But go anyway and anyhow, ready or not ready! Everyone must go to the Promised Land." The unrelenting toil soon soured some and they returned to Ontario. But others stayed, were subsequently joined by several hundred friends and relatives, and their descendants remained through the century ahead.

Meanwhile Americans began heading north in search of farmland, with Mormons forming the biggest single contingent. From Minnesota and the Dakotas came settlers of Norwegian origin who took up land north of the Parry Sounders. Bands of Scandinavians also settled near Olds and east of Wetaskiwin in 1892 and 1893, later spreading to the Stony Plain, Bardo, Camrose and Innisfail areas.

Land pressure in the Dakota territory likewise prompted three Icelanders, Olofur Olafson Espiholi, Einar Jonasson and Sigurdur Bjornson, to investigate the country north of Red Deer. Its rich soil and ample water, they concluded, would be good for dairy farming. Fifty of their compatriots followed in May 1888, and found they were right.[2]

The British bias in immigration policy, and in the Anglo-Saxon territorial establishment, was softening somewhat. These people might not be British, it was reasoned, but they were the next best thing. They were white. They were Protestant. And while they might not necessarily be Anglo-Saxon or speak English, they at least looked much the same. Now, however, came a people who dressed differently, acted differently and spoke a language not remotely like English. Albertans called them all Galicians, in reference to the Austro-Hungarian province of Galicia where most of them originated.

They were met with bald bigotry. Alberta historians Howard and Tamara Palmer, in *Peoples of Alberta: Portraits of Cultural Diversity*, explain that the intellectual justification for

Glenbow Archives, NA-3684-11

POVOZNICTVÍ.	HAULING.
Přivezte (dovnitř — odvezte ven) trochu sena.	Haul (in—out) some hay.
Přivezte (dovnitř — odvezte ven) trochu ovsa.	Haul (in—out) some oats.
Přivezte (dovnitř — odvezte ven) trochu pšenice.	Haul (in—out) some wheat.
Přivezte (dovnitř — odvezte ven) trochu slámy.	Haul (in—out) some straw.
Přivezte (dovnitř — odvezte ven) trochu dřeva.	Haul (in—out) some wood.
KRMENÍ.	**FEEDING.**
Nakrmte krávu.	Feed the cow.
Nakrmte ovce.	Feed the sheep.
Nakrmte krocany.	Feed the turkeys.
Nakrmte prasata nebo svině.	Feed the pigs or hogs.
Nakrmte koně.	Feed the horse.
Nakrmte slepice.	Feed the chickens.
Nakrmte husy.	Feed the geese.
Napojte prasata nebo svině.	Give some slop to the pigs or hogs.

4

Glenbow Archives, NA-3684-12

CPR immigrant Czech phrase book. The Anglo establishment credited the fertility of the land, not the fibre of the east Europeans.

[2] With a second contingent of Icelanders from northern Dakota in 1899, there arrived a man who would exert great influence among Alberta's Icelandic settlers. Stephan Gudmundson Stephansson, political radical and theological liberal, was most of all celebrated for his Norse poetry. He was posthumously declared poet laureate of Iceland (1927), and the Stephansson home in Markerville was declared a provincial historic site.

this was provided by the ideology currently embraced by much of the intelligentsia. It was called at the time "Social Darwinism." The next century, after its implications became clearer, would come to call it racism, or in one of its more virulent forms, Nazism.

Charles Darwin had published his theory of natural selection in 1859, contending that the various species of plants and animals came about through "survival of the fittest." Individuals with superior qualities survived and reproduced; the less fit did neither. Thus a species either gradually adapted and throve, or did not and became extinct. Popular philosophers, notably Herbert Spencer, enthusiastically applied the same concept to all manner of human development. The different human races must represent successive stages of development, they argued: the Negro the most primitive; the Mongolian (including Asians and American Indians) the next higher level; the Caucasian (British, Germans and Scandinavians) highest of all.[3]

Entrenched in Canadian immigration policy, this notion meant that British settlers were preferred, followed by American, Scandinavian and German. Eastern Europeans — Ukrainians, Poles, Romanians, Slovenians, Ruthenians — were contemptuously lumped together as Galicians. Subscribers to Social Darwinism did not want them at all. Particular disdain fell upon Russian Jews. These "are a people whose filthy habits and usurious character have made them detested in the country from which they come...the very dregs of the most ignorant and barbarous country in Europe," declared the *Lethbridge News* in July 1893.

Two facts, however, gradually forced official policy to yield. One was that too few Britons could stand the tough conditions of prairie pioneering, the other that most so-called Galicians could. Some of the Galicians who landed in the future Alberta were in fact Germans, who had migrated to Galicia at the invitation of Catherine the Great of Russia. When Galicia was appended to the Austro-Hungarian empire they found themselves being persecuted. Moving to Canada, most settled in Assiniboia, but in 1889 a few tackled the unbroken and arid Prairie near Medicine Hat.

[3] Both Darwin's theory of evolution and its supposed social ramifications clashed directly with Christian doctrine. Theologians contended that species differ from each other because God designed them so in the first place, as recounted in the Old Testament, not because of survival of the fittest. As for human racial superiority, St. Paul had asserted (in his *Letter to the Colossians*, for example) that among Christians there is "neither Jew nor Greek, Barbarian nor Scythian."

Rev. Brick's astonishing wheat won world acclaim

Wheat-growing in Alberta before the turn of the century was far from being an unqualified disaster. Although the renowned Red Fife matured too late to be reliable, it could produce notable results when conditions were right. One such instance came in Peace River in 1893.

The Reverend John Gough Brick began a small farm in 1887 to help support his remote Anglican mission at Shaftesbury, between Dunvegan and Peace River Crossing. The operation was decidedly primitive. Seed had to be brought in by trail wagon, then riverboat and finally canoe. Brick harvested wheat with a scythe and threshed it with a flail on the floor of his church.

One bushel of seed, however, produced 72 bushels in 1892. Hearing about the upcoming World's Fair at Chicago, Brick decided to send a sample south, to show what could be done in the Peace country. Son Thomas Allen Brick transported it to Edmonton (then a 10-day trip). Thence, noted the *Edmonton Bulletin*, it was "to be forwarded to the Indian Commission for exhibition at the World's Fair."

Glenbow Archives, NA-3858-1

Farmer Brick. He threshed on the church floor.

Subsequently a story developed that it won the world wheat championship that year, but Alberta historian Hugh A. Dempsey says this is a myth. He checked in 1954 with the U.S. Archives where all the World's Fair papers are preserved, and no mention of any Brick entry could be found in the competition records.

He concludes that it was an exhibit, not a competition entry, and the story an exaggeration based on an 1893 *Bulletin* report from the fair: "The single exhibit that caused most astonishment was a globe of Red Fife wheat grown in the Peace River district, 680 miles north of the United States frontier." Not so spectacular as a world championship, of course — but not so bad either. *M.S.*❦

Stories that the German settlers were starving were investigated and discounted by the North-West Mounted Police. Reported the *Medicine Hat Times*: "Inspector Davison speaks highly of the thrift displayed by these settlers in the construction of good houses and stables. The reports of destitution among them, he found to be greatly exaggerated. Two heads of families who, while lost on the prairie had their feet and hands frozen, are unable to work, but both they and their families are being well cared for by neighbours."

All was far from well with them, however. After two years of steady drought, the Germans picked up and moved to new and fertile land around Stony Plain, Horse Hills and the area east of Fort Saskatchewan. There they established Josephburg, 22 miles northeast of Edmonton, named for their home town in Galicia, and their determined efforts were rewarded.

Provincial Archives of Alberta, A-11,151

'Galician' promoter John Pylypow at Lamont with early Ukrainian arrivals in 1894. 'We are not yet prepared to admit that they are a desirable class,' grumbled Strathcona's Plaindealer.

Their non-German countrymen were watching their progress. Ukrainian Ivan Pylypow had been a schoolmate in Galicia of John Krebs, one of the Josephburg settlers. When Pylypow and his companion Wasyl Eleniak came to investigate Canada's North West in 1891, they naturally sought out their German-speaking friends. Difficulties notwithstanding, they were impressed by what they found and more Ukrainians began to arrive.[4]

The *Alberta Plaindealer*, Strathcona's weekly, reacted with suspicious approval, regretting of course that they were not British, and attributing their success to the merits of the land rather than the settlers: "To a person who saw those people step from the train in South Edmonton last spring it seems almost incredible that their condition is so encouraging. It speaks volumes for Northern Alberta as a poor man's country and indicates the probabilities of success are in almost any man's favour...It proves beyond a shadow of a doubt that these people are industrious. We are not yet, however, prepared to admit that they are a desirable class of settlers or that the government has done right in bringing them in. If such poor settlers can do well what may not well-to-do British or American immigrants do?"

A rather condescending wonderment remained the dominant note when the *Calgary Albertan* reported:

> A mixed party of Romanian and Bulgarian immigrants excited a great deal of comment, by their curious clothing and footgear, at the CPR depot yesterday afternoon and evening. The party, which numbers about twenty, are on their way to Edmonton. While waiting for the train this morning, they encamped at one of the old waiting rooms at the depot.
>
> In appearance they are very dark, and particularly the children possess more than their share of good looks. All wore big earrings, the women and the girls excelling in this particular, and also in the matter of varicoloured clothing. Bright shawls draped over one shoulder formed a part of everybody's outfit. The men all wore top-boots and even the small boys of the party had gaily coloured trousers tucked into the tops of small top-boots, reaching midway between the knee and ankle.
>
> None of the party can speak English, but they were apparently enjoying themselves and in the best of spirits, when visited by an Albertan reporter and a CPR policeman. The new arrivals are of exceptionally fine physique, and altogether appear to be a desirable class of immigrants.

One newcomer group that fared especially badly is described by James MacGregor in

[4] An enthusiastic booster of Ukrainian immigration to the West was Galician agricultural expert Joseph Oleskiw. He toured Canada in 1895 and produced two books on western immigration prospects. Dr. Oleskiw also personally financed an incentive plan for his countrymen from 1895 to 1900. Adding to the attraction of free homestead land, he offered $5 to every adult of the farming class who decided to go to western Canada.

A History of Alberta. This was a little band of Russian Jews who, likely sponsored by the Young Men's Hebrew Benevolent Society of Montreal, were recruited from the Chicago slums and brought to Canada's West. Deposited at Ghostpine Lake near Red Deer in the summer of 1893 with a few axes, shovels and a pair of horses, they were left to farm or fail.

The amazing thing is that these inexperienced city-dwellers managed to survive at all in the winter that followed. They lived in caves dug in a hillside and snared rabbits for food. When one of the two workhorses died, some of the younger men sought work in Red Deer. One returned in triumph with some cash, supplies and a .22 rifle for partridge hunting. During the joyous but chaotic reception of the young hero, however, the new gun — which was being passed around for excited inspection — went off accidentally and killed the other horse. The little party had scattered by the following year.

So did many other settlers. "In driving about," observed Elizabeth Mitchell, "one could not help seeing these sinister weed-grown abandoned farms." Nevertheless, by the

The two-generation quest of the Saunders family

IT TOOK 19 YEARS, BUT RED FIFE AND RED CALCUTTA COMBINED TO BEAT THE FROST

Red Fife wheat, miraculous though it had been in Ontario, was proving a bitter disappointment in the West. It needed 120 days to ripen, leaving it frequently vulnerable to killer prairie frosts. Thus a concentrated search began for an equally good wheat variety that would mature more quickly. This would not be found until the first decade of the next century — but then it would transform prairie agriculture.

William Saunders, a London, Ontario pharmacist and plant breeder, had already attracted the attention of the dominion government with his promising varieties of raspberries, gooseberries, currants and grapes. His consequent government-commissioned study of the American experimental farm system had led to the creation of a similar one in Canada, with farms at Ottawa; Nappan, Nova Scotia; Brandon, Manitoba; Indian Head, Saskatchewan; and Agassiz, British Columbia. Appointed director of them all, Saunders tackled the western need for an early-maturing wheat variety in 1888.

He and his two sons, Dr. Charles E. Saunders and A.P. (Percy) Saunders all went to work on the project. Seeking to retain Red Fife's strength, colour and yield as well, they concentrated on hybridizing Red Fife with Russian and Asian varieties. By 1892, Percy tested the results on the prairie experimental farms. The wheat matured early all right, but the quality wasn't there.

For another decade new varieties were planted, harvested and the best of their progeny replanted the next season. Finally in 1904 son Charles, by then appointed "dominion cerealist," selected the best prospect, a cross made at the Agassiz farm between Red Fife and an Indian wheat, Hard Red Calcutta.

Charles Saunders.

Provincial Archives of Alberta, E. Brown Collection, B-605

He planted the kernels of a single head and coaxed 12 plants to maturity. By 1906 he had tested more than 100 variations of this cross. In his most curious test of quality, he chewed a dozen kernels for five minutes, carefully examining the whitish goo that resulted to assess its elasticity. The more elastic the goo, he would smile, the bigger the loaf of bread it would produce.

With 40 precious pounds of seed ready for field testing in 1907, Charles Saunders sent 23 pounds to Indian Head. Horrifyingly, the sack of seed was stolen. Frantic farm officials posted notices, stressing its vital importance to western agriculture. Next day the all-important sack mysteriously reappeared.

In its first season wheat grown from this seed survived a frost that destroyed all other species at Indian Head. It had the unmistakable short, plump kernels of Red Fife, but matured more than a week earlier, a week that would be worth billions to the West. Furthermore, its flour was the desired cream colour and its yields up to 20% greater than Red Fife. Within 10 years it was seeded on thousands of prairie farms and had won first prize at the New York World's Fair. The Saunders brothers called it Marquis. In the entire history of the West, no development would matter more. *M.S.*❦

late 1890s it was becoming equally evident that many settlements would survive, and that circumstances were turning in their favour.

On the southern prairie, irrigation was believed to be the answer, although the dominion government seemed in no great rush to foster it. The *Lethbridge News* blamed this negligence on the death of the great prime minister who had created Canada. On October 5, 1893, it wrote:

> The government with that pertinacious determination against innovation which has characterized their every act since the death of Sir John Macdonald, will steadily decline to move in the matter of irrigation. Liberal offers of land have already been made to them for the irrigation of this district but every proposal or suggestion has been persistently rejected...For ourselves, disgusted as we are with the apathy and lack of interest displayed by the government in regard to North-West affairs, we have ceased to hope for irrigation as long as the government of Sir John Thompson remains in power.

The next year, however, Ottawa did pass the North West Irrigation Act, giving the Crown control over this crucial resource. Diversion of surface waters without a licence became illegal. Charters were granted to private companies, beginning with the Macleod Irrigation Company. By 1898 some 100,000 acres were under irrigation. The Canadian Pacific became a major participant. It swapped some of its scattered property along the main line for large parcels of farmland west of Medicine Hat, which the Bassano dam was eventually built to service.

Other notable developments were also under way. Before very long the new Marquis wheat variety would offset the long winter of the northern Prairies. Four- and five-horse ploughs and mechanical seed drills were common in the 1880s. "Self-binding harvesters" and steam threshers were making their first appearance.

Finally, as early as 1881, there appeared at Gretna, Manitoba, a strange tall building that would spare farmers the back-breaking job of hoisting the 650 bags of wheat needed to fill a railway car. It contained equipment that would lift the grain for them, then drop it into the car below. The number of these towers more than quintupled, from 90 to 454, in the century's last decade. The grain elevator had arrived on the western landscape.

Yet it was on the political front that the greatest strides would be made. Already the Crow's Nest freight rate agreement had terminated what farmers saw as outright robbery by the railways. Now it was the elevator companies that must be somehow checked. Moreover, there was still a terrible need for people. Too many farms had been abandoned; too much farmland had never been occupied.

Thus it was that in 1896, the front line of prairie development shifted to Ottawa. One convulsive election had swept the Tories from office, introducing the era of Sir Wilfrid Laurier and with him the man who would spectacularly change Alberta and the West. His name was Clifford Sifton. Under his direction the immigration gates would open wide, and the trickle would become a torrent.❦

A turn of the century threshing crew at lunch. Despite reversals, by 1900 there were 454 grain elevators across the Prairies.

Provincial Archives of Alberta, E. Brown Collection, B-289

Provincial Archives of Alberta, E. Brown Collection, B-1544

North and south, coal was immediately useful, and a viable commercial proposition. Workmen at Milner's Coal Mine, one of many in the Edmonton area, posed for a pioneer photographer at the turn of the century.

The oil search goes back to '94, coal and gold are early winners

A GAS FIND ON THE ATHABASCA WAS LEFT BLOWING FOR YEARS ❦ A CIVIL WAR VETERAN'S MODEST COAL MINE LED TO LETHBRIDGE ❦ KLONDIKERS SET OFF A SHORT-LIVED GOLD RUSH IN EDMONTON

The lure of wealth and adventure to be gained from the new great West began with fur and evolved rapidly into cattle and grain. From the beginning, however, some few sought their fortunes elsewhere — in oil, gas, coal and, most particularly, gold. Others thought the gold fever was madness, as indeed it would turn out to be.

The Athabasca tar sands, the last mineral resource to be developed, was the first to be discovered. Fur trader Peter Pond noted the oil sands in the lower Athabasca valley in 1788. Geologist George Dawson made a technical study of them 90 years later. In 1893, after a dominion geological survey also mentioned oil in the territorial District of Athabaska, which lay north of the District of Alberta, the dominion government allotted $7,000 to drill three experimental holes.

Glenbow Archives, NA-302-11

Dominion government attempts to drill for Alberta oil in the 19th century were not a great success. The second well, at Pelican Portage, produced natural gas in a spectacular blow-out and then burned for years. The third, 70 miles east of Edmonton, pictured here in 1898, was abandoned at 1,870 feet.

Drilling equipment arrived in Edmonton the following summer from Petrolia, Ontario, and was wagoned 80 miles north over the old portage trail to the former Fort Assiniboine, now called Athabasca Landing. Two miles upstream, in September 1894, the drillers hit natural gas 400 feet down. The presence of gas was taken to be evidence that oil was there too. Dr. Alfred Selwyn, retiring director of the Geological Survey of Canada, waxed eloquent on the well's possibilities. "If oil is found in large quantities, as there is every reason to expect, Canada will own the largest oil fields in the world, and we will be able to supply oil from Athabaska to Manitoba, British Columbia and all the Pacific states of the Union and to the islands of the Pacific. The greatest market for oil not yet exploited is Asia, and if we have the oil in Athabaska it can be exported from there to the millions of Asia cheaper than from any other oil field."

No sooner had he made this prophecy than fortune turned. In October, with drilling at 1,000 feet, the bit struck quicksand and exploration stopped for the winter. Work continued the next spring, but at 1,770 feet the drillers could bore no further and the well was abandoned. Although some of Selwyn's optimism about Athabasca oil would one day be vindicated, he would not live to see it. He died in 1902.

The equipment then made the hazardous passage by barge 150 miles down the raging Athabasca to Pelican Portage, where drilling began in the summer of 1897. That fall they hit natural gas at 820 feet. The chief engineer reported walnut-sized nodules of iron pyrite blown out at great velocity "like bullets from a rifle." The gas field "blew every drop of water out of the bore, the roar of gas could be heard for three miles or more. Soon it was completely dry and the gas was blowing a cloud of dust 50 feet into the air...It was impossible to do anything with the bore that day, so we were forced to let it stand just as it was." Next day the crew tried to resume drilling but found that water couldn't be put down the well because of the strong gas flow. Drilling stopped for the winter; the gas was left to blow off.

As soon as the drillers cleaned out the hole in the spring of 1898 the gas flow increased in power. Clouds of sand and gravel blew higher than the derrick. Thus drilling ceased at 837 feet. The well eventually caught fire and burned for years before it was finally capped, serving in that time as a preferred Indian winter campsite. A third hole, at Victoria Mission, about 70 miles east of Edmonton, proved even less satisfactory. The paddlewheeler *Northwest* moved gear to the site and drilling went on until 1899. Then the well was abandoned at 1,870 feet, just before the North Saskatchewan River flooded and inundated the boiler and some of the equipment. The search for oil was then, for the time being, called off.

In the south natural gas was common, so common at Medicine Hat that some householders drilled private wells to heat their houses. The prime search in the south was for water, needed by Canadian Pacific locomotives as they crossed the Prairies. The CPR first struck gas in 1883 while searching for water near the siding of Cassils. This immediately prompted Minnesota and Manitoba speculators to form the Winnipeg and Northwest Petroleum Co. — the future oil province's first oil company. They took out leases north of Medicine Hat, but likely never drilled a hole. In 1885 the company folded, claiming to have been driven off the site by hostile Indians. But natural gas at a depth of 650 feet would later become a boon to local industries.

A promising oil discovery was made in the Pincher Creek-Waterton Park area in 1889, when a local homesteader began selling oil he skimmed off a pool on Cameron Creek. A number of claims were filed; Imperial Oil sent an agent to have a look. Imperial wasn't interested but local residents were, and in 1890 they formed the Alberta Petroleum and Development Co., with offices in Pincher Creek. Within a year a derrick had been built, but the drillers struck water only 240 feet down and the boom was over. Speculation revived in 1898, the village of Oil City was established in Waterton Park at the turn of the century, and grandiose claims of dramatic strikes were made. The area did produce oil, too, but never in commercial quantities.

Coal, on the other hand, had a more immediate commercial success. In the late 1850s, John

An industrious gold-seeker dumps North Saskatchewan River gravel into the locally manufactured sluice arrangement called a 'grizzly.' Other Edmontonians found their gold by acting as outfitters to Klondike-bound hopefuls.

Palliser's exploratory expedition had drawn attention to its abundance. For decades Fort Edmonton blacksmiths had pulled coal out of the river banks for their forges. Settlers had gopher-holed it out all along the North Saskatchewan. Commercial coal mining began at Edmonton in 1880 when businessman Donald Ross sank a shaft into the side of McDougall Hill. By 1900 mines were operating at Beverly, seven miles downstream from the fort.

Meanwhile coal led to the development of an entire new town in the south. Nicholas Sheran was an Irish adventurer and Civil War veteran who drifted from Montana to Canada around 1874, looking for gold. He found coal instead, at the junction of the Oldman and St. Mary rivers, a locale known to the Blackfoot as the "place of the black rocks." Later, deciding that site unprofitable, he selected a new one a few miles away, prosaically naming it Coal Banks. From there, Sheran shipped coal down the Whoop-up Trail to Fort Benton on the Missouri, and to the new North-West Mounted Police post at Fort Macleod.

Sheran's modestly successful enterprise attracted big-money attention after a while. In 1882 Elliott Torrance Galt, son of the Montreal financier and father of Confederation Sir Alexander Galt, organized the North Western Coal and Navigation Company. He included as a shareholder a man who would leave his name on the map of Alberta, William Lethbridge. Galt knew that the CPR's demand for coal would make large-scale mining profitable; excess production could find other markets. Moreover the coal could reach the CPR's main line by steamer and barge down the Oldman River.

In July 1883, the hull of the 173-foot *Baroness* was built at Coal Banks (by now renamed Lethbridge), floated down to Medicine Hat and fitted out as a steam sternwheeler with equipment brought in on the newly arrived CPR. She began plying the Oldman and South Saskatchewan, but the plying went badly. Sandbars in both rivers proved so obstructive that only 200 tons of coal reached the railway in the first season. Two more vessels were acquired in 1884, the 120-foot sternwheeler *Alberta* and the 35-foot tug *Minnow*. The company's expanded fleet, three boats and 25 barges, delivered 10,000 tons that year, but it still wasn't enough. Low river levels allowed them to operate for one month only; another method of transport had to be found.

The following year the company began building a narrow-gauge railway that weaved around the rolling hills for 107 miles from Lethbridge to Dunmore station, just east of Medicine Hat. The line did the job, although the spectacle of its careering cars and the heaves and plunges of its roadbed caused it to be dubbed the Turkey Track. The CPR leased the route in 1893, converted it to standard gauge, and bought it outright in 1897.

The quest for gold had meanwhile begun in the north. Some prospectors journeyed home from the Fraser River rush of 1858 and the Cariboo rush (1860 to 1866) by way of Fort Edmonton. One of these was Tom Clover,[1] who arrived in 1860 and stayed to prospect the North Saskatchewan upstream to Rocky Mountain House. There he found gold in paying quantities, and word of gold in prairie rivers quickly spread. Some 60 miners, bound for the Cariboo in 1862, heard of Clover's fortune and stayed to work the North Saskatchewan. Although the river never yielded a bonanza, it was enough to spur prospectors for the next half-century.

Farther south, gold discoveries in Montana and Idaho convinced prospectors that the mineral would also be found on the British side of the border. This idea seemed to be confirmed in 1862, when a white man living with the Blackfoot claimed he had discovered gold and would share his secret with anybody who wished to join him. A party was organized to that end, but neither the elusive white Indian nor his lode was ever found. Later that year a number of prospectors were killed by Indians near southern Alberta's Porcupine Hills. Such discouragements notwithstanding, the search for gold continued. "At Bow River there are now some 300 miners, and small parties are scattered here and there," a Winnipeg newspaper reported in 1864.

Although it never unearthed any great quantity of the precious metal, the search gave Alberta one of its genuine legends: the saga of the mysterious Lost Lemon Mine. According to one version of the tale, two partners named Blackjack and Lemon were returning from the Edmonton diggings in 1870 when they discovered a rich lode in the mountains west of High River. In an argument as to whether they should camp there for the winter, Lemon killed his partner with an axe and fled to the Tobacco Plains in Montana. But the experience left him half-crazed; when he tried to take a party back to his find the following spring, he became violently insane.

Many have since searched for the Lost Lemon. For years King Bearspaw, a Stoney Indian who lived in the region, made a comfortable living guiding hopeful prospectors every summer. As recently as 1983 an Ontario couple claimed they had found the lode. They established Lost Lemon Mine Ltd. to raise capital. In 1989 an Edmonton geological technician disclosed plans to extract gold from the volcanic rock of the Crow's Nest Pass. But as of 1991 no fortune had been made from southern Alberta gold discoveries.

The Edmonton area also had its share of gold stories. The *Edmonton Bulletin* of June 6, 1895, recapitulated 30 years of North Saskatchewan mining and confidently proclaimed: "More gold is being taken out of the river this season than ever before." Again in 1897 the *Bulletin* glowed: "Already the rush has commenced, and impatient miners and prospectors, local experts, wandering fortune seekers and businessmen not waiting for the ice to leave the river, have staked claims all along the banks from high to low water mark, all seeking to secure a share whose name is a magnet to millions."

Three weeks later came the even bigger news of the Klondike strike, and other enterprising Edmontonians saw their town as lying virtually on the Klondike's doorstep. Standing in the way was about 1,200 miles of almost impenetrable geography, of course, but that did not inhibit the *Alberta Plaindealer*. "We firmly believe," the paper affirmed, "that the routes through here are the cheapest, easiest and best available." Besides, the *Plaindealer* suggested on October 14, 1897, there is also gold "somewhere about the head waters of the Peace." And the Edmontons (Old and New) "are the outfitting points for any part of the Peace river country." The newspaper clinched its case with the testimonial of one William Cust, who had dug gold in the Peace country 35 years before "and now enjoys the fruits of his toil in early life on his magnificent farm near St. Albert."

Soon the North Saskatchewan flats blossomed with tents and the streets were clogged with northbound sleds. Almost all this activity was in vain, however. More than 1,500 men and nine women headed through Edmonton for the Klondike. About 700 made it, most of them by way of the Mackenzie River. Seventy perished. Three found gold. By late 1898, unpleasant truths had to be faced. The North Saskatchewan was no more a bonanza gold river than Edmonton was a shortcut to the Klondike. In a letter to the *Alberta Plaindealer*, F.H. Herbert of south Edmonton summed up the reality. "It seems to me that hard persistent work does not count for anything here. It seems to be just pure luck."

But gold fever did one thing for Edmontonians. It revived their hopes. Things had gone badly for their town in the closing decades of the 19th century, but perhaps its fortunes would improve in the 20th. Indeed they would, and far more rapidly than even the most chronic gold optimist would have dared to imagine. *Terry Johnson*❦

[1] The Edmonton district of Clover Bar commemorates prospector Tom Clover.

Prime Minister John A. Macdonald and Lady Macdonald on a CPR tour of the West in 1886, at Stave River near Vancouver
Glenbow Archives, NA-4967-132

Section Eight

The Politicians

Chapters by George Koch
Sidebars by Greg Heaton and Ted Byfield

Chapter One

Canada buys itself a vast colony without knowing how to govern it

THE AMERICAN TERRITORIES WERE GIVEN A FORMULA FOR STATEHOOD BUT CANADIAN POLICY CONSIDERED ONLY THE FOUNDING PROVINCES; THE INTERESTS OF THE AREA TO BE GOVERNED WERE NOT DISCUSSED

The February 28, 1891 cover of Prairie Illustrated. *From the 1860s onward both Ottawa and westerners were acutely conscious that the West had other options.*

The visionaries who achieved Confederation in 1867 wanted to turn Canada into a great continental power. They had one prize in their sights: British Columbia. But between it and the four original Canadian provinces, Ontario, Quebec, New Brunswick and Nova Scotia, lay the vast Hudson's Bay Company territory of Rupert's Land. To the romantic soldier-geographer William Butler it was "the Great Lone Land." Nearly everything about it was unknown: its physical limits and content; its agricultural and resource potential; and most important, what obstacles it might present to railway construction and therefore to settlement. To Canadians, even its peoples were largely unknown.

Rupert's Land, says George F.G. Stanley,[1] one of its foremost historians, "was without government of any form." It derived its legitimacy from the British Crown under the Hudson's Bay Company's Charter of 1670, as well as the 1821 and 1838 Licences to Govern the Indian Territory. It functioned as a gargantuan trading concession, however, not as a real political jurisdiction. In contrast to most British possessions, Rupert's Land was devoid of a British military or civilian presence. And except for the Metis colonies in the Red River and Assiniboine River valleys, there were only tiny, scattered settlements of Hudson's Bay employees and their families, along with a few missions serving the Indians of the area.

Prime Minister John A. Macdonald had little vision for the West beyond a determination to acquire it. He and the other framers of Confederation knew that if they were to fulfil their ambition to create a sea-to-sea Canada, then British Columbia must become Canadian. So, therefore, must that enormous gap between. Historian Lewis H. Thomas[2] calls this expansion to the Pacific "one of the important objectives of the Fathers of Confederation." The Quebec Resolutions of 1864, a key

1 George F. G. Stanley was professor of Canadian Studies at Mount Allison University in Sackville, New Brunswick, and a lieutenant-governor of New Brunswick. *The Birth of Western Canada*, published in 1936, is considered the first example of Canadian history from a western perspective.

2 Lewis Herbert Thomas was professor of history at the University of Alberta, and provincial archivist of Saskatchewan before that. In *The Struggle for Responsible Government in the North-West Territories 1870-1897* he presents a complete and authoritative account of the early years of prairie government.

precursor to Confederation, declared the West's indispensability to the new country. The resolutions held that its acquisition "was of the greatest importance, not to the territories but to the confederated provinces," writes C.C. Lingard.[3]

Macdonald's goals were commercial rather than philosophic, concludes W.L. Morton.[4] He was not aiming to create a state founded on principles of justice and liberty, but to open the interior to commercial exploitation for the benefit of the East. While it was clear Canada needed the territories, Lingard observes, it was not at all clear that the territories needed Canada. For them, Thomas says, Confederation was a mixed blessing. What might be in the best interests of the West was nowhere discussed by Canadian politicians, however. "A strong government, in the view of the Conservative administration," Thomas writes, "meant a system in which the territorial government would not be permitted to obstruct federal authority and policy." To the people in the territories, this sounded as though they were about to become Canada's colony. Their fear would be realized, and for many years.

Moreover, they had other options. They could become, like British Columbia, a Crown colony. They could remain under HBC control. They could join the United States. The last possibility was far from hypothetical. Settlement south of the border was exploding. From 1849 to 1860, the white population of the Minnesota Territory vaulted from fewer than 5,000 to 172,000. Already the Union Pacific spanned the United States and the Northern Pacific was pushing into the American Northwest. Top congressional leaders were expansionists, as was President Ulysses S. Grant, victor of the Civil War.

Underlining the West's vulnerability to a take-over were the U.S. whisky traders and other interlopers, who were encroaching into British territory from outposts along the Missouri River. Even more problematic were the battles between the Indians and U.S. cavalry. In 1870, American troops massacred 170 Peigans not far from the border, and Indians began fleeing into Canada. That was only the beginning of a long series of Indian wars. Inter-tribal strife was rampant in the Canadian territories. For example, a large Cree force attacked a Blackfoot encampment on the Oldman River, also in 1870. The Blackfoot repulsed the poorly armed Cree, killing up to 300. Ottawa had no means of preventing such chaos nor of securing its southern prairie border.

Lack of any coherent western policy is evidenced in Section 146 of the British North America Act itself, Canada's constitution. Written in Britain, but heavily influenced by the "founding fathers" in Canada, it gave Ottawa power to annex the North West "on terms to be arranged." What terms? Nobody had thought to say, because nobody had thought about it.

There was a noteworthy precedent to draw on, but Macdonald ignored it. When the new nation known as the United States of America decided to push beyond the Appalachian Mountains into the area that was called the Old Northwest, the lands south of the Great Lakes, west of the Ohio River and east of the Mississippi, it articulated a complete constitutional plan before the first settler headed west. As early as 1780, Congress resolved that major new lands should be "formed into distinct republican States," with "the same rights of sovereignty, freedom and independence" as the original 13.

A committee headed by Thomas Jefferson formulated the Northwest Ordinance, stipulating that the area should be surveyed, then divided into three to five territories. These would be ruled by federally appointed governors, but have their own constitutions. Once a territory counted 5,000 men of voting age, it could elect a legislature and send a non-voting delegate to Congress. When voting-age males numbered 60,000, the territory automatically became a state, a status making it instantly equal with other states in the powerful U.S. Senate.

Thus statehood, and settlers' political rights, were set out in advance and not subject to the whim of a given president. The Northwest Ordinance, which U.S. historian Earl Pomeroy considers "less a unit of control than a framework for self-government," became the basis for settlement of the whole western United States. Such a formula for new Canadian territories was apparently not seriously considered in Ottawa.

Macdonald's approach was based entirely on what was good for the East, and for Conservative

Glenbow Archives, NA-1375-1

Prime Minister Macdonald. A business proposition.

[3] C.C. Lingard, a University of Toronto historian who received his doctorate from the University of Chicago, is best remembered for *Territorial Government in Canada*, his detailed study of Frederick Haultain's nine-year battle with Wilfrid Laurier for the provincehood of the Prairies beyond Manitoba.

[4] W.L. Morton, professor of history at the University of Manitoba, chairman of the history department at Trent University in Peterborough, Ontario, and chancellor at Trent, was the son of William Morton, who served 31 years as a Liberal-Progressive MLA in Manitoba. W.L. Morton further developed what Stanley had begun: a western school of Canadian history. His works include: *The Progressive Party in Canada*, a history of the Progressive movement; the authoritative *The Kingdom of Canada*; *Manitoba: A History*; and "Clio in Canada," an essay which argues that the basic structure of Canada is exploitative.

Glenbow Archives, NA-644-30

The legendary 1886 'wet' council. Front row (from left): Mayor George Murdoch; treasurer C. Sparrow; clerk T.T.A. Boys. Back row: S.J. Hogg; assessor J. Campbell; solicitor H. Bleeker; Dr. N.J. Lindsay; J.H. Millward; S.J. Clarke; Chief J.S. Ingram; collector J.S. Douglas; I.S. Freeze. 'You're out!' said the judge.

A 'dry' judge fired Calgary's council and jailed a publisher

But the city's determined drinkers fought back furiously until there were two rival councils in office

Prohibition on the Prairies began by decree of the North West Territories Act in 1875, and ended when the territorial legislature gained jurisdiction over the liquor trade in 1891 and started licensing saloons in 1892. In that 17-year interval, however, the region was far from dry. Whisky still flowed north across the U.S. border. Liquor could also be imported from the East by means of a special permit that could be extended ad infinitum. Booze control occupied a great deal of police time, and there are even stories of drunken rowdiness in various NWMP barracks. It was also political dynamite, as Judge Jeremiah Travis painfully discovered in Calgary.

Travis was appointed as a law-and-order judge in 1885 to "dry out" the town, and he was determined to do it. Thus he has gone down in local lore as the man who jailed a town councillor and the court clerk, and fired the mayor and his entire council — all for obstructing his efforts to suppress illegal saloons.

In pre-Travis days, Mayor George Murdoch, a harness maker and a "wet" sympathizer, had also functioned as justice of the peace. Murdoch had not tried to dry out the town. His own sympathies aside, he regarded full enforcement of the territorial liquor law as simply hopeless anyhow. An 1884 entry in his journal explains: "[Some] say I wink at the whiskie business. Plenty to do without taking on myself to turn Policeman."

Quentin Cayley, publisher of the *Calgary Herald* and also court clerk, predicted trouble from the Travis appointment. "He will come here a totally inexperienced man, a stranger to the country, its people, its laws and customs," he wrote. "Consequently he will labour under a great disadvantage." Cayley had it right. The tall, gaunt Scot from New Brunswick arrived in September. Two months later he jailed town councillor S.J. Clarke for interfering when the Mounties tried to search his illegal saloon.

But a crowd had gathered, declared themselves a public meeting, and passed a resolution denouncing the jailing. The police had been in plain clothes and carried neither badge nor warrant, they complained. (This was allowed by the act, which bestowed such immense powers on the Mounties that they did not always use them.) The citizens also objected to the fact that the act allowed for no appeal. Councillor Clarke was a crusader, not a criminal, they said; he was establishing a "test case." They collected $500 and dispatched Mayor Murdoch to Ottawa to get the prohibition law repealed.

Jeremiah Travis rose to the challenge. He wrote to the

lawyer who had advised the crowd, threatening a contempt-of-court citation. Cayley roared back in the *Herald*. Travis was a temperance preacher not a judge, he stormed, who was defending himself more than the town. So Travis fired Cayley as court clerk. Given reason: drunk on the job.

Moreover, Judge Travis warned him, just one more word in the *Herald* and he'd be up for contempt as well. The newspaper answered a week later with the provocative headline: "Is This Contempt of Court?" Cayley had dug out an old Travis indictment of the appeal courts back east which lambasted them for "ignorance — plain, stupid, stolid ignorance."

Cayley was cited for contempt, found guilty, fined $200 and ordered to print an apology. He refused, was fined another $200 and jailed for three months. Travis also barred his lawyer from appearing for him again. So Cayley marched to jail, escorted by a brass band and cheering supporters who stopped at all the illegal bars along the way.

By then Travis was a national issue, cited by the eastern press as an example of judicial tyranny. Prime Minister John A. Macdonald is said to have urged him in a telegram to "Let the little beggar go!" But it was the Justice minister who ultimately ordered Cayley's release.

The booze issue now consumed Calgary municipal politics. Mayor Murdoch and the wets were all returned in the 1886 election, but Travis charged that the voters' list had been tampered with. He fined Murdoch, ordered his harness shop auctioned off to pay his fine and declared runner-up James Reilly and his dry faction the true winners.

Chaos ensued. The sheriff refused to carry out the auction order. Town employees, all Murdoch appointees, hid the town seal and council records so Reilly couldn't govern. Reilly made up his own seal. His council and Murdoch's began governing simultaneously, each passing bylaws. The lieutenant-governor stepped in, nullified both councils, and called a new election.

The next year a royal commission was struck to investigate the anarchy in Calgary. It concluded that Travis had no authority to convict Cayley for his published comments or to disqualify the Murdoch election. Travis, already under suspension, was removed from the bench and went back east.

Murdoch and Reilly both lost in the next election. Murdoch quit politics; Reilly was elected mayor in 1899. As for Travis, he returned to Calgary in 1893, became a prosperous and quite popular resident, and died there in 1911.

Elsewhere in the territories, prohibition produced results that were usually less dramatic but equally problematic. The law proved largely unenforceable from the start. Before 1892, for example, a citizen could get a permit allowing him to import a single bottle. But the permit was never cancelled nor collected; its holder could refill his bottle indefinitely with bootleg liquor, producing his dog-eared slip if anyone challenged him. Bootleggers meanwhile transported their goods in hollow canes, cans marked "fruit," and (in at least one instance) inside hollowed-out Bibles.

Medicine Hat Museum, PC525.215

'Nigger Molly' as nursemaid (1899) with 'Baby Nichol.' After an illustrious bootlegging career, respectability.

Renowned in the trade was "Nigger Molly," who with a partner, "Slippery Annie" Barclay, ran an establishment outside Medicine Hat. According to local historian Ed Gould, Molly wore a specially designed rawhide brassiere and bustle, capable of concealing two and six quarts respectively for her sales trips into the construction camps. When liquor became legal in 1891, so did Molly, opening a proper saloon. Her career also included work as a laundress, and as a nursemaid for more respectable Medicine Hatters.

Molly's partner, Slippery Annie, capped her bootlegging career by marrying a chap from Quebec. Ed Gould describes the wedding as a gala one, at which the bride arrived quite drunk with her similarly handicapped bridegroom in tow, and began pounding out "Pop Goes the Weasel" on the church organ. They had better come back some other time, the clergyman suggested, when they were sober. Oh no, Annie protested: "The trouble, your Riverence, is he won't come back when he's sober."

Problems with liquor did not end when the territorial legislature assumed authority over it. Few prohibitionists were elected in 1891, said Ruth Elizabeth Spence in her 1919 book *Prohibition in Canada*, and many who favoured licensing. At their first sitting the territorial legislators produced a bill that set up a licence system, and also allowed for local option votes whereby a town could decide to remain totally dry.

But this did not please the prohibitionists. "Prohibition was broken down," author Spence mourned, "and the liquor traffic had fully opened up to it our great, new, rich North-West Territories." *G.H.*❦

[5] **Unlike other provinces, Manitoba was not granted control of natural resources, the foundation of every other provincial government's economic policy. Moreover, the entire province at first consisted of an 11,000-square-mile "postage stamp" that later was enlarged to the present size.**

political fortunes. It was unquestioned in central Canada that government in this new territory must be entirely the creation of Ottawa. Hence the Temporary Government Act of June 1869 established a lieutenant-governor with an appointed advisory council of seven to 15 members. Neither governor nor council had any real power. To many, observes Thomas, Ottawa plainly "intended to fasten despotic rule on the North West for an indefinite period."

The first consequence of this attitude and policy was the Red River Rebellion. The Metis correctly regarded the sale of the HBC land as heralding annexation by a new and unknown ruler. They barred at the border the first governor Ottawa sent out, then established their own provisional government until they won partial provincehood[5] under the Manitoba Act of 1870.

But what was to become of the rest of the territories? The dominion government's answer reflected much the same indifference, bolstered by ignorance, that led to the Red River insurrection and 16 years later would cause another rebellion farther west. Manitoba's lieutenant-governor and an appointed council were to run the North West Territory from Fort Garry (Winnipeg).

The first governor, Adams G. Archibald, was a competent, thinking man who fully grasped what had prompted the rebellion. But given his tiny staff and budget, Archibald's tasks were simply impossible. He was to study and report on "the state of laws now existing in the Territories," "the system of taxation now in force," the condition of roads, "such lands in the Territories as it may be desirable to open up at once for settlement," plus "all subjects connected with the welfare of the Territories," and "the state of the Indian tribes now in the Territories."

Except for a couple of cart tracks around the Red River settlement and other posts, plus the trans-prairie trails, there were no roads. There were no taxes. The whites could be numbered in the hundreds. As for the Indian population, who could say? Some put it at 25,000. Ottawa's main concern was to make sure the natives didn't interfere with future railway construction and hoped-for settlement.

Ottawa therefore kept political control tightly within its fist. Archibald appointed the council and had to approve any regulation or legislation it produced, but nothing was valid until the dominion cabinet also approved it. His first ordinances, to set up a working council and ameliorate a smallpox epidemic, were promptly annulled. "It would be hard to find a more striking example of distrust of local self-government," Thomas observes. In 1872 Archibald left Fort Garry in disgust as soon as his first two-year term was over.

His successor, Alexander Morris, struggled mightily and with similarly scant results. His first three acts, sent to Ottawa for approval, were (it seems hard to credit it) lost — mislaid in Macdonald's office. When they were eventually found, two were disallowed. Equally incomprehensible are the numbers in the territorial budget. To undertake his enormous responsibilities Morris asked for $10,000 in 1873. Macdonald approved $4,000 and the next year cut this to $3,000, a sum he still considered exorbitant.

Meanwhile, in 1873 the Metis of the North and South Saskatchewan River valleys, concluding that Ottawa did not have their interests at heart, decided to govern themselves. They proclaimed their own provisional government, set up an assembly,

Glenbow Archives, NA-1406-214

Louis Riel (centre), sympathetically portrayed in the Canadian Illustrated News *in 1874. Surrounding him are: William McDougall (lower right), appointed governor of Rupert's Land in 1869 but turned back by Riel's rebels; successors Adams Archibald and Alexander Morris (top right and left), who held the office under strict Ottawa control; and Dr. John C. Schultz, MP, who began as a convinced 'Canada Firster' but ended by condemning the dominion's treatment of Indians in the territories. Ten years later the eastern media would view Riel in a very different light.*

When politics became too important to trust to the public

For the first four years after its incorporation as a town in 1884, municipal politics in Calgary was lively — too lively, some thought. Certainly civic elections were vigorously contested. In Tom Ward's *Cowtown*, an oldtimer recalls how on nomination day "a regular flock" of would-be candidates would crowd into the fire hall, along with most of the town, to seek nominations for the positions of mayor and six councillors.

"The hecklers got oiled up before the meeting, and when some of them started to show signs of hoarseness, they dropped back to the nearest saloon to oil up again, ready for more." Three mayoral and 18 council candidates were named: merchants, professionals, tradesmen and one describing himself as a "gentleman."

By 1889, however, leading citizens had decided that their town's politics needed to become more serious — a great deal more serious. That unfortunate interlude in 1886 when two rival councils tried to function simultaneously had been particularly deplorable. Calgary historian Max Foran furthermore notes (in *Calgary: An Illustrated History*) that in 1888 the budget stood at $24,000. This was big money, and a five-fold increase in three years. The merchants, who paid most in taxes (and derived benefit through town contracts), decided municipal politics was too important to entrust unreservedly to the public.

As one of them put it, what the town needed was a mayor and council possessed of "thorough business training and sound judgement." A select group of merchants therefore met before the 1889 election, chose a slate of candidates and submitted the names to a public meeting as the sole nominees. Amazingly, it was accepted. The whole slate went in by acclamation.

Municipal elections never did return after that to their initial unfettered exuberance. After all, said the merchants, the business of Calgary was business. *G.H.*❦

and passed laws, thereby sowing the seeds of the second rebellion.

The dominion government could cite some solid accomplishments, however. The Mounties trekked west. The Indian treaties were signed. The telegraph line reached Edmonton. The great land survey was begun. But settlement moved forward at a glacial pace. So did the development of territorial government.

Western hopes had risen when the Liberal administration of Alexander Mackenzie took office in 1873. The Liberals had loudly deplored Macdonald's western policy, and in 1875 tabled their own North West Territories Act. Westerners, the people it was intended to govern, remained as usual unconsulted as to its contents. This legislation provided for a resident governor to run the area, advised but not controlled by an appointed council. Local laws would no longer need cabinet approval. When any area of 1,000 square miles or less attained a population of 1,000 white adult males, it could elect a council member. When there were 21 or more elected members, the council would become a legislative assembly.

The council sat at Fort Livingston on the Swan River in Assiniboia until 1876, farther west in Battleford until 1882, and in Regina thereafter. Over an area of more than 500,000 square miles, the territorial administration was supposed to safeguard property and civil rights, administer justice, provide police and public health services, build and maintain roads and bridges, and provide for all other matters in which Ottawa did not want to interest itself directly.

The council's power to tax and legislate remained ill-defined and largely nonexistent, however. People asked: What can it actually do? The answer: Very nearly nothing. The Department of the Interior watched over its every activity, on the one hand inhibiting its power to act, on the other refusing to act on its behalf. In education, for example, although the dominion government had no plans for schools in the territories (the BNA

Liquor control was one of the territorial government's few areas of real authority. This six-month personal licence was issued in 1890.

Glenbow Archives, NA-4889-1

Act assigns this responsibility exclusively to the provinces), it forbade the council to set up school districts on its own. The council then formally requested permission to do so; Ottawa took six years to respond.

The council's taxing authority was equally circumscribed. It could only issue liquor licences and levy fines for liquor infractions, activities whose net proceeds in one year amounted to $250. Nevertheless, it was forbidden to incur debt and hence was entirely dependent on federal largesse. This proved notably parsimonious. While the dominion government funded the provinces generously, territorial grants were hopelessly inadequate (although resented nonetheless by the donors).

The North West Territories Act admittedly guaranteed an eventual legislative assembly, but nothing in the act bestowed power on the assembly if and when it came about. As for a voice in the dominion parliament itself, no provision for territorial representation was made. It would take Riel's second armed rebellion to attain that. In the meantime, the Prairies remained in every respect Canada's colony.❦

City of Edmonton Archives, EA-10-242

St. Albert, Father Lacombe's notable experiment in self-government, looking north across the Sturgeon River bridge to the Roman Catholic mission and the bishop's palace. St. Albert history buffs claim this was the first permanent bridge in the District of Alberta.

The amazing case of the 'republic' of St. Albert

Before Canadian law and governance came to the vast tract of North America between the Great Lakes and the Rockies and north to the Arctic, such settlements as existed had to provide their own government. None in Alberta afforded itself a more complete constitution than the Metis settlement of St. Albert, 10 miles northwest of Fort Edmonton.

Oblate missionary Albert Lacombe arrived at the hilltop overlooking the Sturgeon River in April 1861, with three of his Metis parishioners from Lac Ste. Anne, 30 miles to the west. Others joined them. Within six years St. Albert* was a thriving village of 1,000 Indians and Metis, raising vegetables, livestock and some of the first grain crops in the region.

Any community must somehow be governed, however. The townsfolk approached the HBC, owner of the whole region, for direction. None was forthcoming, possibly because the sale of Rupert's Land to Canada was already thought to be inevitable. Therefore, in 1867, the villagers held a meeting and established a system of their own.

In charge of administration was the *chef du pays* (literally chief of the country, a sort of president), assisted by two councillors. The legislative branch consisted of nine elected committee members. A magistrate provided the judiciary. A constable was added later.

In three years the St. Albert government enacted 39 bylaws that together form a remarkably comprehensive system of criminal and civil law. The legislation, although it bears the signatures of the nine committee members, also carries the unmistakable stamp of one raised in the tradition of the French civil code. This very likely was Lacombe himself.

The laws were carefully tailored to the needs of a small, agrarian, Christian community with few resources, whose members were utterly dependent upon one another for survival. A citizen convicted of committing assault, theft, adultery or "depredations of any kind" was to be fined. Murderers were to be transported to Red River at public expense.

In the area of civil law, fines were imposed on those deemed to have broken promises to perform work, pay debts or marry. Provision was made for the estates of those who died without leaving a will. Certain minutiae were covered, such as damage done by loose pigs or dogs, or oxen improperly yoked. There was even a traffic law: "Any person who drives a sleigh of any kind without bells, on the public road," would be fined three shillings.

The "St. Albert Code" endured nearly 10 years, until the laws of Canada arrived with the NWMP. Many saw these as no more effective, and far less democratic, than St. Albert's. Some still do. *G.H.*❦

*The name was bestowed by Bishop Taché of St. Boniface, according to Eric J. and Patricia M. Holmgren in *Place Names of Alberta*. On a pastoral visit he is said to have planted his cane in a snowbank and declared, "This will be the site of your new mission and I will name it after your patron St. Albert."

CHAPTER TWO

Haultain fights for self-government in the first big clash with Ottawa

THE GROUP THAT MET IN KAMOOSE TAYLOR'S MACLEOD HOTEL GAINED A DEGREE OF DEMOCRACY IN SPITE OF MACDONALD'S 'NATIONAL POLICY' THAT ENVISIONED THE WEST AS A COLONY

Glenbow Archives, NA-510-1

F.W.G. Haultain, de facto *premier of the territories, author of responsible government in the territories, and in private life an enigma.*

Manitoba escaped outright colonial subjugation to Canada by means of armed rebellion. A second violent insurrection in the remaining territories in 1885, however, did not meet with the same success. It remained for the next towering figure of western Canadian politics to lead the West in such blatant, albeit non-violent, defiance of Ottawa that the Macdonald government eventually had to relent and confer on the territories a measure of democracy. Much of the life of Frederick William Alpin Gordon Haultain of Fort Macleod, Alberta, has remained shrouded in mystery — his marriage to an invalid for 32 years, for instance, was kept secret until after his death. But he was known from Manitoba to the Rockies as "premier of the West."

Haultain was the scion of an old Huguenot family whose sons had served for generations as officers of the British Empire. Born in England and raised in Peterborough, Ontario, where his father was stationed, the young Haultain found few opportunities for a military career in Canada. "F.W.G.," as he styled himself, broke with family tradition and studied law. In 1884 he took the new railway to Calgary, hopped a stagecoach for Fort Macleod and hung out his shingle.

An engaging and soft-spoken man of medium height and athletic build, he joined the Anglican church choir and the polo club, played soccer with the Mounties, started defending accused whisky traders and horse thieves, and soon became a popular figure on the local scene. In 1887 a seat on the territorial legislative council opened through resignation and Haultain contested the by-election. He won decisively.

Whether a council seat conferred any real political power, however, was greatly in doubt. The council's authority was severely limited. It still had almost no taxing power and got almost no money from Ottawa. The lieutenant-governor ran things, as one telegram from the Department of the Interior put it, "under instructions from this department."

Like many other westerners, Haultain knew Ottawa's goals were not the territories' goals. The dominion government viewed the area as a place from which to extract resources for the enrichment of central Canada. "The public domain in the territories," writes historian C.C. Lingard, was "employed for purely federal purposes." Haultain knew also that the fundamental explanation for this attitude lay in the central tenet of the Macdonald government, the one that had won it re-election after the disaster of the Pacific Scandal: "the National Policy."

Developed over a decade, this multi-pronged program was aimed at making the new Dominion of Canada a great nation. Haultain realized, however, that to Ottawa planners Canada meant essentially Ontario and Quebec, as it would continue to do. Already the Atlantic provinces, Nova Scotia and New Brunswick, now joined by Prince Edward Island, were becoming junior partners. British Columbia had been added to give the new nation a sea-to-sea dimension, and the pseudo-province of Manitoba to secure the territories and fend off the American threat.

Under the National Policy, industry would be nurtured through tariffs, both a general duty of 15% on all imports and incidental protection for selected industries, nearly all based in Ontario and Quebec. Indian treaties and a land survey would open the West to settlers. An immigration policy would procure them. A railway would get them there, and ship back the staples they would produce. The North-West Mounted Police would cement Canada's claim to the interior. Ottawa would control land policy and other resources. Altogether these measures would counter American expansionism, provide cheap commodities for central consumption and export, and create a market for central manufactured goods.

Glenbow Archives, NA-9-16

Interpretations of the National Policy vary. In the second volume of his biography of Macdonald, *The Old Chieftain*, historian Donald Creighton[1] focuses on the tariff established in 1879.[2] In an age free of income tax, the tariff eventually accounted for 60% of dominion government revenue. The term "National Policy" was an inspired euphemism that avoided the word "protection," which notoriously aroused 19th-century political passions.

Creighton concludes that Macdonald was aiming to secure the allegiance of central

Glenbow Archives, NB-9-15

The Macleod crowd held their salons at Kamoose Taylor's hostelry (right). Taylor is fourth from the right, holding his bowler hat. (Above) the Macleod Hotel participants are: (front row, from left) D.W. Davis, W. Pocklington, H. Taylor, Haultain; (back row) D.J. Campbell, A.F. Grady, A.J. McDonald, J. Black. It might not be Paris, but it was power politics nonetheless.

[1] **Donald Creighton was professor of history at the University of Toronto. Dean of the centrist school of Canadian historical thought, he is the foremost biographer of Sir John A. Macdonald (*The Young Politician* and *The Old Chieftain*). He also rejects the thesis, first propounded by Quebec nationalists in the 1960s, that Canada is fundamentally a compact between two founding races, the English and the French. Such a concept, he contends, was never evident in the Confederation negotiations.**

[2] **Historian Creighton does not examine the effect of the National Policy upon the territories, whose farmers would have to pay the tariff on all agricultural equipment. This factor apparently did not strike him as important, any more than it did Macdonald.**

[3] **Gerald Friesen is professor of history at St. Paul's College, University of Manitoba. In *The Canadian Prairies: A History* he provides what is perhaps the most readable full account of the region's four centuries of exploration and development, ending with the Lougheed era.**

[4] **Harold Adams Innis was an economic historian, best known in the West for his seminal study, *The Fur Trade in Canada*, published in 1930.**

industrialists and voters, gain support for his railway scheme, and win power back from the Liberal foes who had unseated him with the Pacific Scandal. He could also count on virulent anti-Americanism in central Canada, a United Empire Loyalist stronghold. (It was a sentiment never strong in the West, where many newcomers were Americans of a different stamp.) Macdonald hoped to "make considerable capital" out of this, he confided to a friend.

Gerald Friesen[3], in his analysis of the National Policy, also finds it entirely dedicated to the interests of central Canada. "The millions of acres of western real estate were expected to serve the interests of 'Old Canada,'" he writes in *The Prairie West.* "Mile after mile of farmsteads would...provide a hinterland for the manufacturing plants of central and Maritime Canada." Harold Adams Innis[4] goes farther. "Western Canada has paid for the development of Canadian nationality," he declares.

None of this was lost on the little circle of cattlemen, newspapermen, remittance men and others who gathered regularly for "bull sessions" in the dining room of Harry "Kamoose" Taylor's Hotel Macleod.[5] If democracy in the Canadian Prairies has an equivalent for the Paris salons that led to the French Revolution, Kamoose's dining club, however improbable, would be it. They found Ottawa's policy thoroughly distasteful, and resolved to do something about it. What was it about the Prairies and its treatment by Ottawa that turned many an Ontario blueblood into an ardent Westerner? Historian Lewis H. Thomas attributes it to culture. Many early westerners were of British background and simply unwilling to have Ottawa deny them rights they considered theirs by birth.

Glenbow Archives, NA-2307-4

Edgar Dewdney in 1893. He was approvingly described by Sir John A. as a 'paternal despot...governed by instructions from Head Quarters.'

Similar sentiments found voice beyond Kamoose's. In 1886, a group of Calgarians, among them James Lougheed, grandfather of a future Alberta premier, formed the "North West League." It was put together, as the *Calgary Tribune* explained, "for the purpose of uniting the people of the Territories...to work for the interests and advancement of the Territories."

A powerful debater and shrewd political tactician, Haultain quickly rose to prominence. He did not hesitate to declare the West "a colony within a colony." Like the settlers who supported Riel up to the very point of rebellion, and those who assembled at Winnipeg the year before it broke out, he hated the attitude of Macdonald, sitting in Ottawa, stating smugly that "government proceeds from here."

Declared the *Calgary Tribune* in its opening editorial in 1885: "There is at the present time nothing in common between the politics of this District and those of Ontario or Quebec." The *Medicine Hat Times* raged year after year against the tariff. The *Regina Leader* complained in 1891: "Nearly half the House [of Commons] do not believe in the North West, nearly half the House do not realize what the North West is going to be." One resolve emerged. They must fight Ottawa, and fight they did.[6]

Haultain quickly became the champion of what was called responsible government, the principle whereby bureaucrats are responsible to cabinet ministers, cabinet ministers to the premier and elected assembly, and the assembly to the electors. The Macdonald government, determined that the West should serve the Centre, was in no hurry to confer such power on a territorial legislature.

The lieutenant-governor at the time was Edgar Dewdney, a surveyor from British Columbia and an intense Macdonald partisan. A huge man, his face framed by enormous sideburns, he was an implacable opponent of territorial autonomy. Macdonald approvingly described him as "a paternal despot...governed by instructions from Head Quarters." In 1885 he had dismissed as "petty grievances" the Metis land claims, petty grievances that led immediately to the North West Rebellion. Inevitably, therefore, territorial politics became an increasingly inflammatory clash: Haultain with his group of reformers on the one side; Dewdney (on occasion referred to by the *Edmonton Bulletin* as "Dirty Dewdney") and his Ottawa-appointed successors on the other.

By the 1880s the prairie situation was beginning to change. Settlers were arriving in somewhat

[5] Like the much-travelled Kamoose himself, originally from the Isle of Wight, his guests at the Macleod Hotel were an extraordinary group that included Howell Harris, the pioneer cattleman who started ranching the area in 1872; *Macleod Gazette* editor C.E.D. Wood, whose paper consistently supported Haultain; merchant D.W. Davis, an early MP; and the eccentric Lord Boyle (who became the 6th Earl of Shannon in 1890), the first local representative on the territorial council.

[6] The hardships posed by the National Policy and Ottawa's indifference are not, as it later became fashionable for centrist historians to argue, the result of revisionist history or manipulative latter-day prairie politicians. The first generation of settlers wholly believed they were in conflict with a dominion government out to exploit the West. Their actions, letters and editorial voices were unmistakably clear on this point.

The fiery invective of Edmonton's first newspaper editor

Tories and Indians ranked high up on Frank Oliver's list of hatreds but 'Dirty Dewdney' led them all

Early portraits of Frank Oliver depict a short, wiry man with a face that would be rather boyish if it weren't for that enormous moustache. But it is the quality of his gaze that sets the paintings of Oliver apart from the often stiff, glassy-eyed faces in museums and archives. It is so intense and unflinching that he seems to be trying to see through a wall, or perhaps compel it to fall down. And this is in fact an accurate impression of the pioneer Edmonton publisher and politician who in many crucial aspects foresaw the future Alberta and knew its problems would require the same fierce vision his portraits disclose.

He was born Francis Bowsfield in 1853 at Brampton, Ontario. His mother died while he was still in school, and his father remarried soon afterwards. Young Frank never forgave him for it. He adopted his mother's maiden name as his own and left the family farm in his teens. Having apprenticed as a printer, he moved to Toronto and found a job in the printing shop of the *Globe*, where he became a political disciple of its editor, Liberal luminary George Brown.

Many of Brown's tenets became Oliver's: militant teetotalism; mistrust of the fur and railway monopolies; a belief that the expansion of the West was best achieved through aggressive immigration and land policies; and passionate espousal of the right of all men to responsible government.

Provincial Archives of Alberta, E. Brown Collection, B-8347

Militant MP Oliver. The West, he charged, was treated with malevolent neglect, punctuated by periods of outright brigandage.

He went west at 20, and worked at the *Manitoba Free Press* for three years as a printer before starting a freight business, running goods on oxcarts between Winnipeg and Fort Edmonton. Moving to Edmonton in 1878, he set up the town's first store outside the walls of the fort. Like hundreds of others, he saw this as the smart move. After all, the transcontinental railway was surveyed to pass through the town. Oliver's mistrust of railway interests grew into open hostility when the southern route was chosen instead.

In the meantime, however, he had returned to his first profession. With a second-hand printing press, a masthead hand-carved from a piece of firewood, a lively mind and an acid pen, he set up the *Edmonton Bulletin* in an old smokehouse behind the Edmonton Hotel. Opinionated, anti-Indian, and belligerent to a degree that shocks modern sensibilities, Oliver saw himself as fulfilling his oft-repeated claim that he "stood for principles, not men."

The principle he stood for most ferociously was his advocacy of the West, even to the point that he loudly endorsed the Metis cause up to the very brink of the rebellion of 1885. But he turned against the Metis when they made common cause with the Indians, and he urged brutal justice when the fighting was over. "Every effort should be made to meet the demand for dead Indians by a reasonable supply," he wrote.

Oliver raged against federal, railway and Hudson's Bay Company land reserves as grievously discouraging settlement. He castigated the dominion government for its slowness in surveying Edmonton properties. But he hurled his most furious salvos against the denial of democratic process in the territorial government. He blamed the rebellion on the Macdonald government's policy towards the West which, he said, was one of malevolent neglect, punctated by periods of outright brigandage.

In the same spirit, he fanned and endorsed the citizenry's armed defiance of the NWMP in the incident of the Edmonton Land Titles Office. When hoodlums, terming themselves "vigilantes," pushed the shacks of some alleged claim jumpers into the North Saskatchewan River, he approved their actions too. What else can people do, he demanded, when the lack of a survey means they can't prove ownership?

In 1883, Oliver was elected to the territorial council, where he made himself heard in his usual style. He lost the next election, however, to Dr. H.C. Wilson, a "wet" on the liquor question. For a while he had to content himself with blistering editorial invective against the Tories, the railroads and the Macdonald-appointed lieutenant-governor, Edgar Dewdney.

Frank Oliver's loathing of "Dirty Dewdney" became almost pathological. He marked the occasion of Dewdney's retirement as lieutenant-governor with this observation: "His appointment was a calamity, his administration a crime, its results a disaster and his retirement his most acceptable act." (To his chagrin, however, his nemesis was then appointed minister of the Interior, a position of even greater power and influence over the West.)

In 1896 the Laurier Liberals swept the Tories from power at Ottawa, and Oliver won for them the federal constituency of Alberta. It was in the new century and in the federal field that some of his major contributions would be made. *G.H.*❦

more substantial numbers. The railway reached Calgary; the link to the Pacific was completed. Along the tracks, and around some of the old trading posts, towns were springing up. Newspapers began publishing. The territorial government's responsibilities grew apace. There were schools to fund, roads to build, merchants and professionals to regulate, squatters' rights to assess, and epidemics to fight.

In 1882 Ottawa divided the territories into four districts: Alberta and Athabaska, occupying the approximate area of the future Alberta; Assiniboia and Saskatchewan that of the future Saskatchewan. The dominion government officially explained the division as being "for the convenience of settlers and for postal purposes." What this meant, no one knew. Some historians believe Macdonald was preparing for the day he would create four small, weak provinces. If this was in fact his motivation, he never acted on it, although the division was to have far-reaching consequences.

A more immediately significant change occurred through the North West Territories Act adopted by the Mackenzie administration in 1875. Its provisions allowed members to be elected as the local population increased. Once the council counted 21 elected members, the body was to be transformed into a legislative assembly. Election conferred a legitimacy that appointed council members lacked, and changed the nature of territorial politics. With the public behind them, the elected members made it clear they did not intend to be Dewdney yes-men. They made their first appearance in 1881, serving at the beginning without pay; the first was Lawrence Clarke from Lorne, the region around Prince Albert. By 1883, there were six.

Glenbow Archives, NA-546-1

Quebecker and Manitoban Joseph Royal, a lieutenant-governor friendlier towards western aspirations. But 'concessions' no longer would suffice. Haultain and the entire legislative assembly of the territories resigned to force Royal to concede responsible government.

Notable among them was Frank Oliver, publisher of the *Edmonton Bulletin*. Noted the *Calgary Herald*, looking characteristically askance at Edmonton (as it would continue to do), Oliver "swore like a mule driver." He was the council's first major voice for territorial rights. In one memorable tirade, Oliver compared territorial residents to Siberian serfs. "The North West is under a despotism as absolute, or more so, than that which curses Russia," he wrote. In 1885, the year of the rebellion, Oliver cast the non-Metis people of the North West perilously close to the Metis cause, forcefully arguing that short of rebellion they too could expect nothing from Ottawa.

In the legislative session following immediately upon the rebellion, Dewdney realized from the opening day that the climate had fundamentally changed. Eleven seats were now elective. Almost to a man, the members demanded immediate responsible government and local control of territorial funds. Dewdney's throne speech produced a raucous denunciation, the assembly voicing its uneasiness about Ottawa's intentions. Dominion hints of early provincehood were met with scorn, and the members reminded the governor they had repeatedly warned him the rebellion would occur.

In 1886, several prominent citizens travelled to Ottawa and presented a 21-point petition demanding a host of local economic and infrastructure improvements, plus representation in parliament and more authority for the council. The dominion government conceded some MPs, but not increased local autonomy or economic aid. The next year the new member from Macleod took his seat on the territorial council and the Haultain-Dewdney struggle began. Dewdney no doubt hoped he could control Haultain. Both were Tories, and for a lawyer patronage was important. The firebrand Oliver, on the other hand, was a Grit. Dewdney's hope was short-lived.

From the start, Haultain made it clear that the West meant more to him than his party. National parties could not serve the western cause, he argued, because they must of necessity take their direction from Ontario and Quebec. Besides, he considered the council (and the legislative assembly that succeeded it) too small for partisan blocs. Perhaps westerners could afford to be opponents on the national scene, but they must agree on the territorial objectives. Tory or not, therefore, Dewdney was his foe and the Liberal Oliver his ally.[7]

[7] Not all historians ascribe Haultain's non-partisanship to a disinterested championing of the West. Stanley Gordon of the University of Alberta argues in his essay "F.W.G. Haultain: Territorial Politics and the Quasi-Party System" (*Prairie Forum*, 1981, Vol. 6, No. 1) that he used it to keep himself in power. By including the outnumbered Liberals in what amounted to the first cabinet, he contends, Haultain kept them beholden to him and "was able to consolidate the growing impression of his own indispensability and strengthen his firm grip on local political activity."

Haultain opted for an aggressive, at times confrontational, style. He began introducing draft bills embodying the policies he believed Ottawa should follow, while knowing full well Ottawa would disallow them, which Ottawa nearly always did. His strategy was to "make the best use of the machinery and tools" he had, looking for ambiguities in the North West Territories Act or lapses in dominion responsibility he might exploit. His bills confronted, as the dominion government would not, the issues the West faced: alcohol regulation (with all its social, economic and religious implications); sluggish immigration;[8] and most of all, money.

Money was a constant problem. Ottawa refused to give the territories meaningful taxing authority. Royalties from local lands, mines and forests went straight to the dominion government. Nor could the council tax CPR assets, which could have brought in about $300,000 annually. Haultain defiantly tabled a bill to tax the Canadian Pacific. Though the *Calgary Tribune* approved, Ottawa did not. And instead of the fixed per capita subsidies it gave to provinces, Ottawa reluctantly sent the territorial governor an annual grant that varied according to prime ministerial mood. For the 1889 fiscal year, the governor (at the direction of the Department of the Interior) controlled $142,900. The council had at its disposal just $16,500 in revenue from licences and fines.

There were also some peculiar accounting decisions. The cost of putting down the Riel insurrection went on the books as a loan to the territories, for instance — although defence was clearly a federal responsibility — and the North West Territories Act prohibited the territorial government from incurring any debt.

[8] From 1867 to 1899 only 1.5 million immigrants landed in Canada. The United States attracted 5.5 million in the 1880s alone, Australia, 2.5 million. Moreover, as the *Calgary Tribune* lamented, one million left Canada during the 1880s, a "calamity...unparalleled in the history of new countries." The newspaper blamed an over-taxing, debt-ridden and indifferent Ottawa, and incompetent immigration agents.

It seems undeniable the West benefited from Riel's revolt

For years Ottawa wouldn't provide territorial seats in the Commons; then suddenly four were established

Western historians disagree as to a causal connection between the Metis rebellion of 1885 and Ottawa's establishment of four seats for the territories in the dominion parliament two years later. A mere coincidence, some say — but others find the timing a bit too much of a coincidence.

Territorial demands for parliamentary representation had been increasing ever since Manitoba was made a province in 1870. True, it was a province restricted in area and denied control of natural resources, but it had been given an amazing four seats in the House of Commons and two senators — very generous for a population of 12,000. Manitoba admittedly only made these gains after rising in armed rebellion. But surely, moderate westerners argued, the other territories wouldn't have to follow that example.

So from the beginning the territorial council had included parliamentary representation in nearly every list of demands upon Ottawa. Western newspapers were all for it too; it was practically the only thing they agreed on. Even Prime Minister John A. Macdonald had once spoken favourably of it, back in 1867 when the question of future additional provinces arose in the Confederation negotiations. He said he didn't like the American model where territorial congressmen could sit but not vote.[a] They ought to have a vote, he said then, but he had done nothing about it since.

Glenbow Archives, NA-2882-23

Nicholas Flood Davin. He tried to use his Tory connections.

In 1884, the year before the rebellion, a delegation from Regina travelled east to present the case once more, and one member stayed on for months to lobby for it. Nicholas Flood Davin, a staunch Macdonald man and convinced of the rightness of the National Policy, was one of the West's more curious spokesmen.

He had founded the *Regina Leader* two years earlier, with money from local Conservatives, but his Tory connections predated that. In 1878 he had contested the Grit riding of Haldimand in Ontario and nearly won. To recoup his financial losses he asked Sir John to appoint him to something and Sir John did, commissioning him to study and report on Indian education. It was the first of several such government assignments.

Davin was convinced, however, that the territories should be represented in parliament. He persuaded a Tory senator to make a speech representing the territorial

But the struggle for responsible government transcended all other issues, absorbing most of the political energy of the 1880s. In 1887 Haultain boldly put forward a draft bill that in effect created a legislative assembly to which a cabinet would be responsible, and which would control all territorial funding. The bill was rejected by "Head Quarters." In 1888, Nicholas Davin, one of the first territorial MPs (Assiniboia West) and an early Haultain ally, tabled in the dominion parliament a bill for quasi-provincehood. This too was promptly killed.

Haultain meanwhile held together on the council his disparate coalition of Grits and Tories, no easy job. Like any politician, he had enemies. Catholics in particular resented his opposition to sectarian schools. When he appointed an old political foe as speaker of the council (a typical Haultain action), the *Alberta Tribune* wrote sarcastically, "The breast of the young pseudo-premier appears to be bursting with the milk of human kindness." This act was purely self-serving, the paper opined. Haultain's opponents might otherwise "brand him as a hypocritical tergiversator and force him from the office he has so grossly prostituted."

Haultain's interminable legislative conniving had an erosive effect. In 1888, Ottawa introduced limited reforms. The council would become a legislative assembly. There would be 22 elected members, chosen from districts as drawn up by the council, serving three-year terms. Any adult male citizen, regardless of wealth, could vote. But balloting would remain open, as opposed to secret (meaning of course that patronage recipients could be watched).

There was no provision for a cabinet either, only an "advisory council on matters of finance."

Glenbow Archives, NA-3012-16

NICHOLAS FLOOD, THE GOVERNMENT'S CANDID FRIEND.

One more appeal to Ottawa, as drawn for GRIP *magazine by J.W. Bengough, October 10, 1885.*

case. The response was cautious. It was an interesting idea, a government spokes-man said. It had much merit. Perhaps there should be an inquiry. But clearly none of the territories had enough population to justify a seat in the House of Commons. They might be home to more than 48,000 people, but most were non-voting natives.

Undaunted, Davin turned to the Commons. A backbencher put forward a private member's bill to effect territorial representation. It died on the order paper. A very worthy idea, said a front-bench spokesman. Perhaps it could be brought up next session. Davin returned to Regina with the case no farther advanced, so far as he could see, than it had been 15 years before.

Eleven months later, in March 1885, the Metis declared their provisional government at Batoche in Saskatchewan Territory. In the ensuing weeks thousands of Canadian soldiers moved west on the Canadian Pacific to suppress the rebellion, with considerable bloodshed. And two years later the Macdonald government introduced a bill granting four seats to the three southern territories — two for Assiniboia, one each for Alberta and Saskatchewan. (Athabaska contained hardly any settlers at the time.) It passed both Commons and Senate in short order.[b]

What about the population argument? the chiding Liberals demanded. How strange that nearly the same population, hopelessly inadequate in 1884, was suddenly altogether sufficient in 1886. Macdonald replied smoothly: "The population would scarcely allow of so many members, but although the settlers are very few in number, the country is large and has many different interests requiring different legislative measures."

It was left for Frank Oliver, writing in his *Edmonton Bulletin*, to state the obvious: "If history is to be taken as a guide, what could be plainer than that without rebellion the people of the North West need expect nothing, while with rebellion, successful or otherwise, they may reasonably expect to get their rights." *G.H.*❦

[a] Under the American Northwest Ordinance, however, a territory with 60,000 males could automatically become a state, making it equal with other states in the powerful U.S. Senate.

[b] Davin, who had meanwhile covered the Riel trial for the *Leader*, ran for and won the Assiniboia West seat in 1887 and as an MP tried to do what he could for the West until 1900. Subject to bouts of depression, he shot himself in 1901.

Most territorial funds remained the governor's to spend. As the *Qu'Appelle Vidette* put it, the governor could spend public money "according to the freaks of his own fancy." Thus, without real control over the purse-strings, the assembly was ultimately powerless.

Dewdney was gone from the territories by now, though he had been promoted to the even more lethal position of minister of the Interior. His successor as lieutenant-governor was Joseph Royal, an urbane Quebecker who lived in Manitoba from 1870 to 1893, where he founded *Le Metis* newspaper in Winnipeg, practised law and served as MLA and MP. Royal, says Haultain biographer Grant MacEwan,[9] carried out Ottawa's mission to "perpetuate the elected body as a democratic phoney." Lewis H. Thomas disagrees. He holds that Royal "supported the movement" for responsible government, in sharp contrast to Dewdney's "obtuse and stubborn resistance."

At first Royal seemed charmed by Haultain, but the infatuation was short-lived. Haultain had resolved that the time had come for a showdown. "Concessions" were no longer enough, he

[9] **Grant MacEwan is the dean of Alberta's popular historians. A former mayor of Calgary and lieutenant-governor of Alberta, his *Frontier Statesman of the Canadian North West* is the only biography of F.W.G. Haultain.**

The day they called Edmonton's militia out against Ottawa

Hundreds of armed citizens were ready to fight it out with the Mounties over an order to move an office

Before the Metis at Batoche took up arms against the Ottawa government in 1885, there were repeated warnings from the territories that other settlers harboured many and similar grievances, possibly to the point of armed rebellion. Dominion government officials discounted these warnings. An incident seven years later gave them a delayed credibility, however, when Edmonton citizenry did, in fact, take up arms against Ottawa.

In 1892 the historic fur trade centre on the north bank of the North Saskatchewan River was chronically resentful of the fact that the railroad builders had ignored it. Even the Calgary & Edmonton Railway ended on the south bank at "New Edmonton," the separate and rival community that would soon become Strathcona. Then on Satur-day, June 18, 1892, came more bad news. The government had approved removal of the Dominion Land Titles Office across the river to New Edmonton, where it would be handier for settlers arriving by rail.

Virtually every one of Old Edmonton's 700 adult citizens knew what this meant. The land office was one of several factors that bolstered their claim to importance in the district. They responded with raw fury. When a dray from New Edmonton showed up about 3 p.m. and workmen quietly began loading all the land titles records into it, the citizens were ready for a fight.

Within minutes a small crowd gathered. Then the fire alarm rang. Soon several hundred people had turned out. NWMP reports said the crowd was well-behaved until Mayor Matthew McCauley addressed them: "We have been too long dead! (Cheers) We don't want to be called rebels. (More cheers, the reference to the rebellion being clear) But it has come to this — we must fight for our rights! (Loud cheers) And we will fight for them too." (Pandemonium) The crowd, now wild, ripped the wheels off the wagon and led the horses away to hide them.

City of Edmonton Archives, EB14-40

The much-disputed Dominion Land Titles Office. Old Edmonton's 'Home Guard' was entirely ready to fight the NWMP in its defence – but 'Dirty Dewdney' backed down just in time.

The dominion land agent and office manager, Thomas "Timber Tom" Ander-son, was a Tory patronage appointee. Frank Oliver had charged in the *Bulletin* that Timber Tom owned a half-interest in the property the office was slated to occupy in New Edmonton. Anderson now called for more wagons and horses. The mob met them at the ferry and turned them back.

Mayor McCauley was meanwhile dispatching a series of telegrams to Ottawa, declaring the move an outrage and demanding Anderson be sacked. Anderson had arranged the whole thing, he said, for "personal and pecuniary interests." Alarmed, Inspector William Piercy of the NWMP offered to have his men guard the wheel-less wagon and its contents until the dispute could be resolved.

The crowd, though suspicious, withdrew. But "excited groups

declared. Only "rights" would do. In the fall of 1889 he engineered the resignation of the entire assembly. Astonishingly, Royal relented, agreeing to make the administration responsible to the legislature. But did a governor have power to do this? No, said dominion government lawyers, he did not.

In Ottawa the outraged Dewdney decided to meet Haultain's challenge head on. If the elected members wouldn't serve, fine. He would go back to appointing them. He began looking for replacements. Dr. R.G. Brett of Banff, representing the Red Deer constituency, proved tractable. He agreed with Haultain's goal — there wasn't a man in the assembly who did not — but objected to his tactics. Haultain was too confrontational, too flamboyant, too impatient. Brett was a let's-sit-down-and-discuss-it-like-sensible-people man. He proposed names for the Dewdney council, which encountered a roar of hostility. Brett found that in becoming "Ottawa's man" he had lost all credibility at home, and resigned his seat.

remained around the streets until a late hour," the *Bulletin* reported, "and a proposition to burn the land agent in effigy found such favour that, although the police interfered in one case, the project was finally carried out amid much enthusiasm at the flagpole between McDougall's store and the Imperial Bank."

Next day, Sunday, nothing happened, but on Monday morning Ottawa cracked down. NWMP Superintendent A.H. Griesbach rode in from Fort Saskatchewan with 20 Mounties, diplomatically left his men on the edge of town, and came to the town office for "discussions." He found the situation ominous.

Provincial Archives of Alberta, E. Brown Collection, B-1967

Superintendent Griesbach. Diplomatically, he left his troop on the edge of town, and avoided an ugly confrontation.

Posted at the town office was an order for all members of Edmonton's "Home Guard" to assemble under arms at the town centre. It was signed by Councilman Colin Strang, who ran a hardware store with Fred and Jim Ross. Already about 40 members of the militia unit, inactive since the rebellion, were being issued 80 to 100 rounds of ammunition each for their long Schneider rifles and were taking up positions outside the land office.

A telegram had by now arrived from the minister of the Interior. It was not Anderson who had ordered the "temporary" removal of the office, the telegraphed message said. It was he, Edgar Dewdney who had done so, entirely for the convenience of settlers. "Dirty Dewdney is in the steal," blared a special edition of the *Bulletin*, adding that the wrong man had been burnt in effigy.

But Dewdney had also decided to get tough. "Mounted police instructed to effect removal," said his telegram to the mayor, "and it is expected that the mayor and council will assist in maintaining order."

In fact the NWMP had no such order, but Dewdney's telegram set the fire bell ringing again. By 4 p.m. every able-bodied man in town, most carrying arms, had joined the Home Guard at the land office, ready if necessary to battle the NWMP. Two hours later Griesbach assured McCauley he intended to do nothing until he received instructions from Ottawa.

The crowd dispersed, but remained vigilant. Tuesday it began to rain and the Mounties who had been guarding the land office supplies decided to move them back inside the building to keep them dry. Instantly the alarm rang again, reported the *Bulletin*, and within eight minutes 150 men were on the scene.

Ottawa, finally aware of the gravity of the situation, changed its tune. Telegrams to McCauley became conciliatory. On Wednesday Dewdney advised that the main office of the land agent would remain in Old Edmonton, with a sub-agent doing business across the river in a boxcar. This had actually been his intention all along, he claimed.

A more light-hearted sequel followed a few days later, when a group of New Edmonton youths decided to steal the alarm bell of the Old Edmonton fire brigade. As they struggled to muscle the 800-pound load onto a wagon they were discovered. The ensuing brawl lasted 20 minutes; the invaders went home with an empty wagon.

Some Edmontonians thought they saw a salutary lesson in the Battle of the Land Titles Office. Facing really determined resistance, they concluded, Ottawa would back down. It was a lesson that would have to be learned over and over again, however, as the coming century would demonstrate. *G.H.*❦

Glenbow Archives, NA-334-6

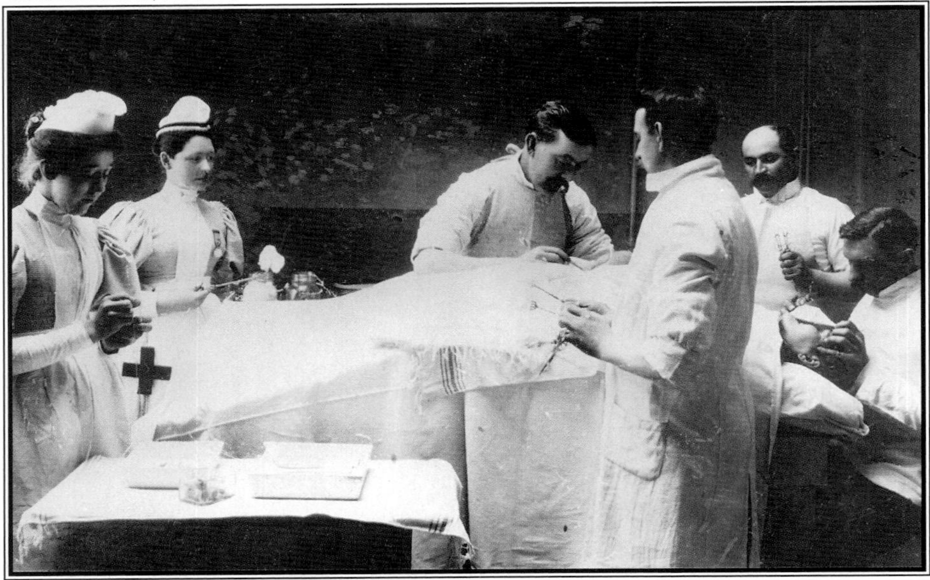

Dr. Brett, MLA for the Red Deer constituency, at work in his Banff hospital. His political career didn't do so well after he opted to become in effect 'Ottawa's man.'

What was Lieutenant-Governor Royal to do now? He could hardly govern without a council of some kind. Late in the year he decided to name one on his own, a monarchical tactic that threw the whole territory into an uproar. The following year, 1890, the elected council reappeared at Regina to hear Royal's throne speech. Haultain's withering reply amounted to the manifesto of the reform forces.

He decried "the disregard for and violation of all constitutional rules, the infringement upon the rights and privileges of the house and usurpation of its prerogatives." He and his 12 allies — the "13" as they were known — demanded full responsible government. He announced a boycott of all legislative proceedings, including budgetary matters. Most papers in the North West backed him. The *Calgary Herald* was one exception. It attacked him bitterly.

So did Royal, infuriated by the incessant legislative machinations of the Fort Macleod lawyer. He was, the exasperated governor declared, "the driftwood that necessarily floats towards all new countries." The "driftwood" was doing more than float, however. Ottawa responded to the Haultain-engineered breakdown by amending the North West Territories Act. The lieutenant-governor would no longer sit in, "like a chaperon" as MacEwan puts it, on proceedings of the assembly. Furthermore, about 75% of spending would henceforth be by the lieutenant-governor on the advice of the assembly, not at the order of the Interior Department. The assembly gained increased powers over electoral districts, alcohol regulation and the use of French. But there was still no provision for a cabinet.

Whatever its achievements, Haultain's strategy had nevertheless been risky. Justice Minister John Thompson threatened to dissolve the assembly if it got too obstreperous. Would he actually do this? Or was it a bluff? Haultain decided it was bluff, and pressed on with his next and final device.

Ambiguities in Ottawa's amendments allowed him to put together an "Executive Committee of the Territories...to aid and advise in the Government of the Territories." This amounted, as Thompson, Royal and everyone else well knew, to a cabinet. The Macdonald government let it stand. Responsible government was established. Democracy had arrived on the Prairies. It was, says Thomas, "a major landmark."

Even Lieutenant-Governor Royal, whose term in office lucklessly coincided with the final and decisive challenge, congratulated Haultain as the author of responsible government in western Canada when he retired. The cabinet was established December 31, 1891, and Haultain moved to the territorial capital, Regina. Technically he was chairman of the executive committee. But he was *de facto* premier, a position he would hold until 1905.

He remains nevertheless an enigma. Although he was socially active and a well-known public figure for five decades, his marriage to Marion, the physically and psychologically troubled daughter of Herbert Mackintosh (a territorial lieutenant-governor) remained secret even beyond his death in 1942.[10] Little is known of Marion. She was said to be a pretty but erratic woman who fled to England, with her one child, after an unhappy marriage to a Saskatchewan merchant. There she is thought to have become involved with a ne'er-do-well who soon deserted her. Haultain took pity, supported her financially, then married her.

But they never lived together and had no children. MacEwan was able to offer little insight into the relationship. Haultain left no private papers; only his public record survives. But that public record is unimpeachable, and in one respect almost unprecedented: a half-century of distinguished service without the slightest hint of scandal.❦

[10] The Haultain marriage remained secret, in fact, until Grant MacEwan discovered it while researching material for his biography, published in 1985.

CHAPTER THREE

Hopes soar and then are dashed after the pivotal election of '96

LAURIER'S LIBERAL VICTORY PROMISED A NEW DEAL FOR THE WEST AND SIFTON UNLEASHED A MASSIVE AD CAMPAIGN TO FIND SETTLERS BUT HAULTAIN'S PLAN FOR 'ONE BIG PROVINCE' FRIGHTENED OTTAWA

After a long Saturday night dinner party on May 23,1891, at Earnscliffe, his home overlooking the Ottawa River, John Alexander Macdonald, the "old chieftain," took to his bed with a cold. Four nights later he suffered a stroke. Two nights after that he was hit with another, this time devastating. He never spoke again. On June 6 the foremost of Canada's founding fathers was dead, and as the long funeral cortège moved towards the railway station and his final resting place at Kingston, Ontario, people knew that the entire Tory era would soon follow.

Its death throes proved so chaotic that they made it a challenging task for Canadian schoolchildren, when they were expected to know such things, to remember the names of all the country's prime ministers. Four administrations, each headed by a former Macdonald cabinet minister, came and went in five years.[1] Many in the West mourned Macdonald too, if more out of nostalgia than gratitude. They also pined, however, for the day when his Conservative Ottawa would become Liberal Ottawa instead. A change of government, they were sure, would make all the difference.

The Tory term finally ran out in the summer of 1896; the prime minister, Sir Charles Tupper, called the election for June 23. From Manitoba to the Rockies, as in the rest of the country, the implications were momentous. The territories had only four MPs out of the total 213, so that even in a tight election they were scarcely a significant factor, but the campaign nevertheless had powerful symbolic value. Defeating western Conservative candidates[2] would at least signal that the West was rejecting Macdonald's National Policy and colonial treatment generally. Returning them would show a sort of political "hit us again, we love it" masochism.

Glenbow Archives. NA-3901-1

Sir Charles Tupper, last of 'the old chieftain's' four immediate successors. The death throes of the Macdonald government were chaotic.

The election resulted in what would become familiarly known in central Canada as a "prairie protest vote," a phenomenon as recurrent in Canadian politics as it is misunderstood. To the centrist, it is nothing more than a knee-jerk response to misfortune, bad weather, bad economic conditions or bad luck. To westerners it is a cry against a system that leaves the West wholly vulnerable to exploitation by the more populous central provinces, an exploitation so effective they can never gain sufficient numbers of people to threaten the central ascendancy of Ontario and Quebec in the House of Commons.

The electoral event of 1896 would represent such a protest. So too had the military event of 1885 as some few, like Edmonton's Frank Oliver and territorial "premier" F.W.G. Haultain, had been shrewd enough to observe at the time. Riel's real cause, it was now becoming plain, had not been that of the Metis alone, but of the whole prairie region. However, in 1896 as in a dozen or

[1] The four administrations of the Tory sunset were headed by Sir John Abbott, Sir John Thompson, Sir Mackenzie Bowell and Sir Charles Tupper.

[2] The Macdonald followers were officially known at the time as the "Liberal Conservatives."

Collection of Glenbow Archives

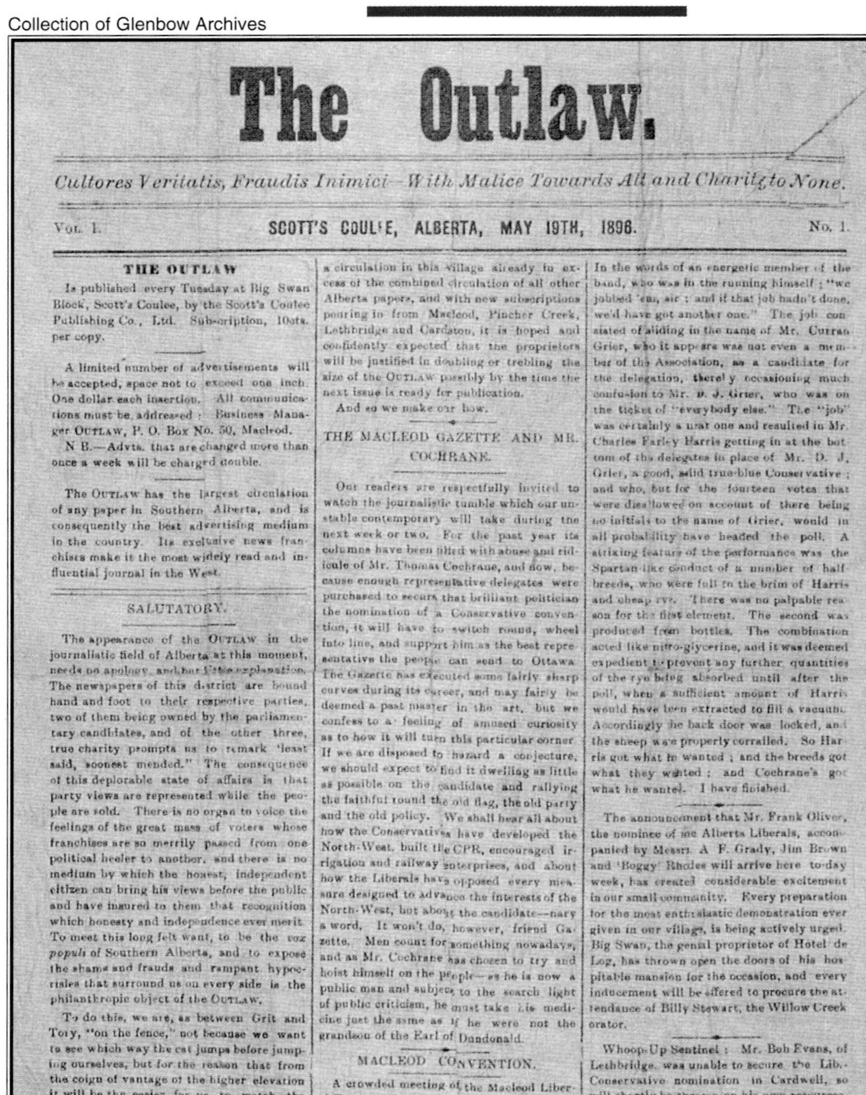

The Outlaw.

Cultores Veritatis, Fraudis Inimici—With Malice Towards All and Charity to None.

Vol. 1. SCOTT'S COULEE, ALBERTA, MAY 19TH, 1896. No. 1.

THE OUTLAW

Is published every Tuesday at Big Swan Block, Scott's Coulee, by the Scott's Coulee Publishing Co., Ltd. Subscription, 10cts. per copy.

A limited number of advertisements will be accepted, space not to exceed one inch. One dollar each insertion. All communications must be addressed: Business Manager OUTLAW, P. O. Box No. 50, Macleod.

N. B.—Advts. that are changed more than once a week will be charged double.

The OUTLAW has the largest circulation of any paper in Southern Alberta, and is consequently the best advertising medium in the country. Its exclusive news franchises make it the most widely read and influential journal in the West.

SALUTATORY.

The appearance of the OUTLAW in the journalistic field of Alberta at this moment, needs no apology, and but little explanation. The newspapers of this district are bound hand and foot to their respective parties, two of them being owned by the parliamentary candidates, and of the other three, true charity prompts us to remark 'least said, soonest mended." The consequence of this deplorable state of affairs is that party views are represented while the people are sold. There is no organ to voice the feelings of the great mass of voters whose franchises are so merrily passed from one political heeler to another, and there is no medium by which the honest, independent citizen can bring his views before the public and have insured to them that recognition which honesty and independence ever merit. To meet this long felt want, to be the *vox populi* of Southern Alberta, and to expose the shams and frauds and rampant hypocrisies that surround us on every side is the philanthropic object of the OUTLAW.

To do this, we are, as between Grit and Tory, "on the fence," not because we want to see which way the cat jumps before jumping ourselves, but for the reason that from the coign of vantage of the higher elevation it will be the easier for us to watch the struggling mobs below and point out the foibles and vanities, the vices and tricks that will make up the contest on which the people of Alberta have entered. "Spare none, praise none" will be one of our mottoes

a circulation in this village already in excess of the combined circulation of all other Alberta papers, and with new subscriptions pouring in from Macleod, Pincher Creek, Lethbridge and Cardston, it is hoped and confidently expected that the proprietors will be justified in doubling or trebling the size of the OUTLAW possibly by the time the next issue is ready for publication.

And so we make our bow.

THE MACLEOD GAZETTE AND MR. COCHRANE.

Our readers are respectfully invited to watch the journalistic tumble which our unstable contemporary will take during the next week or two. For the past year its columns have been filled with abuse and ridicule of Mr. Thomas Cochrane, and now, because enough representative delegates were purchased to secure that brilliant politician the nomination of a Conservative convention, it will have to switch round, wheel into line, and support him as the best representative the people can send to Ottawa. The Gazette has executed some fairly sharp curves during its career, and may fairly be deemed a past master in the art, but we confess to a feeling of amused curiosity as to how it will turn this particular corner. If we are disposed to hazard a conjecture, we should expect to find it dwelling as little as possible on the candidate and rallying the faithful round the old flag, the old party and the old policy. We shall hear all about how the Conservatives have developed the North-West, built the CPR, encouraged irrigation and railway enterprises, and about how the Liberals have opposed every measure designed to advance the interests of the North-West, but about the candidate—nary a word. It won't do, however, friend Gazette. Men count for something nowadays, and as Mr. Cochrane has chosen to try and hoist himself on the people—as he is now a public man and subject to the search light of public criticism, he must take his medicine just the same as if he were not the grandson of the Earl of Dundonald.

MACLEOD CONVENTION.

A crowded meeting of the Macleod Liberal-Conservative Association was held last week in the Court House to elect delegates to the Conservative Convention for Alberta. The meeting was in fact packed ram-jam full to the doors—whether it was a Conservative meeting is "another story." It is no

In the words of an energetic member of the band, who was in the running himself; "we jobbed 'em, sir; and if that job hadn't done, we'd have got another one." The job consisted of sliding in the name of Mr. Curran Grier, who it appears was not even a member of the Association, as a candidate for the delegation, thereby occasioning much confusion to Mr. D. J. Grier, who was on the ticket of "everybody else." The "job" was certainly a neat one and resulted in Mr. Charles Farley Harris getting in at the bottom of the delegates in place of Mr. D. J. Grier, a good, solid true-blue Conservative; and who, but for the fourteen votes that were disallowed on account of there being no initials to the name of Grier, would in all probability have headed the poll. A striking feature of the performance was the Spartan-like conduct of a number of half-breeds, who were full to the brim of Harris and cheap rye. There was no palpable reason for the first element. The second was produced from bottles. The combination acted like nitro-glycerine, and it was deemed expedient to prevent any further quantities of the rye being absorbed until after the poll, when a sufficient amount of Harris would have been extracted to fill a vacuum. Accordingly the back door was locked, and the sheep were properly corralled. So Harris got what he wanted; and the breeds got what they wanted; and Cochrane's got what he wanted. I have finished.

The announcement that Mr. Frank Oliver, the nominee of the Alberta Liberals, accompanied by Messrs. A. F. Grady, Jim Brown and 'Boggy' Rhodes will arrive here to-day week, has created considerable excitement in our small community. Every preparation for the most enthusiastic demonstration ever given in our village, is being actively urged. Big Swan, the genial proprietor of Hotel de Log, has thrown open the doors of his hospitable mansion for the occasion, and every inducement will be offered to procure the attendance of Billy Stewart, the Willow Creek orator.

Whoop-Up Sentinel: Mr. Bob Evans, of Lethbridge, was unable to secure the Lib.-Conservative nomination in Cardwell, so will shortly be thrown on his own resources. "Bob" is a truly typical backwoods tavern keeper, nothing more, and should endeavor to curtail his vanity within bounds, attend to his veterinary duties (if any) and leave well enouuh alone."

'We hate and detest the Liberals almost more than we despise the Conservatives,' shouted southern Alberta's anonymously published newspaper The Outlaw. Specifically inspired by the 1896 dominion election, The Outlaw published just six invective-strewn issues – which became collectors' items.

more elections to follow, many saw the West's salvation in simpler terms. Throw out the Macdonald Tories and all will be well, they cried (as 88 years later they would cry for the throwing out of the Trudeau Liberals). Was not Wilfrid Laurier, the silver-tongued leader of the Liberal resurgence, himself running for the territorial seat called Saskatchewan in the Commons?[3]

For the West, the key election issues were Ottawa's refusal to allow effective local government on a sound financial footing, high tariffs on crucial imports, the question of whether Catholics should have the right to separate schools, the failure of immigration policies to procure sufficient settlers, the slow pace of railway building and the CPR's steep freight rates.

The Liberals seemed pro-West on all questions. At their seminal 1893 policy convention they "denounce[d] the principle of protection as radically unsound and unjust to the masses of the people." They championed "freer trade" with the United States and Britain, lower deficits and lower taxes. They said the school question should be a provincial matter. They promised early attention to the territories' constitutional concerns and a new deal with the Canadian Pacific on freight rates.

The Conservatives ran in 1896 on their record of territorial expansion, railway and waterway construction, industrial development, close ties to Britain and the National Policy. Their record on most of these matters would not endear them to the West. But the party was in grim shape generally. The 75-year-old Tupper, like his three predecessors, could nowhere near approach Macdonald in personality, presence of mind, or guile. The party was split over the separate schools question and racked by ministerial resignations. Drought and economic depression had struck simultaneously in 1892.

Conservatives and Liberals collided fiercely in every constituency, and a third party had made its appearance. Farmers, sick of Ottawa, the tariff and the high-handed ways of the CPR and the new grain-elevator companies, had formed the Patrons of Industry. Their candidate, the Reverend J.M. Douglas, was considered a strong contender in Assiniboia East. Although they were not to last long, the Patrons were the forerunners of the great agricultural movements that would dominate western politics for the next 40 years.

What a campaign it was! Political meetings frequently lasted well past midnight, rival candidates plumbing the depths of their vituperative vocabularies. The media outdistanced them all, the newspapers chiding and lashing at one another in an orgy of bombast they obviously enjoyed immensely.

Just look, said the *Lethbridge News*, there's Frank Oliver of the *Edmonton Bulletin* advocating some of the self-same policies he's spent the last 15 years condemning. The paper helpfully quoted numerous earlier *Bulletin* editorials, heavily dosed with Oliver vitriol, that had castigated positions which now, as Liberal candidate in the constituency of Alberta, Oliver must defend. The *Bulletin* in truth had never been unswerving Liberal; it had never been unswervingly anything. Unabashed,

[3] Laurier, a Montreal lawyer, won his seat in the 1896 election by only 44 votes. He had chosen to run in the locale of the North West Rebellion in order to emphasize his support of Louis Riel and the Metis after Riel's execution largely destroyed the Tory party in Quebec.

and however inconsistent with its past, Oliver's paper plunged into the Laurier campaign with the fervour of a catechumen. Across the river the *South Edmonton News* looked on appalled, lavishly quoting Oliver speeches in order to ridicule and deplore them. When Oliver won, though, the *News* heartily congratulated him. His victory, *News* readers were doubtless bewildered to learn, had been "anticipated" all along.

One sheet, however, exceeded everything else in the West for raw venom. Called *The Outlaw,* it was the product of the 1896 campaign, published for the sole purpose of commenting on it. It was ostensibly produced in Scott's Coulee, nine miles west of Macleod, and ran just six issues. Only four are preserved at Calgary's Glenbow Institute, although a retired Calgary judge is said to have a complete collection.

The Outlaw's motto was, "With malice towards all and charity to none." It adhered to this principle with awesome fidelity in a constant barrage of sarcasm, fictitious "interviews" with Conservatives making fools of themselves, and uproarious personal attacks (though it failed to conceal a professional admiration for Frank Oliver, every bit its equal in invective when he wanted to be). *The Outlaw* announced itself as "the most widely read and influential journal in the West." This claim might actually have held up; copies were cherished as memorabilia for years afterward.

The Outlaw stance was essentially supra-partisan: "We hate and detest the Liberals almost more than we despise the Conservatives." Since all other papers were the mere tools of party politicians, *The Outlaw* would serve as the *vox populi*, the voice of the people, an alternative to "the shackled and servile press." It would "expose the shams and frauds and rampant hypocrisy that surround us on every side." It had, it jeered, "a circulation in this village already in excess of the combined circulation of all other Alberta papers."[4]

Collection of Glenbow Archives

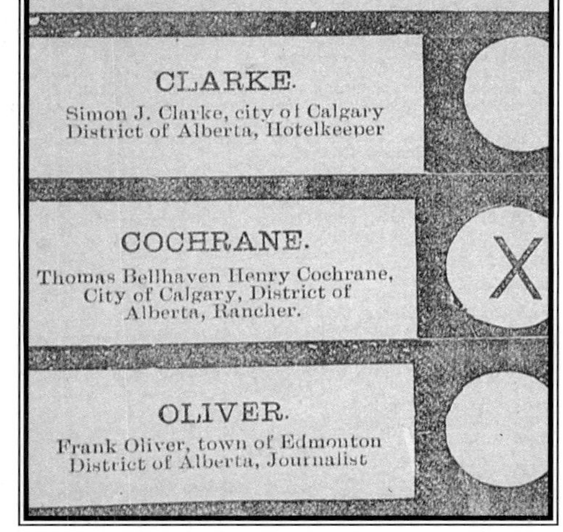
elow is published an illustration of the new ballot t
n the Dominion elections on Tuesday next. E
g to his polling station on Tuesday will be handed a
instructed to mark a X opposite the name of the ca
to vote for; and it is to every intelligent man's int
well wisher of the future of the North West, or any
erests in the Territories to mark that X in the circl
chrane's name.

CLARKE.
Simon J. Clarke, city of Calgary
District of Alberta, Hotelkeeper

COCHRANE.
Thomas Bellhaven Henry Cochrane,
City of Calgary, District of
Alberta, Rancher.
X

OLIVER.
Frank Oliver, town of Edmonton
District of Alberta, Journalist

A Calgary Herald *ad, June 18, 1896, leaves voters in no doubt about what they must do. But Oliver won.*

Of the Tory candidate for Alberta, Lieutenant T.B.H. Cochrane, *The Outlaw* sneered: "He has been forced by circumstances to enter a sphere for which he is as much fitted as the editor of the *Macleod Gazette* is to conduct the *New York Herald*. Nature did not think it necessary to bestow on him the gift of expression." Cochrane, *The Outlaw* snickered, posed a problem for the inexorably Tory *Gazette*. Macleod's sheet had dumped on the man all year, but now as the party candidate he had suddenly gained its unreserved support. To *The Outlaw* this clearly evidenced the hypocrisies of party politics, to which the West's newspapers were not immune. Look at them "wheel into line," it jeered.

In the vote of June 23, the Liberals swept in with 117 seats to the Conservatives' 89. In Alberta, Oliver beat Cochrane. Laurier won Saskatchewan. Douglas, supported by local Liberals, took Assiniboia East. The Conservatives held on to one seat, Assiniboia West, where Nicholas Davin, the *Regina Leader* editor, squeaked in by one vote. Elsewhere in the West, the results were not so decisive. British Columbia elected four Liberals and two Conservatives, Manitoba two Conservatives and two Liberals.[5]

In its June 30 final issue, *The Outlaw* solemnly published the "obituaries" of leading Conservatives. Its verdict on Calgary lawyer James Lougheed: "a harmless but windy mortal" who "spake with feebleness." Then, taking an advance shot at the Liberal patronage it knew would inevitably follow, it ran a list of high-level public "appointments" of local Liberals. It closed with a few comments on the Alberta media, in particular the *Calgary Herald*: "It has ever been a mixture of pretentious mediocrity and asinine stupidity...We should be glad to believe its course the result of insanity, but insanity presupposes the existence of intellect."

The Conservative establishment was not the only casualty of the 1896 campaign. The other, as gradually became evident, was the spirit of non-partisanship through which Haultain had been winning solid gains for the West. In the euphoria attendant on the Liberal take-over in Ottawa, his exhortations for everyone to work together in advancing the territories' interests seemed naive and out of date. The West must now think "nationally," many urged. Besides, as every aspiring local politician knew, allegiance to a party could do a lot for a man's career. The promises of power, privilege, position and wealth were real. Haultain's arguments were mere abstractions. Partisanship was becoming incarnate in two powerful westerners — R.B. Bennett, the Tory, and Clifford Sifton, the Liberal.

Bennett, junior partner in the law firm of the ambitious Lougheed, was 28 years old when he

[4] There is no settlement now at Scott's Coulee, and there never was much. It has only ever rated a listing as a "physical feature," namely a creek flowing southeastward into the Waterton River across the Peigan Reserve. Possibly *The Outlaw*'s supposed publishing locale just fitted its general style.

[5] Athabaska, the fourth district of the territories, lay beyond latitude 55°N and was too sparsely populated to be given an MP. Though the district had a northern boundary, it was considered one with the Far North that ran to the Arctic islands. Out of this huge tract, the Yukon territory was carved in 1898. The District of Athabaska, north to latitude 60°N, was split between Alberta and Saskatchewan when they became provinces in 1905.

entered the territorial assembly in 1898. Discerning that Haultain's non-partisanship was eroding support for the national Conservatives, he quickly became Haultain's chief opponent.[6] This display of opposition gave Ottawa the comforting impression that territorial opinion was far from united behind Haultain. (In the following decade, Bennett would help work the political destruction of Haultain, and finally go on to become Canada's 15th prime minister. His own political fate, however, would in the end turn out little better than Haultain's, and the latter would live to see that happen.)

Glenbow Archives, NA-166-1

The young R.B. Bennett. He became Haultain's nemesis in the territorial assembly and, in dominion politics nearly four decades later, Canada's 15th prime minister.

Sifton, Laurier's undisputed first lieutenant in the West, was the more immediate danger to Haultain. The MP for Brandon constituency, Sifton became Minister of the Interior after the 1896 election, seemingly exploding onto the political scene. In truth, at 35 he was already a seasoned political operator. With his six-foot frame, piercing eyes, clipped moustache and boundless energy, he was known as "the Young Napoleon of the West." He had been active in the Manitoba and North West Farmers' Union, an MLA at 26, and Manitoba's attorney-general at 29.

His father, John Wright Sifton, an old Ontario Grit and longtime ally of Alexander Mackenzie, had secured several construction contracts on the Canadian Pacific's Thunder Bay-Winnipeg section thanks to his Grit connections. He ended his long political career as speaker of the Manitoba legislature. J.W.'s two sons, Arthur and Clifford, were to become distinguished westerners, the easy-going Arthur, the elder, as MLA and premier of Alberta, the iron-willed Clifford as the author and architect of a new Canadian West.[7] A complex, contradictory character, a workaholic and voracious reader, Clifford had been a gold medallist in law school, and had then gone into partnership with his older brother.

As a political operator, Sifton became a master of patronage, staffing his department with Liberals, handing out government timber leases to in-laws, and unapologetically indoctrinating new immigrants to vote Liberal. He seemed to break most other rules of practical politics, however. He shrank from no controversy, fiercely proclaiming himself anti-Catholic and anti-French, positions that would eventually cause a breach with Laurier. In an age when alcohol was the lubricant of all politics, he was a defiant teetotaller, though he would use whisky as readily as patronage in the pursuit of his goals.

Moreover, Sifton was an aristocrat and so presented himself, flaunting his diamond rings, his mansions in Winnipeg and Ottawa, his elegant carriages and his yacht. While in office he secretly acquired ownership of the *Manitoba Free Press* (later the *Winnipeg Free Press*), publicly denying he had anything to do with the paper. Its editor, the renowned John W. Dafoe, would begin in the next decade to make "the Old Lady of Carlton Street" the foremost editorial voice of western Canada.

In one respect more than any other, Sifton would leave an indelible mark upon the West. His contention that Ottawa had failed utterly in populating the Prairies was more than political cant. It was a deep conviction. Even more than most other westerners, he had cause to despise the Department of the Interior. He well recalled the day he led a delegation from the North West Farmers' Union to the office of the department's tyrannical deputy, A.M. Burgess, only to be told

[6] Bennett came closer than anyone ever would in finding a stain on the otherwise spotless Haultain career. He "discovered," he said, $20,000 "missing" from the public accounts, suggesting Haultain had pilfered it. The money was later accounted for by J.C. Pope, the territorial auditor, and the charge was withdrawn.

[7] Two good biographies of Clifford Sifton are *Clifford Sifton in Relation to His Times* (1931) by J.W. Dafoe, and *Clifford Sifton* by Daniel J. Hall (two volumes, 1981 and 1985). An excellent word portrait of him appears in Pierre Berton's superb sketch of the great migration to western Canada, *The Promised Land* (1984).

after a seven-hour wait that Burgess had no time for him. An intimate Burgess colleague was social engineer Hayter Reed, the incompetent architect of the Indian "peasant farmer" program, whose chief accomplishment (as described in Section II) had been to wreck the early attempts at Indian agriculture.

Though Conservative appointees, both these men had seen Sifton coming and had taken care to buttress themselves with strong support in the Laurier caucus. They believed themselves wholly conversant with western problems and therefore indispensable to any administration. To Sifton they were worse than incompetent; they were actively hostile, and would subvert anything he attempted. His first act therefore was to fire them both, although it took eight months to actually clear them out. He appointed a Brandon Grit, James Smart, his political ally of a decade, to succeed them both.

Sifton soon issued the bold declaration that effectively summed up the immigration policy for which he would long be remembered: "I think a stalwart peasant in a sheep-skin coat, born on the soil, whose forefathers have been farmers for ten generations, with a stout wife and half-a-dozen children, is good quality." To later generations of westerners, familiar with the Ukrainian or Polish ancestry of local doctors, professors, judges, mayors, business leaders or deputy prime ministers, the declaration seems either obvious or patronizing. But at the time it was startling, taunting and bristling with controversy.

Here, for instance, is a letter of protest "on behalf of the white and Indian inhabitants of these territories" that appeared in the *Alberta Plaindealer* of Strathcona on May 18, 1898:

> Is this fair land to be given to the off-scourings of humanity? If so the government would confer a favour by

Western Canada Pictorial Index

Liberal Clifford Sifton (left). Once he expelled the Tory mandarins from the Department of the Interior, his immigration policies exerted an indelible effect upon the West. (Below) a crowd photographed at the Calgary station, circa 1900.

Glenbow Archives, NA-4069-3

The religious issue that bitterly split territorial politics

Behind the Catholic schools debate lay a deeper educational question with grave consequences no one foresaw

Although the struggle for democracy was F.W.G. Haultain's top priority, and the defining theme of the first three decades of prairie politics, no issue caused more heated debate and personal animosity in territorial politics than the language and schools questions. The issue was religious — Protestant versus Catholic — but beyond this, lay an even deeper question, affecting the whole shape and quality of the society being created. However, no one at the time suspected this dimension of the controversy, and it would take 100 years before the full implications became clear.

Superficially, the issue in the territorial council was whether the state should allow tax money to be used in support of a Catholic school system. Early on, nearly all Catholics in the territories were French, so that supporting the Catholic schools meant supporting a French language culture, alongside the English one. This, Haultain feared, would implant the same cultural dichotomy in the West that had already split Ontario from Quebec in the East.

He therefore favoured a "public" school system from which all religious sectarian interest was prohibited. If Catholics wanted their own schools, he argued, they should be prepared to pay for them, while at the same time supporting the public system with their tax money. Protestants on the council agreed with him; Catholics fiercely opposed him.

Haultain wanted the same public school system in the West that was already being created in Ontario by the educator and Methodist Minister Egerton Ryerson. Like Haultain, Ryerson too had to fight for a non-sectarian public school system. However, his fight had not been with the Catholics who had already gained the right to tax-supported schools. Ryerson's fight had been with the Anglicans, in particular with the Anglican bishop of Toronto, John Strachan (pronounced *Strawn*).

Strachan, himself a teacher, argued that education must always express some philosophical or religious assumptions. If the public schools were divorced from religion, he said, there was no telling what they might ultimately wind up teaching. Therefore the church should always play a dominant role in the public school system. Since most Ontarians at the time were Anglicans he meant this to be the Anglican church.

Ryerson countered that Canadian society was Christian, and would always be so. Therefore the public school system could be depended on to reflect Christian values in general — whether Methodist or Anglican didn't matter — and religious sectarianism should be kept out of the schools.

Metropolitan Toronto Library Board

Bishop John Strachan. His worst fears would be vindicated.

Ryerson carried the day, and the Ontario public schools thereupon became the model for the public schools in the territories, where Haultain became their champion. Had Ryerson, a devout Christian, been able to look a century ahead to a day when the washrooms in his public schools would feature condom machines for the use of the children, he would no doubt have been aghast. For Ryerson's assumption that the schools would remain Christian was to prove wrong. Strachan's worst fears would be vindicated, and by the 1980s, many Protestant denominations themselves were frantically trying to establish their own schools as an alternative to the public system.

But such a prospect was impossible for Haultain or anyone else on the territorial council at the time to foresee.* They considered the issue as merely one of English Protestantism versus French Catholicism, and it went back to the roots of territorial government.

Under the terms of the Manitoba Act which created that province in 1870, the French (meaning the Metis) were guaranteed rights to their own language, schools and the practice of their religion. A system of French Catholic schools was thereupon established.

The North West Territories Act, passed by the federal Liberal administration of Sir Alexander Mackenzie in 1875, similarly declared the right of Catholics to separate schools in the territories. An 1877 amendment gave French equal status to English in the territorial government and courts. These provisions recognized, of course, that French was as commonly spoken as English in the territories when Canada took them over.

As new settlers came in, many of them from Ontario and the United States, English became by far the dominant tongue. The newcomers were aware, moreover, that these guarantees did not prevail in the original four provinces. The British North America Act assigned authority over education, for instance, to the provinces and not to the dominion government.

The crisis first came to a head in Manitoba. Thousands of non-Catholics, arriving from Ontario in the 1870s and '80s, soon made their influence felt in Manitoba's new legislative assembly. Thus in 1890 the Liberal provincial government abolished public funding of French Catholic schools, despite the Manitoba Act guarantee.

The Manitoba Schools Question quickly became a national issue that helped bring down the federal Tory government at Ottawa. The Tories, taking the side of the Manitoba French Catholics, introduced a bill to disallow the Manitoba legislation. (A little-used power of the federal parliament under the BNA Act enabled it to void a provincial statute.)

Paradoxically, Sir Wilfrid Laurier's Liberals fiercely fought the remedial bill, and forced the Tories to withdraw it. If Ottawa could intervene in the affairs of Manitoba, Laurier argued, then it could also intervene in the affairs of Quebec. In the 1896 election the French clergy therefore supported the Tories — but Quebec voted for Laurier, thereby betraying the French people in Manitoba.

Provincial Archives of Alberta, E. Brown Collection, B-3894

The 'Schools Question' in the territories pitted F.W.G. Haultain, who favoured strictly secular education, against Father Albert Lacombe, who sent him an open letter in defence of Catholic education. Meanwhile, schooling continued. Edmonton teacher Joe Carson posed with pupils in 1881.

The schools question was meanwhile proving an inflammatory issue in the remaining territories as well. "Premier" Haultain, firmly committed to the Ryerson concept, believed in secular education, and opposed all "religious training" in the schools. He also believed that dual school systems, Protestant and Catholic, unnecessarily segregated children. This raised the ire of Father Albert Lacombe, who sent Haultain a strongly worded open letter.

But it was when the issue became linguistic, rather than religious, that the fight became the sharpest. By the 1880s, English-speakers outnumbered French by a ratio of 13 to 1 in the territories. As of 1890 nobody had ever asked for a French-language copy of assembly proceedings either. For both reasons, Haultain considered dual-language printing a waste of money.

In 1892 he supported a resolution introduced by Regina MLA Daniel Mowat to abolish French-language recording (though not speaking) in the assembly. It was passed 20-4. In the same year the School Ordinance, modelled on a B.C. statute, eliminated separate school boards by establishing a single "Council of Public Instruction," dominated by the territorial cabinet. It also made English the sole language of instruction, mainly to ensure that children of German, Ukrainian and other immigrants learned English.

These moves outraged not only the local French population but the Tory government at Ottawa, and occasioned a ferocious editorial battle among local newspapers. Many modern historians agree in heaping scorn on Haultain on this account. Even Lewis H. Thomas, a Haultain admirer, calls him "anti-Catholic" and unsympathetic towards French.

Haultain's bigotries, if such they were, were unquestionably shared by much of the population. In 1890, the *Macleod Gazette* expressed the common view: "It is very properly urged that the necessity for the use of French as an official language, if it ever existed, does not exist now; that it entails useless expense upon the territories, and that it was never contemplated to insert the clause in the Act relating to it."

A year earlier the *Calgary Tribune* had said: "The separate school system is strongly denounced by all liberal-minded people...We have witnessed the folly of allowing any one sect or denomination to dictate to the legislatures. Therefore, let us agitate for the abolition of the iniquitous octopus of separate schools that has gained a foothold and is rapidly fastening itself upon us."

Few of these editorial writers at the time would have supported "non-sectarian" education quite so unreservedly if they could have foreseen what it would become, for most of these men were at least nominally Christian, and some devoutly so. But that change, like so many other things, lay beyond the century's turn.

In the meantime, as provincehood was demanded for the territories, the question naturally arose: Will they or will they not have separate schools? In Ottawa, the issue would split the Laurier cabinet and cost it its most powerful minister.
T.B.❦

* The Catholic clergy of the day would have disputed the assertion that no one could really see what was coming. The fact that education cannot be divorced from religion had always been the Catholic contention. That's why the church had always insisted upon Catholic schools. They would also contend that the later efforts of Protestant groups to establish Protestant schools demonstrated the Catholics right.

Glenbow Archives, NA-1514-1

Prime Minister Laurier. Many westerners thought his triumphant Liberals would give the West a better break. But not much changed.

> telling us, so we can look for other quarters. Moving is unpleasant to say the least, but life in the midst of these filthy and untutored beings will be unendurable...Quantity rather than quality is what counts with Mr. Sifton, he evidently wants so many head in the Northwest within a given time...If the thing can't be stopped in any other way we would advise that the land office volunteers of Edmonton get out their shooting irons, send recruiting officers around the country for a day or two and then meet the next train that brings such rubbish with the firm resolve that they shall not land in this district.

This was the opposition that Sifton faced and defied. Sending his agents (invariably Liberal) across Europe and the United States, he sought immigrants with the most expensive advertising campaign the world had yet seen. The result in the coming decade would transform the West, raising the population from under 100,000 in 1896 to 360,000 in 1905. Moreover, the tide he had unleashed would continue to flood the Prairies for years afterwards.

But in the quest for direct political power for the West, the kind of power all other provinces had, Sifton's success was wholly undistinguished. In truth, he didn't care about it. The man who continued to do so was "premier" Haultain. The two could scarcely have differed more. Sifton had inherited wealth and position in the West; Haultain was self-made and had come west on his own. Sifton was vitriolic, ostentatious and blatantly ambitious; Haultain was measured, moderate and self-effacing. Sifton revelled in working the system; Haultain, wary of seduction by Ottawa, remained the perennial outsider. Sifton put the party first; Haultain the West first. Sifton felt that if he had power, then the West had power; Haultain believed that power must flow from the system, not from the fortunes of a single man.

Responsible government within the territories had been achieved in principle. Their legislative assembly had considerable law-making power, and above all spending by the governor was subject to the control of an "executive committee" (in effect a cabinet) made up of MLAs and responsible to the assembly. But because Ottawa limited local taxing authority, most of territorial revenue continued to come from Ottawa. Haultain's funding requests were consistently cut back by a parsimonious dominion government; in 1896 he asked for $380,000 and got $240,000.

Much worse was the fact that the assembly's entire estimates were subject to federal cabinet veto, making a mockery of the notion that the assembly was really responsible to the electorate. The latest lieutenant-governor, Charles Herbert Mackintosh, an Ottawa Conservative appointed in 1893, was perhaps the worst ever. He resisted any furtherance of legislative power, considered funding for schools a frivolity, and dismissed Haultain as "inclined to pig-headedness."[8]

Problems meanwhile mounted for the territorial assembly. School expansion, road-building, well-drilling and relief payments for the devastating drought of the mid-1890s all lagged. After the 1896 election, therefore, Haultain and the pro-reform MLAs formally asked the new Laurier government to give the assembly additional legislative and administrative authority, full control over spending decisions, a per capita grant and a per capita debt allowance such as the provinces got (rather than piecemeal handouts), a grant in lieu of the natural resource control that had been bestowed on all provinces but Manitoba, and finally to transform the executive committee, the *de facto* cabinet, into a real one.

In 1897, Sifton tabled an amendment to the North West Territories Act. The cabinet was granted, but nothing else. And the cabinet, as Davin's *Regina Leader* was quick to point out, had been established already in everything but name. Historians consider this event the end of the struggle for responsible government within a territorial setting.

Just one year after a grateful West had seen the obstructionist Tories dumped in favour of the reformist Liberals, Haultain and his MLAs became conscious of an irrefutable fact: Ottawa continued to do almost nothing to accommodate the West. The territories' "nationally conscious" MPs were of little help. Davin often seemed more concerned with his party's national position than with Haultain's efforts. Even Haultain's old partner, Frank Oliver, could no longer be counted on for unequivocal support. All were hobbled by partisan considerations and the new-found "national perspective."

As the *Calgary Weekly Herald* observed, Haultain was fighting an entrenched attitude to the effect that, "We bought you. We own the territories." Therefore Haultain decided he must change his strategy. Rather than the old method he had used so successfully under the Tory regime, the

[8] Most curiously, it was this man's unfortunate daughter that Haultain later secretly married and never lived with, as described in the previous chapter.

gradual, step-by-step institution of self-government, he must go the whole way. He must seek full and complete provincehood.

As early as 1887 the *Macleod Gazette* had declared: "If the North West is ready for a sweeping change at all, and we think it is, it is ready to enter Confederation as a province." Now the idea of provincehood was leaving the arena of mere speculation. James Reilly, who would become mayor of Calgary in 1899, prodded the territorial chieftain to take a radical course. Reilly took to holding town meetings in which he decried Haultain's role as the region's "chief mendicant," travelling to Ottawa on "begging expeditions." Premiers of provinces, he assumed, wouldn't have to stoop so low. "The lands, minerals and forests of the Territories are commoded by the Dominion government," said the *Alberta Plaindealer*. "Entering confederation under proper terms would change all this."

Some had doubts, of course. They feared provincehood would bring higher taxation. Others argued that by delaying a push for provincehood until the region was more populous, Ottawa would have less cause to make the territories into pseudo-provinces, as it had done to Manitoba. Still others feared a third possibility: outright annexation to Manitoba, which would make Winnipeg another Montreal or Toronto, dominating an enormous region, nearly half of Canada.

Haultain shared these fears and had another. The Atlantic provinces, he noted, were already in eclipse. Small, disunited, easily exploited by the dominant powers of Montreal and Toronto, they were becoming sub-provinces. Their industries were declining; the Bank of Nova Scotia, once the proud financial possession of Halifax, was talking of moving its executive offices to Toronto. If the territories were fragmented into four provinces, or even two, would the same thing not happen to them?

Furthermore, Haultain argued, the Prairies were one geographical and political entity. United as one province, the largest in Canada (Ontario and Quebec got the bulk of their northern lands only in 1912), stretching from the Rockies to Manitoba, the region would be potent. He dreamed, he told his audiences, "of one large province, holding its own in Confederation, the most powerful province in Confederation. Would this not be much more desirable than a number of small areas confined in their powers and in their influence?"

The very idea made Ottawa shudder. Without ceasing to remind prairie residents they were too few to justify even one province, it nevertheless found no inconsistency in the contention that they must form two or even four, if they were to achieve provincehood at all.

In this they found much local reinforcement, the fruit of Ottawa's division of the territories into four districts back in 1882. In an astonishingly short time, the subtle geographical and economic differences had begun to foster local identities. Calgary-area ranchers and civic boosters, supported by Bennett, wanted separation from the sodbusters in a grassland province stretching across the southern prairie with, obviously, Calgary as its capital. Regina wanted a north-south split, with itself as one of the two capitals. There were centralists like Yorkton MLA T.A. Patrick, who wanted an Ottawa government so strong as to leave scarcely any provincial powers at all.

The *Macleod Gazette*, citing the territories' "community of interests," agreed with Haultain, who ridiculed his opponents' case by taking it to its absurd conclusion. Why not, he chided, "cut the whole country into small plots, so that every man might be a province unto himself with three acres and a cow?"

Laurier Ottawa, like Macdonald Ottawa before it, remained largely aloof from all this talk. In 1898, the territorial assembly formally requested provincial status. The "reformist" Laurier rejected it. Provincehood seemed no closer in 1899 than it had three years earlier when the Liberals took office, or for that matter in the later Macdonald years.

Eventually Haultain would turn to the Tories who, in a bitterly ironic example of the manoeuvring endemic to partisan politics, would carry the torch for provincehood — the very development they had opposed with tooth and claw for 21 years. This move would bring Haultain face-to-face with Bennett, the essence of the partisan, a man who thought very "nationally" indeed. The coming years would not to be kind either to Haultain or the two second-class provinces that eventually emerged out of the North West Territories.❦

CHAPTER FOUR

To the western school of history, Canada was a business proposition

THE PRINCIPLES OF JUSTICE AND LIBERTY IN THE U.S. CONSTITUTION WERE SIMPLY TAKEN FOR GRANTED IN THE CANADIAN CONFEDERATION, THE PROSPERITY OF THE FOUNDING PROVINCES WAS THE OBJECTIVE

By the mid-1890s, the major themes of the prairie political experience had been cast. Because the basic attitude of central Canada towards the West was and has remained, in the western view, exploitative if not antagonistic, these themes were to shape prairie politics not only during the territorial era, but for the entire 20th century. The political movements that continued to spring out of the Prairies have been a direct result of the structural inequalities inherent in the Canadian political arrangement, inequalities that have been regarded in the West as offensive to the principles of justice. It was the founding inequities of the 19th century that created the prairie political movements of the 20th. They represented the West's challenge to perceived injustice.

For 35 years after the Hudson's Bay territory was acquired by Canada, and effectively for decades thereafter, the Prairies were in every sense Canada's colony. This was no happenstance. They were conceived specifically to fulfil that role. In the Quebec Resolutions, in the Confederation debates, in John A. Macdonald's letters and pronouncements, the western interior was viewed as a means to enrich central Canada. Settlement, development, the CPR, Indian policy and local government were all planned with this in mind.

Such a view of Canadian history is no latter-day revisionism. It is the conclusion of many of the great historians of English-speaking Canada. The Canadian state, they agree, was established primarily for economic rather than philosophical reasons.

In his profound essay, "Clio in Canada," W.L. Morton states it categorically: "The Canadian peoples were brought together in Confederation, not for the increase of liberty or the ends of justice, which were taken for granted, but to meet certain commercial, strategic, and imperial purposes." Canada, he writes, was fundamentally "a scheme of commercial exploitation...imperialistic in its methods, aiming not at political justice but at commercial profits." The West "was annexed as a subordinate territory." And this, he observes, is in sharp contrast to the powerful founding premises of the United States, which aimed at procuring liberty for its citizens.

Morton founded his view of Canadian history upon an analysis known as the Laurentian Thesis. It depicts Canada, not as an idealistic attempt to preserve the British identity and tradition in North America, but as a system in which an industrialized, populated centre prospers by drawing resources and staples from a hinterland that remains relatively undeveloped. The Laurentian Thesis was recognized not only by Morton but by other prominent Canadian historians and economists like Donald Creighton and H.A. Innis.

For the nascent West, this ideology held ominous implications. "It was the fate of the West to become the colony of a colony which brought to its new imperial rule neither imagination, liberality, nor magnanimity," Morton contends. "For Confederation was brought about to increase the wealth of central Canada, and until that original purpose is altered...Confederation must remain an instrument of injustice." Innis arrives at an equally condemnatory conclusion: "Western Canada has paid for the development of Canadian nationality, and it would appear that it must continue to pay."

Other respected historians acknowledge that this was and is Canada's political/economic arrangement, but regard it as entirely justified both then and now. They argue that the less populous, resource-producing provinces must remain forever subordinate to the dynamic, industrialized centre for the good of Canada. Some centralists even contend that resource ownership should never have been given to any province. Political scientist Peter Russell, and historians Jack Granatstein and Desmond Morton, all of Toronto, are leading centralists. So were Pierre Trudeau and his ministerial and bureaucratic allies.

Brock University political scientist Garth Stevenson, in his 1989 book *Unfulfilled Union*, demonstrates the basic centralist outlook. In an analysis of Canada's 1982 constitution, which strengthened provincial rights to some extent, he writes: "Even more than the original model of 1867, the 'new' Canadian constitution was an untidy collection of miscellaneous provisions reflecting sordid and undignified compromises with a variety of provincial interests...In the last analysis the compact theory [which holds that Confederation is a voluntary union of equal provinces], that malignant legacy of Canadian history, triumphed over democracy, freedom and national unity."

The whole historic purpose of Confederation was to make possible a great industrial heartland controlling staple-producing territory from Atlantic to Pacific, the centralists agree. Thus when Macdonald in the 1870s was faced with hostile Ontario voters and sluggish Ontario industry, the welfare of Canada demanded that he introduce the National Policy.

Glenbow Archives, NA-3055-13

STARTLING AFFAIR IN LONDON!

A PROMISING YOUNG WOMAN OFFERED FOR SALE TO THE HIGHEST BIDDER.

A GRIP magazine cartoon (December 31, 1880) castigates the Macdonald Tories for selling out the territories. The cartoonist's specific targets are the huge subsidies, enormous land grants and the monopoly given the CPR. But in a wider sense too, says historian W.L. Morton, Canada was structured as 'a scheme of commercial exploitation' – not least of its new western colony.

In effect, then, according to this interpretation, Ontario's interest is the national interest. One consequence of this identification is that Ottawa becomes Ontario's agent, removing the need for strong provincial governments. In any event, Stevenson argues, provincial grievances are usually of dubious merit, the product of unscrupulous, manipulative local politicians. So is it not logical to conclude that whenever the interests of one small element on the periphery threaten the hegemony or economic dominance of the centre, they threaten the very nation itself? Clearly, for the good of Canada, the hinterland must give way or be forced into line.

Whether or not this was in fact the intent of the Fathers of Confederation, or of Macdonald, critical western historians condemn it as an impossible basis for a just democracy. "The mantle of 'imperial' pretensions was donned with alacrity in Ottawa, and only put off with reluctance," writes Lewis H. Thomas in *The Struggle for Responsible Government in the Northwest Territories.*

In case westerners did not voluntarily embrace the goal of advancing central Canada's interests at the expense of their own, the dominion government developed a whole battery of mechanisms to ensure the desired result. It retained firm control over western lands and resources (and would continue to do so for more than half a century until the West finally adopted the course advocated by F.W.G. Haultain and divorced itself from the national political parties). It conferred a monopoly on the Canadian Pacific Railway. It furnished hand-picked lieutenant-governors with near-absolute powers and appointed compliant councillors. Some, like Edgar Dewdney and Herbert Mackintosh, were openly hostile to any aspirations of the territories.

It cannot be said that Macdonald was anything but candid about the National Policy. He seemed to assume that everyone, including westerners, would concur with it. Thus his utter astonishment in 1885 when the Metis up took arms. Thus his casual description of Dewdney as "a paternal despot...governed by instructions from Head Quarters." Not in jest did Canada's first minister of the Interior, Senator Alexander Campbell, call himself "Secretary for the Colonies." As Thomas observes, the senator merely "expressed the prevailing Canadian philosophy."

And since the dominion government, the principal agent of the central Canadian colonizers, was not bound by such American imperatives as equal liberty and opportunity for all, inequities were built into prairie administration. As the West was populated, these inequities soon became apparent to the settlers and they found themselves locked into enduring conflict with Ottawa. The West wanted responsible government; Ottawa sought to sustain colonial despotism. The West wanted commercial freedom; Ottawa pushed protectionism. The West liked populism and political pragmatism; Ottawa depended upon national partisanship and, later, upon executive federalism.

Fundamentally, westerners of the 19th century, like those of the 20th, wanted an equal part in national life. As a whole they never were, and did not become, separatists. They wanted justice, not independence. Neither did they ever seriously favour annexation by the United States. Yet some saw in the American system an example to bring about justice in Canada, a means of giving the less populous provinces some measure of equality with the more populous in directing national policy. This they discerned in the U.S. Senate, the most powerful legislative body in the American system, where all states, no matter how small or sparsely populated, are equally represented.

This equalizing function, of course, had ostensibly been one of the primary purposes of the Canadian Senate also. From the start, however, that body was regarded with scorn in the West. As early as the 1890s, westerners were demanding it be changed. In an 1899 editorial, the *Lethbridge News* described the Senate as "a sort of political dumping ground for worn out political hacks," and charged that genuine reform had been "kept down by the greed for place and power of those who pulled political strings." Laurier was by then proposing Senate reforms, but they were, said the *News*, so superficial as to be "a disgrace to an enlightened and educated people."

The clearest early voice of prairie dissent was Haultain's. Over two decades, he led the Prairies from political serfdom to provincehood. His 20,000-word Autonomy Resolution, delivered in the territorial assembly in Regina on May 2, 1900, and passed unanimously, was in fact a western manifesto. No one had yet used the term Laurentian Thesis, but Haultain knew all about it, describing the prairie West as "a colony within a colony." His resolution was the first wholly articulated and categorical rejection of such subjugation. The British North America Act had given Ottawa power to make laws for "peace, order and good government." That meant the West must be governed in the interests of the people who live there, Haultain argued, not as the instrument of central Canadian prosperity.

In the next volume of this series, Ottawa will thwart Haultain. His worst fears will be realized when second-class, pseudo-provincehood is conferred upon Alberta and Saskatchewan. Most egregiously, Ottawa will withhold control over lands, forests and minerals — something granted to the four original provinces, plus Prince Edward Island and British Columbia — contrary to the BNA Act, Canada's constitution. As late as 1946, Toronto historian C.C. Lingard was to write: "At the very heart of the problem stands, of course, the indisputable fact that in 1905 the Dominion Parliament created two inferior provinces in a federation that connotes equality...Equality of treatment and a just allotment of powers and revenues appear even today the requisites of a happy relationship among the various members of the Canadian federation."

But Ottawa failed to thwart the spirit of resistance represented by Haultain. Eventually, the West would develop its own unique response to Ottawa's refusal to listen, and to the impossibility of reforming the national Liberal or Conservative party from within. The West would create its own political movements to attack the institutional inequities directly. This spirit would rise again and again throughout the coming century, both in the form of populist, western-based, so-called protest movements, and as powerful provincial governments taking an active role in national affairs.

It would rise under names like Wood, Brownlee, Aberhart, Manning and Lougheed, leading movements like the Progressives, Social Credit, Alberta's provincial Conservatives, and the Reform party, as the colony became a province and the province continued to struggle against those who had created it for purposes of their own.❦

EPILOGUE

Soon to be born, a province vast and fair

The Marquis of Lorne, first governor-general of Canada to visit the North West Territories, promenaded onto the western Prairies in 1881. Accompanying him came correspondents from *The Times* and four other British newspapers. Officials and newsmen alike were captivated by the foothills country with its shining backdrop of mountains. If he weren't occupied in his official position, said the marquis, he would like to be a rancher near Pincher Creek. (A comparable stir might be provoked today if a mayor of Toronto suggested that he'd like to become a reindeer herder in the Yukon if only he wasn't stuck being a politician.)

A year later, upon his return to Ottawa, the governor-general dedicated this verse to his wife Princess Louise Caroline Alberta, fourth daughter of Queen Victoria:

> In token for the love which thou hast Shown
> For this wild land of freedom, I have Named
> A Province vast, and for its beauty Famed,
> By thy dear name to be hereafter Known.
> Alberta shall it be!

Though Alberta's provincehood remained no more than poetic licence for another quarter-century, the marquis's touching tribute to his wife provided the name for the territorial District of Alberta.

In 1905, it would become the name of a province. ❦

Above, Princess Louise Caroline Alberta; left, the Marquis of Lorne

Index